Nomads in the Middle East

A history of pastoral nomads in the Islamic Middle East, from the rise of Islam, through the middle periods when Mongols and Turks ruled most of the region to the decline of nomadism in the twentieth century. Offering a vivid insight into the impact of nomads on the politics, culture and ideology of the region, Beatrice Forbes Manz examines and challenges existing perceptions of these nomads, including the popular cyclical model of nomad-settled interaction developed by Ibn Khaldun. Looking at both the Arab Bedouin and the nomads from the Eurasian steppe, Manz demonstrates the significance of Bedouin and Turco-Mongolian contributions to cultural production and political ideology in the Middle East, and shows the central role played by pastoral nomads in war, trade and state-building throughout history. Nomads provided horses and soldiers for war, the livestock and guidance which made long-distance trade possible, and animal products to provision the region's growing cities.

Beatrice Forbes Manz is Professor of History at Tufts University where she teaches the history of the Middle East and Inner Asia, with a particular interest in pastoral nomads. She is the author of *Power, Politics and Religion in Timurid Iran* (Cambridge University Press, 2007), which was awarded the Houshang Pourshariati Book Award in Iranian Studies, and the best-seller *The Rise and Rule of Tamerlane* (Cambridge University Press, 1989). She is also the author of numerous articles and chapters in collected words on the history of the Timurids, the Mongol Empire and nomad societies, including in *The New Cambridge History of Islam*, *The Cambridge History of Inner Asia* and *The Cambridge History of War*.

THEMES IN ISLAMIC HISTORY comprises a range of titles exploring different aspects of Islamic history, society and culture by leading scholars in the field. Books are thematic in approach, offering a comprehensive and accessible overview of the subject. Generally, surveys treat Islamic history from its origins to the demise of the Ottoman Empire, although some offer a more developed analysis of a particular period, or project into the present, depending on the subject-matter. All the books are written to interpret and illuminate the past, as gateways to a deeper understanding of Islamic civilization and its peoples.

Other books in the series:

Nomads in the Middle East

Beatrice Forbes Manz

Tufts University, Massachusetts

CAMBRIDGE
UNIVERSITY PRESS

CAMBRIDGE
UNIVERSITY PRESS

University Printing House, Cambridge CB2 8BS, United Kingdom

One Liberty Plaza, 20th Floor, New York, NY 10006, USA

477 Williamstown Road, Port Melbourne, VIC 3207, Australia

314–321, 3rd Floor, Plot 3, Splendor Forum, Jasola District Centre, New Delhi – 110025, India

103 Penang Road, #05–06/07, Visioncrest Commercial, Singapore 238467

Cambridge University Press is part of the University of Cambridge.

It furthers the University's mission by disseminating knowledge in the pursuit of education, learning, and research at the highest international levels of excellence.

www.cambridge.org
Information on this title: www.cambridge.org/9780521816298
DOI: 10.1017/9781139028813

First published 2021

Printed in the United Kingdom by TJ Books Limited, Padstow Cornwall

A catalogue record for this publication is available from the British Library.

Library of Congress Cataloging-in-Publication Data
Names: Manz, Beatrice Forbes, author.
Title: Nomads in the Middle East / Beatrice Forbes Manz.
Description: Cambridge ; New York. NY : Cambridge University Press, 2021. |
Series: Themes in Islamic history | Includes bibliographical references and index.
Identifiers: LCCN 2021025028 (print) | LCCN 2021025029 (ebook) | ISBN
9780521816298 (hardback) | ISBN 9780521531634 (paperback) | ISBN
9781139028813 (ebook)
Subjects: LCSH: Nomads – Islamic Empire – History. | Pastoral systems – Islamic
Empire – History. | Nomads – Sedentarization – Islamic Empire – History. | Tribes –
Islamic Empire – History. | Islamic Empire – Ethnic relations. | Islamic Empire –
Civilization. | Islamic Empire – History. | BISAC: HISTORY / Middle East /
General
Classification: LCC DS58 .M28 2021 (print) | LCC DS58 (ebook) | DDC
305.9/06918056–dc23
LC record available at https://lccn.loc.gov/2021025028
LC ebook record available at https://lccn.loc.gov/2021025029

ISBN 978-0-521-81629-8 Hardback
ISBN 978-0-521-53163-4 Paperback

Dedicated to the memory of

Thomas T. Allsen, 1940–2019

and

David O. Morgan, 1945–2019

Figure 0.1 Nomadic Encampment, probably a folio from a manuscript of Layla va Majnun by Jami, Harvard Art Museums/Arthur M. Sackler Museum, Gift of John Goelet, formerly in the collection of Louis J. Cartier, Photo @ President and Fellows of Harvard College, 1958.75.

Contents

Figures and Maps

Preface

A number of organizations facilitated the research for this book. A membership in the School of Historical Studies, at the Institute for Advanced Study in Princeton in 2003–4 gave me a year in which to begin this work in the best possible surroundings, and encouragement to explore fields I had not previously dealt with. Funds for the year were provided by a postdoctoral Research Fellowship from the American Council of Learned Societies and a Faculty Research Semester from Tufts University. Tufts University also provided a Research Semester grant in the spring of 2012. To all these institutions I express my heartfelt gratitude.

This book covers periods well outside my sphere of expertise, and I could not have written it without the assistance of other scholars. A number of generous colleagues have provided indispensable help by reading the chapters of the book as they were written, saving me from many potential errors. I want to thank Thomas Barfield, Tzvi Abusch, Marc van De Mieroop, the late Patricia Crone, Fred McGraw Donner, Louise Marlow, Kurt Franz, David Durand Guédy, Jürgen Paul, the late Thomas Allsen, Patrick Wing, Charles Melville, Rudi Matthee, Linda Darling, Rhoads Murphy, Lois Beck and Hugh Roberts for their generous gift of time and expertise. I am also grateful to Margaret Fearey for reading through the manuscript as an "educated reader." I owe a particular debt to the Research Technology, TTS team at Tufts University, notably Patrick Florance, Carolyn Talmadge and Yuehui (Aurora) Li, for their painstaking work mapping often obscure locations, under the difficult conditions of the COVID-19 pandemic.

I have dedicated this book to the memory of two scholars who died in 2019, both of whom contributed enormously to the history of nomads, and particularly of the Mongol Empire. The work of Thomas Allsen transformed the field of Mongol history and serves as an inspiration to all writing in this field. David O. Morgan spent a long and productive career promoting the study of both medieval Iran and the Mongol Empire, and also helping to advance the careers of younger scholars.

I first came in contact with him when he wrote me a very kind letter as a reader for my first book, and from that time on I profited continually from his help and guidance. I am also grateful to him for encouraging me to widen my field by inviting me to write the chapter on the Mongols for the *New Cambridge History of Islam*.

Note on Usage and Maps

This book is designed for an audience that includes both specialists and non-specialists. I have tried to keep transcription as simple and as consistent as possible. For Arabic and Persian in the pre-modern period, I have used the classical Arabic transcription. Turkic and Mongolian names are transcribed according to systems specific to those languages. For the Ottoman Empire and modern Iran, I have retained the classical transcription for Arabic and Persian terminology, but for well-known figures I have used common modern spelling. For larger cities, likewise, modern spelling is used, while for smaller locations I use the classical transcription. I have omitted most diacriticals in the text but have retained them in the index.

In addition to maps showing cities and regions, I have included maps showing land use and pasture locations, based on a combination of modern maps representing primarily nineteenth- and twentieth-century conditions and information about earlier periods taken from historical texts. Since these maps are on a small scale and represent a period of more than a millennium, for any given time they must be viewed as approximations.

Black Sea

RUMELIA

GEORGIA

Caspian Sea

Sea of Marmara

Istanbul

Samsun

Trabzon

SHIRWAN

ARMENIA

Aegean Sea

ANATOLIA

Erzerum

ARRAN

Mughan Steppe

KONYA

Sivas

Mush

Akhlat

Ardabil

NIGDE

Kayseri

Amid

Tabriz

GILAN

Aydin

Konya

Mar`ash

DIYAR BAKR

TUR ABDIN

DAYLAM

Taurus Mts.

Mardin

AZARBAIJAN

Antioch

Aleppo

JAZIRA

Mosul

Qazwin

al-Rafiqa

KURDISTAN

SYRIA

Kermanshah

Hamadan

Mediterranean Sea

Hims

Palmyra

Euphrates

Baghdad

JIBAL

Damascus

Syrian

Tigris

Dizful

PALESTINE

HAWRAN

Desert

IRAK

Shushtar

Acre

BALQA

Kufa

Wasit

KHUZISTAN

GAZA

Ramla

Wadi Sirhan

LURISTAN

TRANSJORDAN

Dumat al-Jandal

Basra

Abadan

Cairo

Negev

Petra

KUWAIT

An Nufud Desert

BAHRAYN

Area of Detail

Nile

Tayma Oasis

Hail

Ad Dahna'

HIJAZ

Jabal Shammar

Dedan Oasis

NAJD

Medina

Diriyya

Riyadh

Yamama

Red Sea

Hajar

Jidda

Mecca

Ta'if

Rub

(Empty

○ City

□ Oasis

▦ Fortress

N

0   200   400 Miles

0   200   400 Kilometers

YEMEN

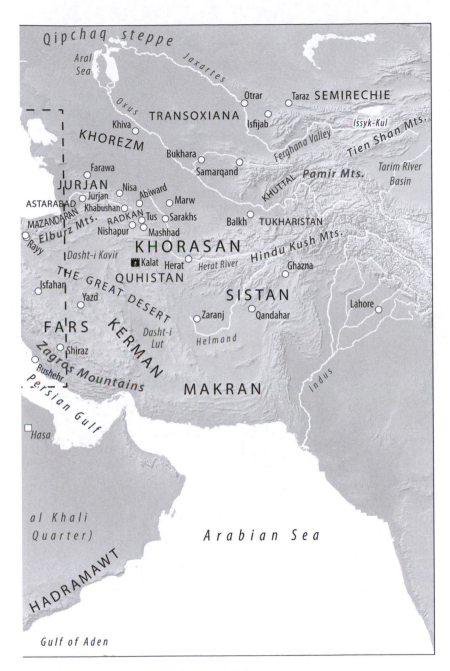

Map 0.1 The Middle East and Central Asia

Map 0.2 Central Regions of the Middle East

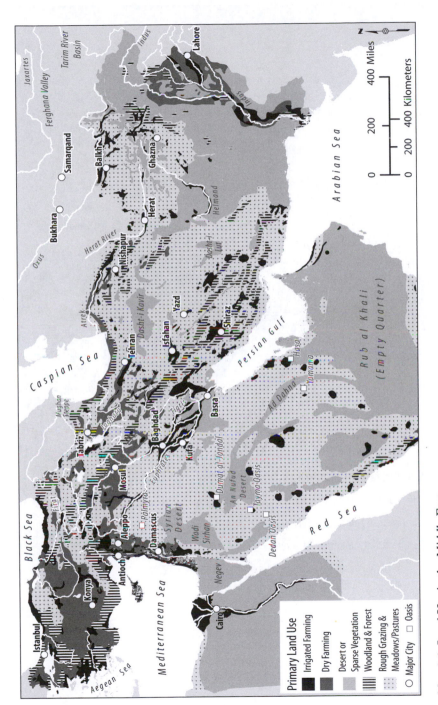

Map 0.3 Land Use in the Middle East

Primary Land Use

- Irrigated Farming
- Dry Farming
- Desert or Sparse Vegetation
- Woodland & Forest
- Rough Grazing & Meadows/Pastures
- ○ Major City □ Oasis

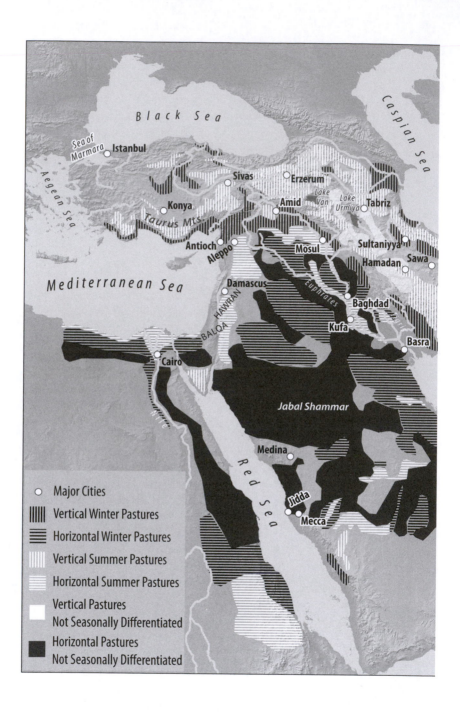

Black Sea

Caspian Sea

Sea of Marmara

Istanbul

Aegean Sea

Sivas

Erzerum

Konya

Taurus Mts

Amid

Lake Van

Lake Urmiya

Tabriz

Antioch

Aleppo

Mosul

Sultaniyya

Hamadan

Sawa

Mediterranean Sea

Damascus

HAWRAN

Euphrates

Baghdad

BALQA

Kufa

Basra

Cairo

Nile

Jabal Shammar

Medina

Red Sea

Jidda

Mecca

○ Major Cities

||||| Vertical Winter Pastures

≡ Horizontal Winter Pastures

|||| Vertical Summer Pastures

≡ Horizontal Summer Pastures

Vertical Pastures Not Seasonally Differentiated

Horizontal Pastures Not Seasonally Differentiated

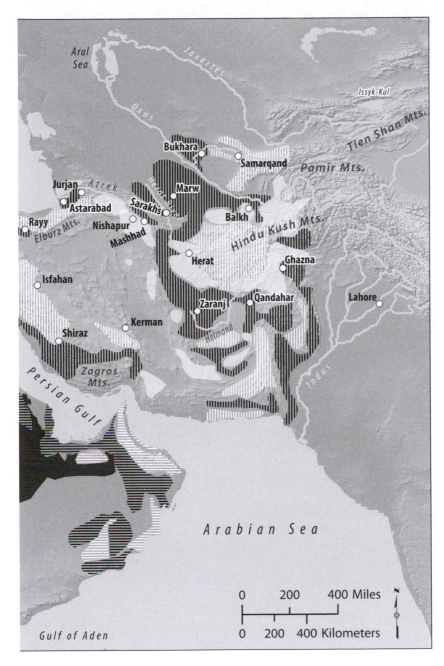

Map 0.4 Nomad Pastureland

Debate between Sheep and Grain

1–11 When, upon the hill of heaven and earth, An spawned the Anuna gods, since he neither spawned nor created Grain with them, and since in the Land he neither fashioned the yarn of Uttu (*the goddess of weaving*) nor pegged out the loom for Uttu – with no Sheep appearing, there were no numerous lambs, and with no goats, there were no numerous kids, the sheep did not give birth to her twin lambs, and the goat did not give birth to her triplet kids; the Anuna, the great gods, did not even know the names Ezina-Kusu (*Grain*) or Sheep. . . . .

26–36 At that time, at the place of the gods' formation, in their own home, on the Holy Mound, they created Sheep and Grain. . . . For their own well-being in the holy sheepfold, they gave them to mankind as sustenance.

43–53 Sheep being fenced in by her sheepfold, they gave her grass and herbs generously. For Grain they made her field and gave her the plough, yoke and team. Sheep standing in her sheepfold was a shepherd of the sheepfolds brimming with charm. Grain standing in her furrow was a beautiful girl radiating charm; lifting her raised head up from the field she was suffused with the bounty of heaven. Sheep and Grain had a radiant appearance.

54–64 They brought wealth to the assembly. They brought sustenance to the Land. They fulfilled the ordinances of the gods. They filled the store-rooms of the Land with stock. The barns of the Land were heavy with them. When they entered the homes of the poor who crouch in the dust they brought wealth. Both of them, wherever they directed their steps, added to the riches of the household with their weight. Where they stood, they were satisfying; where they settled, they were seemly. They gladdened the heart of An and the heart of Enlil.

65–70 They drank sweet wine, they enjoyed sweet beer. When they had drunk sweet wine and enjoyed sweet beer, they started a quarrel concerning the arable fields, they began a debate in the dining hall.

71–82 Grain called out to Sheep: "Sister, I am your better; I take precedence over you. I am the glory of the lights of the Land . . . .

83–91 "I foster neighbourliness and friendliness. I sort out quarrels started between neighbours. When I come upon a captive youth and give him his destiny,

1

he forgets his despondent heart and I release his fetters and shackles. I am Ezina-Kusu (*Grain*); I am Enlil's daughter. In sheep shacks and milking pens scattered on the high plain, what can you put against me? Answer me what you can reply!"

92–101 Thereupon Sheep answered Grain: "My sister, whatever are you saying? An, king of the gods, made me descend from the holy place, my most precious place. All the yarns of Uttu, the splendour of kingship, belong to me . . . .

102–106 "The watch over the elite troops is mine. Sustenance of the workers in the field is mine: the waterskin of cool water and the sandals are mine. . . .

107–115 "In the gown, my cloth of white wool, the king rejoices on his throne. My body glistens on the flesh of the great gods. After the purification priests, the incantation priests and the bathed priests have dressed themselves in me for my holy lustration, I walk with them to my holy meal. But your harrow, ploughshare, binding and strap are tools that can be utterly destroyed. What can you put against me? Answer me what you can reply!"

116–122 Again Grain addressed Sheep: "When the beer dough has been carefully prepared in the oven, and the mash tended in the oven, Ninkasi (*the goddess of beer*) mixes them for me while your big billy-goats and rams are despatched for my banquets. . . .

123–129 "Your shepherd on the high plain eyes my produce enviously; when I am standing in the furrow in the field, my farmer chases away your herdsman with his cudgel. Even when they look out for you, from the open country to the hidden places, your fears are not removed from you: fanged (?) snakes and bandits, the creatures of the desert, want your life on the high plain. . . . .

143–155 Again Sheep answered Grain: . . . .

156–168 "When you fill the trough the baker's assistant mixes you and throws you on the floor, and the baker's girl flattens you out broadly. You are put into the oven and you are taken out of the oven. When you are put on the table I am before you – you are behind me. Grain, heed yourself! You too, just like me, are meant to be eaten. At the inspection of your essence, why should it be I who come second?

169–179 Then Grain was hurt in her pride, and hastened for the verdict . . . .

180–191 Then Enki spoke to Enlil: "Father Enlil, Sheep and Grain should be sisters! They should stand together! . . . But of the two, Grain shall be the greater.

192–193 Dispute spoken between Sheep and Grain: Sheep is left behind and Grain comes forward – praise be to father Enki![1]

---

[1] The Electronic Text Corpus of Sumerian Literature, Faculty of Oriental Studies, Oxford University, Oxford, 1998. http://etcsl.orinst.ox.ac.uk/section5/tr532.htm

1   Introduction

For almost all people, a comfortable lifestyle requires both animal and vegetable products. While livestock and agriculture are easily combined in subsistence farming, a complex society encourages specialization. In arid and mountainous regions, concentration on livestock breeding led to the development of a separate lifestyle – pastoral nomadism – which has had an enormous impact on the history of the world. The owners of large herds can utilize lands too dry or too high to yield reliable crops by moving from one pasture to another, usually in regular migrations between known seasonal pastures. Thus they live in tents which can be moved, and their other possessions must also be easily portable. Pastoral nomadism presents a number of paradoxes. Although it is in some ways a limiting lifestyle, which discourages the development of a high civilization and centers its people outside the major cultural centers, it is a specialized economy which developed out of agriculture and involves exchange with sedentary populations. For thousands of years nomads[1] and settled agriculturalists have defined themselves against each other, each expressing distrust and disdain for the other lifestyle. Nonetheless both have continued to coexist, to trade, and to influence each other.

Although theoretically nomads could live largely from their herds, in practice many have also practiced some agriculture and have further depended on agricultural populations for many of their needs, from grain and vegetables to metal and ceramic wares. Settled societies are less fully dependent on pastoral goods, but over history nomads have offered much more to the settled than the animal products in which they specialize. Their lifestyle gave nomads several skills of great importance – and of use to their settled neighbors. The most famous nomad skill was that of war. The need to migrate required organization and survival skills which translated easily into military action, and the protection of livestock and pasture rights required the ability – and willingness – to use arms. As large sedentary states formed and

---

[1] Throughout this book I use the term nomad to refer to pastoral nomads only.

developed armies, they soon sought out nomadic populations as soldiers. Pastoral nomads also have the ability to live in difficult terrain, to move long distances and to mobilize manpower. Thus, they made trade possible through areas of steppe and desert which were difficult for settled populations to access and impossible for them to control. Nomads provided both pack animals and guidance, and likewise some level of security along the routes.

For the purpose of this book, I define the Middle East as the region between the Oxus and Nile rivers, stretching in the north through Anatolia. I have omitted North Africa due to constraints of space and time but include the eastern regions of Iran and modern Afghanistan, which have been controlled by nomad dynasties through much of the Islamic period. The Middle East has had a particularly close relationship with nomadic peoples. First of all, it interacts with large nomad societies on two sides. To the north, the region borders the Eurasian steppe, a vast tract of grassland stretching from Mongolia to Hungary, which was dominated by nomads for three millennia. In the south lie the Arabian and Syrian deserts, inhabited largely by pastoralists. What has been most important in determining the role of nomads in the Middle East, however, is the topography of the region itself. This is a land fertile but arid, characterized by small areas of productive agricultural land separated by mountain ranges, deserts and plateaus. In the west, great rivers provide two regions of intensive agriculture which were the seats of the first great civilizations of the Middle East – the Nile in Egypt and the Tigris-Euphrates system in Mesopotamia. Between these areas stretches an expanse of desert and arid steppe extending from southern Arabia to the inland region of northern Syria. The Arabian and Syrian deserts are interspersed with oases and in rainy seasons can provide some pastures, but much can be considered hospitable only by the hardiest of men and animals. The northern Middle East – from Anatolia through Iran and Afghanistan – is a combination of mountain and high plateau. There are few sand deserts, but also no river systems as rich as those in the southwest. Some areas – particularly in Anatolia and Azerbaijan – can support farming without irrigation; elsewhere water is conducted from mountains and rivers into the plains through canals and underground conduits.

The regions supporting intensive agriculture are a small percentage of the total area and much land is best exploited by pastoralists or mountain peoples. In the marshy riverbeds, arid steppes and the foothills of the mountain ranges, nomads can find winter and summer pastures, while the smaller remote mountain valleys remain the seat of mountain peoples living from subsistence farming and livestock. Neither population is easy to control, and both have remained a constant and significant presence from the beginnings of written history to the present.

Nomadic Lifestyles

For this book I have adopted a broad definition of pastoral nomads, to include all populations living primarily from livestock breeding and practicing regular migration. Many populations practiced a mixed economy, sometimes living in houses or huts for part of the year and using tents only for the summer months; many also planted crops and harvested them when returning along their migration routes. Sometimes such populations are characterized as semi-nomadic. It was also not uncommon for populations to move back and forth between settled and nomad economies, as weather conditions or political unrest made a change desirable. However, I have not usually tried to distinguish among different levels of nomadism for a simple reason: the paucity of historical evidence. The sources available to us for most periods covered in this book give us almost no information on the lifestyle or economic strategy of individual groups, and therefore do not allow us to differentiate among populations according to the length of the migration, winter habitation, or degree of dependence on agriculture.

While mobility and economic specialization create similarities among all pastoral nomads, very significant variations do exist.[2] Two groups have been most visible in the history of the Middle East: the Arabian and Syrian nomads in the southwestern regions, and nomads from the Eurasian steppe in the northern and eastern provinces. The Arab nomads exploit the desert and semi-desert areas of Arabia, Mesopotamia and Syria to raise sheep, goats, horses and most famously camels. In this region the scarce resource is water, and wells are a central necessity. Summer is the season in which groups congregate most closely around water sources, while in winter after the rains they disperse to make full use of seasonal pastures. Most migration takes place between areas where water is available in summer, and those that can be used only during cooler periods of greater precipitation, often at the same level. For this reason, this type of nomadism is often called horizontal nomadism. The tent used by the nomads of Syria and Arabia is usually made of woven goat hair, which allows the circulation of air in dry weather, but swells when wet and becomes a protection against rain (Fig. 1.1).

Because the needs of camels are significantly different from those of sheep and goats, most nomad groups have specialized in one or the other. Groups raising smaller livestock must remain fairly close to the edge of the desert, where sufficient pasture and above all water can be found throughout the year. Camel nomads (*a'rāb* or *badū*) – known in European languages as Bedouin – can retreat more deeply into the desert and travel

---

[2] See A. M. Khazanov, *Nomads and the Outside World*, 2nd ed. (Madison: University of Wisconsin Press, 1994); Thomas J. Barfield, *The Nomadic Alternative* (Englewood Cliffs, NJ: Prentice Hall, 1993).

Figure 1.1 Bedouin black tent, er-Riha, Jordan, 1898. On the way to Jericho (Er-Riha), Jordan, etc. Bedouin tent American Colony, Jerusalem. 1898. (Photo by: Sepia Times/Universal Images Group via Getty Images)

greater distances in search of pasture, since the camel requires water at most once every four days, and in cool weather with sufficient grazing can go for several weeks without drinking.[3] Like sheep and goats, female camels are used for milk, which forms a major component of the Bedouin diet. Their greater mobility gave the Bedouin both freedom from settled control and enhanced military skill. As a result they held greater prestige than the nomads relying on smaller animals.

The northern regions of the Middle East, from Afghanistan to Anatolia, have been inhabited since the eleventh century largely by nomads of Turkic and Mongolian descent, originally from the Eurasian steppe. These populations differ from Arab nomads in a number of important ways. The livestock raised is usually a mix of sheep, goats and horses, sometimes with Bactrian (two-humped) camels. Sheep and goats form the economic basis of the herd, while horses and camels serve for travel, war and transport. Although horses have somewhat different grazing preferences from sheep and goats their grazing habits are complementary,

[3] Khazanov, *Nomads and the Outside World*, pp. 53–56; Barfield, *The Nomadic Alternative*.

and the pasture benefits from the mix. Herds can thus be pastured in the same areas and be raised by the same group. While for desert nomads the summer is the time of greatest population concentration, for the steppe and mountain nomads the winter pasture is the more intensive, usually requiring a river valley with water and dried forage. Pasture is less dependent on the vagaries of weather and while migrations may be short or long, a given tribe will migrate spring, summer, fall and winter to the same places. Within Iran and Anatolia, tribes usually migrate vertically, with a winter pasture in a river valley and summer pasture in the mountain highlands which, unlike the lowlands, remain green through the summer. In general, nomads remain relatively stationary in winter and summer and move more frequently and for longer distances in the fall and spring migrations. This is known as vertical nomadism. In the past, the steppe nomads used tents made of heavy felt attached to a circle formed by wooden lattice work, with a hole for smoke in the center. These were heavier but also far warmer than the goat hair tents of the south-western nomads (Figs 1.2 and 1.3). Within the Middle East, many Turkic nomads, especially in the warmer regions, have adopted the black goat hair tent.

Among both Arab and Turco-Mongolian nomads, daily tasks are apportioned by gender and women play a major role in production, enjoying a higher position than most settled women. Women set up and take down the tents, and the black goat-hair tents used now by most nomads in the Middle East were until recently woven by them. Herding is usually done by men, but in times of need women can also do this. Among camel nomads milking is done by the men; sheep and goats are usually milked by women, who also process milk products for consumption and sale. Among the Bedouin it is common for extended families to share one tent, which can be separated into public spaces for men and private ones for women, and women are sometimes veiled. Nonetheless they are not segregated and have considerable freedom of movement. Among the nomads of Iranian and Turco-Mongolian descent, the nuclear family is more common, while women are rarely veiled and enjoy both authority and freedom.

The Question of Tribes

The most common social and political unit of organization among pastoral nomads is the tribe, a political and territorial unit often expressed in kinship idiom and requiring little formal administrative structure. Livestock is owned by individual households, and these have usually organized themselves along kinship lines in camping groups which share

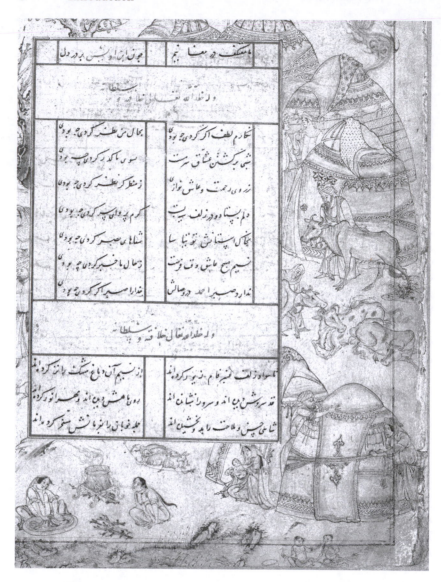

Figure 1.2 Nomad encampment with yurts, from the Diwan of Sultan Ahmad Jalayir, ca. 1400. Ink, color and gold on paper. Freer Gallery of Art, Smithsonian Institution, Washington, DC: Purchase – Charles Lang Freer Endowment, F1932.34, verso.

Figure 1.3 Setting up a Kazakh yurt, Altai Mountains, China, 1987. Courtesy of Thomas Barfield, Boston University.

resources and migrate together. The higher level of organization, dealing with the defense and distribution of pasture, is provided by the tribe. Tribes will usually include several thousand people, and may unite into confederacies, or break up into smaller entities. Although the tribal system is in many ways antithetical to a centralized bureaucratic state, the two systems have coexisted over millennia, and their relationship will be one of the concerns of this book.

There is considerable controversy over the use and meaning of the terms, "tribe" and "tribal," which have been tarnished in part by an implied connection with societies considered primitive and with an earlier stage in the development of political organization. Thus it is necessary to explain why and how I use the word tribe. In early scholarship, up into the twentieth century, tribes were usually seen as large kinship groups, defined by common descent from an ancestor in the fairly distant past. More recently, scholars have recognized the changing composition of tribes over time; unrelated groups may join a successful leader and members may desert for another tribe in times of stress or weak leadership. Individuals may also join as the client of a tribal member, accepting subordinate status. Actual kinship therefore has been seen as important primarily in the smallest divisions within the tribe – camping collectives and limited descent groups accepting collective responsibility for avenging their fellow members. At a higher level, kinship is often claimed but may well be fictive; as new groups join an existing tribe, a real or presumed ancestor can be grafted onto the tribal genealogy. Thus, the tribe is seen as a political grouping, providing a corporate identity, the possibility of collective action and access to pasture for its members. The chief of the tribe provides leadership in the mediation of disputes, the management of seasonal migrations, mobilization for the protection or acquisition of pastures, and for warfare. Tribal society also provides a basis for law and a means of keeping order through mediation among tribal leaders, and through the practice of collective responsibility to avenge harm done to a member. Despite the importance of tribal structure, we need to recognize that nomadism and tribalism are not synonymous; it is quite possible for nomad societies to exist without tribal structure, or to change back and forth between tribal and non-tribal structures. Such a change can occur at times of conquest when nomad rulers create decimally organized armies and move into conquered territories, a phenomenon which will be discussed in this book.[4]

Recently the anthropologist David Sneath, working on Mongolian nomads, has proposed that the concept of tribe should be abandoned for nomad societies – at least for steppe societies – and instead we should recognize named groups formerly seen as tribes as being aristocratic lineages. This reinterpretation is accompanied by a return to the earlier definition of tribes as actual kinship groups, and of tribal societies as egalitarian. In this model, the state is also redefined, as an entity not requiring or even necessarily aspiring to any form of centralization. Sneath suggests that steppe societies were usually stratified, and state-like processes were distributed through a number of authorities.[5] I have not adopted Sneath's model in this book for several reasons. First of all, in my own work on steppe societies in the pre-modern period I see evidence of named corporate groups with hereditary membership and leadership in which it is clear that not all members are aristocrats. Another problem

---

[4] The literature on tribes is too vast to survey here. For a review of the controversies concerning the definition and discussion of tribes, see for instance, Richard Tapper, *Frontier Nomads of Iran: A Political and Social History of the Shahsevan* (Cambridge: Cambridge University Press, 1997), pp. 5–24; Jeffrey Szuchman, "Integrating Approaches to Nomads, Tribes, and the State in the Ancient Near East," in *Nomads, Tribes, and the State in the Ancient Near East: Cross-Disciplinary Perspectives*, ed., Jeffrey Szuchman, Oriental Institute Seminars # 5 (Chicago, IL: Oriental Institute of Chicago, 2009), pp. 4–5.

[5] David Sneath, *The Headless State: Aristocratic Orders, Kinship Society, and Misrepresentations of Nomadic Inner Asia* (New York: Columbia University Press, 2007).

with the replacement of the concept of tribe by that of aristocratic lineage is that it does not address the central question of what sort of power base aristocrats possessed, or what bound their followers to them. These are crucial issues for the analysis attempted in this book.

I have therefore chosen to use the term tribe and have defined it very broadly, as a group of people with a common named corporate identity and a recognized leadership which is able to mobilize at least a portion of the tribe. Membership in a tribe is hereditary but at the same time it is elective; smaller groups may join or leave. A tribe may or may not use a kinship idiom, and its leading lineage may come from within the tribe or may be genealogically unrelated to the majority of its members. One thing which in my view distinguishes a tribe from other political groupings of similar size is that its territory does not define its membership. While tribes often contain members of different lifestyles – nomads, agriculturalists and some townsmen – membership is not necessarily coterminous with the population of the areas a tribe controls. Taxes can be levied, and protection extended to people not seen as members of the tribe, while some tribal members may live in towns not fully controlled by the tribe in question. Furthermore, while at any one time a tribe will have the use of a given territory or territories, nomad tribes can migrate to new regions without dissolving, something extremely difficult for a state or a village.

Because the pre-modern sources do not allow us to discern the details of tribal structures or to test extensive genealogical claims, I have identified only three levels of tribal structure. One is the leading lineages, in which it is usually possible to recognize actual descent. Another is the body of the tribe, usually several thousand people. At a higher level, one can identify tribal confederations with a common name, often claiming preeminence over a significant region. Turkic and Mongolian tribal confederations had a recognized tribe and lineage at the top, controlling several other tribes, each with its own leader subordinate to the chief of the confederation. This was sometimes, but more rarely, the case among the Arabian and Syrian nomads.

We see different tribal systems in the two major nomadic populations I have discussed – the nomads of the Arabian and Syrian desert on the one hand, and the Turkic and Mongolian nomads from the steppe on the other. Among the desert nomads the tribe has been a central institution, defining social and political life; social order, law, and identity all depended on tribal affiliation. Tribal laws have maintained relative peace in the area through mediation among tribes and by means of laws of vengeance, similar to the system of the blood feud. These laws assigned collective responsibility for harm done against a member of the tribe or a subgroup; thus if one member of a tribe or lineage killed someone of another group, any one of his male relatives could be killed in retaliation. Since a violent crime put the entire group in danger, there was strong social pressure against it and though raiding was frequent, most raids did not result in casualties. The tribal values and the achievements of individual tribes were celebrated in poetry and tales about tribal exploits. The importance of tribe was not limited to the pastoralists but seems to have applied to almost all segments of the Arabian population, at least those within the peninsula, where town life was also organized along tribal lines.

Despite the importance of the tribe in the life of its members, among Syrian and Arabian tribes authoritative leadership has not been the ideal. Tribal chiefs have been traditionally chosen by reputation, and even when leadership has remained within one or two families, they have been considered the first among equals, ruling by consensus. Even in the past, when tribes controlled significant territory, the exercise of power depended heavily on the personality of the tribal leader – the *shaykh* – and his ability to command respect through hospitality, skill in war and talent in mediating disputes. It also depended on success. A larger tribe, or confederation, consisted of many smaller sections, which could develop and change according to circumstances. Leadership at this level was in part theoretical, and it was rare that one man or one tribe would control all the sections identified with a major confederation.

The tribes of steppe origin, who became the primary nomad population of Anatolia, Iran and Afghanistan, have had different structures from those of the Arabs. Leadership was usually stronger and was held for generations within one family. In practice, the mobility of pastoralist life gives the ordinary nomads the possibility of defection to other tribes, so that leadership must always depend to some extent on persuasion and consensus. Nonetheless, the power of the chiefs has given them sufficient authority to create larger confederations which have at times controlled significant territory and formed regional states. Unlike many confederations of Arab tribes, these groups had clear leaders within a recognized lineage. While the political role of the tribe was greater among the steppe nomads than among the Arabs, its social and legal influence was less pronounced. Though the practice of vengeance is attested, it held a less central role. The etiquette and cult of honor that has been associated with Arab tribalism was less characteristic of Turco-Mongolian nomads.

One reason for the difference in tribal culture was the connection of the Turco-Mongolian tribes to the imperial tradition of the European steppe. The mounted nomads of the steppe began early on to create states exercising at least loose control over large territories, and able to exert influence on the settled civilizations on their borders, from China, to the Middle East, to the northern Black Sea. From about 200 BC, the

Mongolian steppe became the birthplace of successive nomad empires, most famously those of the Turks and the Mongols. The experience – and later the memory – of these empires gave the steppe nomads a broader identity beyond the tribal one, and a political culture which encouraged military ambitions and state building. It is notable that from the eleventh century on, when the steppe nomads began to enter the Middle East in large numbers, almost all major states were founded and ruled by people from the steppe.

Nomad–Sedentary Relations

The habitat and the lifestyle of pastoralists distance them from urban and agricultural populations but the three groups remain interdependent. Although nomads spend part of the year in terrain useable only for pasture, at certain seasons many graze their flocks on harvested fields and in return they provide useful fertilizer and sometimes also payment. During migration, pastoralists must frequently pass through agricultural regions and, particularly in times of scarcity, their passage often causes conflict. Villagers suffer from flocks that find their way into growing fields; both villagers and nomads suffer from the theft of livestock. Most nomads depend on trade for income and consumer goods. While they have several products to offer – livestock, meat, clarified butter, wool and skins – their need to move and their lack of familiarity with city life often put them at a disadvantage with city merchants. The result can be a resort to credit, sometimes at exorbitant rates. In past times, the balance of power was different. The nomads' skill in warfare allowed them to achieve equality and often dominance over agricultural regions and brought them grudging respect. Their ability to mount raids on villages and to retreat rapidly into the desert or steppe gave them a powerful tool. Nomadic tribes often held responsibility for caravan routes, collecting dues from traders and taxes from villagers in return for protection. This also made them useful to the rulers of sedentary states; nomads frequently controlled border regions, serving as a buffer between different states, and soldiers were perhaps the most sought-after product of nomad society.

However involved they were with the settled population, nomads remained by definition separate and, in the view of settled societies, to some extent barbarian. The dynamic of interaction between the tribally organized nomads and the settled village or state set up a tension felt by both sides and mirrored in their mythologies. We find on each side a sense of competition and threat from the other. One of the best-known stories dealing with the relationship between peasants and pastoralists is that of Adam and Eve's sons Cain and Abel.

---

1 And Adam knew Eve his wife; and she conceived, and bare Cain, and said, I have gotten a man from the LORD.

2 And she again bare his brother Abel. And Abel was a keeper of sheep, but Cain was a tiller of the ground.

3 And in process of time it came to pass, that Cain brought of the fruit of the ground an offering unto the LORD.

4 And Abel, he also brought of the firstlings of his flock and of the fat thereof. And the LORD had respect unto Abel and to his offering

5 but unto Cain and to his offering he had not respect. And Cain was very wroth, and his countenance fell.

6 And the LORD said unto Cain, Why art thou wroth? and why is thy countenance fallen?

7 If thou doest well, shalt thou not be accepted? and if thou doest not well, sin lieth at the door: and unto thee *shall be* his desire, and thou shalt rule over him.

8 And Cain talked with Abel his brother: and it came to pass, when they were in the field, that Cain rose up against Abel his brother, and slew him.[6]

God favored the offering of livestock over that of grain, and when murder was done, it was the farmer who killed the shepherd; there is thus a suggestion of the vulnerability of pastoralists, and of God's favor towards them.[7]

In Mesopotamian mythology the relationship between pastoralist and farmer is also addressed, though with a different judgment. The Sumerian "Debate between Sheep and Grain," quoted at the beginning of this book, expresses an ideal of coexistence, together with openly expressed rivalry. At the beginning of the world, people were naked and ate grass. Then the gods created sheep and grain, and sent them down to earth, where they created wealth and sustenance for the population. However, when success – and sweet beer – went to their heads, they began to quarrel about precedence, each touting her own excellence and hinting at the vulnerability of the other. Finally, Grain appealed to the gods for a judgment:

169–179 Then Grain was hurt in her pride, and hastened for the verdict . . . .

180–191 Then Enki spoke to Enlil: "Father Enlil, Sheep and Grain should be sisters! They should stand together! . . . But of the two, Grain shall be the greater.

192–193 Dispute spoken between Sheep and Grain: Sheep is left behind and Grain comes forward – praise be to father Enki![8]

---

[6] King James Bible, Gen. 4:1–8.

[7] It is interesting to note that Dumuzi, the shepherd god of Mesopotamia, was also killed; in some accounts the sheepfold was also destroyed. Gwendolyn Leick, *A Dictionary of Ancient Near Eastern Mythology* (London; New York: Routledge, 1991), pp. 31–34; Thorkild Jacobsen, *The Treasures of Darkness: A History of Mesopotamian Religion* (New Haven, CT: Yale University Press, 1976), pp. 47–55.)

[8] J. A. Black, G. Cunningham, G. Fluckiger-Hawker, E. Robson and G. Zólyomi, *The Electronic Text Corpus of Sumerian Literature*, Oxford 1998–https://etcsl.orinst.ox.ac.uk/

Challenges to Understanding

Before we can discuss the history of nomads, we must face the issue of our distance from their lifestyle and the limitations of our source material. All historians of the pre-modern Middle East face problems, but the difficulties attached to the history of nomads are particularly great. We are more distant in lifestyle and experience from the society we are studying, and we have even fewer sources. Most historians studying the ancient and medieval periods have turned to ethnographic studies of nomad societies to fill in gaps left in the record. We can use such studies to bring us closer to the level of understanding we would start from in studying a settled society, but they must be used with caution. Modern nomad societies have traits in common and they may have changed less over the last several millennia than settled societies, but they do differ from each other, and they have changed. I have discussed above some of the most salient differences among nomad populations, and within the major groups I have mentioned, there are significant variations from one group to another. The problem of change is a more difficult one since we have detailed descriptions of nomads largely from the last 150 years, and scholarly ethnographic studies only from the last eighty.

One important difference between the recorded ethnography and the more distant past lies in the loss of military and regional power.[9] Through most of history nomads were a crucial element in many armies and often controlled the areas surrounding their pastures. These activities must have influenced their economy, their migration patterns, their social organization, and their leadership. Pastoralism has always been associated with marginally productive lands, and thus often with peripheral status, and it has been technologically limiting as well. However, when nomads held significant military power their position in relation to the settled was of course a much stronger one; they could choose their pastures, threaten neighboring towns and offer protection in return for payment both from towns and from caravans. When they incurred losses of livestock, they were quite certain of finding ways to replenish their herds at the expense of others, and their role in trade and regional government offered them sources of income beyond the sale of livestock products.

---

[9] Jean-Pierre Digard, "À propos des aspects économiques de la symbiose nomades-sédentaires dans la Mésopotamie ancienne," in *Nomads and Sedentary Peoples. XXX International Congress of Human Sciences in Asia and North Africa*, ed. Jorge Silva Castillo (Mexico City: Colegio de México, 1981), pp. 14, 20–22; Michael B. Rowton, "Economic and Political Factors in Ancient Nomadism," in *Nomads and Sedentary Peoples XXX International Congress of Human Sciences in Asia and North Africa*, ed. Jorge Silva Castillo (Mexico City: Colegio de México, 1981), pp. 26–27.

There are also more subtle differences from the past attached to changes in society at large. In earlier times the technological gap between nomad and settled was a much smaller one. Neither world was mechanized, and while settled societies predominated in most technological development, in the crucial field of military technology advances often sprang from interactions between settled and nomad peoples. In another sphere, that of health, the situation has largely reversed itself. In the premodern world, no population had access to effective medical care and the populations of cities and villages, living closely together, were more often prey to periodic epidemics, in addition to the constant pressure brought by problems of diet and sanitation. Nomads lived in smaller groups and their diet, if not varied, at least contained sufficient protein. In the contemporary world, people living in more central locations have a clear advantage over those in the marginal lands, for whom hospitals and clinics are hard to reach.

When we apply modern studies to earlier conditions, therefore, we must assume very basic differences in the balance of power and of privilege. The nomad lifestyle is still attractive to many of its adherents and in some places still retains prestige, at least within the populations who practice it. Nonetheless, nomadism in the contemporary world plays a far narrower role in economy and politics and presents few avenues to advancement. The nomadic societies studied by modern ethnographers have a more limited economic base and a lower place in the larger society than those of the past.

When we try to trace the history of nomads our problems start before the beginning of written history; the archaeological record for nomads is less rich than that of settled peoples, and harder to interpret. It is almost impossible to tell whether a site showing temporary residence belonged to nomads or to settled people leaving their village for a summer pasture.[10] In the historical period, information on nomads comes almost exclusively from the writings of their sedentary neighbors and usually represents an unfriendly viewpoint. The historical texts available to us which describe nomads and their relation to settled societies thus present significant problems of interpretation. Above all, coming from a different society, they present a simplified view of nomad populations, focusing on the strangeness of nomad societies and their distance from high culture, as

[10] Karim Sadr, *The Development of Nomadism in Ancient Northeast Africa* (Philadelphia, PA: University of Philadelphia Press, 1991), pp. 13–22; Richard H. Meadow, "Inconclusive Remarks on Pastoralism, Nomadism, and Other Animal-Related Matters," in *Pastoralism in the Levant*, ed. Ofer Bar-Yosef and A. M. Khazanov (Madison: University of Wisconsin Press, 1992), p. 262; C. C. Lamberg-Karlovsky, *Archaeological Thought in America* (Cambridge; New York: Cambridge University Press, 1989), p. 285.

people outside the circle of civilization.[11] In order to understand how nomads and settled have interacted in the past, it is important to use ideologically shaped texts as sources for ideology and to search elsewhere for evidence about what actually existed.

For most of the period covered in this book we have almost no original documents and thus very little knowledge of everyday life, especially outside the major cities.[12] The medieval and early modern histories which have shaped our understanding of the pre-modern Middle East focus largely on rulers, courts and armies, while biographical literature gives us some information on learning and urban life. Nomads appear almost exclusively as soldiers – either attacking under their own leaders or serving in the armies of others. For many years scholars, both medieval and modern, described pastoralists as foreign, raw and aggressive peoples, who came in waves to attack the cities and agriculturalists of the central lands. Among ancient and medieval historians, we find the model of an outer world of nomads who periodically invaded and conquered the settled world, then assimilated to urban culture, lost their barbarian strength, and eventually became settled, to be conquered by new and purer nomads from the reservoir on the borders of settled lands. This theory was most persuasively argued by the medieval North African historian Ibn Khaldun and has been enormously influential over the last several centuries.

Ibn Khaldun saw the nomad and mountain people as populations closer to nature than the sedentary oasis dwellers. The camel-herding Bedouin were the prime example; others were Berbers, Kurds, Turkmen and Turks. These were the most savage human beings in existence, on a level with wild, untamable animals. At the same time, they were the most virtuous, had the greatest fortitude, bravery and strength. Unlike the settled populations living in luxury, they had maintained a simple lifestyle and a purity of lineage which translated into a group feeling allowing both effective leadership and mobilization. Thus, nomads gave rise to leaders who could harness this group feeling into military success; since it was natural to covet wealth, they aimed at conquest of settled states. Once

---

[11] Pierre Briant, *État et pasteurs au Moyen-Orient ancien*, Collection Production pastorale et société (Cambridge; New York; Paris: Cambridge University Press; Maison des sciences de l'homme, 1982), pp. 13–40; François Hartog, *Le miroir d'Hérodote: essai sur la représentation de l'autre*, Bibliothèque des histoires (Paris: Gallimard, 1980), pp. 23–30; Brent D. Shaw, "'Eaters of Flesh, Drinkers of Milk': The Ancient Mediterranean Ideology of the Pastoral Nomad," in *Rulers, Nomads and Christians in Roman North Africa*, ed. Brent D. Shaw (Aldershot, Hampshire, Great Britain; Brookfield, VT: Variorum, 1995), pp. 25–31.

[12] The exception is the Ottoman Empire, for which archives exist from the seventeenth century onwards.

they were in power, however, younger generations became increasingly weakened by luxury, lost their group feeling, and by the fourth generation had become corrupt and incompetent, easy prey for the next conquest from outside.[13] One can certainly find examples in Middle Eastern history to illustrate Ibn Khaldun's model. However, not all nomadic dynasties were short-lived; nor were all settled ones lasting. The popularity of this paradigm can tempt the historian to notice particularly the foreign nomad traits of the founder, while discerning primarily assimilation in subsequent generations. Ibn Khaldun's cyclical formulation need not be abandoned, but it does need to be applied with caution. I have chosen to use a more evolutionary, less cyclical model here.

Early Nomads in the Middle East

This book deals with the Islamic period, but we must recognize that many of the practices and ideologies which defined nomad-sedentary relations were developed over several millennia before the rise of Islam. Indeed, the interactions between pastoralist and sedentary agriculturalists were integral to the development of Near Eastern civilization. Arab conquest and rule were a continuation and a result of earlier interactions. For this reason, it is useful to give a brief sketch of earlier history here. Although settled societies might portray pastoral nomads as intruders enviously looking in, people of pastoralist background were the founders and the rulers of many Middle Eastern states, from the beginning of the second millennium BC. The region of Mesopotamia, which gave birth to the most important imperial tradition of the Middle East, was one in which city states based on intensive irrigation dealt continually with pastoralists both on their borders and within their own territories. The state developed in lower Mesopotamia and gradually expanded outward. Pastoralists in the borderlands were recruited into the armies, and thus moved into the realm. As the territory of the state grew its center moved north, and the proportion of land and population represented by cities and irrigated agriculture became smaller. Control over the realm required frequent campaigning, and troops from peripheral populations were conscripted for the army, sometimes still tribally organized.

The history of Mesopotamian dynasties illustrates this dynamic. The dynasty of Agade founded by Sargon in 2334 BC marked the first move away from city states towards empire; conquests increased the area of the

---

[13] 'Abd al-Rahman Ibn Khaldun, *The Muqaddimah: An Introduction to History*, trans. Franz Rosenthal, abridged ed., Bollingen series (Princeton, NJ: Princeton University Press, 1967), pp. 93–114.

state to include mountain and steppe areas on the borders. A number of troops were recruited from the partly pastoralist Amorites.[14] The Amorites appear with increasing frequency in Mesopotamian sources from this time on, active particularly on the upper Euphrates. By 2000 BC they were an integral part of the state's population, and it is not surprising to find them emerging as rulers over the next several hundred years. The Mesopotamian political world extended north to what is now southern Kurdistan and west to the kingdom of Aleppo; thus, much of what had been the periphery now formed the central territories. The importance of the Amorite period for state development is illustrated by the reign of the famous Hammurabi of Babylon (1792–1750 BC). Like other Amorite rulers, Hammurabi used earlier imperial legitimation based on religious beliefs, but he also viewed his Amorite descent as central to the right to rule. Elaborate genealogies connected the ruler to Amorite tribes with fictive kinship lines, organizing the population into a recognized hierarchy of tribes.[15]

In the middle of the second millennium, Mesopotamia was taken over by dynasties of Kassite and Hurrian descent. These were again people originally from peripheral regions of steppe and mountain who had been present in the region for several centuries. The Kassites at least had probably been partially nomadic. Kassite and Hurrian rule coincided with the introduction of the horse-drawn chariot into warfare. Whereas up to this period the armies of the Near East had consisted of infantry, in the second half of the second millennium chariots made up an important part of essentially all armies in the region.[16] Over time, horse breeding developed into a systematic enterprise, and improvements, particularly stronger and lighter wheels, made chariots increasingly effective. Babylonian expertise with horses and chariots became a source of strength and provided products for export.[17] By the end of the second

[14] Amélie Kuhrt, *The Ancient Near East: c. 3000–330 BC*, 2 vols., Routledge History of the Ancient World (London; New York: Routledge, 1995), p. 55.

[15] J. J. Finkelstein, "The Genealogy of the Hammurapi Dynasty," *Journal of Cuneiform Studies* 20 (1966): pp. 98–102, 116–118; Piotr Michalowski, "History as Charter: Some Observations on the Sumerian King List," *Journal of the American Oriental Society* 103 (1983): pp. 240–243.

[16] Marc Van De Mieroop, *A History of the Ancient Near East* (Oxford: Blackwell, 2003), pp. 16–17; Glenn M. Schwarz, "Pastoral Nomadism in Ancient Western Asia," in *Civilizations of the Ancient Near East*, ed. Jack M. Sasson (New York: Simon Schuster Macmillan, 1995), p. 255.

[17] I. M. Diakonoff, "Media," in *Cambridge History of Iran*, ed. Ilya Gerschevitch (Cambridge: Cambridge University Press, 1985), p. 40; Walter Sommerfeld, "The Kassites of Ancient Mesopotamia: Origins, Politics and Culture," in *Civilizations of the Ancient Near East*, ed. Jack M. Sasson (New York: Simon Schuster Macmillan, 1995), pp. 925–926.

millennium therefore, horses had become an important element in warfare. They did best in uplands which could provide pasture through the summer, particularly plentiful in the Zagros and the plateaus of Iran, Armenia and Anatolia.[18] From now on any state with pretensions to power needed to have access to lands which were likely to be populated by pastoralists and mountain peoples.

The last and most expansive of the early Mesopotamian empires was that of the Assyrians, who began their rise to power about 1200 BC, using the improved war chariot. Given the importance of horses to their power, it is not surprising to find them centered in territories also inhabited by pastoralists. Like the dynasties before them, they recruited nomads for their armies, often in special regiments.[19] In their imperial legitimation the Assyrians grafted themselves onto the dynastic genealogy of the Amorite rulers, including the fictive tribal genealogy which began with a list of "seventeen kings who lived in tents."[20] Thus, like the earlier Amorite rulers, they chose to emphasize pastoralist origins. By the end of the ninth century BC the state system of the Middle East encompassed many of the areas inhabited by mountain and pastoral populations, stretching from the kingdoms of Lydia, Phrygia and Urartu in Anatolia through western Syria to Egypt, and in the east through Assyria and Mesopotamia to Elam in southwestern Iran. Pastoral nomads were present in most of these states, and for many they represented an important sector of the economy and the military.[21]

The Development of Mounted Nomadism

Early nomads moved on foot, using donkeys and horses primarily as beasts of burden, and most lived quite close to the settled populations. At the beginning of the first millennium BC, a breakthrough occurred

---

[18] Stephanie Dalley, "Ancient Mesopotamian Military Organization," in *Civilizations of the Ancient Near East*, ed. Jack M. Sasson (New York: Simon and Schuster Macmillan, 1995), pp. 416–417; Diakonoff, "Media," p. 47; Niels Peter Lemche, "The History of Ancient Syria and Palestine: An Overview," in *The Civilizations of the Ancient Near East*, ed. J. M. Sasson (New York: Simon & Schuster Macmillan, 1995), p. 1201.

[19] Florence Malbran-Labat, "Le nomadisme à l'époque néoassyrienne," in *Nomads and Sedentary Peoples. XXX International Congress of Human Sciences in Asia and North Africa*, ed. Jorge Silva Castillo (Mexico City: Colegio de México, 1981), 68–71; Dominique Charpin, "The History of Ancient Mesopotamia: An Overview," in *Civilizations of the Ancient Near East*, ed. Jack M. Sasson (New York: Simon Schuster Macmillan, 1995), pp. 820–825.

[20] Finkelstein, "The Genealogy of the Hammurapi Dynasty," pp. 112–113.

[21] Paul E. Zimansky, "The Kingdom of Urartu in Eastern Anatolia," in *Civilizations of the Ancient Near East*, ed. Jack M. Sasson (New York: Simon and Schuster Macmillan, 1995), p. 1137; Malbran-Labat, "Le nomadisme à l'époque néoassyrienne," pp. 62–75.

with the development of mounted nomadism, based on horse riding
in the north and on camel riding in the south. In the Eurasian steppe
the combination of horse riding and animal husbandry developed
into the powerful economic and military system known as mounted
steppe nomadism.[22] Riding saddled horses – though at first without
stirrups – nomads gained speed and mobility, allowing them to move
over greater distances and to become formidable warriors. The appeal of
this way of life is shown by its rapid spread; by about 700 BC much of the
Eurasian steppe was dominated by nomads who shared important elements of culture in addition to their nomadic lifestyle. They had a stratified
society with a warrior ethos, using new technology and equipment, and
they produced strikingly similar art based on stylized animals. The level of
communication nomadism fostered is shown by the rapid spread of this
art, known as the animal style, which is found from China to the steppes
above the Black Sea.[23] One of the new technologies which enhanced the
power of the steppe nomads was a compound bow of wood, horn and
sinew, which could be drawn effectively on horseback.[24] The Eurasian
steppe thus became a vast reserve of mounted archers. The mounted
nomadism of the steppe soon influenced settled states, which were quick
to adopt new military techniques. As riding techniques continued to
improve over the next two centuries, cavalry replaced chariots as the elite
branch of the military, allowing armies much greater mobility and
flexibility.[25]

At about the same time that mounted horse nomadism became predominant in the steppe, camel nomadism arose in the Syrian deserts. As
with horses, the efficient use of the dromedary depended on technological
innovations, and in this case the invention of a new type of saddle allowed
the camel to be used effectively both for riding and for transport. Earlier
the Mesopotamian states had been blocked from expansion in the

[22] Nicola Di Cosmo, *Ancient China and Its Enemies: The Rise of Nomadic Power in East Asian History* (Cambridge; New York: Cambridge University Press, 2002), pp. 23–26; Peter B. Golden, *Nomads and Sedentary Societies in Medieval Eurasia*, Essays on Global and Comparative History (Washington, DC: American Historical Association, 1998), p. 5; Khazanov, *Nomads and the Outside World*, p. 92.

[23] Di Cosmo, *Ancient China*, pp. 31–42; David Christian, *A History of Russia, Central Asia, and Mongolia*, Blackwell History of the World (Malden, MA: Blackwell Publishers, 1998), pp. 124–134; T. Sulimirsky, "The Scyths," in *Cambridge History of Iran*, ed. Ilya Gershevitch (Cambridge: Cambridge University Press, 1985), pp. 167–170.

[24] Edward McEwen, Robert L. Miller, Christopher A. Bergman, "Early Bow Design and Construction," *Scientific American* (June 1991): p. 81; A. I. Melyukova, "The Scythians and Sarmatians," in *The Cambridge History of Early Inner Asia*, ed. Denis Sinor (Cambridge: Cambridge University Press, 1990), p. 98; Diakonoff, "Media," pp. 92–94; Christian, *A History*, pp. 123–128.

[25] M. A. Littauer and J. H. Crouwel, *Wheeled Vehicles and Ridden Animals in the Ancient Near East* (Leiden: Brill, 1979), pp. 96–98, 134–143.

southwest by the Syrian desert, passable only through the river valleys. With the full use of the camel, travel and trade became possible here as well.[26] Camel nomadism gave a new level of power to the pastoral peoples who pursued it.[27]

From this time on, the Syrian and Arabian deserts became important centers for camel breeding. The widespread domestication of the camel fostered the development of an overland trade route connecting the Arabian Peninsula directly with the Euphrates through the oasis of Tadmor, near the later city of Palmyra.[28] Another route linked southern Arabia with northern Syria and Palestine, supplementing the sea route which connected eastern Africa with Egypt and Mesopotamia. Camel nomads provided both the camels and the guidance needed for trade. Throughout the eighth century BC nomads appear as part of the power structure in the Syrian desert; we find them mentioned among local powers sending tribute and sometimes as part of a coalition formed against Assyrian domination. Several confederations appear to have been ruled by women; the story of the famous Queen of Sheba in the Old Testament reflects this.

By the beginning of the seventh century BC, land routes carried two types of resin – frankincense and myrrh – from Southern Arabia to the centers of civilization. This trade was lucrative, since both products were important for ritual purposes and had become a valued commodity throughout Mesopotamia and the eastern Mediterranean.[29] At about the same time, a large confederation of camel nomads known as the Qedar developed and for about 300 years controlled the Syrian desert between the oasis towns of Tadmor (Palmyra) and Dumat, on the southern end of the Wadi Sirhan.[30] The economy of the desert confederations was dependent on camel raising, but also included oasis agriculture and above all the caravan trade. It is at about this time that we first hear of several major towns on the Arabian Peninsula, now connected to Mesopotamia and Egypt.[31]

---

[26] Van De Mieroop, *A History of the Ancient Near East*, p. 10.

[27] Richard W. Bulliet, *The Camel and the Wheel* (New York: Columbia University Press, 1990), pp. 45–58, 67–77; Jan Retsö, "The Domestication of the Camel and the Establishment of the Frankincense Road from South Arabia," *Orientalia Suecana* 40 (1991): pp. 199–206; Jan Retsö, *The Arabs in Antiquity: Their History from the Assyrians to the Umayyads* (London; New York: RoutledgeCurzon, 2003), pp. 122–123.

[28] Retsö, *The Arabs in Antiquity*, p. 122.

[29] Retsö "Domestication of the Camel," pp. 187–199.

[30] M. C. A. MacDonald, "North Arabia in the First Millennium BCE," in *Civilizations of the Ancient Near East*, ed. Jack M. Sasson (New York: Simon & Schuster Macmillan, 1995), 1359, 1366–1367; Retsö, *The Arabs in Antiquity*, pp. 131, 166–168, 179–184.

[31] MacDonald, "North Arabia in the First Millennium BCE," pp. 1362, 1366; Bulliet, *The Camel and the Wheel*, p. 78.

Although the settled states had incorporated most areas used by pastoralists specializing in sheep and goats, camel breeders such as the Qedar could move deeper into the desert using areas too distant from large agricultural territories to allow domination by the major settled states. Nonetheless these nomads required wells for the summer months; this and their interest in controlling trade made the more powerful confederations center themselves in desert oases, while many others used summer pastures on the borders of settled regions.[32] Camel nomads therefore remained vulnerable to the armies of the central empires, who could often defeat them in battle and plunder their summer camps. What the empires could not do was to control the desert themselves.

While the Assyrian Empire could dominate the Syrian desert, it faced a threat from the mounted horse nomads of the Eurasian steppe, who were a more effective military force than the camel nomads, both because the horse is better suited to battle and because of their new archery technology. The first of many nomad groups to enter the Middle East from the steppe were the Cimmerians, belonging to the Iranian language family; they established a center of power in what is now Georgia in the early eighth century BC. When they attempted to invade Assyria they were defeated, but the Assyrians recognized the military opportunity they offered and almost immediately incorporated a regiment of Cimmerians into their army.[33] From this time on, the mounted steppe nomads remained a force in the political balance of the Middle East.

During the seventh century a new group of Iranian nomads, the Scythians, defeated the Cimmerians and became masters of northern Iran. From about the sixth to the third century BC they formed a state ruled by nomads who exerted political and economic power over northern Iran and a large part of the western steppe, along with several Greek city states on the Black Sea coast. Unlike most nomads the Scythians left a rich archaeological record, particularly in spectacular royal graves where horses were buried along with the ruler, accompanied by gold artifacts, some of which picture Scythian life in naturalistic detail. They show a nomad warrior culture of expert mobile archers living off their livestock and drinking the milk of their mares. The finds of Scythian-style arrowheads through much of the western Middle East and beyond suggest that the Scythian military technology was copied well beyond the Scythian realm.[34]

---

[32] Stefan Leder, "Towards a Historical Semantic of the Bedouin, Seventh to Fifteenth Centuries: A Survey," *Der Islam* 92, no. 1 (2015): pp. 92–96.

[33] Diakonoff, "Media," pp. 94–95.

[34] "Media," pp. 115–119; Melyukova, "The Scythians and Sarmatians"; Willem Vogelsang, "Medes, Scythians and Persians: The Rise of Darius in a North-South Perspective," *Iranica Antiqua* 33 (1998): pp. 212–214.

The Greek historian Herodotus described their lifestyle and military practice, including the classic nomad tactic of defeating enemies by retreating before them and luring them forward into terrain where they could be attacked.[35]

While the most powerful tribes appear to have remained fully nomadic, agriculture and trade played an important part in the Scythian economy. Grain was grown within the Scythian domains from the beginning, and by the fourth century it was a major export. A fortified settlement north of the Black Sea known as Kamenskoe was begun in the late fifth century, and it became a kind of capital city and a center for trade and production, including metallurgy.[36]

The Imperial Tradition of the Steppe

From the time of the Scythians onwards, the kingdoms of the Middle East faced nomad confederations on their northern borders, and these were more powerful and more strongly organized than the powers of the Syrian and Arabian deserts. The Iranian Achaemenid Empire (558–331 BC) which took over from the Assyrians dealt with the Royal Scythians in the Black Sea area, and with the eastern Scythians in the Oxus region. This was not an entirely defensive relationship; Achaemenid rulers campaigned beyond the Oxus, bringing new nomad regions into their empire. They were also eager to enlist nomads into their armies, particularly the mounted archers of the steppe.

The Cimmerians and Scythians were both Iranian populations, active primarily in the western and central Eurasian steppe. Later the major locus of nomad power shifted to Mongolia, and to the Turkic and Mongolian nomads of the eastern steppe, both belonging to the Altaic language family. A series of powerful states arose in this region, which controlled enormous territories and produced an independent imperial tradition that was passed down and adapted through many centuries. The history of the Eurasian nomad empires is deeply intertwined with that of the Middle East, both through direct relations in times of strength and through population migrations on the Middle Eastern borders at times of disorder. It is worthwhile therefore to provide a brief sketch here.

The imperial tradition of the eastern steppe began with the nomad Hsiung-nu empire of Mongolia, which dominated the steppe and parts of eastern Turkistan from about 200 BC to 90 AD. We do not actually know what ethnic group the Hsiung-nu belonged to, since they left no

---

[35] Briant, *État et pasteurs*, pp. 201–202; Sulimirsky, "The Scyths," pp. 161–199.
[36] Melyukova, "The Scythians and Sarmatians," pp. 101–109.

written sources, and we learn about them exclusively from outside histories. The Hsiung-nu ruler claimed to rule through heavenly mandate; the dynasty collected taxes from its subjects and organized its army in decimal units, with the largest troop unit at 10,000. Below the ruler, the realm was administered through an appanage system with major posts divided between right and left. Although the ruler was theoretically absolute, he ruled through an aristocratic council. Rulers were also elected by the aristocracy at a great gathering, during which the assembly transferred its authority to the ruler.[37]

The decline of the Hsiung-nu was followed by several centuries of decentralized rule in the eastern steppe. The next long-lasting empire in Mongolia was the T'ü-ch'üeh or Türk Khaghanate, which arose in Mongolia in 552 AD and for most of two centuries dominated the Silk Road and much of the Eurasian steppe. This was the state which gave the Turks their original identity; they were the ruling class of the state and provided its official language. The T'ü-chüeh negotiated and fought with the states of China, Byzantium and the Middle East; the empire's supreme ruler, known as *khaghan*, was recognized by both the Iranian Sasanians (240–651 AD) and the early caliphate as one of the world's major powers. The *khaghan* and the Ashina clan to which he belonged were considered to be distinguished by special, God-given good fortune, which allowed the ruler to serve as intermediary between his subjects and supernatural powers.[38] Succession to the throne was usually lateral, with rule passing first to brothers and then to sons. According to outside sources, there was also a formal election ritual, as with the Hsiung-nu.[39] The main belief system of the Turks was shamanism, and in addition they worshiped a sky god known as Tengri.

Although the Hsiung-nu and the Türk Khaghanate fostered agriculture, the Turkic elites were self-consciously nomadic and saw their distance from settled norms as part of their strength.[40] This sentiment was expressed in some of the inscriptions they have left behind written on stones, first in the Iranian Soghdian language and later in Turkic. The

---

[37] Peter B. Golden, *An Introduction to the History of the Turkic Peoples: Ethnogenesis and State-Formation in Medieval and Early Modern Eurasia and the Middle East*, Turcologica, Bd. 9 (Wiesbaden: O. Harrassowitz, 1992), pp. 57–59, 65; Di Cosmo, *Ancient China*, pp. 175–185.

[38] Golden, *Introduction*, pp. 146–147.

[39] Denis Sinor, "The Establishment and Dissolution of the Türk Empire," in *Cambridge History of Early Inner Asia*, ed. Denis Sinor (Cambridge: Cambridge University Press, 1990), p. 315.

[40] Nicola Di Cosmo, "Ancient Inner Asian Nomads: Their Economic Basis and Its Significance in Chinese History," *The Journal of Asian Studies* 53, no. 4 (1994); Sören Stark, *Die Alttürkenzeit in Mittel- und Zentralasien: archäologische und historische Studien* (Wiesbaden: L. Reichert, 2008), pp. 289–291.

neighboring Chinese Empire, tempting their subjects with luxuries and comforts, was to be avoided:

Deceiving by means of (their) sweet words and soft materials, the Chinese are said to cause the remote peoples to come close in this manner. After such a people have settled close to them (the Chinese) are said to plan their ill-will there. (The Chinese) do not let the real wise men and real brave men make progress .... Having heard these words, you unwise people went close to (the Chinese) and were (consequently) killed in great numbers. If you go towards those places, oh Turkish people, you will die! If you stay in the land of Ötükän, and send caravans from there, you will have no trouble! If you stay at the Ötükän mountains, you will live forever dominating the tribes![41]

In the seventh century, an offshoot of the Türk Khaghanate, the Khazars, took over the western steppe, controlling the trade of the great river system from the confluence of the Volga and Kama rivers, connecting them to Scandinavia in the north and more closely to Byzantium in the south. The Caucasus became a battleground between them and the caliphate.[42] The Türk Khaghanate remained under the charismatic Ashina clan up to 744, when another related people, the Uighurs, restored the failing eastern khaghanate and took over as its rulers until the empire's final collapse in 840. The tribes and confederations that had made up the khaghanate remained important over a large area, and subsequent Eurasian states preserved both the alphabet developed by the Turks and many of their political traditions.

Conclusion

While pastoralism has long been recognized as a specialized economy which functioned best in collaboration with agricultural societies, there has been relatively little discussion of the other side of the equation: the usefulness of pastoralists to agricultural states. As I have shown, the early rulers of Mesopotamia expanded into mountainous regions and steppes inhabited by herders despite the difficulties they met in controlling nomad populations. We need not assume that states simply expanded out of a natural urge; the peripheral populations also had something useful to offer.

Pastoral populations were central to two major processes, the creation of increasingly large regional states – eventually empires – and the

---

[41] Talât Tekin, *A Grammar of Orkhon Turkic* (Bloomington: Indiana University Press, 1968), p. 262.

[42] Peter Golden, "The Peoples of the South Russian Steppe," in *The Cambridge History of Early Inner Asia*, ed. Denis Sinor (Cambridge; New York: Cambridge University Press, 1990), pp. 264–265.

development of military strategy involving animals. Once these developments had begun, the process of expansion fueled itself. Nomads were from the beginning considered useful as soldiers, but their importance increased markedly with the development of chariot warfare. Like many later advances in military technology, the development of light chariots seems to have occurred on the frontier between nomad and settled. Once the chariot became an asset in warfare, horses became a necessity and the regions where they were raised took on strategic importance. New advances in military technology connected with mounted nomadism made the horse essential for military might, while the camel became central to trade and useful in war. The nomads who raised these animals were recruited into the army as mercenaries or auxiliaries.

By the middle of the first millennium BC the imperial states based on agriculture had advanced almost as far as they could – in the west and south up to the Syrian and Arabian deserts, and in the north up to the borders of the Eurasian steppe. Beyond these limits, the land did not offer sufficient agricultural potential to maintain a settled empire and could not be effectively controlled. By this time, both the camel herders and horse nomads had developed sufficient technology and mobility to create states – or confederations – based primarily on pastoralism, with agriculture and trade as secondary economies. We now find the familiar worlds of settled and nomad populations facing each other on borders that remained relatively stable over two millennia. Neither side, however, had an economy based exclusively on one strategy. Within the great states of the Middle East, pastoralist populations exploited areas which were more suitable for herding than for agriculture, and in both desert and steppe, agricultural communities continued, sometimes indeed expanded, under nomadic overlordship.

Early in the seventh century, the Prophet Muhammad began preaching in the small merchant city of Mecca; by his death in 632 his community included – nominally at least – the whole population of the Arabian Peninsula. Within two decades his followers had conquered much of the heartland of the Middle East, overturning the Iranian Sassanian Empire and taking over the eastern section of the Roman one. Despite the novelty of its result, the Arab conquest arose from regional dynamics similar to those of earlier Middle Eastern dynasties. Imperial expansion and rivalry brought outlying peoples into the political sphere of settled states, and a population which had been peripheral became the ruling class. What was new and perhaps unique was the extent of the conquests and the originality of the resulting civilization. The Arabians, as the carriers of their own religion and heir to two separate empires, created a new cultural tradition. After the conquest, as the Muslim ruling elite sought to create an identity distinct from that of their more sophisticated subjects, they made use of their desert past and its pastoralist heritage. Here again, they resembled the Amorites and Assyrians, whose tribal and nomad background appears to have been an asset.

To understand the early Islamic state – and the role of nomads within it – we need to examine the milieu within which Islam arose and to determine how early Islamic society changed under radically new circumstances. The Arabians of the Peninsula evolved from a tribal population of varied religions and lifestyles into an army of conquest and quickly became the rulers and soldiers of a new empire. The Arabian Peninsula, a region poor in resources but strategic for trade routes, first became the seat of a new empire, and then returned to the status of a periphery, important primarily for religious reasons. The role that nomads played in this drama was complicated and is not always easy to decipher. It is sometimes difficult to distinguish between ideal and practice; both are important, but they were often quite different.

The geography of the Arabian Peninsula and Syrian hinterland were central to the structure of society, and I shall begin with a description of the terrain and the lifestyles used to exploit it, then proceed to history, from the last century before the rise of Islam to the fall of the Umayyad dynasty in 750. Throughout the discussion I attempt to distinguish the role that nomads played, the policies developed towards them, and the impact of new political structures on the lives of pastoralists.

The Arab Territories

Muhammad and his community were Semitic people belonging to a language family and a genealogical tradition – known primarily from the Old Testament – that placed them within the wider world. The Arabians of the pre-Islamic period were a mixture of sedentary farmers and merchants, mountain peoples, camel nomads, and nomads specializing in sheep and goats. The Syrian and Arabian deserts contain land suitable for sheep herding but many of the central areas will support only camels. Camel nomads,[1] the Bedouin, were not the majority of the population but they enjoyed a prestige and cultural importance disproportionate to their numbers and economic power. Medieval texts and modern travelers have shown more interest in the desert life and military exploits of the Bedouin than in their economic activities. The vast and forbidding desert was their domain, and they could emerge from it to raid their sedentary neighbors, then retreat into areas inaccessible to others. Nonetheless, it is important to remember that camel pastoralism was connected to the rise of the trade routes through the desert and the usefulness of the dromedary as a means of transportation. The nomads lived off the products of their herds and the needs of desert caravans. Thus, they required contact with settled merchants as well as with peasants, and the largest confederations came into being along major trade routes. Relations between nomad and settled populations were central to the life of Syria and Arabia. Almost all Arab tribes, including those dominated by camel nomads, had sedentary sections living in the towns and the surrounding countryside.[2] The tribal confederations which often dominated larger regions contained a mix of lifestyles.[3]

---

[1] The camels of the Arabian and Syrian deserts are dromedaries, with one hump rather than two. The nomads of the northern Middle East and the steppe used the Bactrian camel, with two humps, less suitable for deep desert but more tolerant of cold.

[2] See, for example, Fred M. Donner, "The Bakr b. Wā'il Tribes and Politics in Northeastern Arabia on the Eve of Islam," *Studia Islamica* 51 (1980): pp. 16–25; David Frank Graf, "Rome and the Saracens: Reassessing the Nomadic Menace," in *Rome and the Arabian Frontier: from the Nabataeans to the Saracens*, ed. David Frank Graf (Aldershot: Variorum, 1997); L. Gardet and J.-C. Vadet, "Kalb," in *Encyclopaedia of Islam* (hereafter *EI*) 2nd, ed. P. Bearman et al. (Leiden: Brill, 1960–2005).

[3] Donner, "The Bakr b. Wā'il," pp. 18–23; M. J. Kister, "Mecca and the Tribes of Arabia," in *Studies in Islamic History and Civilization in Honour of David Ayalon*, ed. M. Sharon (Leiden: Brill, 1986), pp. 34–8, 42; Michael Lecker, *The Banū Sulaym: A Contribution to*

The close interaction between settled and nomad was due in part to the seasonal organization of pastoralism. The towns of the Hijaz, the settled lands on the west bank of the Euphrates, and the eastern flanks of the coastal range in Syria were all a regular part of Bedouin life in the summer months.[4] The settled populations controlled resources in water and agricultural produce that they could withhold from their nomadic neighbors, and a strong power in the agricultural sphere could often dominate nearby nomads. For their part, the Bedouin could use military force, particularly in the form of raids on border villages. When the settled power was strong, however, raids elicited punitive expeditions.[5] It is important to recognize that military skill was not limited to the Bedouin, and many sedentary Arabs were also excellent fighters, notably the tribes of the mountainous regions. In the Yemen and the Asir mountains, sedentary power prevailed.[6]

The relative importance of nomad and settled populations varied but almost all regions had a mix of the three lifestyles. The southeastern section of the Arabian Peninsula – the Hadramawt and the Yemen – has sufficient rainfall to maintain agricultural states, and nomads here were a minority. The rest of the peninsula ranges from semi-desert to sand deserts, usable only by camels, interspersed by oases which offer rich farmland and significant water supplies over a small area. Three major regions should be distinguished. The Hijaz, the birthplace of the Prophet, contains numerous oases where settled populations predominated, though camel and sheep nomads occupied deserts and hills. To the northeast lies the Najd, stretching from the borders of the Hijaz to the Persian Gulf and the lower Euphrates, where camel nomads were more prominent. Finally, there is the Empty Quarter, the famous sand desert which separates the fertile coastal region from the interior. Here the lack of water limited the population to a few small tribes.

---

the Study of Early Islam, The Max Schloessinger memorial series. Monographs; 4 (Jerusalem: Hebrew University of Jerusalem, 1989), pp. 5–11, 63, 99–101, 202–203.

[4] Eva Orthmann, *Stamm und Macht: die arabischen Stämme im 2. und 3. Jahrhundert der Hiğra* (Wiesbaden: Reichert, 2002), pp. 153–155; Gustav Rothstein, *Die Dynastie der Laḥmiden in al-Ḥīra; ein Versuch zur arabisch-persischen Geschichte zur Zeit der Sasaniden* (Hildesheim: G. Olms, 1968), p. 121. See also Suzanne Pinckney Stetkevych, *The Poetics of Islamic Legitimacy: Myth, Gender, and Ceremony in the Classical Arabic Ode* (Bloomington: Indiana University Press, 2002), p. 90.

[5] For an example of the relationship of border towns and Bedouin, see Jibrail Sulayman Jabbur, Suhayl Jibrail Jabbur, and Lawrence I. Conrad, *The Bedouins and the Desert: Aspects of Nomadic Life in the Arab East*, SUNY series in Near Eastern studies (Albany: State University of New York Press, 1995), pp. 1–8.

[6] Ella Landau-Tesseron, "Review of F. McGraw Donner, *The Early Islamic Conquests*, Princeton 1981," *Jerusalem Studies in Arabic and Islam* 6 (1985): pp. 499–500.

In the Syrian desert, settled populations along with sheep and goat nomads predominated on the desert edges, and camel nomads in the center. The eastern and western edges of the desert formed the frontier of the great imperial states, which could usually control border regions and punish nomads who attempted to impose their will. To achieve independence and above all to dominate the lucrative trade to Syria and Iraq, a nomad confederation had to control the central oases which offered summer grazing and water. It is worth listing the larger oases here, since they were the key to power over trade routes and the center of successive desert kingdoms. Al-Yamama is the largest oasis area in the Najd desert, and the well-watered Bahrayn coast also provided agricultural goods and summer pasture. Both regions were closely connected to southern Iraq. Further west, a series of oases have defined the trade routes between the Arabian Peninsula and the Syrian lands. Dedan, Tayma and Dumat al-Jandal lead from the Hijaz and Najd to southern Syria, and from Dumat a string of small oases, the Wadi Sirhan, leads to the Fertile Crescent. Near the western edge of the desert a series of oases provided an alternate route leading through Petra and Bostra to Damascus. In the north Tadmur, site of the famous Arab city of Palmyra, was a key point in the route between the upper Euphrates and the coast.

While the desert oases allowed nomads to achieve considerable power, they could not be maintained or defended without year-round population. Therefore, we find in them a mix of tribal populations – some sedentary tribes, some who specialized in sheep and goats, and sections of primarily Bedouin tribes. The most famous of the Arab desert powers, the Nabataean kingdom centered at Petra, combined sedentary and nomadic manpower to dominate trade along the western edge of the desert from about 300 BC to 100 AD. The original founders of the kingdom were nomads, who are thought to have become increasingly sedentary over time as their oases became large and flourishing agricultural centers. Nonetheless, the nomadic population remained an important element in the kingdom's structure up to the end of its existence.[7]

Throughout these regions, the tribe was a central institution, defining social and political life. Religion, law and identity all depended on tribal affiliation. The importance of tribe was not limited to the pastoralists, but also seems to have applied to almost all segments of the population within the peninsula, where town life was also organized along tribal lines. Both the tribal system and the pastoral economy were constantly changing; they were self-replicating but not static. Both before and after the rise of

---

[7] G. W. Bowersock, *Roman Arabia* (Cambridge, MA: Harvard University Press, 1983), pp. 13–24.

Islam, tribes and tribal sections moved towards the north from the Yemen, through the Najd, into Syria, reacting to economic or political pressures. These were often slow population movements, with people moving group by group over long periods of time. Thus, over time in each region power, pasture and water rights had to be renegotiated or won through military might.

The Arabs and Surrounding Powers before Islam

What brought the Arabians into a wider political field was the development of three major powers to their south, north and west. In Chapter 1, I discussed the Middle Eastern imperial tradition up to the Achaemenid Empire (558–331 BC), which centered in southern Iran but inherited the Mesopotamian tradition and stretched to include the western lands. After this, Iranian dynasties took over the eastern territories while the western section gradually came under the control of a new power – the Roman Empire. By 106–107 AD the Romans controlled much of Syria, creating the new province of Roman Arabia, and reached into the Peninsula.[8] Beginning in 240 AD a new Iranian dynasty, the Sasanians, created an empire which stretched from Central Asia to the Caucasus and from the border of India to the Arabian Peninsula. Laying claim to the imperial tradition of the Middle East, the Sasanians constructed their capital in Mesopotamia, north of Babylon. The two empires faced each other across the Syrian hinterland and competed for the control of the desert and its trade routes. Towards the end of the third century, a southern Arabian dynasty, the Himyar, united most of the southern end of the Arabian Peninsula, and began to extend its influence north, thus becoming involved in the conflict between the Sasanians and the Romans.[9]

The nomads of the Syrian desert and steppe were now in a strategic position; they could threaten imperial borderlands and could also offer their military services to the neighboring states. The Romans instituted a defense system along the western Syrian desert, using nomadic Arab tribes as frontier armies. Some tribesmen became citizens living within Roman boundaries; others were allies offered salaries through individual treaties. The Sasanians established their presence on the southern shore of the Persian Gulf and eastern Arabia; another area important for the

---

[8] Bowersock, *Roman Arabia*, pp. 81–97.
[9] C. E. Bosworth, "Iran and the Arabs before Islam," in *Cambridge History of Iran*, ed. Ehsan Yarshater (Cambridge: Cambridge University Press, 1983), pp. 603–606; Robert G. Hoyland, *Arabia and the Arabs. From the Bronze Age to the Coming of Islam* (London; New York: Routledge, 2001), pp. 44–57.

Sasanians was the Najd, whose camel nomads controlled the approaches to southern Mesopotamia.[10]

The three powers surrounding the Arab lands – the Himyarites, Byzantines and Sasanians – used client Arab confederations to support their goals rather than attempting to rule the desert directly. The Syrian and Arabian deserts thus became involved in the rivalry of the surrounding states, and their inhabitants entered the Byzantine and Sassanian armies. Client rulers received land and subsidies in return for controlling neighboring tribes and providing troops against rival powers. The leaders of the Kinda tribe in central Arabia served as governors for the Himyarite kingdom. The Lakhmid dynasty, established on the Euphrates at the beginning of the fourth century, served the Sasanians. Their capital at al-Hira developed from an encampment into a permanent city and a center for the developing literature in Arabic. From 502–503 on, the Byzantines promoted another dynasty, the Ghassanids, bestowing official ranks as well as subsidies. The major Ghassanid court was in Jabiya, on the edge of the desert south of Damascus.

The client kings exerted power in the desert more through promise of reward than threat of retaliation. There appears to have been a gradation of power, first subjects, then allies, then tribes considered independent and not expected to pay taxes. The settled tribesmen closest to the Ghassanid and Lakhmid courts could be considered subjects, and the nomads raising sheep and goats likewise. Distant tribes, particularly camel nomads, were more difficult to incorporate. The Lakhmid and Ghassanid kings, about whom we have the best information, attracted the Bedouin elite in several ways. They offered court and military positions to tribesmen and handed out fiefs to some. A particularly advantageous appointment was that of tax-collector to one's own tribe – a position which offered both income and position. Service also provided opportunity for military activity on a larger scale than was available in intertribal conflicts, and thus a path to wealth and prestige.[11]

The client kings had only modest standing armies and when they came into conflict with inimical tribes, they were not certain of victory. Nonetheless their influence was felt throughout the peninsula. Even in the Hijaz, which was only loosely connected to this system, some lineages sought advantage at the northern courts.[12] The Lakhmids and Ghassanids reached

---

[10] Hoyland, *Arabia and the Arabs*, pp. 27–28; Bosworth, "Iran and the Arabs before Islam," p. 603.

[11] Fred McGraw Donner, *The Early Islamic Conquests* (Princeton, NJ: Princeton University Press, 1981), pp. 45–48.

[12] Donner, "The Bakr b. Wā'il," p. 27; Kister, "Mecca and the Tribes of Arabia," pp. 42, 46; M. J. Kister, "Al-Ḥīra: Some Notes on Its Relations with Arabia," *Arabica* 15 (1968).

their apogee in the sixth century, then collapsed quite suddenly at the turn of the seventh. The Kinda rulers, clients of the Himyarites, succeeded twice in taking over the Lakhmid court for several years.[13] It is not entirely clear why the system was abandoned, though the difficulty of controlling the client kings may have been one reason. The Lakhmids and Ghassanids, fighting each other on behalf of their patrons, became personal enemies and did not always feel bound by treaties between the two empires.

The Lakhmids and Ghassanids undoubtedly contributed to the development of stronger political traditions among the tribes and their impact in the cultural sphere was even more important. Their courts are linked with two types of early literature in Arabic, the odes (*qaṣīda*) and accounts of the tribal battles remembered as *ayyām al-'arab*, both of which remained popular through the rise of Islam and formed the base for later historiography and poetry. The *ayām* and *qaṣīda* were connected to the tribe, whose glory they commemorated and extolled. Later commentators described the tribal gatherings at which poetry was recited, often in the Arabian market towns, and the yearly poetic contest which brought prestige to the tribe whose poet performed the best.[14] Many of the most famous poets are known also to have sought fame at the courts of the client kings, and some lived there permanently. Since much of the biographical material recorded about pre-Islamic poets apparently originated later as commentary on their verse, we do not know the details of their relations to the Ghassanids and Lakhmids, but the number of poems addressed to these monarchs attests to the importance of courtly patronage.[15]

Pre-Islamic literature expresses a tribal tradition closely connected to the Bedouin, whose habits and ideology came to symbolize an ideal for Arabians of all lifestyles.[16] Theirs was an egalitarian ethos which emphasized military bravery, generosity, the pursuit of vengeance, and the protection of guests and dependents. The honor of individual and tribe required that no suppliant be turned away and that any guest, however inconvenient, be fed and given protection. If one someone was killed, the close relatives had to exact recompense or, preferably, vengeance, no

---

[13] Irfan Shahid, "Lakhmids," *EI* 2nd ed.; Irfan Shahid, "Tanūkh," "Ghassān," *EI* 2nd ed.

[14] Abdulla el-Tayib, "Pre-Islamic Poetry," in *Arabic Literature to the End of the Umayyad Period*, ed. A. F. L. Beeston (Cambridge: Cambridge University Press, 1983), pp. 28–33.

[15] "Pre-Islamic Poetry," pp. 29–33, 45–49, 65–73.

[16] This literature was preserved orally and was edited and glossed only in the Islamic period; thus, our current texts must be considered only an approximation of the pre-Islamic poetry. Fred McGraw Donner, *Narratives of Islamic Origins: The Beginnings of Islamic Historical Writing*, Studies in Late Antiquity and Early Islam; 14 (Princeton, NJ: Darwin Press, 1998), pp. 5–20; James E. Montgomery, *The Vagaries of the Qaṣīdah: The Tradition and Practice of Early Arabic Poetry*, Gibb literary studies; no. 1 (Cambridge: E. J. W. Gibb Memorial Trust, 1997), pp. 38–39.

matter how much danger this brought them. The claims of honor often went against the interest of the individual and the family and even more against those of the state, but that only enhanced the ideal. These were the virtues which, as the Bedouin saw it – or at any rate as it was expressed in literature – distinguished the Bedouin from other peoples and gave them superiority. What is striking about the image enshrined in early works and continued in later writing is the emphasis on the difference and distance between Bedouin and settled peoples; much greater in literary traditions than it probably was in real life.[17] Connected with this separation is an attachment to the desert as the locus of nomadic life and personal freedom. The classic pre-Islamic ode began with a lament over a deserted campsite, followed by an amatory adventure and a journey on either a horse or a camel. All of these were normally set in the desert, adorned with place names and a description of the landscape, weather and wildlife:

> Oh abode of Mayyah on height and peak!
>   It lies abandoned
> And so long a time has passed it by.
>
> I stopped there in the evening
>   to question it;
> It could not answer, for in the vernal camp
>   there was no one.
>
> Nothing but tethering pegs
>   that I made out only slowly,
> And the tent trench, like a water trough,
>   hollowed from the smooth hard ground.[18]

It is odd to find a tone of nostalgic melancholy associated with what must have been everyday objects and experience. Scholars have pointed out that in some cases neither poet nor patron was in fact nomadic; thus, the poetry was not Bedouin but Bedouinizing.[19] There may also be a more fundamental reason for the tone of the *qaṣīda*. Arab camel nomadism contained a certain paradox. The nomads' military prowess and their considerable prestige stemmed from their wide-ranging migrations in the desert, when groups were dispersed and self-sufficient. It was this life which nourished the tough egalitarian code of the Bedouin. The true desert was a region of danger that required specific highly developed skills, possessed only by the Bedouin. One had to be able to find remote wells in a shifting landscape and to read traces in the sand which betrayed

---

[17] Sara Binay, *Die Figur des Beduinen in der arabischen Literatur 9.-12. Jahrhundert* (Wiesbaden: Reichert, 2006), p. 30.
[18] Al-Nābigha, "Oh abode of Mayyah," in Stetkevych, *Poetics*, p. 20.
[19] Montgomery, *The Vagaries of the Qaṣīdah*, pp. 7–9.

the identity of those who had passed by, sometimes by recognizing the print of an individual camel.[20] Many, perhaps most, Bedouin, however, spent only the cold months in the desert and the summer under tighter authority at desert wells or among settled peoples. This was the time at which taxes were collected, either by tribal leaders or outside powers. It was sometimes the most prestigious tribal lineages who maintained the closest ties to settled society.[21] The tension between the ideal of desert life as lived for part of the year and the need to accept greater control during summer months may be one reason that the desert is emphasized, along with the ideal of the pure Bedouin, disdaining the constraints of settled life.

There was also a question of authority within the tribe itself. In the ideal, the tribal *shaykhs* was first among equals but the organization of large-scale trade or warfare undoubtedly required the imposition of additional discipline. The pre-Islamic Arabic poetry we know originated in the sixth century when the system of client states was at its height, and this situation probably threatened the autonomy of individual tribesmen. The client kings offered wealth and authority to tribal *shaykhs* and in return expected them to control their followers. The appointment of tribal clients as tax collectors to their tribes underlined the subordination of the tribesmen both to their own chief and to his outside patron. This demand appears to have been resented, and taxes were sometimes refused.[22]

The emphasis in many poems on personal freedom – sometimes indeed transgression – may be in part a response to the diminution of these very things. Poets who came to the courts to gain recognition sometimes stressed their claim to equality, and their audience – then and later – appears to have appreciated their sentiments. The famous ode of 'Amr b. Kulthum addressed to the Lakhmid king 'Amr b. Hind (554–569), asserting tribal and personal honor in response to tyranny, has been enshrined among the most famous odes:

> With what purpose in view, Amr bin Hind,
> do you give heed to our traducers, and despise us?
> With what purpose in view, Amr bin Hind,
> should we be underlings to your chosen princelet?
> Threaten us then, and menace us; but gently!
> When, pray, were we your mother's domestics?[23]

[20] These skills are vividly described for the twentieth century in Wilfred Thesiger, *Arabian Sands* (New York: Dutton, 1959).
[21] Donner, "The Bakr b. Wā'il," pp. 22, 27, 29; Jabbur, Jabbur, and Conrad, *The Bedouins and the Desert*, pp. 31–32.
[22] Kister, "Al-Hira," pp. 159–163.
[23] A. J. Arberry, *The Seven Odes; The First Chapter in Arabic Literature* (London, New York: G. Allen & Unwin; Macmillan, 1957), p. 206.

The early poetry that has come down to us illustrates the ideals and tensions of a period in which the rivalries of the great powers and of their client kingdoms offered opportunities for power and wealth that were hard to resist. The nomad and mountain lifestyles fostered military skills that made tribesmen valuable to the great powers, and alliance opened new fields of military action to the tribes. On the other hand, involvement with outside powers threatened the egalitarian nature of tribal life. While Arab tribesmen accepted the opportunities offered, they also needed to reassert the power of their ideals and the locus of their independence.

The First Years of Islam

Before beginning the discussion of the rise of Islam, I must state that I am here using the traditional narrative based on Arabic sources. Unfortunately, no narrative based on outside sources can provide sufficient material for an analysis of nomad activities. Thus, my conclusions must be taken as tentative. According to tradition, the Prophet Muhammad was born about 570 into a merchant family of Mecca in the Hijaz. Mecca was a city whose population depended largely on trade but was closely connected to neighboring farming and nomadic communities. During the sixth century it appears to have emerged as a regional trading center, in cooperation with the rich oasis of Ta'if, which provided the city with much-needed food. The city and its dominant tribe, the Quraysh, also profited from control over several pilgrimage sites. The possession of holy sites was a common base for supratribal leadership within the fluid politics of the region, since it provided both divine authority and a nucleus for local trade. There is some dispute among scholars over the nature and extent of Meccan trade and over the level of control that the city exerted over the major routes.[24] The primary exports were probably leather and leather goods, clothing, perfume, and perhaps precious metals mined in the region. The imports were often finished goods, along with grain from the Yamama oasis.[25] The major trading partners appear to have been Syria and the Yemen.[26]

---

[24] Patricia Crone, *Meccan Trade and the Rise of Islam* (Princeton, NJ: Princeton University Press, 1987), pp. 87–108; F. E. Peters, *The Arabs and Arabia on the Eve of Islam* (Brookfield, VT: Ashgate, 1998), Introduction, xxxvi, note.

[25] Róbert Simon, *Meccan Trade and Islam: Problems of Origin and Structure*, Bibliotheca orientalis Hungarica, v. 32 (Budapest: Akadémiai Kiadó, 1989), pp. 63–70, 91–95; Crone, *Meccan Trade*, pp. 87–108.

[26] Crone, *Meccan Trade*, 117–131.

The rise in Mecca's trade may have been due in part to the fall of the client states; in 581–582, the Byzantines deposed the last of the Ghassanids kings and in 602 the Sasanian emperor executed the Lakhmid king and established a Persian governor in Hira. The Sasanians and Romans now dealt directly with the Arab tribes, but they did not become fully involved in the Arabian Peninsula, because for almost three decades, from 603 to 628, they were locked in a bitter war with each other. It is possible that the Roman-Sassanian war benefitted Meccan trade, since leather was a crucial material for military use and the Roman army consumed it in large quantities. Leather was one of the more important pastoral products, so growing demand would also have increased the prosperity and importance to the nomad population.[27]

The Quraysh were sedentary, but the nomads of the region provided many of their trade partners and helped maintain the security of their caravans. Some members of nomadic tribes lived in Mecca, and intermarriage with city tribes was not uncommon.[28] Like many other Meccans, Muhammad appears to have been suckled by a woman from a nomad tribe, but his early career, both as merchant and as prophet, was among the settled population.[29] When he and his followers left Mecca, the community that offered him a new home was the agricultural oasis of Medina, where he and his followers arrived in 622.

Muhammad's religious message reflected his settled background. The emphasis on loyalty to the religious community – the *umma* – over the tribe, and social responsibility over individual glory was not designed to appeal to Bedouin. During Muhammad's first years in Medina, he made some attempts to ally with surrounding tribes, but most of the nomads of the Hijaz supported the Meccans against him. This was not surprising, considering the Meccans' long-standing alliances.[30] The lack of sympathy between Bedouins and early Muslims is shown in the Qur'an, where references to Bedouin are few and largely negative. The word most often used for camel nomads is *a'rāb* or *a'rābī* and it is usually applied in a pejorative sense. The few Qur'anic passages on the Bedouin

[27] Patricia Crone, "Quraysh and the Roman Army: Making Sense of the Meccan Leather Trade," *Bulletin of the School of Oriental and African Studies* 70, no. 1 (2007).

[28] Lecker, *The Banū Sulaym*, pp. 107–134; Kister, "Mecca and the Tribes of Arabia," pp. 33–34, 38; W. Montgomery Watt, *Muhammad at Mecca* (Oxford: Clarendon Press, 1953), p. 89.

[29] Watt, *Muhammad at Mecca*, pp. 34–36.

[30] W. Montgomery Watt, *Muhammad at Medina* (Oxford: Clarendon Press, 1956), pp. 17–36; Fred M. Donner, "Muḥammad's Political Consolidation in Arabia up to the Conquest of Mecca: A Reassessment," *The Muslim World* 69, no. 3 (1979): pp. 236–239. The existence of numerous small oases throughout the Hijaz encouraged a mixed economy among local tribes; except for those in the major oases, most apparently depended primarily on pastoralism.

portray them as inferior in religion, self-serving and deceptive. They are mentioned as those who make excuses instead of turning up for battle; they claim to be believers but have no real faith (Qur'an 9:90, 97 and 49:14). To some extent these traits represent the view of the settled population towards nomads, but the context in which they are placed suggest frustration with a group of people who resisted Muslim efforts to attract them.[31]

The situation changed somewhat with the conclusion of the treaty at al-Hudaybiya in 628, when the Muslims and Meccans agreed to a ten-year truce. The Muslims were now apparently free to seek allies among the regional tribes; this is certainly what they did.[32] Muhammad used a mixture of attraction and force to gather a sizeable following among the Hijazi tribes and when he took over Mecca in 630 he was accompanied by contingents from former Meccan allies including several primarily nomad tribes. The key to control lay in the oases, and Muhammad immediately set about taking over the major ones, thus depriving the Meccans of key allies and giving himself an advantage over the nomads of the Hijaz, since he controlled local markets and sources of water.[33]

According to Islamic tradition, the two last years of the Prophet's life saw a rapid expansion of the Muslim confederation and numerous conversions to Islam, as tribes from all over the peninsula sent deputations to Medina to declare allegiance. It is likely that the deputations represented only sections of tribes and that most treaties did not require a firm commitment. Towards the end of his life the Prophet decided to place greater demands on the tribes of his confederation and sent out followers to oversee the implementation of treaties and the collection of tax. It is not clear however that his agents had collected any dues before Muhammad died on June 8, 632.[34]

Muhammad's death was sudden and unexpected. In choosing a new leader for the community, his companions agreed on his aged father-in-law Abu Bakr, known for his skill as tribal negotiator. Abu Bakr's two-year reign was a continuation of Muhammad's policies in both internal and external affairs. He appears to have favored the Quraysh aristocracy, who provided most of the leadership for his military campaigns. With the death of Muhammad many tribes saw little reason to send on the taxes

---

[31] Binay, *Die Figur des Beduinen*, pp. 78–89.

[32] Donner, "Muḥammad's Political Consolidation," pp. 240–245; Watt, *Muhammad at Medina*, pp. 48–55.

[33] Watt, *Muhammad at Medina*, pp. 66–73; Donner, "Muḥammad's Political Consolidation," pp. 245–246.

[34] Elias Shoufani, *Al-Riddah and the Muslim Conquest of Arabia* (Toronto: University of Toronto Press, 1973), pp. 10–46; Donner, *The Early Islamic Conquests*, pp. 102–111.

so recently demanded of them, while powers who had never accepted an alliance now became enemies and had to be subjugated. The campaigns against recalcitrant tribes in Arabia are subsumed in Islamic tradition under the rubric of the Ridda.[35]

During his lifetime Muhammad had sent several expeditions to the north, and the subjugation of the southern Syrian region began during the Ridda wars. During the lifetime of Abu Bakr, campaigns concentrated on securing the oases and tribal territories on the desert fringes, avoiding major engagements.[36] In Syria, many of the Muslims' opponents in early battles were the Arab clients and allies of the Byzantines and they often remained faithful to the Romans.[37] In the Iraqi campaigns, aimed against the towns along the Euphrates which had long connections to the desert tribes, regional tribesmen took different sides.[38] By the time of Abu Bakr's death in 634, the new Islamic community had been consolidated and expanded to include almost the whole of the Arabian peninsula and the southern Syrian desert. The new elite of the community was also formed, and was securely Hijazi, with the settled tribes of Mecca, Medina and Ta'if in ascendancy. The Hijazi nomads, along with a few faithful allies from nearby tribes, also participated in the campaigns of the Ridda and shared in its rewards but they did not achieve the level of prestige granted to new converts from Mecca and Ta'if.[39]

The next caliph, 'Umar (634–644), at first continued to rely primarily on the tribesmen of the Hijaz and the Yemen. After 636, when the Muslim armies began to conquer cities and clash with major Byzantine and Persian armies, 'Umar expanded the army, using soldiers and commanders even from tribes which had opposed the Muslims during the Ridda.[40] The Muslim armies, which were the major path to wealth, power and prestige, now included large, primarily nomadic tribes.

Tribes and Nomads in the Founding of the State

As we examine the policies that Muhammad and his successors adopted to maintain control over their followers, we should recognize two particularities of the Arabian population which presented potential challenges. One was the centrality of the tribal system, which encouraged numerous

[35] Shoufani, *Al-Riddah*, pp. 58–96.
[36] Donner, *The Early Islamic Conquests*, pp. 112–119.
[37] Donner, *The Early Islamic Conquests*, pp. 103–148; Walter Emil Kaegi, *Byzantium and the Early Islamic Conquests* (Cambridge; New York: Cambridge University Press, 1991), pp. 68, 79, 114.
[38] Donner, *The Early Islamic Conquests*, pp. 173–188.
[39] Donner, *The Early Islamic Conquests*, p. 88.
[40] Donner, *The Early Islamic Conquests*, pp. 204–211.

power centers. The other was the presence of nomad populations with a mobile lifestyle and control of inaccessible terrain. It is important to remember that while tribalism and nomadism were often connected, many – probably most – Arabian tribesmen were not nomads. Thus, the policies towards tribes and those towards nomads should be distinguished from each other. Neither is easy to discern, since the sources at our disposal were not written down until the eighth and ninth centuries. We can learn more about cultural attitudes towards tribes and nomads than about reality. When examining tribes, we can discover something about the policies of the central government, and the histories pay loving attention to inter-tribal politics and rivalries; what is less clear is how tribes were organized. On the question of nomadism there is very little material. Even when historians were interested in determining the actions of the Bedouin, they were dependent on traditions which distinguished among various tribes, but not between their nomadic and settled sections.

The control of tribes was clearly a major concern from the beginning of Muhammad's career. The Muslim army required tighter discipline than tribal structure would allow, and much of it was made up of individuals or sections of tribes who campaigned under commanders close to the ruler. Members of the same tribe often belonged to different regiments.[41] There was also a systematic effort to detach potential soldiers from their tribes. Muhammad and his successors called on new converts to perform the *hijra*: to leave their homeland to devote themselves to the expansion of the Muslim community. During Muhammad's lifetime the invitation was to settle in Medina. Clearly such a move could be difficult for farmers, who would have to give up their land, but it was even harder for nomads, whose livelihood depended on livestock, territory and social cooperation. Muslim traditions (*ḥadīth*) record exceptions granted by Muhammad which permitted sincere converts to remain in their original tribal regions, but this appears to have involved a lower status.[42]

Once the conquests were underway the caliph 'Umar and his successors invoked the concept of *hijra* to encourage immigration into the conquered lands and to control new arrivals. Muslims were deliberately kept apart from the local populations and settled in garrison cities. Muslims who were active in government or army were allotted regular stipends inscribed in the official register (*dīwān*), calculated according to the date of conversion and service to the Muslim cause; this created a new hierarchy based on religious primacy, which favored the largely sedentary early converts. Those who performed the *hijra* to settle in the garrison

---

[41] Donner, *The Early Islamic Conquests*, pp. 119, 221–226; Kaegi, *Byzantium*, pp. 72, 123.
[42] Patricia Crone, "The First-century Concept of Hiğra," *Arabica* 41 (1994), p. 356.

cities – known as *muhājirūn or muqātila* – received regular salaries. People who remained in their own territories might fight in the army but received only the booty of the campaigns in which they participated.[43] Taxation fell most heavily on non-Muslims, while Muslims originally paid only an alms tax on wealth: for the settled the *zakāt*, and for nomads a tax in animals, known as the *ṣadaqa*.[44] There is controversy over whether the *hijra* was part of a deliberate policy to weaken nomads, who might threaten an orderly state. Whether or not the policy was aimed against nomads, it must certainly have been designed to increase government control.

The promotion of the *hijra* suggests a policy aimed against tribalism, but nonetheless within garrison cities immigrants were organized along tribal lines. Members of a tribe were settled in the same quarter, and often shared a mosque and a guest house. It was the tribal *shaykhs* who were responsible for paying salaries and who recruited soldiers for campaigns.[45] The continued use of tribal organization in the army and cities may have been a concession to Arab traditions, but it also offered significant advantages to the state. The system brought the tribes into the sphere of government and, what may have been equally important, stabilized their leadership. The connection of tribal structures to stipends and recruitment permitted the state to interfere in the choice of tribal *shaykhs*, traditionally chosen within the tribe. The chiefs, appointed as pay masters and as commanders, now depended partly on the state for their authority and were responsible to the central government for the actions of the men under them.[46]

The retention of tribal organization had another major advantage, as a tool for the exclusion of the conquered population from membership in the ruling elite. The Caliphs naturally relied heavily on the men who had served the Romans and Persians to administer their new lands. It was desirable to consider these people inferior and foreign to the Arab Muslims, and the tribal system provided a useful marker. The organization of military power along tribal lines helped to underline Arab exclusivity even as the Muslim armies accepted increasing numbers of non-

---

[43] F. Løkkegaard, "Fay," *EI* 2nd ed.; Wilferd Madelung, "Has the *Hijra* Come to an End?" in *Mélanges offerts au professeur Dominique Sourdel*, Revue des Études Islamiques, vol. LIV (Paris: Paul Geunther, 1986), pp. 232–234.

[44] As usual with administrative terminology, the usage of these terms is not entirely consistent. Orthmann, *Stamm und Macht*, pp. 173–174.

[45] *Stamm und Macht*, pp. 81–97; Donner, *The Early Islamic Conquests*, pp. 228–240.

[46] Donner, *The Early Islamic Conquests*, p. 259; Martin Hinds, "Kûfan Political Alignments and Their Background in the Mid-Seventh Century A.D.," *International Journal of Middle East Studies* 2 (1971), p. 347; Hugh Kennedy, *The Armies of the Caliphs: Military and Society in the Early Islamic State*, Warfare and History (London; New York: Routledge, 2001), p. 22.

Arab and particularly Persians troops, highly respected for their mastery of military arts.[47] In the matter of religion, tribal structures were used even more effectively. The Arabian Muslims defined themselves both by religion and by origin, and as the ruling stratum they had every reason to keep themselves distinct. Most land was left in the hands of its previous owners, and only land owned by non-Muslims was subject to tax. For the conquered peoples therefore, conversion to Islam could bring financial advantage, and for the government a loss of revenue. One barrier used to prevent large-scale conversion was based on the centrality of tribalism to Arab identity. To become Muslim, the convert had to affiliate himself with an existing Arab tribe, accepting low status as *mawla*, or client, the status given to freed prisoners of war.[48]

The Umayyad Caliphate

'Umar's continued promotion of early converts over other tribesmen, including those with more prestigious lineages, alienated many Arabs in the garrison cities who felt insufficiently rewarded for their contributions. The resulting tensions helped to bring about the murder of the third caliph, 'Uthman, in 656 and the civil war in which Muhammad's cousin 'Ali b. Abu Talib was murdered. The victor was the governor of Syria, Mu'awiya, member of the Umayyad branch of the Quraysh. He moved the capital to Damascus, not far from the former capital of the Ghassanid kings, putting the Syrian army at the center of his power structure. Mu'awiya is credited with a policy which favored the older tribal aristocracy – the *ashrāf*. While he established a royal court, he ruled primarily through balance and persuasion and became famous for the quality of *ḥilm* – patience and subtlety – associated with tribal leadership. His family cultivated close political and matrimonial ties with the powerful Quda'a confederation, particularly the largely nomadic Kalb tribe which dominated the northern Syrian desert. Thus, a number of Bedouin rose to prominence during his reign. On the other hand, most of the governors he appointed were from the sedentary Quraysh and Thaqif. The troops who conquered Syria and thus made up the core of its early army were almost exclusively from settled tribes. Some scholars believe that Mu'awiya curtailed Bedouin influence.[49]

---

[47] Kennedy, *Armies of the Caliphs*, pp. 4–5.
[48] Ignaz Goldziher, *Muslim Studies*, trans. C. R. Barber and S. M. Stern, 2 vols. (London: Allen and Unwin, 1967–1971), vol. 1, pp. 101–104; A. J. Wensinck and P. Crone, "Mawla," *EI* 2.
[49] Nancy A. Khalik, "From Byzantium to Early Islam: Studies on Damascus in the Umayyad Era," unpublished PhD dissertation, Princeton University (2006), p. 51; Gerald Hawting, *The First Dynasty of Islam: the Umayyad Caliphate AD 661–750* (Carbondale; Edwardsville: Southern Illinois University Press, 1987), pp. 32–35, 42–43; H. A. R. Gibb, "An

During his reign and those of his descendants, known as the Sufyanids, the soldiers of the garrison cities were the regular armies, and whatever their origins, they themselves were separated from a nomadic lifestyle. The policy of *hijra* continued and the garrisons circled the desert, thus potentially exerting control over its nomad populations.

Mu'awiya's death in 680 unleashed a new civil war, as candidates from other branches of the Quraysh attempted to win the caliphate. The two most important challengers were 'Abd Allah Ibn al-Zubayr, the son of one of Muhammad's companions, and Husayn, the son of 'Ali b. Abu Talib. The dynasty was rescued by Marwan, a member of a different Umayyad lineage, whose descendants held the caliphate to the end of the dynasty. Marwan had first to rise within the Umayyad camp, and then to win over the Syrian army, a significant part of which favored Ibn al-Zubayr, particularly the tribes centered in the Jazira and northern Syria. Marwan achieved success with the help of the Kalb and several tribes of more local power in Syria.

Even the Kalb, who had intermarried with the Umayyad house, had to be won over, and they were powerful enough to impose conditions for their support. The terms proposed by the tribe's leader, Ibn Bahdal, provide a telling illustration of the position of Bedouins and their *shaykhs* in the early Umayyad period. Ibn Bahdal demanded that he continue to hold same high position he had under Mu'awiya and his son Yazid: 2,000 Kalb would get yearly pay of 2,000 dirhams, which was the highest stipend for non-Quraysh aristocracy, and Ibn Bahdal would have unrestricted control, presumably over the people and territory of his tribe. He also wanted assurance that he would have leadership of the tribal council and that after his death either his son or his cousin would lead the Kalb.[50] These are large demands and show the centrality of the Kalb position, but they also suggest the dependence of the tribe on the state. There is an assumption here that the caliph had the power to appoint the tribal leader, and that the caliph, not the tribes themselves, determined the membership of the tribal council. The Kalb held significant power within the state, but their tribe was not a totally self-governing entity.

The decisive victory for Marwan and the Umayyad dynasty was achieved in a long and destructive battle at Marj Rahit, north of Damascus, during the summer of 684, during which the coalition opposing Marwan was defeated and a large number were killed. When the Marwanid lineage replaced Mu'awiya's line, the organization of the

Interpretation of Islamic History," in *Studies on the Civilization of Islam*, ed. Stanford Shaw and William R. Polk (Boston: Beacon Press, 1962), p. 7.
[50] Gernot Rotter, *Die Umayyaden und der zweite Bürgerkrieg (680–692)*, Abhandlungen für die Kunde des Morgenlandes; Bd. 45, Nr. 3 (Wiesbaden: Steiner, 1982), p. 147.

army and the role of the Arab tribes in dynastic politics underwent a change. Marwan's successor 'Abd al-Malik (685–705) centralized the realm and created a more professional army. While Mu'awiya had chosen his major commanders from the tribal aristocracy, from the time of 'Abd al-Malik commanders of more modest descent were preferred and the army contained significant numbers of non-Arabian troops. Over time, moreover, the garrison armies of Basra and Kufa were marginalized, and the Syrian army was used to maintain control even outside its own province.[51]

Although army units no longer mirrored the tribal structure of the conquest, tribes remained important in politics and in the military. The battle of Marj Rahit, which was devastating to the defeated tribes, marked the beginning of factional rivalry between two parties envisioned in tribal terms: the Qays, consisting of tribes identified as being of northern origin, most of whom supported Ibn al-Zubayr; and the Yamani, to which the Kalb belonged, identified with southern origins.[52] The continuing factional struggle between Qays and Yaman incorporated local struggles over land use and regional preeminence. Starting with Marj Rahit, the desire for vengeance – justified as a tribal obligation – ensured a constant succession of raids and battles, both small and large. The resulting disorder and factionalism lasted to – indeed through – the end of the Umayyad dynasty and was a major cause of its weakness.[53] The schism spread to other regions, taking on a variety of names. There has been a great deal of debate about what these factions meant and how they functioned.[54] Whatever their actual nature, they kept alive the concept of tribalism and its relevance to politics. Only after the 'Abbasid revolution and the remodeling of the caliphate on a more Persian model did the factions gradually die out.

The Role of Nomadism in the Early Islamic State

So far, I have written largely about tribalism; in this section I will explore the results of Muslim policies on the practice of nomadism, posing three major questions: whether nomadism increased in conquered territories under Muslim rule; what level of power and prestige nomads held; and

[51] Kennedy, *Armies of the Caliphs*, pp. 18–19, 22–23, 34–42; Patricia Crone, *Slaves on Horses* (Cambridge: Cambridge University Press, 1980), pp. 37–39.

[52] Rotter, *Die Umayyaden*, pp. 133–151; Julius Wellhausen, *The Arab Kingdom and Its Fall*, trans. Margaret Graham Weir (Calcutta: University of Calcutta, 1927), pp. 201 ff.

[53] See, for example, Abd al-Ameer Abd Dixon, *The Umayyad Caliphate, 65–86/684–705: (A Political Study)* (London: Luzac, 1971), pp. 89–119.

[54] For some discussion, see Patricia Crone, "Were the Qays and Yemen of the Umayyad Period Political Parties?" *Der Islam* 71 (1994); Orthmann, *Stamm und Macht*, pp. 9–20.

finally whether divisions between nomad and settled populations were an important factor in politics. The central lands of the new Islamic empire lay on either side of the Syrian desert; thus, communication within the empire depended on the state's relations with the Bedouins inhabiting it. Whatever policy the leadership espoused, nomads could neither be eliminated nor entirely marginalized. The Muslims had also conquered territories which lent themselves to a combination of pastoralism and agriculture – mountain areas such as the Jazira, the desert border along the Euphrates, and the hilly steppes of Trans-Jordan. The first question to examine is whether the influx of Arab tribes from the peninsula resulted in an increase in pastoral lifestyle in these mixed regions.

The scholarship on the period suggests that despite the influx of new partly nomadic tribes, the ratio between nomad and settled population did not change significantly. In western and southern Iraq, local pastoralists were encouraged to settle in garrison cities. Agriculture and urban settlement were significantly expanded, but the pastoral economy apparently continued to be important. In the southern Iraqi border regions, the desert and steppe appear to have remained largely in the hands of the tribes already controlling the area, but in central Mesopotamia several largely pastoral tribes were pushed north by new arrivals.[55] In northern Syria and the Jazira, there was a larger influx of new tribes from the south. The Kalb extended their territories northward to the Tadmur oasis and several tribes such as the B. Sulaym moved sections into the Jazira, where they competed for land with tribes previously there and with new arrivals from central Iraq.[56] Despite the evidence of competition over pasture, however, there is no clear indication of a long-term increase in the number of nomads or a growth in the proportion of pastoral to settled populations.[57]

Likewise, for the region between Damascus and Palestine studies suggest a continuance of settled and nomadic populations without major change in their proportions. The northern cities of Syria – Aleppo, Hims and Damascus – were home to numerous immigrants in the city and

---

[55] Michael G. Morony, *Iraq after the Muslim Conquest* (Princeton, NJ: Princeton University Press, 1984), pp. 229–232.

[56] Morony, *Iraq after the Muslim Conquest*, p. 231; Rotter, *Die Umayyaden*, pp. 126–133; Claus-Peter Haase, "Untersuchungen zur Landschaftsgeschichte Nordsyriens in der Umayyadenzeit," unpublished PhD dissertation, Universität Hamburg (1975), pp. 140–144.

[57] Haase, "Untersuchungen zur Landschaftsgeschichte," pp. 121–126, 147–169; Chase F. Robinson, "Tribes and Nomads in Early Islamic Northern Mesopotamia," in *Continuity and Change in Northern Mesopotamia from the Hellenistic to the Early Islamic Period*, ed. Karin Bartl and Stefan R. Hauser, Berliner Beiträge zum Vorderen Orient, Band 17 (Berlin: Dietrich Reimer, 1996).

countryside, but these were both nomads and agriculturalists. Sections of formerly nomadic tribes, finding themselves in territories favoring agriculture, became at least partially settled.[58] In Palestine likewise, immigration did not cause a major change in the relationship between nomad and settled; in the Negev region north of the Gulf of Aqaba there appears to have been a gradual move towards sedentarization.[59] The regions along the western edge of the desert from Balqa to Hawran show continuity across the Arab conquest without significant increase in nomad population.[60] It is important to remember that nomads sometimes used cultivated fields as summer pastures; thus the expansion of agriculture did not necessarily entail a decline in pastoralism.[61] The increased irrigation in the desert fringes of Hawran and Balqa', along the Mesopotamian rivers, and in the northern oases all occurred in regions still used as summer pastures by nomads.[62]

The importance of the Bedouin population for the Umayyads is illustrated by the residences the dynasty constructed at the edges of the desert, most particularly in Transjordan, at the head of the Wadi Sirhan. Settlements were also scattered southwest from Damascus, with a few along the northern edge of the desert. Many of these had highly developed systems of irrigated agriculture. Early scholars attributed the location of Umayyad palaces primarily to a nostalgia for the desert, but over the last decades researchers have suggested additional reasons for their location, both economic and political. Many are built along important routes. Most are on the edge of agricultural districts and could be meant to expand the agricultural base. Finally, these were locations which allowed the dynasty to maintain relations with nomad tribes, most notably the Judham in Trans-Jordan and the Kalb to the north. The Qasr al-Khayr al-Sharqi in Tadmur may have been built specifically with the Kalb in mind, since they centered in that region.[63] There is nothing contradictory in

---

[58] Haase, "Untersuchungen zur Landschaftsgeschichte," pp. 149, 153–155; Orthmann, *Stamm und Macht*, pp. 81–98.

[59] Gideon Avni, *Nomads, Farmers, and Town-Dwellers: Pastoralist-Sedentist Interaction in the Negev Highlands, Sixth-Eighth Centuries C.E* (Jerusalem: Israel Antiquities Authority, 1996), pp. 55–57, 90–91.

[60] G. R. D. King, "The Umayyad Qusur and Related Settlements in Jordan," in *The IVth International Congress of the History of Bilad al-Sham*, ed. Muhammad 'Adnan al-Bakhit and Ihsan 'Abbas (Amman: al-Jami'a al-Urduniya, 1987), pp. 74–79. For a good discussion of the literature to 1995, see Michael Wood, "A History of the Balqā' Region of Central Transjordan during the Umayyad Period," unpublished PhD dissertation, McGill University (1995), pp. 71–96: for nomads particularly 94–96.

[61] Sonderforschungsbereich 19 "Tübinger Atlas des Vorderen Orients," *Tübinger Atlas des Vorderen Orients* (Wiesbaden: Reichert, 1977), compare AX 1 (Kopp, 1989) and AX 11 (Scholtz, 1989).

[62] *Tübinger Atlas*, map AX 11.

[63] King, "The Umayyad Qusur," pp. 76–77, 79; "The Distribution of Sites and Routes in the Jordanian and Syrian Deserts in the early Islamic Period," in *Proceedings of the*

these various purposes, since the use of the desert routes, the provisioning of the army, and the security of the settled region all depended on relations with Bedouin tribes. In the Jazira as well, the Umayyads showed concern for the control of partly nomad tribes.[64]

The place of nomads in the Umayyad army is difficult to ascertain. The Umayyad army was largely Syrian, and thus presumably included recruits from the tribes of the desert. We should remember also that the regular army enrolled in the *dīwān* did not provide all the troops used by the Umayyads. Important commanders, often members of the dynasty, increasingly recruited their own troops, whose pay may still have come from the central government.[65] There were also auxiliary troops raised for particular campaigns; primarily nomadic tribes certainly contributed to some of these units.[66] However, the sources rarely specify what section of the tribe troops came from, or whether regular soldiers were recruited from regions beyond the garrison cities and their attached lands.[67] We can conclude that Umayyad armies included soldiers from nomad groups and some auxiliary troops were in tribal formation at least at the lower levels. We cannot judge, without more detailed research, what proportion of the army was nomad and whether significant numbers of Bedouin were among the elite troops.[68]

Finally, we must attempt to determine the importance of nomadism in political life. Did nomads represent a distinct group in conflicts within the state? Were they a threat to stability or the economy on their own account? In general, the answer to these questions should be a qualified "no." While nomad concerns added fuel to some rivalries and nomads contributed manpower to several revolts, the political fault lines were religious and regional. The factional rivalry between the Qays and Yamani blocks began with the battle at Marj Rahit in 684, which was fought over the issue of the caliphate. Over the next years, continued contests over land

---

Twentieth Seminar for Arabian Studies held at London on 1st–4th July 1986 (London: Seminar for Arabian Studies, Institute of Archaeology, 1987); Wood, "A History of the Balqa-Region," pp. 61–70.

[64] Robinson, "Tribes and Nomads," p. 443.

[65] Kennedy, *Armies of the Caliphs*, pp. 47–49.

[66] Kennedy, *Armies of the Caliphs*, p. 49; Dixon, *Umayyad Caliphate*, p. 56; Morony, *Iraq after the Muslim Conquest*, pp. 249–250.

[67] Orthmann, *Stamm und Macht*, pp. 40–41.

[68] Scholars have come to different conclusions about the proportion of Bedouin troops active at this time. See, for instance, Patricia Crone, "The Early Islamic World," in *War and Society in the Ancient and Medieval Worlds. Asia, the Mediterranean, Europe and Mesoamerica*, ed. Kurt Raaflaub and Nathan Rosenstein (Washington, DC: Center for Hellenic Studies, Harvard University, 1999), pp. 316–317; Kurt Franz, *Vom Beutezug zur Territorialherrschaft. Beduinische Gruppen in mittelislamischer Zeit*, vol. 5, Nomaden und Sesshafte (Wiesbaden: Reichert, 2007), pp. 120, 199.

combined with the desire for vengeance to keep the tribes of Syria in a state of feud, contributed to the ill-feeling between the two factions.[69] Some land in dispute was pasture, but some may well have been agricultural. In the Qays-Yamani split, as in the division between the supporters of Ibn Zubayr and the Umayyads, regional issues were more central than the division between settled and nomadic. Thus, in general the northernmost region, the Jazira, contained primarily Qaysi tribes, often at odds with the more southern Syrian regions. The division between Iraqi and Syrian interests is also well known; here the discontents appear to have centered around the distribution of wealth and privilege and, in Kufa, questions of religion. Although there were some raids and occasional problems with routes, the relations between the Bedouin and townspeople seem not to have been a source of serious trouble.

When we examine the position of nomads – as nomads – in the early Islamic state, we find a situation which had elements in common with pre-Islamic Syria and Arabia. There does not appear to have been a major shift in the ratio of nomad and settled populations, and the Umayyads seem to have been successful in their attempt to co-opt the chiefs of the Syrian Bedouin. Aside from the interior deserts, there was no one region totally dominated by nomads, and almost none were free of them. Thus, the system earlier visible in the Arabian Peninsula, in which almost all regions, tribes, and states included farmers, Bedouin and nomads with mixed flocks, seems to have spread to the new heartland of the Islamic state. What is probably most different is the level of integration of the nomadic population into state structures. Nomads were now less excluded, but probably more controlled.

The Bedouin Image

The Umayyad period was one of intensifying assimilation to the conquered populations. By the eighth century the Arab elite were intermarrying with their new subjects and adapting to the life of the great cities and imperial traditions. As rulers over the population of two highly developed empires, they required both a more sophisticated legitimation and a political and cultural identity as an Arab ruling class.[70] The effort to create these involved the nomads, particularly the Bedouin, though less as

---

[69] Dixon, *Umayyad Caliphate*, pp. 84–119; Rotter, *Die Umayyaden*, pp. 133–146.

[70] Fred M. Donner, "Umayyad Efforts at Legitimation: The Umayyads' Silent Heritage," in *Umayyad Legacies: Medieval Memories from Syria to Spain*, ed. Antoine Burrut and Paul M. Cobb (Leiden: Brill, 2010); Fred M. Donner, *Muhammad and the Believers at the Origins of Islam* (Cambridge, MA: Belknap Press, Harvard University Press, 2010), pp. 217–220.

actors than as an iconic image. The Bedouin came to stand for the pre-Islamic past of the Arabs and for their separate identity within the larger world. For many city Arabs, Bedouin provided the definition of the inferior society they had left behind with the *jāhilīya* – the age of ignorance before the rise of Islam.[71] At the same time, the desert and the Bedouin formed the base for much of the best-loved literature of that period, which remained highly popular. The desert nomad became an ambivalent figure; he was uncouth, irreligious and lawless, but also brave and generous.

As we have seen, references to nomads in the Qur'an were largely negative. The number of *ḥadīth* describing Bedouin as inferior Muslims suggests disapproval among some of the population also in the first centuries of Islam. Muhammad was reported to have made disparaging remarks about them. He was said to have forbidden Bedouin from leading *muhājirūn* in prayer; Bedouin were lax in prayer, tending to put off the evening prayer until they had milked their camels; women of the *muhājirūn* should not marry them lest they slide back into Bedouin ways.[72] However, one finds some traditions which suggest a more positive view. One *ḥadīth*, for instance, concerns a Bedouin who entered a mosque during Muhammad's lifetime, and casually urinated inside it. Incensed, the Muslims yelled at him, but Muhammad ordered that he be let go and simply poured water over the urine.[73]

It was in the literary sphere that the Bedouin became useful. The art of tribal Arabic poetry was actively promoted by the Umayyad caliphs, who sponsored a return to pre-Islamic poetic traditions. Mu'awiya set up his court at Damascus, near the former capital of the Ghassanids, and like them, he patronized poets. Thus, the pre-Islamic poem of eulogy and denigration – the *qaṣīda* – continued to flourish. Since Mu'awiya and his successors chose to rule through the tribal system, it is not surprising to find that the *qaṣīda* continued to be used also in the service of tribal rivalry. The form and imagery of the *qaṣīda* were highly stylized, and its nomad references firmly set. For poets remaining within the genre, the locus remained the desert, and the mores those of the nomad.[74] The famous poem composed by the poet al-Akhtal for the caliph Marwan after the victory at Marj Rahit in 684 both praises the caliph and claims for his own

---

[71] Binay, *Die Figur des Beduinen*, pp. 3–7, 26.
[72] Robinson, "Tribes and Nomads," pp. 441; Crone, "The First-Century Concept of Hiğra," pp. 360–371; Sulayman Bashir, *Arabs and Others in Early Islam*, Studies in Late Antiquity and Early Islam; 8 (Princeton, NJ: Darwin Press, 1997), pp. 10–14; Binay, *Die Figur des Beduinen*, pp. 106–125.
[73] Bukhārī, vol. I, bk 4, numbers 218, 221; Sahih Muslim, vol. II, numbers 558, 559. www .hadithcollection.com
[74] Jaroslav Stetkevych, *The Zephyrs of Najd: The Poetics of Nostalgia in the Classical Arabic Nasīb* (Chicago: University of Chicago Press, 1993), pp. 111–122.

tribe, the Taghlib, a greater prestige than they probably held. The Taghlib was a tribe on the central Euphrates which raised primarily sheep, goats and horses, and thus did not enjoy the cachet of the camel Bedouin. At this time, moreover, they were still largely Christian, and therefore presumably ranked low in both the religious and the tribal hierarchies.[75] In the ode, nonetheless, the pure-bred camels appear with the Taghlib, while their enemies, many of them originally Bedouin, are associated with the inferior animals – sheep, goats and asses.[76] The many battles associated with the Qays/Yamani rivalry were commemorated both in poetry and in prose, and rivals also recalled their pre-Islamic exploits, thus keeping alive the pre-Islamic historical tradition of the *ayyām al-'arab*.[77]

Interest in poetry and the use of Bedouin imagery was not confined to court and army. The reconstitution of tribal structure under the early caliphs and later the Qays-Yamani factionalism ensured that rivalries would take on a tribal nomenclature; thus, the historical and legendary traits ascribed to particular tribes became the object of scholarly research. The creation of a subordinate class of recent converts, the *mawālī*, and their attempt to gain greater status encouraged the political use of pre-Islamic Arab traditions, which could be mined to find weapons against rivals and upstarts. The science of genealogy soon became important, and its practitioners sought after.[78] The new learned classes of the cities in Iraq pursued knowledge of the Bedouin for other reasons – ironically as a tool for understanding the Qur'an, a text hardly friendly to the Bedouin ideal. The Bedouin were seen as great masters of speech and moreover, as desert dwellers who had remained away from the cities, they were the key to the understanding of earlier language and habits necessary to the urban commentators, most living outside the Arabian Peninsula.[79] The greatest centers for the elaboration of Bedouin studies were the cities in Iraq – Kufa and most especially Basra – which although they started as garrisons soon had a mixed population and an active economy supporting a learned leisure class. Basra, closer to the desert, stood out, perhaps because of its famous market, the Mirbad, which attracted desert Bedouin conveniently to the doorstep of city scholars.[80] Iranian converts

---

[75] Stetkevych, *Poetics,* Chapters 2–3 (pp. 51–108).

[76] Stetkevych, *Poetics,* pp. 90, 96–97.

[77] Dixon, *Umayyad Caliphate,* p. 89; Donner, *Narratives of Islamic Origins,* pp. 196–197.

[78] Morony, *Iraq after the Muslim Conquest,* pp. 237–238, 254–258; Claude Cahen, "History and Historians," in *Religion, Learning and Science in the 'Abbasid Period,* ed. J. D. Latham ; R. B. Sergeant ; M. J. L Young, *Cambridge History of Arabic Literature* (Cambridge: Cambridge University Press, 1990), p. 189; Goldziher, *Muslim Studies,* pp. 126–131, 167–175; el-Tayib, "Pre-Islamic Poetry," pp. 389, 393, 409.

[79] Binay, *Die Figur des Bedouinen,* pp. 50–52.

[80] Charles Pellat, *Le milieu baṣrien et la formation de Ǧāḥiz* (Paris: Librairie d'Amérique et d'Orient Adrien-Maisonneuve, 1953), pp. 5–12, 34–35, 37–47; Morony, *Iraq after the Muslim Conquest,* pp. 195, 198, 208–209, 271.

began to write in Arabic, and the literary language started to include Persian words, while the first translations of Persian literature into Arabic were undertaken. In response, many poets and philologists sought out Bedouin lexicography to enshrine in their works.[81]

When the Arab elites defined themselves against their non-Arab subjects, the Bedouin ceased to be the uncouth "other" and became the unpolluted "self." Fear that the prestige and the fighting strength of Arabs could be damaged by too close an association with their subject peoples was openly expressed. The problem was particularly acute in Iraq, where Persian influence was strong, and became sharper as the governors 'Ubayd Allah b. Ziyad (675–684) and al-Hajjaj (694–714) worked to develop a more centralized administration.[82] In 683, 'Ubayd Allah reportedly declared in the Friday sermon (khuṭba) in Basra, "We have worn silk, the striped cloth of Yaman, and soft clothing until our skins have become disgusted with it. We must replace it with iron."[83] Likewise among the religious classes, settled and Persian ways were frowned upon, and we find ḥadīth warning against such Persian habits as using a knife at meals or rising as a mark of respect.[84] By the end of the Umayyad period there was a significant bilingual elite within which people of different origins and traditions worked closely together, but nonetheless the Arabs as rulers and the military class had managed to retain – or to create – a consciously separate character, based in part on a carefully preserved corpus of Bedouin lore and literature.

Conclusion

In some ways the dynamics of Arabian conquest and rule resemble those of earlier dynasties in the Middle East. The Arabian population began as a peripheral society using a variety of methods to wrest a living from marginal lands. It was brought into the orbit of the neighboring states first because the territory lay across important trade routes, and second because Arabians were useful as troops. After several centuries of service, strife, and mutual political interference, the Arabs organized and conquered not one empire, but all of one and part of another. Once in power

---

[81] H. A. R. Gibb, "The Social Significance of the Shuubiya," in *Studies on the Civilization of Islam*, ed. Stanford J. Shaw and William R. Polk (Boston: Beacon Press, 1962), p. 63; C. E. Bosworth, "The Persian Impact on Arabic Literature," in *Arabic Literature to the End of the Umayyad Period*, ed. T. M. Johnstone A. F. L. Beeston, R. B. Sergeant and G. R. Smith (Cambridge: Cambridge University Press, 1983), p. 492.
[82] Morony, *Iraq after the Muslim Conquest*, pp. 51–53, 59–61, 66–68, 74–75, 79.
[83] Morony, *Iraq after the Muslim Conquest*, pp. 262–263.
[84] Bosworth, "The Persian Impact," p. 484.

they adopted many of the traditions of their subject peoples while retaining an elite identity as outsiders.

The people of the Arabian Peninsula did not have a common economic strategy or belong to one political tradition, but they did share a poetic language and a tribal tradition in which leadership by consent combined with an egalitarian ethic and a code of conduct covering most aspects of life. While the tribal code was powerful in towns and agricultural districts, it reflected Bedouin society in its emphasis on warfare, hospitality and equality. Effective leadership, however, came most often from settled tribes or sections, particularly from those who had access to additional religious legitimation which could transcend tribal separatism.

If we examine the history of nomad and settled through the formation of the caliphate, what we see could be understood as the expansion of settled power. In the first centuries of camel nomadism, largely nomad confederations had controlled several of the major trade routes by centering themselves in the larger oases, and while the oases developed a strong agricultural base, the Bedouin remained crucial to the control of trade. After the Roman takeover of the Syrian coast, nomads remained important as troops and were courted by the client kings of the Romans and Sasanians. From the time of Muhammad, the balance appears to have changed. It is notable that Muhammad's community, centered in towns living from trade and agriculture, succeeded in building up a coalition able to expand through the whole of the peninsula and beyond. The early outside conquests were the work of primarily sedentary soldiers, with the Hijazis at the center. The need for new manpower in the conquest army after 634 led to the inclusion of tribes who converted later, some of whom were largely Bedouin, but at the same time the creation of garrison cities and the emphasis on the *hijra* discouraged a fully nomadic lifestyle within the central army.

The Umayyads controlled three sides of the desert, leaving only southern and eastern Arabia relatively independent, and these were no longer critical areas. Thus, the nomad tribes of the central deserts could no longer play one power against another. On the other hand, the Umayyads had to deal more closely with the desert. While the Byzantines and Sasanians had used client kings to protect themselves from raids by desert nomads or attacks from the rival empire, the Umayyads had to incorporate nomads and their habitat in order to keep their state together. Many Arabs did remain nomadic, and Bedouin continued to make up part of the army. We cannot characterize the Umayyads as a tribal confederation, but the dynasty did bring both tribalism and nomad populations into state structures. The chiefs of largely Bedouin tribes such as the Kalb were now part of the central elite, intermarrying with the dynasty and holding important positions, and tribal support was crucial to the second civil war and the triumph of the Marwanids.[85] The nomads had lost some independence of action, but they were more fully included in the power structure.

The nomads also played a central role in the development of Arab identity. Unlike earlier nomad rulers in the Middle East, the Muslims brought with them a new religion and with it their own language and literary tradition. Here the Bedouins played a crucial role, and one that has influenced the understanding of Arab culture and history. Two forms of oral pre-Islamic literature helped to form the basis of later literature: the *qaṣīda* and the tales of the *ayyām al-'arab*; both furthered a tribal image tied to a Bedouin ideal. The emphasis on the desert, on freedom and on a particular set of personal characteristics may have arisen in opposition to a reality which limited the autonomy of the camel nomads. The highly colored image of a separate people who represented both the Arab homeland and the pre-Islamic past was more ideal than reality. Nonetheless it proved useful and durable, both in expressing tensions among the early Muslim Arabs and in demonstrating their cohesion and difference from other peoples.

[85] Crone, *Slaves on Horses*, pp. 93–94.

3   The Rise of New Peoples and Dynasties

On their victory in 750 the 'Abbasids moved the capital of the caliphate from Syria to the old imperial center in Mesopotamia and brought a shift in the composition of court personnel and the standing army. For the nomads of the Islamic lands the first 250 years of Abbasid rule represented a period of relative exclusion, followed by a rise to power and importance. As nomads regained power, the Bedouin were joined by new groups who enlarged the sphere of nomad control. Abbasid commanders and the Persian bureaucrats who dominated the Abbasid administration brought a more eastern geographical consciousness. For the Bedouin and the Arab tribesmen of Syria, early Abbasid rule meant a drop in status and probably in prosperity. In other partly nomadic areas, on the other hand, the Abbasids brought new energy for expansion and consolidation. As the Jazira, Azerbaijan, Kurdistan and the Caspian provinces gained importance, the nomads and mountain peoples of these regions developed into political powers.

In the ninth century a new military class emerged as the troops that the 'Abbasids had brought with them were first supplemented and then gradually replaced by Turkic soldiers. This was the first appearance of an ethnic group which has played a central role in the history of the Middle East. The Turks were imported from the Eurasian steppe in small groups or as individuals, some originally slaves, and they were used as highly trained cavalry. By the middle of the ninth century, the three leading ethnic groups of the central Islamic lands – Arabs, Persians and Turks – were all recognized as an integral part of the governing elite.

It seems ironic that it should have been under the Abbasids that the Bedouin developed into independent political powers, since the Abbasid revolution appeared to shift power away from their lands. During the Umayyad period the Syrian desert had held a central position. Bedouins therefore could not be excluded, but when they were active, they were usually led by settled powers; tribal leaders were active forces in government politics but did not establish independent dynasties.

Bedouin political development in the Abbasid period was gradual and the result of a number of separate factors. In their first years, the Abbasids were a strong expanding power, but within a century they began to face serious problems. The first and most intractable of these was the decline in the agricultural base of Iraq; this brought with it financial difficulties that made the maintenance of a large standing army difficult. Thus, the dynasty became increasingly dependent on neighboring areas for both grain and manpower. As a result, dynasties of mountain and nomad provenance gained increasing power in the center. Both they and the 'Abbasids, seeking additional soldiers, turned to Bedouins and Kurds for auxiliary troops. Tribal chiefs, gaining authority and wealth from outside, strengthened their position over their tribesmen. In the tenth century, Bedouin tribal groups began to take part in local politics under their own leadership, and over the century leading lineages strengthened their power sufficiently to found regional dynasties. During the same period the Iranian Kurds likewise became organized and emerged as a significant historical force. From this time on, the Middle East was never without dynasties of nomad provenance.

When the Abbasids established themselves in Iraq, they were implicitly claiming all of Iran and the eastern caliphate, since these had been conquered by the Iraqi army. The early 'Abbasid period was a crucial one for the nomads of both the western and the eastern parts of the caliphate. However, developments in the two regions proceeded along different lines and would be difficult to trace in one chapter. I have therefore limited myself here to the history of the western provinces, from Egypt to central Iran, and will discuss eastern Iran and Central Asia in Chapter 4, on the Seljukid period.

The Changing Caliphal Army

The Abbasids defeated the Umayyads with the help of a large army they brought with them from Khorasan, and their rule ended the Syrian domination of the standing army. When they sought additional soldiers from outside, they turned to new sources of manpower in the northern and eastern regions. Arabs – including Bedouins – did not cease to serve in caliphal armies, but they became one among many different peoples. The 'Abbasids settled the core of their Khorasanian army in Iraq as elite troops; these included Arab soldiers from Khorasan, some of whom had probably remained nomadic, and Iranian troops.[1] These armies and their

---

[1] The region of Marw, which was the garrison center for Khorasan, was on the edge of the desert and noted for camel raising; many Arabs also inhabited Qumis, also a region known

descendants became a separate, privileged group, known as the *abnā* (sons). However, the new military order was not a complete or sudden reversal for either the Syrian military or the nomads. The Bedouin had ceased to play a central military role before the fall of the Umayyads.[2] During the first years of Abbasid rule, moreover, Syria remained a strategic region. The Abbasid family had been centered in the town of Humayma in the southern desert, now southern Jordan, and in their contest with the Umayyads, they had successfully courted many of the northern Syrian tribesmen.[3] During the first decades of Abbasid power, Syrian troops, both nomad and settled, were still active, and Abbasid representatives forged close links with nomad tribes, particularly within the Qays faction.[4]

The position of western troops was eroded in the succession struggle which followed the death of caliph Harun al-Rashid in 809, which pitted the armies of the eastern and western regions against each other. Harun had divided his realm – the west under his first heir apparent, Amin, and the east under another son, Ma'mun. Amin was stationed in Baghdad and had the allegiance of most of the standing army; he also recruited Kalb from Homs and Damascus, and from the north, including the Jazira. Al-Ma'mun was stationed in Khorasan, and when he took over Baghdad in 819 he brought with him a largely eastern army. Among the soldiers al-Ma'mun recruited in the east were a number of Turks. This was a fateful move, since Turkic soldiers came to play a central role in military and political history, and in the history of nomads.

The Turks had long been familiar as formidable enemies and occasional allies along the northern frontier in Central Asia and the Caucasus. They owed much of their military prowess and their reputation as soldiers to their background as steppe nomads. In particular, they were renowned for their skill in mounted archery; here they were superior to the Bedouin. It was not only fighting skill which distinguished the Turks; they also had the prestige of belonging to a major imperial system, since they were connected with the Türk Khaghanate. Furthermore, they were available.

---

for livestock. Heinz Gaube and Thomas Leisten, *Die Kernländer des 'Abbāsidenreiches im 10./11. Jh.: Materialien zur TAVO-Karte B VII 6*, Beihefte zum Tübinger Atlas des Vorderen Orients. Reihe B, Geisteswissenschaften; Nr. 75 (Wiesbaden: L. Reichert, 1994), 37, 110; Vladimir Minorsky, V. V. Bartol'd, and Clifford Edmund Bosworth, *Hudūd al-'Ālam; "The Regions of the World": A Persian Geography, 372 A.H.–982 A.D.*, 2nd ed., E. J. W. Gibb memorial series; new ser., 11 (London: Luzac, 1970), p. 104.)

[2] Franz, *Vom Beutezug*, pp. 120, 199.

[3] Hugh Kennedy, *The Prophet and the Age of the Caliphates: The Islamic Near East from the Sixth to the Eleventh Century* (London; New York: Longman, 1986), pp. 126–131.

[4] Hugh Kennedy, *The Early Abbasid Caliphate: A Political History* (London; Totowa, NJ: Croom Helm; Barnes & Noble, 1981), pp. 59–60, 67–68, 74.

Over the two centuries of its existence, the khaghanate had broken down and fragmented several times. Some Turkic tribes moved west and became the dominant groups on the Transoxanian frontier; many also moved into Transoxiana and Khorasan. With the break-up of the western section of the khaghanate in 737–738, these groups became independent and available for recruitment. The Turkic borderlands provided opportunity for volunteer fighters for the faith who could at once spread the banner of Islam and acquire prisoners of war to sell as slaves.

The Turks were brought in largely as individuals or small groups, separated from their own society, many of them originally purchased as slaves. There is some controversy over the extent of actual slavery within the Turkic forces. Some clearly came in as free men, often prestigious, while others were purchased but later freed, and fought as free men.[5] The purchased slaves, ideally young men or adolescents, were given intensive training in military arts, and usually converted to Islam. They were kept together and separate from the population, to encourage loyalty to the dynasty. Fully trained as professional soldiers, many achieved high rank in the army. Known as *mamlūk* or *ghulām,* or often simply as Turks, they became a standard part of standing armies, and often a considerable political force.

Ma'mun had recruited Turkic military from the eastern borderlands and when he took Baghdad from al-Amin he used them, along with Khorasanians, to augment the standing army. During al-Ma'mun's reign his brother, the future caliph al-Mu'tasim, also began gathering a personal guard of Turkic slave soldiers from Transoxiana and the Caucasus. A number of these were slave soldiers but there were also several powerful Turkic military families in Baghdad, some of them apparently of aristocratic background.[6] From this time on, mamluks were part of most major Middle Eastern armies.[7] When al-Mu'tasim became caliph in 833, the Turkish soldiers still formed only a personal guard, but their numbers grew over time. Estimates of the size of the Turkic guard vary widely, from a few thousand to over 100,000.[8]

A foreign standing army quartered in the capital city is likely to show signs of arrogance. This had happened with the Khorasanian army and became an even greater problem with the Turkic troops, who were

---

[5] See, for example, Kennedy, *Armies of the Caliphs,* pp. 120–123; Matthew Gordon, *The Breaking of a Thousand Swords: A History of the Turkish Military of Samarra, A.H. 200–275/815–889 C.E* (Albany: State University of New York Press, 2001), pp. 6–8.

[6] Gordon, *The Breaking,* pp. 2, 157–160.

[7] For a more skeptical view of Mamluk importance, see Deborah G. Tor, "The Mamluks in the Military of the Pre-Seljuq Persianate Dynasties," *Iran* 46 (2008).

[8] Gordon, *The Breaking,* pp. 71–73.

resented by the Khorasanians as well as the city population. After a number of unpleasant incidents, al-Mu'tasim built a new capital for the court and army at Samarra, about 70 kilometers north of Baghdad.[9] However the guard in Samarra became involved in politics, and by 847 when the caliph al-Mutawakkil (847–861) came to the throne, Turks were among those deciding the succession.[10] Al-Mutawakkil's moves against the Turks, along with his difficulty in paying their salaries, led to his murder and to a period of anarchy, in which members of the Turkic guard supporting a rival caliph attacked Baghdad, causing great destruction to the city and surrounding districts.[11] Finally, under the caliph al-Mu'tamid (872–892) the dynasty regained control, and the caliphate moved back to Baghdad.[12]

While the Samarra caliphate lasted only a short time, the Turkic elite remained a central part of the power structure, connected to the bureaucracy and surrounding powers. As trusted commanders, Turkic *mamluks* were appointed to governorships, and when power weakened at the center, several achieved first autonomy and then independence. Two dynasties of Turkic soldiers controlled Egypt for about a century, and will figure in this chapter: the Tulunids (868–905) and the Ikshidids (935–969). Such dynasties became a common phenomenon in the central Islamic lands.

Ethnic Rivalries and Characterization: The Bedouins and the Turks

By the mid-ninth century Khorasanians and Turks had largely supplanted the Syrians – Bedouin and settled – who had dominated the Umayyad army. The bureaucracy underwent a similar change. Persian bureaucrats now held the highest offices, introducing elements of Persian culture and legitimation. Thus the 'Abbasids were an Arab dynasty with a ruling elite made up largely of non-Arab peoples, particularly in the center of the caliphate. One might expect that these changes would destroy the iconic place of the Bedouin in cultural identity; however, this was not the case. The adoption of foreign culture and increasing equalization among the ethnic groups making up the empire provoked a deliberate promotion of a separate Arab consciousness. The need for Persian and Turkic elites was accepted – tacitly at least – but not their equal cultural worth. 'Abbasid rule, therefore, brought new elaboration to

---

[9] Gordon, *The Breaking*, pp. 27–30, 48–50. [10] Gordon, *The Breaking*, pp. 80–87.
[11] David Waines, "The Third Century Internal Crisis of the Abbasids," *Journal of the Economic and Social History of the Orient* 20, no. 3 (1977), p. 299.
[12] Gordon, *The Breaking*, pp. 141–143.

the theme of ethnic particularism, which became enshrined in literature for future generations.

In seeking to define a unique and superior character for the Arabs, writers turned again to the Bedouin as the archetypical inhabitant of the desert lands. Increasing enthusiasm for the study of their language, history and lifestyle created a lively market for Bedouin lore, with the accompanying problems of exploitation and fabrication. The Muslim scholars of the ninth century already faced the question of how to preserve the purity of primitive objects of study and how to judge the reliability of informants.[13] The famous essayist al-Jahiz (d. 869) praised the speech of the cultured, eloquent Bedouin, but railed against those "who pitch their tents in the neighborhoods of main roads and busy markets."[14] The bookseller Ibn al-Nadim, who wrote a valuable treatise on Arabic literature in 987, lists the Bedouin teachers of earlier scholarly generations, noting several who artificially heightened their desert cachet.[15]

The trumpeting of Arab superiority irritated the non-Arabs and led to an intellectual movement in the early Abbasid period known as the Shu'ubiyya, in which some scholars of non-Arab origin asserted the worth of their own people and mocked the Arab glorification of Bedouin lifestyle.[16] The Arabs answered in kind. This was a literary contest not to be confused with nationalism in the modern sense. Many people defending their own heritage against that of the Arabs were themselves experts in Arab ethnography and history; indeed, it was their knowledge of Arab lore which allowed them effectively to lampoon ancient Arab ways.[17] The Shu'ubiyya and its refutation produced a wealth of ethnic characterizations of Arabs and their subjects – particularly the Persians, who were chosen as the effete counterpart to the Arab. Disagreement seems to have centered less around the character of each group than around the question of whether the traits observed were

[13] Zoltan Szombathy, "Fieldwork and Preconceptions: The Role of the Bedouin as Informants in Mediaeval Muslim Scholarly Culture (Second–Third/Eighth–Ninth Centuries)," *Der Islam* 92, no. 1 (2015), pp. 128–137.

[14] Charles Pellat, *The Life and Works of Jāhiẓ* (Berkeley: University of California Press, 1969), p. 105.

[15] Muḥammad ibn Isḥāq Ibn al-Nadīm, *The Fihrist of al-Nadīm; A Tenth-Century Survey of Muslim Culture*, trans. Bayard Dodge (New York: Columbia University Press, 1970), pp. 100, 106, and for further examples 115; Pellat, *Le milieu baṣrien*, pp. 127–128.

[16] The epithet *shu'ūbī* comes from Qur'an 49:13, where it is stated that God created man in *shu'ūb* and tribes, which was taken to advocate judging nobility according to righteousness rather than tribal descent. Roy Mottahedeh, "The Shu'ūbiyah Controversy and the Social History of Early Islamic Iran," *International Journal of Middle East Studies* 6 (1976), pp. 164–165.

[17] Ibn al-Nadīm, *Fihrist*, pp. 230, 244–245; Goldziher, *Muslim Studies*. pp. 148–149, 177–180, 189.

admirable ones. Much of the writing was satirical, making full use of irony and caricature.[18]

In the literature of the Shu'biyya and its opponents, the character sketched out for Arabs is that of the Bedouin and the warrior. In al-Jahiz's characterization, the Arabs were not merchants, artisans, scholars, or farmers (all of which they were in fact by this time); rather, they lived in the plains and grew up in contemplation of the desert.[19] Arab strength was seen as having derived in part from their minimal needs and their ability to bear want and hardship.[20] The group of people thus imagined was the ruling class, whose supposed traits of simplicity and honesty were connected to the legitimacy of their rule.[21] The subject elite, particularly the Persians, are portrayed in opposite terms, – overdressed, pretentious, at once proud, servile, and fearful.[22] The deprived life and faintly repulsive habits of the Bedouins, lampooned by the Persian, are thus turned around to become sources of virtue for the Arabs:

Our life, by God, is a life which can in no way be called deprived. Our food is the tastiest and most wholesome: colocynth, lizards, jerboas, hedgehogs and snakes. Sometimes by God, we eat lambskin, roasting the hide.[23]

The poet al-Akhlab, writing in 684 after the battle of Marj Rahit, had characterized such foods as "vile provender" and attributed them to his enemies as a source of ridicule.[24]

The fashion for ethnic characterization extended to other groups, including those serving in the army. The Turks were a frequent subject. As a military class from an inhospitable region, they shared the traits of simplicity and martial character for which the Arabs claimed superiority. At the same time, they were clearly resented and feared. Much of the ambivalence shown towards the Bedouin, which I described in Chapter 2, can also be found in writings about the Turks. Both Bedouins and Turks are distinguished by their bravery and independence, their ability to bear discomfort and to survive on a limited diet, and their straightforward behavior. On the negative side, both are uncouth, often ugly, uneducated, violent and given to

---

[18] Göran Larsson, "Ignaz Goldziher on the Shu'ūbiyya," *Zeitschrift der deutche morgenländische Geselschaft* 155, no. 2 (2005).

[19] Pellat, *Life and Works*, pp. 96–97.

[20] al-Jāḥiẓ, *Nine essays of al-Jahiz*, trans. William M. Hutchins (New York: P. Lang, 1989), pp. 126–133 ("Homesickness"), 205–206 ("Turks"); Gérard Lecomte, *Ibn Qutayba (mort en 276/889). L'homme, son oeuvre, ses idées* (Damascus: Institut français de Damas, 1965), pp. 350–351.

[21] Lecomte, *Ibn Qutayba*, pp. 250–253.   [22] Pellat, *Life and Works*, pp. 272–274.

[23] Jāḥiẓ, *Nine Essays*, 128.   [24] Stetkevych, *Poetics*, pp. 96, 108.

plunder.[25] The most positive portrayal of the Turks is that of al-Jahiz, who praised the martial abilities of the Turks, resulting from their hardiness as a steppe people and their particular expertise in mounted archery. They are the "Bedouin of the non-Arabs," sharing one virtue, that of homesickness for a native land of purity and discomfort.[26]

The writings of al-Jahiz and other early Abbasid authors, which have enjoyed enduring popularity, suggest a recognition of peoples of varied ethnic backgrounds within the caliphate, with a distinct sphere and character assigned to each. In the military, the groups more recently added, Khorasanians and particularly Turks, take place alongside the Arab, typified as the Bedouin. The Persians, with others of urban and non-military origin, are given a contrasting and equally exaggerated set of traits. Underlying the opposite characterizations lies the expectation of a military and ruling class that was foreign to the subject population in origin and character. The dichotomy set up at this period lasted throughout the Abbasid period and even beyond when new Turkic and Mongolian rulers from the Eurasian steppe took the place of Arabs.

Changing Regional Dynamics

The rise of Persians and Turks at the Abbasid court was part of a more general shift in regional power. Changing routes and growing wealth were bringing new regions to preeminence and their populations into a broader political sphere. From the beginning Khorasan was a major source for military manpower, and from the time of the caliph al-Ma'mun, Transoxiana became one as well. Thus, northern Iran gained strategic importance. The northern Khorasan road ran from Iraq through Hamadan to Rayy, and along the southern edge of the Caspian. Soon after coming to power, the Abbasids conquered much of Mazandaran and began to settle at Rayy. Arab penetration into Azerbaijan also increased, and at the end of the eighth century Abbasid forces began to move into Armenia.[27] As the eastern regions became more important, Syria lost some of its stature and prosperity. Since the protection and taxation of trade caravans was part of the Bedouin economy, it is likely that the decline of these routes affected the nomads of the Syrian deserts.[28]

---

[25] Susanne Enderwitz, *Gesellschaftlicher Rang und ethnische Legitimation: der arabische Schriftsteller Abū 'Uṯmān al-Ğāḥiẓ (gest. 868) über die Afrikaner, Perser und Araber in der islamischen Gesellschaft* (Freiburg im Breisgau: Schwarz, 1979), pp. 118–124; Ulrich W. Haarmann, "Ideology and History, Identity and Alterity: The Arab Image of the Turk from the 'Abbasids to Modern Egypt," *International Journal of Middle East Studies* 20, no. 2 (1988), pp. 178–180; Binay, *Die Figur des Beduinen*, pp. 48–49, 154–155.
[26] Jāḥiẓ, *Nine Essays*, pp. 193–208.   [27] Kennedy, *Early Abbasid*, p. 123.
[28] Kennedy, *Early Abbasid*, pp. 23–25; Franz, *Vom Beutezug*, pp. 56, 162–168, 187, 231–232.

Not all western regions declined under the Abbasids. Under the Umayyads, Egypt had held little power; now it achieved a position commensurate with its wealth in grain and its favorable location for trade. The rulers of Egypt – Tulunids and Ikshidids – began to extend their power over the cities of Syria. The Jazira also gained importance. In 772, ten years after founding the city of Baghdad, the caliph al-Mansur built the city al-Rafiqa near al-Raqqa on the upper Euphrates as a garrison for frontier troops and a center for the collection of grain to ship to Iraq.[29] Since the Mesopotamian crown lands – the Sawad – were not sufficient for the demands of an enlarged court and army, the Jazira, rich in livestock and cereals, became a key supplier.[30] Mosul developed into a major regional center, profiting from rain-fed agriculture and a location between the steppe inhabited by camel nomads, and mountain ranges used by nomads raising sheep and horses.

Over the course of the ninth century the decline of the imperial center further changed the regional balance of power. The most basic problem was the ongoing deterioration of the rich Sawad region south of Baghdad, which had provided grain for the cities of Iraq and a good proportion of the state's revenue. Over the course of the ninth and tenth century, the dynasty lost much of the benefit from this region, partly through a vicious cycle of overuse, need and quick fixes. Internal divisions and disorder added to the problem.[31] From the second half of the ninth century, the caliphs had turned to grants of land in addition to cash salaries to pay their armies, and as it became more difficult to gather taxes, the administration resorted to tax farming. By the tenth century, a significant proportion of the Sawad land of Mesopotamia was thus no longer directly under government control.[32] The weakness at the center led to growing strength in neighboring regions. Some reacted with military adventures and moves towards independence. Others became involved in the politics of the central government.

Bedouin Powers in the Syrian and Arabian Desert

During the late ninth and early tenth centuries rebellious groups began to gather support among both settled and nomadic tribes in the Syrian desert and the Arabian Peninsula. The Bedouins had continued to play

[29] Kennedy, *Early Abbasid*, pp. 89–90.
[30] Muḥammad ibn ʿAlī Ibn Ḥawqal, *Configuration de la terre (Kitab surat al-ard)*, trans. Johannes Hendrik Kramer and Gaston Wiet (Beyrouth: Commission internationale pour la traduction des chefs d'oeuvre, 1965), pp. 207–212.; *TAVO* Atlases AX 1, AX 11.
[31] Waines, "The Third Century," pp. 282–303.
[32] Kennedy, *The Prophet*, pp. 189–192, 199; Kennedy, *Armies of the Caliphs*, pp. 79–87, 128–129; Michael Bonner, "The Waning of Empire, 861–945," in *New Cambridge History of Islam*, ed. Chase Robinson (Cambridge: Cambridge University Press, 2010), pp. 352–354.

an essential function in provisioning and guiding caravans, particularly the pilgrimage caravans that were essential for the prestige of the dynasty. The Abbasids and other neighboring powers usually paid a stipend to local tribes to ensure the safety of the caravan. When the agreements broke down, Bedouins raided the caravans; these raids had occurred sporadically throughout the eighth and early ninth century, sometimes provoking retaliation from the Abbasid government.[33]

At the end of the ninth century, Bedouin activities became more organized and more threatening, though the Bedouin acted not on their own but under outside leadership. In about 867 a Medinan family, the Hasanid Ukhaydirs, gained control of the Yamama oasis and used Bedouin troops to attack Mecca, Medina and Jidda.[34] A larger and longer-lasting challenge came from the Isma'ili Shi'ites, based in the town of Salamiyya on the western edge of the Syrian desert between Damascus and Aleppo. They had begun preaching among the tribes of Syria and Mesopotamia at the end of the eighth century, achieving considerable success among the Bedouin in northern Syria and the Sawad. The movement soon fragmented; one branch, accepting the claim of 'Ubayd Allah of Salamiya as the *imam,* followed him to North Africa and later founded the Fatimid caliphate. Other factions stayed; they called themselves the Ahl al-Haqq but were known by the derogatory term Qarmatians (Qaramita). In the north, a series of leaders attracted a significant following from Bedouin tribes, primarily sections of the Kalb confederation which dominated the northern desert and the trade route through Palmyra. We should note, however, that the tribal section which had responsibility of guarding the caravans – and presumably enjoyed the resulting rewards – did not choose to join up.[35] Military activity apparently appealed most to tribal sections in need of additional income. From 903 to 907 the Qaramita and their army briefly controlled region from Ba'albek to Aleppo, but they were not able to retain the loyalty of the major Bedouin tribes, and when their armies suffered a defeat by the 'Abbasids in 907, the coalition fell apart.[36]

In the southern regions, the Isma'ili movement had more lasting success. A missionary ($d\bar{a}\,\ddot{\imath}$) from Iraq, Abu Sa'id al-Jannabi, established himself in Bahrayn and Hajar in 899, and eventually formed a state, making heavy use of the Bedouin. Al-Jannabi and his successors controlled agricultural lands used by the nomads as summer pastures. Some nomads joined of their own accord, and others were brought into the military through a combination of compulsion and persuasion. The

---

[33] Franz, *Vom Beutezug*, pp. 162–171, 197–199.   [34] *Vom Beutezug*, pp. 174–175.
[35] Kennedy, *The Prophet*, pp. 287–288; Franz, *Vom Beutezug*, pp. 54–57.
[36] Franz, *Vom Beutezug*, pp. 57–83.

Jannabi dynasty organized pasture and migration, and when Bedouin resisted they could be severely punished.[37] The dynasty owed much of its power to the control of the pilgrimage route from Iraq and when, after 923, the Abbasids attempted to withhold payment, the Jannabis organized attacks threatening the pilgrims and thus the prestige of the government. In some years there was no government sponsored pilgrimage along this route. In 929–930 the Bahrayni ruler attacked Mecca and removed the black stone from the Ka'ba, which remained in the possession of the dynasty until 951.[38]

Despite the military importance of the nomads, there was little political development in the ninth to tenth century among the Bedouin of the Arabian Peninsula and the Syrian desert. The most organized movements, under the Ukhaydir and the Ismai'li Jannabis, were led by rulers who centered themselves in oases from which they could control the Bedouins' access to summer pasture, water and markets. The Bedouin were usually powerful enough to claim a share in the income from the pilgrimage, but not to control the state.[39]

Development of Regional Power

The events described above involved the development of local powers able temporarily to challenge government power in regions at a distance from the center. Bedouin involvement did not lead to claims of independent power. As the tenth century progressed, however, in northern Syria and the Jazira the participation of nomad groups in military activity led to closer involvement with the central government, the development of stronger tribal leadership and eventually to the creation of nomad states under tribal leadership. There were two processes going on here. First, as the Abbasids proved incapable of retaining direct control over the regions they had incorporated, local powers gained increasing strength and dealt independently with surrounding nomads. Second, as the politics at the center became increasingly factional, contestants pulled in tribes and nomads as allies and troops.

As the Abbasids claimed more extensive territory in Iran, they found it necessary to delegate authority, and Abbasid commanders in Azerbaijan and central Iran were allowed significant autonomy.[40] Over time, the Abbasids also resorted to treaties with local rulers, recognizing them as "governors" of regions like Fars and Rayy, which the Abbasids claimed

---

[37] Franz, *Vom Beutezug*, pp. 171–172.   [38] Franz, *Vom Beutezug*, pp. 172–182.
[39] Franz, *Vom Beutezug*, pp. 152–156.
[40] Kennedy, *The Prophet*, pp. 178, 184–185, 192; C. E. Bosworth, "Sādjids," *EI* 2nd ed.; Fred M. Donner, "Dolafids," *Encyclopaedia Iranica (Hereafter EIr)*.

but could no longer control.[41] Two mountain populations of northern Iran begin to appear in the histories over this period: the Kurds and the Daylamites. Although Kurds are mentioned from the beginning of the Arab conquest in northwest Iran, we know very little about them before the ninth century. In medieval Arabic sources, the term *kurd* (plural *akrād*) denotes Iranian nomads, or nomads who were neither Arab nor Turkic, and is applied to people well outside the current region of Kurdistan. The Kurds as we now know them are made up almost certainly of a variety of different peoples, among whom Iranian tribesmen have been predominant.[42] In this work I shall use the name Kurd only for the tribal population of primarily nomad or semi-nomad lifestyle raising sheep, horses and goats who inhabited Kurdistan – the mountainous region centered in Kermanshah, reaching in the east almost to Hamadan and in the west to Hulwan. This was a region containing much fertile agricultural land along with rich pastures and inaccessible mountain peaks, and it straddled the road linking Baghdad with Khorasan. Kurdish lands adjoined Bedouin regions to the north and west, and in some cases the two types of nomad appear to have used the same pastures at different seasons; this was the case with the meadows between the two Zab rivers, used in winter by the Kurds and in summer by Bedouin, and may also have been true of the Mosul region, where the geographer Ibn Ḥawqal mentions both Kurds and Arab nomads, and both summer and winter pastures.[43]

The mountains of Gilan in the western Caspian region were the home of the Daylamites, a mountain people known as redoubtable warriors. Unlike the Kurds, who raised and rode horses, the Daylamites fought as infantry. By the end of the ninth century, the Caspian region had become part of wider politics, and Daylami soldiers began to seek employment outside. Within a short time, contingents of Daylamites were found within the armies of numerous regional powers and within the Abbasid army itself.

Over the course of the tenth century, Kurds and Daylamites, along with many tribes of the Jazira, became intimately involved in the politics not only of their own regions, but also of Iraq and even Baghdad. What brought them in was the factional strife which plagued both army and administration. After about 908, power in Baghdad lay less with the

---

[41] Kennedy, *The Prophet*, pp. 177–179, 185, 192.

[42] Martin van Bruinessen, *Agha, Shaikh, and State: The Social and Political Structures of Kurdistan* (London; Atlantic Highlands, NJ: Zed Books, 1992), pp. 15–18, 50–53, 111; V. V. Minorsky, "Kurd, Kurdistan, iii. B History: The Islamic period up to 1920" *EI* 2nd ed.

[43] Ibn Ḥawqal, *Configuration*, pp. 209–210.

caliphs than with their officials; viziers and commanders vied for control amid ever-shifting factions and frequent executions. In 936 the caliphs achieved a partial solution by creating a new position known as *amīr al-umarā'*, which combined military and fiscal responsibility, giving the commander of the army control over the whole administration. This move eliminated some areas of conflict but provided a new office to fight over. Few men remained in the position for more than a year or two.[44]

Problems at the center provided opportunity for surrounding peoples. Some took advantage of Abbasid weakness to raid, plunder, and extort concessions. Many others were brought in by the Abbasid government. Attempting to diversify their army and provide a counterweight to the powerful Turkic slave soldiers, the caliphs recruited numerous other ethnic groups into the standing army including Daylamites and Qaramita – former Bedouin soldiers of the Isma'ilis. The monetary and political cost of the standing army also encouraged the use of auxiliary troops, some of whom were recruited among the Bedouin of the Syrian desert, others from the tribes of the Jazira.[45] Finally, outside powers and their troops were sought out and brought in as allies by people and parties in need of help against their rivals – from caliphs to tax farmers. Some of the power gained by nomad and mountain populations was taken, but more was given.

The Development of Tribal Power

Over time involvement with the Abbasid military led to greater internal organization among tribal peoples and to the formation of new dynasties. As these dynasties in their turn sought manpower and alliance with neighboring peoples, political organization increased among other populations, leading eventually to the creation of regional states governed by Bedouins and Kurds. Such states represent a major change, as both societies are known for their egalitarian social structure and up to this time had usually been dependent on outside organization for any large-scale undertaking.[46]

Two dynasties – the Hamdanids of the Jazira (ca. 905–1004) and the Buyids of Iran (ca. 932–1062) – played a particularly important role in the evolution of nomad states. Both arose out of mountain or pastoral societies and gained power in the center; coming from a tribal society, they

---

[44] Kennedy, *The Prophet*, pp. 187–199.
[45] Kennedy, *Armies of the Caliphs*, pp. 157–164; Franz, *Vom Beutezug*, pp. 119–133.
[46] Franz, *Vom Beutezug*, pp. 1–9.

dealt closely with nomad tribes as mercenaries, allies and competitors. As a result, Bedouin and Kurdish tribes, becoming an integral part of regional politics, developed stronger leadership and greater ambitions. The Hamdanids and Buyids each had one ruler of particular power and skill who managed to reduce the nomads to obedience for the period of his reign. These men interfered in tribal affairs, attacked and defeated the most powerful tribes of the area, and gave regional responsibilities to the leaders of newly favored tribes. By the time they died, leaving weaker successors, the tribes they promoted had developed the political institutions needed to found states in their own right. I will give a brief introduction to the history of each dynasty.

The Hamdanids

The Hamdanids began as chiefs of a section of the Banu Taghlib tribe, between Mosul and Mardin. Part of the tribe was nomadic, though not Bedouin; as I have stated earlier, they raised primarily sheep and horses. Other sections were agriculturalists, and grain was an important product.[47] The first well-known member of the Hamdanid lineage, Hamdan b. Hamdun, became active during the 860s, providing valuable service to the Abbasids against dissidents in the Jazira.[48] His sons held command within the Abbasid army and secured recognition as governors over Mosul along with a considerable portion of the Jazira. At the same time, they became players in the politics of Baghdad at the highest level, involved in the appointment and dismissal of chief viziers and even the choice of caliphs.[49]

Several factors contributed to the rise of the Hamdanids. First, they enjoyed great wealth from their control of pastures and agricultural lands in the district of Mosul. Second, they rose to power at a time of confusion in northern Syria and the Jazira, with new migrations into the region. Tribes were competing for pasture, raiding and aiding rebellions.[50] It is likely that the shortage of pastures left many in need of additional income, and a number served in the Abbasid or regional armies. The unsettled condition of the Jazira made it impossible for the Abbasids to hold Mosul on their own despite several attempts to retake the region.[51]

The establishment of the Hamdanid realm as an independent emirate was the work of one of Hamdan's grandsons, Hasan (ruled ca. 929–967),

---

[47] Marius Canard, *Histoire de la dynastie des H'amdanides de Jazîra et de Syrie* (Paris: Presses universitaires de France, 1953), p. 303; Franz, *Vom Beutezug*, p. 107.
[48] Canard, *Histoire*, pp. 291–302.   [49] Canard, *Histoire*, pp. 308–351.
[50] Franz, *Vom Beutezug*, pp. 109–112, 180.
[51] Canard, *Histoire*, pp. 343–344, 350–351, 398–401.

usually known by his honorific title Nasir al-Dawla. His career provides a good illustration of the dynamics of Hamdanid politics. In 936–937 Hasan and his brother received from the Caliph the accoutrements of regional status – robes of honor, horses and banners – and from this time they were relatively independent rulers of Mosul. In 938 Hasan refused to pay taxes and succeeded in holding his own against an Abbasid attack, largely because Iraq depended on his grain supply.[52] In 942, he achieved the position of *amīr al-'umarā*, given on condition that he restore order in southern Iraq. Both he and his brother received formal titles, Nasir al-Dawla for him, and Sayf al-Dawla for his brother.[53]

The office granted to Nasir al-Dawla was less a grant of power than an invitation to attempt the impossible; the Sawad could not be brought to order. After less than a year the brothers gave up and returned to Mosul. One important result of service as *amīr al-umarā* was the acquisition of armies of professional soldiers – Turks, Daylamites and Qaramita, a great advantage in a situation of tribal upheaval. From this time on, Nasir al-Dawla was the recognized ruler of Mosul and able to expand to the north and west into Azerbaijan, Armenia and Kurdistan.[54] Sayf al-Dawla took Aleppo in 944, acknowledging the caliph and Nasir al-Dawla in the Friday prayers, but controlling northern Syria as a largely independent emirate.[55] The Hamdanid family thus rose to power through a combination of regional strength and office within the central government; they were at once outsiders and insiders. While they usually could not stand against the caliphal army, they had a strong position from which to bargain, both because Iraq depended heavily on their region for provisions, and because the Mosul region was almost impossible for an outsider to hold.

While Nasir al-Dawla worked to retain his hold on Mosul, his brother Sayf al-Dawla achieved equal or greater power in Aleppo and Mayyafariqin. He is remembered particularly for his campaigns against the Bedouin and his success in bringing them under control. He was dealing with a situation of particular difficulty, since the immigration of new tribes strained the resources of the region. The Numayr had migrated north in 921, and new sections of the B. Kilab came into Syria in 936 to compete for the fertile region between Aleppo and Hama.[56]

Sayf al-Dawla should not be seen as an enemy of nomads; he made liberal use of Bedouin in taking and keeping northern Syria. In taking Aleppo he had the encouragement of the chiefs of the B. Kilab, eager to

---

[52] Canard, *Histoire*, pp. 378–407.   [53] Canard, *Histoire*, pp. 416–35.
[54] Canard, *Histoire*, pp. 416–451, 492, 514.   [55] Canard, *Histoire*, pp. 491–504.
[56] Franz, *Vom Beutezug*, pp. 109–112.

unseat the Ikhshidid governors of Aleppo who belonged to other tribal sections. Later we find the B. Kilab in his army along with sections from the 'Uqayl, Kalb and Numayr.[57] Through much of his reign, Sayf al-Dawla's policy seems to have been focused on limiting the aggression of the new arrivals and adjudicating tribal disputes over land. Thus in 948 he settled a conflict over grazing rights in the region between Aleppo and Palmyra between sections of the B. Kilab, predominant around Aleppo, and the B. Kalb of the Palmyra region. Two sections of the Kilab raided the Kalb; Sayf al-Dawla attacked their camp and punished them but stopped the killing fairly soon.[58] Over the next years Sayf al-Dawla continued to deal firmly with Bedouin tribes; he meted out harsh punishment to offenders, followed by a display of mercy towards women and children. At the same time, he continued to give out generous subsidies to his Bedouin allies.[59]

The greatest challenge from nomads occurred in 955, when many people from several tribes including the 'Uqayl, 'Ajlan sections of the Ka'b, and much of the B. Kilab, attacked Za'raya and Qinnasrin. The Numayr, further away, were sympathetic, but apparently sent no troops. As Sayf al-Dawla headed against the tribes, the B. Kilab section submitted; the others were pursued by Sayf al-Dawla, who killed some and pushed others into the desert. It was summer, and many died of thirst. This event changed the balance of power among the Bedouin, leaving the tribes central to the conspiracy considerably weakened, while those who had submitted gained in strength. The B. Kilab were rewarded for their decision with an extension of their lands and became the preeminent tribe of northern Syria and western Jazira. The Numayr, who had also sent in their submission, were left in possession of their territories.[60] This was the last major tribal disturbance before the Byzantine incursion in 962 and Sayf al-Dawla's death in 967. In the confusion and destruction that followed the Byzantine attack, the Hamdanids lost their independence and the B. Kilab stepped into the power vacuum they had left behind.[61] Thus, Sayf al-Dawla's creation of a new order after the suppression of the revolt led to the creation of a new tribal force.

---

[57] Samir Shamma, "Mirdās," in *EI* 2nd ed.; Canard, *Histoire*, pp. 501, 587.

[58] Canard, *Histoire*, pp. 598–600.

[59] Canard, *Histoire*, pp. 606–609, 636; Ramzi Jibran Bikhazi, "The Ḥamdānid Dynasty of Mesopotamia and North Syria 254–404/868–1014," unpublished PhD dissertation, University of Michigan (1981), pp. 664–674.

[60] Bikhazi, "The Ḥamdānid," pp. 765–773; Canard, *Histoire*, pp. 611–617; Franz, *Vom Beutezug*, pp. 113–114, 117.

[61] Canard, *Histoire*, pp. 644–650; Kennedy, *The Prophet*, pp. 281–284.

The Buyids

The other dynasty instrumental in the rise of nomad power was the Buyid lineage from Daylam. The dynasty began its rise to power shortly after the Hamdanids, and soon became a rival for power over the regions north of Baghdad. It was founded in 935 by three brothers, 'Ali, Abu 'Ali Hasan, and Ahmad. Starting as soldiers of fortune, and taking over the lands of their former commander, they gained control over almost all of Iran except for Khorasan.[62] They evolved a system of shared rule with each remaining essentially independent within his territory, but with one member of the family recognized as senior to the others.[63] Within a year of the Buyids' rise, one of the factions in the contest for power over Iraq sought them out as allies. Ahmad, sent to help, soon became an important actor in Iraqi struggles, and in 945 the caliph granted him the office of amīr al-'umarā with the title Mu'izz al-Dawla. Unlike their predecessors, the Buyids were strong enough to pass on the office of amīr al-umarā within their family. From this point on the caliph held no actual power but received a stipend and retained some officials for his personal service.[64]

The Buyids of Iraq, however, had to contend with their relatives in other regions, while in the north they competed with the Hamdanids. Thus, they were frequently at war. Their standing army of Daylamite soldiers was not sufficient for their military needs and they soon turned to the nearby Bedouins. The second Buyid in Baghdad, 'Izz al-Dawla Bakhtiyar (967–978), brought in Shaybani and 'Uqayli troops to fight the Hamdanids, and enlisted some of the Asad tribe between Basra and Ahwaz, along with the Kurdish ruler Hasanwayh Barzikani from Dinawar, northeast of Kermanshah.[65] Other nomads, sometimes from the same tribes, posed a threat, with the Shayban and Kurds raiding from the north and various sections of the B. Asad from the west and south. Buyid rule over Iraq was loose and partial; they controlled only a few major cities. Villages and nomad tribes collected protection money from the population, and within the cities paramilitary organizations undertook similar activities.[66]

Stronger rule was introduced for a short time by 'Adud al-Dawla (949–983), the most powerful of the Buyid rulers, who took over Iraq in 977. 'Adud al-Dawla was not content with the loose rule characteristic of most of his family, and he had access to the resources of several provinces. He

---

[62] W. Madelung, "Deylamites, ii, In the Islamic Period," *EIr*, pp. 343–345.

[63] T. Nagel, "Buyids," *EIr*, pp. 578–579.

[64] John J. Donohue, *The Buwayhid Dynasty in Iraq 334 H./945 to 403 H./1012: Shaping Institutions for the Future* (Leiden: Brill, 2003), pp. 9–14, 17–27.

[65] Donohue, *The Buwayhid Dynasty*, p. 220; Franz, *Vom Beutezug*, p. 149; Ch. Bürgel and R. Mottahedeh, "'Ażod al-Dawla," *EIr*.

[66] Donohue, *The Buwayhid Dynasty*, p. 80.

overthrew the Hamdanid emir of Mosul, then undertook expeditions against the Shayban and Kurds at Shahrazur near the lower Zab, and against the leader of the Asad tribe. In dealing with Kurdish regions, Adud al-Dawla's strategy was to impose order by strengthening one tribe at the expense of others. At the end of 369/980 he campaigned in Kermanshah and installed as local ruler Hasanwayh Barzikani's son Badr, continuing 'Izz al-Dawla's alliance with the family.

'Adud al-Dawla had no hesitation in using harsh measures and deceit. Soon after his campaign in Kermanshah he sent an expedition against the Hakkari Kurds and when they surrendered on condition that their lives be spared, they were crucified along the side of the road for five *farsakhs*.[67] He lured the Shayban tribe back from their retreat in the Zab region only to attack at night, killing or capturing many of them. Within Iraq he disarmed the population; he also introduced a tax on the market sale of horses, asses and camels, a move which may have been aimed at the nomads.[68]

'Adud al-Dawla's use of violence brought the nomad tribes to order, but after his death in 983 their power rapidly increased. His successors depended heavily on Bedouin and other nomad manpower and were willing to grant local authority in return. Buyid control extended only over Baghdad, Wasit and Basra.[69] A new bureau called the *dīwān al-himāya* was created to organize the protection moneys paid to regional tribes.[70] The government attempted to use the system to pay some tribes for protection against others. Tribal disunity made the Bedouin less immediately dangerous to the government, but it probably increased the suffering of the population, both nomad and settled.[71]

Throughout the period of the Hamdanids and the Buyids, therefore, nomad tribes gained in importance regardless of the policies aimed at them. Many tribes of the Jazira and Iraq had served for decades in the Buyid and Hamdanid armies, and they had been pulled into government politics and given responsibility for the regions in which they predominated. Tribal leaders serving as commanders gained increased authority within their tribes. Both Sayf al-Dawla and 'Adud al-Dawla acted aggressively and effectively towards nomads, but their system of reward and punishment left favored tribes in a position of unprecedented strength.

---

[67] V. Minorsky, "Kurds, Kurdistān, iii B: History: Islamic Period up to 1920," *EI* 2nd ed.
[68] Donohue, *The Buwayhid Dynasty*, pp. 80–85; Franz, *Vom Beutezug*, p. 149–151.
[69] Donohue, *The Buwayhid Dynasty*, p. 217.
[70] Donohue, *The Buwayhid Dynasty*, pp. 94–95, 104–105.
[71] Donohue, *The Buwayhid Dynasty*, pp. 106, 223–227.

The Rise of Nomad Dynasties

The late tenth through the early eleventh centuries represents a new phase, with the rise of several independent nomad states among the Bedouin and Kurds. These were not conquest states; most tribal leaders gained power through service to settled powers and eventually assumed power over their own and neighboring territories.[72] What distinguished these states from earlier polities involving tribes was that their leadership was not settled but nomadic in origin and usually lifestyle. We should not ascribe the nomad rise to power to simple military superiority. As the narrative in this chapter shows, in battles with the central government the nomads very often lost. Like the settled population, Bedouins were vulnerable to attack, particularly in their summer pastures, and in summer they could also be pushed out into the desert where they might die of thirst. The poisoning or destruction of wells was an effective tactic frequently used against nomads.[73]

A more important factor in the creation of nomad states was the lack of a single central power able to control the larger region. The Byzantine campaign against Sayf al-Dawla in 962 left a trail of destruction and fatally weakened the Syrian Hamdanids, while 'Adud al-Dawla's defeat of the Hamdanids of the Jazira similarly reduced the power of the western branch of the dynasty. The Hamdanid regions were now contested among local tribes and three neighboring states: the Byzantines, the Buyids, and a new power, the Isma'ili Fatimid dynasty of Egypt and North Africa, which took over Egypt in 969 and extended its power into Syria.[74] Damascus and Aleppo became disputed cities, with Damascus generally under Fatimid control, while Aleppo was usually dominated by tribal powers. The Syrian desert and the Jazira returned to the position they had held before the Arab conquest, with competing powers on either side. The nomads inhabiting them could play neighboring powers off against each other and thus gained in importance and in independence.[75]

The first new dynasties to develop were Kurdish powers in the Jazira and its border regions, where the Buyid 'Adud al-Dawla had defeated the Hamdanids and transformed the landscape of power. Badr of the Hasanuyid Barzikani, whom 'Adud al-Dawla had put in charge of much of Jibal, became independent on 'Adud al-Dawla's death in 883. He and his successors dominated the region from Kermanshah to Hamadan.[76]

---

[72] Franz, *Vom Beutezug*, pp. 251–252.
[73] *Vom Beutezug*, pp. 76, 171, 193; Canard, *Histoire*, pp. 614–615.
[74] Franz, *Vom Beutezug*, p. 210; Kennedy, *The Prophet*, pp. 315–327.
[75] Franz, *Vom Beutezug*, pp. 86–87.
[76] Donohue, *The Buwayhid Dynasty*, pp. 221, 225; Kennedy, *The Prophet*, pp. 250–253.

Meanwhile the city of Nasibin reacted to news of 'Adud al-Dawla's death by giving allegiance to a Kurdish leader, Badh b. Dustak, the founder of the Marwanid dynasty. Badh's forces rapidly gained control over Diyar Bakr and half of the region of Tur 'Abdin, southeast of Mardin, from which they encroached on Mosul.[77] The Marwanids were the most powerful and prestigious of the new Kurdish dynasties, contending and allying with their neighbors – the Byzantines, Georgians and Armenians, and the northwestern Bedouin powers, the Numayr and 'Uqayl. They initiated strong building programs in their two major cities, Mayyafariqin and Amid (the modern Diyarbakr) and, especially under the long-lived ruler Abu Nasr Ahmad (1011–1061), presided over a brilliant court culture.[78]

The first of the Bedouin dynasties in the Jazira was the 'Uqaylids (ca. 990–1096). The 'Uqayl tribe, summering near Mosul and wintering west of Baghdad, had likewise begun to develop a stronger leadership during the reign of 'Adud al-Dawla. 'Adud al-Dawla's successors, unable to hold the Jazira on their own, reinstalled Hamdanids in Mosul; the Hamdanids then turned to the 'Uqaylids to defend them against Marwanid aggression. The 'Uqaylids provided help and in return demanded Jazira and Mosul. Within a few years their leader Muhammad b. al-Musayyib controlled Mosul and received Buyid recognition as a vassal; for about a century the 'Uqaylids remained in control of the region.[79] During much of this time they appear to have remained largely nomadic and often preferred to live in camps outside their cities.[80]

After 'Adud al-Dawla's death Iraq likewise came under tribal control, and was soon dominated by the Mazyadid dynasty, originating in the Asad tribe, which had been deeply involved in the dynastic and tribal rivalries of the later Buyid period and eventually was given responsibility for much of Iraq. By 996–997 the Mazyadids in the south and the 'Uqaylids in the north were between them responsible for almost the whole length of the Euphrates and much of the Sawad.[81] Mazyadid power was centered at al-Jami'ayn, where their camp, or *hilla*, quickly

[77] Donohue, *The Buwayhid Dynasty*, pp. 89, 22; Kennedy, *The Prophet*, pp. 262–266.

[78] Paul A. Blaum, "A History of the Kurdish Marwanid Dynasty A.D. 983–1085, Part I," *International Journal of Kurdish Studies* 5, no. 1–2 (1992); "A History of the Kurdish Marwanid Dynasty, A.D. 983–1085, Part II," *International Journal of Kurdish Studies* 6, no. 1–2 (1993).

[79] C. E. Bosworth, "'Uḳaylids," *EI* 2nd ed.; Kennedy, *The Prophet*, p. 297.

[80] Hugh Kennedy, "The Uqaylids of Mosul: The Origins and Structure of a Nomad Dynasty," in *Actas del XII congreso de la Union européenne d'arabisants et d'islamisants (Málaga, 1984)* (Madrid: Union Européenne d'Arabisants et d'Islamisants), pp. 397–398.

[81] Donohue, *The Buwayhid Dynasty*, pp. 221–222.

developed into a prosperous city, retaining the name Hilla. This was not an easy region in which to retain power, but through astute and shifting alliances the dynasty remained in place well into the Seljuqid period.[82]

In northern Syria, where the Hamdanid Sayf al-Dawla had held power, nomad dynasties developed only a few years later. After Sayf al-Dawla's death in 967 the region became the frontier between Fatimids and Byzantines, and the last of the Hamdanids held on to their territory as vassals of one or the other. Not surprisingly, the gainers were the B. Kilab tribe, who had benefitted from Sayf al-Dawla's favor and now increased their power through astute acts of diplomacy and treachery as the Fatimids and Byzantines competed for control over pliant members of the Hamdanid dynasty in Aleppo. Salih b. Mirdas of the B. Kilab, the founder of the Mirdasid dynasty, is first mentioned as governor of Rahba in 399/1009, when Aleppo was controlled by former slaves of the Hamdanids. His tribe twice saved the Aleppan governors, first from Marwanid and then from Fatimid armies, and naturally demanded recompense, in grants of pasture. The governor agreed, then invited the tribesmen to a feast, where he captured and killed many of them. In 1014 Salih escaped, and some time later managed to take the city. Aleppo proved a slippery prize, and neither Fatimids nor Mirdasids were able to control it consistently, but the dynasty did hold several cities in the region, up to Raqqa on the Euphrates, against both Byzantine and local rivals.[83]

The Mirdasids shared power with another Bedouin dynasty, the Numayrids. After the conspiracy against Sayf al-Dawla in 955 the Numayr had been pushed east where they were allowed to consolidate their power, useful as a shield against the Kurdish dynasties to the north. When the Hamdanids of Aleppo collapsed, the B. Numayr began to issue their own coinage and developed a court in Harran, east of Aleppo. At first, they seem to have remained self-consciously nomadic, camping outside the city; later they became at least partially settled and involved in city life.[84]

The history of these dynasties is a tale of internal and external rivalries; battles, raids and retaliation; the taking, losing and retaking of cities and regions; treaties made, unmade and remade. It was undoubtedly a stirring

---

[82] C. E. Bosworth, "Mazyad, Banū, or Mazyadids," *EI* 2nd ed.

[83] Th. Bianquis, S. Shamma, "Mirdās,– Mirdās b. Udayya," *EI* 2nd ed.

[84] Franz, *Vom Beutezug*, pp. 136–146; Stefan Heidemann, "Numayrid ar-Raqqa: Archaeological and Historical Evidence for a 'Dimorphic State' in the Bedouin Dominated Fringes of the Fāṭimid Empire," in *Egypt and Syria in the Fatimid, Ayyubid and Mamluk Eras. The 9th and 10th International Colloquium at the Katholieke Universiteit Leuven in May 2000 and May 2001*, ed. U. Vermeulen and J. van Steenbergen (Leuven, Belgium: Peeters, 2005), pp. 93–105.

life to live – at least for those who liked battle – but the telling becomes complicated and confusing. The regions held by Bedouin dynasties remained in flux partly because of pressure from outside powers: the Fatimids who wanted to control northern Syria, the Byzantines who were gaining ground in Armenia and along the Syrian coast, and the Kurdish dynasties to the north and west. Most nomad dynasties recognized the suzerainty of one or another of these powers, and sometimes recognized two at once. Thus, local nomad dynasties were threatened by outside powers, but not destroyed.

Most of the dynasties discussed here continued into the Seljuqid period; each was fortunate to have at least one ruler with an exceptionally long reign, and several of these overlapped in the early eleventh century.[85] Although politics was never still, the reigns of these emirs encompassed a period of renewed prosperity and development in the middle of a difficult age. Their contributions went beyond the political sphere. As Baghdad declined in power, scholars, writers and musicians sought patronage at provincial courts, moving from one to another as their favor or the fortunes of various rulers changed. Confusion, economic decline and political fragmentation in fact added to the opportunities open to men of literature and learning. The Buyid courts in Shiraz, Rayy, Isfahan and Hamadan attracted major scholars.[86] The court of the Hamdanid Sayf al-Dawla at Aleppo was also known for its brilliance in both scholarship and literature, with two of the greatest Arab poets of the century – al-Mutanabbi and Abu'l Firas al-Hamdani – as members of his entourage.[87] Another great poet of the 'Abbasid age, al-Ma'arri, wrote for and about the rulers of Aleppo, as the city was transferred from the control of the Hamdanids to that of the Mirdasids, who continued the court culture of Aleppo and the patronage of poetry.[88] The Marwanid dynasty is remembered for flourishing courts at Mayyafariqin and Amid, where medicine, religious scholarship and literature were patronized.

---

[85] The Marwanids rose to the peak of their power under Ibn Marwan, who ruled from 1011–1161. From 1001 to 1051 the 'Uqaylids were ruled by Qirwash, whose reign overlapped significantly with that of Nur al-Dawla Dubays of the Mazyadids (1018–1081), and somewhat less with Thimal Mirdasi, who ruled (with interruptions) from 1041 to 1062.

[86] Joel L. Kraemer, *Humanism in the Renaissance of Islam: The Cultural Revival during the Buyid Age* (Leiden: Brill, 1986), pp. 28, 50–51, 53.

[87] Kraemer, *Humanism*, pp. 90–91; A. Hamori, "al-Mutanabbī," in *'Abbasid belles-lettres*, ed. Julia Ashtiany, T. M. Johnstone, J. D. Latham, R. B. Sergent, and C. Rex Smith, *Cambridge History of Arabic Literature* (Cambridge; New York: Cambridge University Press, 1990), pp. 300–01; Abdullah el-Tayib, "Abū Firās al-Ḥamdānī," in *'Abbasid Belles-lettres*, pp. 317–319.

[88] P. Smoor, "al-Ma'arrī," *EI* 2nd ed.; Suhayl Zakkār, *The Emirate of Aleppo, 1004–1094* (Beirut: Dar al-Amanah, 1971), pp. 263ff.

Even the minor Bedouin dynasty of the Jarrahids at Ramla attracted some poets to its court.[89] Thus the tenth and eleventh centuries saw increasing fragmentation and the movement of political strength and cultural production from the center, through the Buyid and Hamdanid dynasties to the tribal nomadic states which they had helped bring into existence.

The Nature and Impact of Nomad Rule

The impact of nomad power on urban life and agriculture has usually been judged as negative. In the western caliphate the tenth and eleventh centuries have been characterized as a period of "bedouinization," in which pastoralism increased at the expense of settled life, with some former nomads returning to nomadism, and agricultural land being converted to pastures. This formulation helped to explain the decline in settlement and in city building, which has been an object of study. Kurt Franz has recently reopened the issue of nomadization and has determined that the sources yield insufficient evidence to prove it.[90] The concept of Bedouinization appears to rest at least in part on the assumption that nomadism and agriculture must be inversely related, a belief that I called into question in Chapter 2. In the tenth and eleventh centuries, as in the Umayyad period, the two economies often flourished in close proximity, under one ruler. The geographers describe several cities as owing their wealth to both grain and livestock: at this period, these include Nasibin, Mosul, Hims, Antioch, Hamadan and Isfahan.[91] It is clear that the Hamdanids and Marwanids, two particularly successful dynasties, owed their strength to the combination of the two economies.

The decline of cities is more clearly illustrated than the agricultural situation. However, it is important not to draw broad conclusions from studies limited to a few regions. We should recognize that cities, whether under nomad or settled rule, had quite varied experiences, stemming from a number of causes. The major cities of northern Syria – Aleppo, Antioch and Edessa – began to decline in the early 'Abbasid period when the capital was moved east, and they suffered during the disorders of the later period. With the rise of Fatimid power in the eleventh century, the change in trade routes from a system centered in Baghdad to one which brought trade through Egypt was undoubtedly a factor in this decline. The Balikh river valley has been intensively studied and shows a reduction

[89] Thomas Ripper, *Die Marwāniden von Diyār Bakr: eine kurdische Dynastie im islamischen Mittelalter* (Würzburg: Ergon, 2000), pp. 411–424.
[90] Franz, *Vom Beutezug*, pp. 36–38, 250.
[91] Ibn Ḥawqal, *Configuration*, pp. 173, 177, 181–182, 205–210, 350, 354.

in settlement and building.[92] Its two main cities, al-Raqqa and Harran, were impoverished first due to their abandonment by the 'Abbasid caliphs who had occupied them, and then through over-taxation by the Hamdanid rulers.[93] Towards the end of the Numayrid dynasty, however, al-Raqqa became a regular capital with dynastic buildings, and the Numayrids showed an interest in developing it further.[94] Several other cities flourished and grew during this period. In Amid, both the Hamdanids and the Marwanids undertook major building projects. The Mazyadids embellished their capital Hilla with magnificent dwellings and rich markets, which lasted through their reign and beyond.[95] It appears that both nomad dynasties and those that combined nomadic and sedentary lifestyles promoted cities when there was sufficient security and when the region was one in which they were invested.

The tenth and eleventh centuries were a difficult period. There can be no doubt that the population and the land suffered from the constant warfare of the time. Scholars have concentrated on the trials of settled populations, particularly the harm they suffered at the hands of Bedouin raiders. The geographer Ibn Hawqal, who came from the Jazira and described its situation during his lifetime, has been a useful source for this school of thought, since he was inimical to the Hamdanid dynasty and eloquent on the suffering of the region.[96] However, though Ibn Hawqal's references to Bedouin are usually negative, the wrongs he lists were not visited exclusively on the settled. In his lament for the fate of his own hometown, Nasibin, he mentions the departure of the Taghlibid Banu Habib and their neighbors, along with their families and their herds. When the Hamdanid ruler Hasan took over, he cut down trees and changed watercourses; he did this not to create pasture, but to plant grain.[97] New tribes came into the region and pushed out nomad and semi-nomadic populations; when they demanded protection money from the inhabitants, it is quite possible that they were replacing earlier nomads who had done the same.[98] One of Ibn Hawqal's accusations against the Hamdanids was their oppressive taxation, and here again it appears that nomads suffered along with the settled population, since taxes on the sale of livestock are among those frequently mentioned, and in some places, the disappearance of nomads – at least their livestock – is given as an

---

[92] Heidemann, "Numayrid ar-Raqqa."
[93] Stefan Heidemann, *Die Renaissance der Städte in Nordsyrien und Nordmesopotamien: städtische Entwicklung und wirtschaftliche Bedingungen in ar-Raqqa und Ḥarrān von der Zeit der beduinischen Vorherrschaft bis zu den Seldschuken* (Leiden: Brill, 2002), pp. 29–31.
[94] Franz, *Vom Beutezug*, pp. 143–144.   [95] J. Lassner, "Ḥilla," *EI* 2nd ed.
[96] See, for instance, Ibn Ḥawqal, *Configuration*, pp. 173, 204, 215–216.
[97] Ibn Ḥawqal, *Configuration*, pp. 205–208.
[98] Ibn Ḥawqal, *Configuration*, pp. 204, 222–223.

example of decline and destruction.[99] There is no reason to doubt that Bedouin raids contributed to the troubles of the Jazira, but we should recognize that the nomads were victims of violence as well, and their raids were often in reaction to conditions of hardship imposed by others.

Conclusion

The Abbasids began as a centralizing power, but by the eleventh century political power lay in the hands of regional dynasties. A significant number of these were founded by nomads or mountain peoples and from this time on, the Middle East was never without nomad rulers. The rise of the Fatimid dynasty in Egypt made the Syrian desert once again a borderland between two competing powers, allowing its nomad inhabitants to enjoy an independence which had been curtailed by the early caliphate. The greater importance of northern regions, particularly Azerbaijan and the Khorasan Road, added another set of actors. The Bedouin and other Arab pastoralists who had been prominent in the Umayyad period were now joined by Iranian peoples, notably Daylamites and Kurds.

The early caliphate, from the Rashidun to the early Abbasids, was closer to the Bedouin but did not provide favorable conditions for political development. The Bedouin were not excluded, but where they were politically active, they were almost always under outside leadership. The long decline of Abbasid power had a very different result, leading to the political involvement of tribal peoples, first the Hamdanids and Buyids – partly nomadic and mountain populations – and then the more fully nomadic Bedouin and Kurds. Tribal leaders gained fuller authority over their tribesmen and over the regions they inhabited as they were increasingly called in to provide military service to one or another faction in local contests. By the eleventh century they were able to take over the rule of their areas. Much of the central territory of the caliphate was now under the rule of Bedouins or Kurds, from Iraq to Azerbaijan, and across to northern Syria.

Changes within the standing army were also striking; here what was most important for the future was the introduction of Turkic soldiers as skilled cavalry. Though they came in mostly as individuals, the Turks were recognized for their nomadic background and skills, and they were associated with the prestige of an imperial and warlike power. As they began to serve as governors, and eventually as independent rulers, their sphere expanded, both geographically and politically.

[99] Ibn Ḥawqal, *Configuration*, pp. 208, 213, 220–221.

Cultural developments of the Abbasid period were also important for the future. The rise of Persian influence resulted not in an abandonment of the Bedouin image, but in further elaboration of both tribal prestige and Bedouin traits as an important marker of an Arab ruling class. The emphasis on martial accomplishments associated with nomadism, Spartan lifestyle, and peripheral origin brought idealized Arab traits close to those associated with the Turks, "the Bedouin of the non-Arab." All these developments – the rise of nomad dynasties, the introduction of Turks as a military class, and the idealized image of foreign rulers of nomad origin – helped to prepare the way for a new stage in which nomads from the eastern steppe invaded and took over the central Islamic lands.

4   Turkic Tradition and Seljuqid Rule

In 1035 a few thousand ragged nomads crossed the Oxus into Khorasan and wrote a letter to the governor requesting pasture in return for military service. Within six years the Seljuqs had conquered eastern Iran and were heading west to take over the central Middle East, from Transoxiana to Anatolia. Historians recognize the Seljuq conquest as the beginning of a new era in Islamic history. From the eleventh to fifteenth centuries most of the Middle East was ruled by nomads from the Eurasian steppe. The first to arrive were the Seljuqs, whose reign established a set of institutions adapted by later nomad conquerors. The Seljuqs were Oghuz from a western branch of the Turks, different in language and traditions from the eastern Turks and Mongols who succeeded them. Their descendants thus maintained a separate Turkic identity in the Middle East, coming to be known as "Turkmen."[1]

In this chapter we move our focus east, to Iran and its northeastern frontier, an area suited to the animals of the steppe nomads – horses, sheep, goats and Bactrian camels – which became the center of successive nomad states. It has a landscape of mountains and high plateaus, combining oasis agriculture dependent on irrigation with vertical pastoralism in mountain and steppe. There were a number of nomad populations in Iran before the arrival of the Seljuqs; in addition to the Kurds of northwestern Iran, mentioned in Chapter 3, there were Iranian and Arab nomad groups in Fars, Kerman and Khorasan, combining sheep, goats and horses with some camels and a few cattle. The nomads do not appear to have utilized all the pastoral resources of the region, and the arrival of the Seljuqs began a long period of growth in the nomad population of the eastern Islamic world.

---

[1] The term Turkmen was not used entirely consistently and seems to have changed its meaning over time. At first it probably denoted the nomad Turks in the steppe who had converted to Islam. Later, it was used for the Oghuz in the Middle East, particularly the nomad followers of the Seljuqs. See A. C. S. Peacock, *Early Seljūq History: A New Interpretation* (London: New York: Routledge, 2010), pp. 49–53.

The Seljuqs who entered Iran had a different tribal structure and political tradition from those of the Kurds and Arab nomads we have been discussing. Steppe nomads had a hierarchical society that allowed significant authority to the tribal leadership, and many had been at least peripherally involved with the steppe empires centered in Mongolia, most recently the Türk Khaghanate. The khaghanate had also included territories and cities inhabited by Iranians, who had provided the *khaghans* with many of their scribes. Thus, the Seljuqs arrived in the Middle East with a tradition of state building and some knowledge of Iranian culture. Entering through Transoxiana and eastern Iran, where Perso-Islamic administrative practice was strongly developed, they picked up accomplished bureaucrats who accompanied them into central Iran. Their rule created a powerful synthesis of Islamic, Turkic and Iranian political cultures which remained in force until the modern era.

The Eastern Steppe Frontier

The main locus of interaction between the Islamic world and the steppe nomads was Transoxiana, the region between the Oxus and Jaxartes rivers. When the Türk Khaghanate fragmented in the mid-eighth century, increasing numbers of nomads migrated into the steppes north of the Jaxartes. Two groups created confederations that became important for the history of the Islamic world. Along the lower Jaxartes and the Aral Sea region were the Oghuz, western Turks who by the tenth century had developed a separate dialect; and to the East, from Ferghana to the Semirechie, were the Qarluqs, who appear to have had a more eastern origin. Both confederations had leaders with the title Yabghu, the second-rank title in the Türk Khaghanate; thus, whether or not they connected themselves explicitly to the khaghanate, they had inherited some of its political traditions.[2]

The border was complex and porous. We can best chart it as a gradation from the area north of the Jaxartes, where Turkic peoples of nomadic lifestyle were in the majority, to the regions of Transoxiana and Khorasan where settled Iranians were predominant. Turks and Iranians, nomads and settled people traded, allied and fought with each other. The area south of the Oxus, corresponding to what is now southern Turkmenistan and Afghanistan, was also mixed. The region of Balkh just south of the Oxus, and Khuttal to its north, were both known for livestock.[3] The most important part of Khorasan for the caliphate was the region stretching from Nishapur to Marw. Here again agricultural land

---

[2] Golden, *Introduction*, pp. 194–199.
[3] Ibn Ḥawqal, *Configuration*, pp. 428–430, 434–436.

combined with pasture; Jurjan, Marw and Sarakhs were known for camel raising and provided winter pasture for other livestock, while the mountains near Nishapur and Khabushan had excellent summer pastures.[4] The eastern frontier was not quiet on either side, and the populations of Transoxiana and Khorasan were known for their skill in war. The Arabs began their conquest of Central Asia in the 660s, and by the early eighth century had taken Transoxiana along with several cities beyond the Jaxartes.[5] By the eighth century Transoxiana was part of the central Islamic lands. The Turks to the north were soon acquainted with Islamic and Iranian culture. Trading towns on the steppe border served as a conduit for Islam, and by the tenth century Islam was spreading among both the Oghuz and the Qarluq. Since most merchants came from the Iranian population, there was a bilingual population of Iranians speaking Turkic along with Turks familiar with Iranian languages.[6]

The relationship between the Iranians and Turks had begun earlier, under the Türk Khaghanate. In the western regions of the khaghanate a good proportion of the city and agricultural population was Iranian. While the Ashina clan and the tribes attached to it were nomadic, scribes and administrators were usually from the settled population, most often Soghdians – an Iranian people centered in Samarqand with a strong merchant class active along the Silk Road. Both Chinese sources and funerary art indicate close interaction between Turkic and Iranian elites; murals show the two peoples making treaties, hunting together and eating at common banquets, with music, song and dance.[7]

The connection between Iranians and Turks is given expression in the place that the Turks found for themselves within the Iranian epic tradition, popularized in the medieval Middle East through the enormously popular epic poem, the *Shāhnāma* of the Persian poet Firdawsi (932–1025). In both Turkic and Iranian traditions, the Turks became identified as the descendants of the legendary nomad king Afrasiyab, the powerful enemy of successive Iranian heroes. Among the Turks, Afrasiyab came to be conflated with a legendary Turkic figure, Alp Er Tonga, whose heroic

---

[4] *Configuration*, pp. 437–438; Gaube and Leisten, *Die Kernländer des ʿAbbāsidenreiches im 10./11. Jh.: Materialien zur TAVO-Karte B VII 6*, p. 158; Rashīd al-Dīn Ṭabīb, *The History of the Seljuq Turks from the Jāmiʿ al-tawārīkh: an Ilkhanid adaptation of the Saljūq-nāma of Ẓahīr al- Dīn Nīshāpūrī*, trans. Kenneth A. Luther (Richmond, Surrey: Curzon, 2001), pp. 518, 594, 598–599, 605, 609.

[5] H. A. R. Gibb, *The Arab Conquests in Central Asia* (New York: AMS Press, 1970), pp. 29–52.

[6] Golden, *Introduction*, pp. 197–198, 212–213.

[7] Golden, *Introduction*, pp. 190, 198; Stark, *Die Altürkenzeit*, pp. 289–314.

and untimely death had entered into folk poetry.[8] It seems surprising that the Turks should have embraced a connection to the great villain of Iranian tradition; however, Afrasiyab was of kingly blood – related to the Iranian kings – and Iranian epics contain a few favorable stories about him, some of which may reflect originally Turkic traditions.[9] Furthermore, according to legend, the family of Afrasiyab had intermarried with the Iranian dynasty and the exemplary king Kay Khusraw was descended from him on his mother's side.[10] By the time the Turks entered the central Islamic lands, therefore, they and the Iranian populations of Central Asia had a long shared history and tradition.

In the ninth century, Muslim regional dynasties began to arise in eastern Iran and Transoxiana. One of most influential of these was the Samanid dynasty (819–1005), who were appointed as governors over several cities by the caliph al-Ma'mun (813–833), and who became wealthy through eastern and northern trade, particularly the sale of the Turkic military slaves then coming into fashion. In 875 the Samanid family gained caliphal recognition as governors of the whole of Transoxiana and became essentially independent rulers over Transoxiana, Khorezm, and Khorasan, a realm which they held until 999. They enjoyed a subsidiary source of manpower in religious volunteers eager to gain blessing by fighting the infidels, following the tradition established on the Byzantine frontier.[11] Like the Arabs, the Samanids were active campaigners; they soon extended their rule beyond the Jaxartes, to Otrar, Isfijab and Taraz along with most of the Ferghana Valley – thus well into Turkic and nomad territory.[12] These campaigns are often portrayed as a response to Turkish raids, but given the Samanids' expansionist policies and the value of captured Turks, we should not characterize all of their border warfare as defense.[13]

---

[8] Louis Bazin, "Que était Alp Er Tonga, identifié à Afrâsyâb," in *Pand-o Sokhan. Mélanges offerts à Charles-Henri de Fouchécour*, ed. Claire Kappler, Christophe Balaÿ, Ziva Vesel (Tehran: Institut français de Recherche en Iran, 1995).

[9] Maḥmūd al-Kāshgharī, *Compendium of the Turkic Dialects*, trans. Robert Dankoff and James Kelly, vol. 1, Sources of Oriental Languages and Literatures (Cambridge, MA: Harvard University, 1982), pp. 92, 189; E. Yarshater, "Afrāsīāb," in *EIr*.

[10] Dick Davis, "Iran and *Aniran*: The Shaping of a Legend," in *Iran Facing Others: Identity Boundaries in a Historical Perspective*, ed. Abbas Amanat and Farzin Vejdani (New York: Palgrave Macmillan, 2012), pp. 39–40.

[11] Jürgen Paul, *The State and the Military: The Samanid Case* (Bloomington: Indiana University Research Institute for Inner Asian Studies, 1994), pp. 11–23; Golden, *Introduction*, p. 190; D. G. Tor, *Violent Order: Religious Warfare, Chivalry, and the 'ayyār Phenomenon in the Medieval Islamic World* (Würzburg: Ergon, 2007), pp. 66–67, 211–215.

[12] Minorsky, Bartol'd, and Bosworth, *Ḥudūd*, pp. 118–119; S. G. Kliashtorny, "Les Samanids et les Karakhanides: une étape initiale de la géopolitique impériale," *Cahiers d'Asie Centrale* 9, Études Karakhanides (2001), pp. 38–40.

[13] Golden, *Introduction*, pp. 193.

The Samanids are important in the history of the Middle East as creators of a tradition of Iranian culture and administration, which was adopted and spread by the Turkic dynasties that succeeded them. The Samanids were of Iranian origin, and they attached themselves to the memory of earlier Iranian glory while remaining supporters of caliph. Iranian language, social structure and tradition had remained strong in eastern Iran, distant from the center of the caliphate. The dynasty and its landed elite patronized literature in a new Persian language written in Arabic script, which replaced Arabic as the chancellery language and over time became a major literary language. They and their servitors patronized poetry and belles lettres in New Persian, and likewise the collection and recording of Iranian myths. In other ways the Samanids copied Abbasid governance, maintaining an administration staffed by highly trained bureaucrats.[14] The Turkic dynasties that followed them adopted many of their policies and hired their bureaucrats. Thus, the condominium of Turkic rule and Iranian culture, begun under the Türk Khaghanate, continued within the Islamic lands.

Two immediate successors to the Samanids are particularly important to our story. The first of these was the nomad Qarakhanid polity, which controlled Transoxiana and the regions to its north and east from 999 to 1211. This was the first state to combine loyalty to Turkic political traditions with adherence to Islam. The Qarakhanids came to power within the Qarluq confederation which controlled both steppe regions and significant cities.[15] In its political structure the Qarakhanid state adhered to Turkic norms, and the official titles attested are those found in the Türk Khaghanate; however, its legitimation reflects Iranian traditions as well. The name Qarakhanid is an outside designation; the dynasty itself used various names, including "al-Khāqāniyya" and "Āl-i Afrāsiyāb."[16] The first title clearly emphasizes the link to the Türk Khaghanate, laying claim to equal status by claiming the highest title in the steppe. The second one refers likewise to royal origin, but through Iranian myth.

Sometime in the tenth century the Qarakhanids converted to Islam, and in the 990s they began to compete with the Samanids for control over Transoxiana, achieving victory in 999. Their conquest does not appear to

---

[14] Richard N. Frye, "The Sāmānids," in *Cambridge History of Iran*, ed. Richard N. Frye (Cambridge: Cambridge University Press, 1975), pp. 136–145.

[15] Karl M. Baypakov, "La culture urbaine du Kazakhstan du sud et du Semiretchie à l'époque des Karakhanides," *Cahiers d'Asie Centrale* 9 (2001), pp. 142–145.

[16] Jürgen Paul, "Karakhanids," in *The Turks*, ed. C. Cem Oguz, Hasan Celâl Güzel, Osman Karatay (Ankara: Yeni Türkiye Publications, 2002), p. 71; E. A. Davidovich, "The Karakhanids," in *History of Civilizations of Central Asia*, ed. M. S. Asimov and C. E. Bosworth (Paris: UNESCO Publishing, 1998), p. 121.

have caused severe disruption. A number of Samanid military command-ers served under them, and the *ghāzī* activities against pagan Turks continued.[17] Like the Samanids, the Karakhanids developed a new lit-erature in their own language written in the Arabic script. The first known monument of the new literary language, the *Kutadğu Bilig: Wisdom of Royal Glory,* was a mirror for princes – an Iranian genre – written in Turkic with an Islamic tone and a liberal admixture of Persian and Arabic vocabulary.[18] Another work, the *Dīwān Lughāt al-Turk,* was written by a member of the Qarakhanid dynasty in Baghdad about 1070, and it represents an effort to preserve Turkic language and culture and to give Turkic an honorable place among Muslim literary languages.[19]

The Qarakhanid rulers retained a largely nomadic lifestyle for the first century and a half of their rule while actively promoting city life and agricultural prosperity. The rulers relied on nomad armies and preferred to camp outside cities rather than taking up residence within them. This practice changed in the mid-twelfth century, when the dynasty began to inhabit palaces in the city and citadel, but it is not clear whether or not this move represented a decline of nomadism beyond the dynasty itself.[20] Throughout their reign, the Qarakhanids were patrons of urban develop-ment, repairing fortifications and constructing hospitals, religious build-ings and caravansarays.[21] They presided over a period of urban growth in which new cities developed and older ones grew larger. We should note that local trade in livestock products was an important factor in the prosperity of Transoxiana and its borderlands.[22] In this time and place then, nomad rule and the existence of a large and favored pastoral population was not a disadvantage for the settled economy.

---

[17] "The Karakhanids," pp. 123–125; Boris D. Kochnev, "Les frontières du royaume des Karakhanides," *Cahiers d'Asie Centrale* 9 (2001), p. 42.

[18] Jürgen Paul, "Nouvelles pistes pour la recherche sur l'histoire de l'Asie centrale à l' époque karakhanide (Xe–début XIIIe siècle)," *Cahiers d'Asie Centrale* 9 (2001), pp. 23–24; Yūsuf Khāṣṣ Ḥājib, *Wisdom of Royal Glory: A Turko-Islamic Mirror for Princes,* trans. Robert Dankoff (Chicago: University of Chicago Press, 1983), "Introduction," pp. 1–4; Ahmet B. Ercilasun, "Language and Literature in the Early Muslim Turkish States," in *The Turks,* ed. C. Cem Oğuz, Hasan Celâl Güzel, Osman Karatay (Ankara: Yeni Türkiye Publications, 2002), pp. 349–353.

[19] Ercilasun, "Language," pp. 352, 362–364.

[20] Davidovich, "The Karakhanids," pp. 123, 132; Paul, "Karakhanids," pp. 73, 75; Valentina D. Goriacheva, "À propos des deux capitales du khaghanat karakhanide," *Cahiers d'Asie Centrale* 9 (2001), p. 91; Yuri Karev, "From Tents to City. The Royal Court of the Western Qarakhanids between Bukhara and Samarqand," in *Turko-Mongol Rulers, Cities and City Life,* ed. David Durand-Guédy (Leiden: Brill, 2013).

[21] Davidovich, "The Karakhanids," pp. 130, 133.

[22] Baypakov, "La culture urbaine," pp. 144–148, 151–157, 161–162; Michal Biran, "Qarakhanid Studies: A View from the Qara Khitai Edge," *Cahiers d'Asie Centrale* 9 (2001), pp. 78–83.

The other important dynasty was the Ghaznavids, founded by a lineage of Turkic mamluks from the Samanid army who had been garrisoned in the region of Ghazna. The third ruler of the dynasty, Sultan Mahmud (r. 998–1030) undertook a career of conquest both into India and into the Samanid realm, then in 999 joined with the Qarakhanids to destroy the Samanids and divide their territory.[23] Sultan Mahmud acquired a realm stretching from the Oxus to Lahore, and west to Rayy. Bureaucrats, scholars and literati from the Samanid court transferred their services to the Ghaznavids who were famous for the cultural brilliance of their court, where Persian literature continued to flourish. An example is the poet Firdawsi, mentioned above, a native of Tus in Khorasan, who began writing his great *Shāhnāma* under the Samanids, but finished it after their fall and presented it to Sultan Mahmud. In this instance Mahmud was not enchanted and offered only a paltry reward, but other writers were better treated. The dynasty also followed the Samanids in inventing a royal Iranian genealogy, but at the same time both rulers and army appear to have retained some Turkic ethnic loyalty; Mahmud's defeat of the Samanids was portrayed as a victory of the descendant of the Khaqan over descendants of the Iranian kings.[24]

The Early History of the Seljuqs

The Ghaznavids and Qarakhanids had been in control of the eastern regions for about thirty years when they were challenged by new arrivals from the steppe. The Seljuqs originated within the Oghuz confederation in the Aral Sea region. Since the word Oghuz designates a confederation, we cannot be certain that these are the people who are mentioned in the inscriptions of the Türk Khaghanate, and in any case they had apparently mixed with local populations in their new regions.[25] However their use of the title Yabghu does suggest that they were within the Turkic political system. While the Oghuz are portrayed in contemporary sources as primitive, it is important to remember that their winter pastures on the lower Jaxartes had several significant towns and they traded actively with the people of Khorasan and Transoxiana in forest and livestock products, particularly sheep.[26] The eponymous founder of the dynasty was Seljuq, son of Duqaq; both he and his father seem to have made a career of

---

[23] Clifford Edmund Bosworth, *The Ghaznavids: Their Empire in Afghanistan and Eastern Iran 994:1040*, 2nd ed. (Beirut: Librairie du Liban, 1973), pp. 37–40.

[24] Bosworth, *Ghaznavids*, pp. 40, 56.

[25] Peacock, *Early Seljūq*, pp. 17–20; Golden, *Introduction*, p. 207.

[26] Baypakov, "La culture urbaine," p. 143; Ibn Ḥawqal, *Configuration*, p. 437; Minorsky, Bartol'd, and Bosworth, *Ḥudūd*, p. 119.

military service, leading armies of their own followers. Seljuqid sources mention them first serving the Khazars centered in the Volga region, who as members of the Ashina clan held the title Khaghan. At some point the two men broke with the Khazars and Seljuq moved to Jand, in what is now western Kazakhstan. There he apparently converted to Islam, perhaps from Judaism, the religion of the Khazars; several of his sons had the names of Jewish prophets: Mikha'il, Musa and Isra'il. Seljuq and his followers occupied themselves in *jihād* against the pagan Turks and also served as auxiliaries for the Samanids and later for the rulers of Khorezm. Coming into conflict with one of the Oghuz powers, they moved into Transoxiana, with summer pastures near Samarqand and winter ones near Bukhara.[27]

After Seljuq's death some of his descendants, including his son Arslan Isra'il and two of Arslan's nephews, Toghril and Da'ud Chaghri, served the Qarakhanid ruler of Bukhara, 'Ali Tegin. In return they were allotted grazing lands near Bukhara. In 1025 the Ghaznavid sultan Mahmud joined with the Qarakhanid khan to attack 'Ali Tegin and his Oghuz allies, imprisoning Arslan and disbanding his armies. After this he allowed a group of about 4,000 of Arslan's followers to cross the Oxus into the pastures of Sarakhs, Abiward and Farawa, near the border of the desert.[28] At the time of their migration, the Oghuz probably specialized in Bactrian and hybrid camels with some sheep; these were the animals connected with the regions they inhabited and mentioned in their battle tactics.[29]

The Oghuz who came into Khorasan were poor, disorganized and angry. Their new hosts had little patience with them and no desire to provide them with a livelihood. The result was painful for both sides. Khorasan was a fertile region with excellent pasture, but it had been badly overtaxed under the Ghaznavids, and agriculture had suffered.[30] The Oghuz arrived in Khorasan almost destitute and, to make matters worse, they soon broke into segments under separate commanders. By 1027 the people of Nasa and Abiward were complaining. The governor of Tus undertook punitive measures, which were followed the next year by a campaign under Sultan Mahmud Ghaznawi, who defeated and scattered the Oghuz.[31] Some found employment with Mahmud's son Mas'ud

---

[27] Andrew C. S. Peacock, *The Great Seljuk Empire* (Edinburgh: Edinburgh University Press, 2015), pp. 24–27; Jürgen Paul, "The Role of Ḫwārazm in Seluq Central Asian Politics, Victories and Defeats: Two Case Studies," *Eurasian Studies* VII (2007–2008), pp. 6–8.

[28] Peacock, *Early Seljūq*, pp. 64–66; Peacock, *Great Seljuk*, pp. 28–32.

[29] Ann K. S. Lambton, *Continuity and Change in Medieval Persia: Aspects of Administrative, Economic, and Social History, 11th–14th century* (Albany, NY: Bibliotheca Persica, 1988), p. 6; Claude Cahen, "Le Malik-nameh et l'histoire des origines seljukides," *Oriens* 2 (1949), p. 63.

[30] Bosworth, *Ghaznavids*, pp. 86–88.   [31] Bosworth, *Ghaznavids*, p. 224.

and a few moved west to serve regional rulers in Iran. In 1033 to 1034 the Ghaznavids vented their anger on the nomads. They summoned leaders to Nishapur and executed about fifty of them, including the commander who had earlier served Mas'ud. When the survivors moved towards Rayy and continued their depredations, Mas'ud – who had succeeded his father on the throne in 1030– captured their camps and moved their followers to India, where he killed many by cutting off their hands and feet and then gibbeting them. Oghuz men captured raiding on the Karakhanid border were thrown under the feet of elephants and trampled.[32]

The Oghuz who had remained in Transoxiana under Seljuq's grand-sons Toghril and Chaghri had a somewhat better time of it. For a while they continued to serve 'Ali Tegin, but towards the end of his life they apparently quarreled with him. In 1035 they crossed the Oxus into Ghaznavid territories with 7,000 to 10,000 followers, moving into the region of Nasa in northwestern Khorasan. From there they wrote to the Ghaznavid governor offering their services as border troops in return for pasture.[33] These men were to some extent professional soldiers, and when they came into Khorasan they were probably looking for a situation similar to the one they had left.

The Ghaznavids had been fighting the earlier Oghuz for two years and they greeted the new arrivals with frank hostility. The request for pasture was summarily refused and Mas'ud moved against them. The armies met near Nasa in June or July and the Ghaznavid army suffered a severe defeat. The Seljuqs now achieved recognition as governors of the border region from Marw and Sarakhs to the Caspian. Troubles continued, however. According to a tradition originating from the Seljuqids, Sultan Mas'ud acted insultingly against the Seljuqid leaders and did not honor his promise to give freedom to their uncle Arslan. The Seljuqs continued to raid and were joined by new contingents of Oghuz from the steppe.[34]

Events now moved with remarkable speed. The Seljuqs needed live-stock and acquired it by raiding. The lands allotted them were not suffi-cient, and the Ghaznavids had no desire to give them more or to employ

---

[32] 'Izz al- Dīn Ibn al-Athīr, *The Annals of the Saljuq Turks: Selections from al-Kāmil fī'l-Ta'rīkh of 'Izz al-Dīn Ibn al-Athīr*, trans. D. S. Richards (London: RoutledgeCurzon, 2002), pp. 14–15; Bosworth, *Ghaznavids*, p. 224–225; Abū'l Faḍl Muḥammad Bayhaqī, *The History of Beyhaqi (The History of Sultan Mas'ud of Ghazna, 1030–1041)*, trans. C. Edmund Bosworth, 3 vols. (Cambridge, MA and Washington, DC: Ilex Foundation and Center for Hellenic Studies, 2011), vol. 2, pp. 94–96.

[33] Cahen, "Malik-nameh," pp. 53–54; Peacock, *Great Seljuk*, pp. 33–35.

[34] Abū'l Faḍl Muḥammad Bayhaqī, *Tārīkh-i Bayhaqī*, ed. Manūchihr Dānishpazhūh (Tehran: Intishārāt-i Hīrmand, 1997–1998), pp. 708, 730, 750; Cahen, "Malik-nameh," pp. 59–60; Ibn al-Athīr, *Annals*, pp. 35–36.

them as soldiers. The Ghaznavid policy was to punish the Seljuqs, contain them, or push them back, but these tactics could not work against a group which had insufficient sources of livelihood and no place to return to. In battles between the Ghaznavids and the Seljuqs, victory went sometimes to one side and sometimes to another, and as they realized that the Ghaznavids could not decisively defeat them, Toghril and Chaghri set their sights on the larger cities.[35]

In 1036–1037 they took Marw and Balkh, and in 1037 or 1038, Nishapur opened its gates without resistance.[36] We have a vivid description of this event, which illustrates Toghril's tactics and the state of his troops. Toghril's relative Ibrahim Inal first approached the city with about 200 men and sent in a messenger. The notables decided to submit, but when they came out to escort Ibrahim into the city they were appalled at the ragged appearance of his troops. This was a major city, used to having rulers of power and magnificence. The crowd watching the Seljuq entry was likewise taken aback, comparing the ragged Seljuq troops with the imposing Ghaznavid armies. Two days later Ibrahim read the congregational prayer in the name of Toghril, and despite his wearing better clothes, riots broke out. The situation improved when Toghril arrived about ten days later attired in fine silk and linen and accompanied by 3,000 horsemen in armor. He seated himself on the sultan's throne and the few members of the mob still present remained orderly.[37]

After the fall of Nishapur, Sultan Mas'ud brought a Ghaznavid army north and the Seljuqs abandoned the cities to take refuge in the steppes and mountains. However, the region could not support the Ghaznavid army, and while the Oghuz could often be defeated, they could not be eliminated. In May 1040 the full Seljuq force met the Ghaznavid army at Dandanaqan near Marw, and the Seljuqs won a decisive victory. The Seljuq brothers sent an emissary to the Abbasid caliph with news of their victory and from this time increasingly presented themselves as rightful rulers.[38]

The Ghaznavid historian Bayhaqi, who has left us the fullest account of the Seljuqid conquest, blamed the loss of Khorasan on Sultan Mas'ud's failure to act decisively. However, it is hard to see how more military

---

[35] Bosworth, *Ghaznavids*, pp. 242–244, 249; Cahen, "Malik-nameh," pp. 60–61; Erdoğan Merçil, "History of the Great Seljuk Empire," in *The Turks*, ed. C. Cem Oguz, Hasan Celâl Güzel, Osman Karatay (Ankara: Yeni Türkiye Publications, 2002), p. 149.

[36] For the question of the date, see Peacock, *Great Seljuk*, p. 39.

[37] Bosworth, *Ghaznavids*, pp. 254–257.

[38] C. E. Bosworth, "The Political and Dynastic History of the Iranian World (A.D. 1000–1217)," in *Cambridge History of Iran*, ed. J. A. Boyle (Cambridge: Cambridge University Press, 1968), p. 23.

activity could have helped. As the Ghaznavid armies campaigned against Toghril and Chaghri they depleted both local and central reserves, and by the end the Ghaznavid army was living off plunder and causing as much destruction as the Seljuqs.[39] Despite their poverty, the Seljuqs had several advantages: since they controlled the desert border, they could interrupt the caravan trade and cut off the supply of livestock products, for which Khorasan relied heavily on the Oghuz.[40] In a situation of scarcity, the mobile troops of the Seljuqs, which appear to have depended more on camels than horses, were clearly at an advantage.[41] The central problem for the Ghaznavids, however, may not have been the power or military prowess of the Seljuqs but their desperation: they had too little to live from, no place to return to, and thus no choice but to stand and fight.

The Formation of the Seljuqid State

It is not clear how the Seljuqs were organized when they arrived in the Middle East. Our sources give no indication that either army or adminis-tration were set up along tribal lines. The Seljuqs entered the Middle East in three distinct groups. The first Oghuz, who crossed the Oxus in 1025, were the followers of Arslan Isra'il and came to be known as the "Iraqis," because they soon moved west and became active in Iraq. Those who came in with Toghril and Chaghri were made up of two allied groups – the "Saljuqiyan," followers of the brothers, and the "Inaliyan" attached to Ibrahim Inal.[42] It seems likely that the Seljuqid leaders were warriors working outside the tribal system, leading personal followings made up of people from various groups and owing loyalty directly to their new lead-ers. Ambitious men leading a group of personal non-tribal followers were a common phenomenon in the steppes; two great dynastic founders, Chinggis Khan and the later conqueror Tamerlane, began as leaders of personal warbands, separate from their own tribes. Like the Seljuqs, these men spent years leading their armies in the service of several different powers. It is not clear whether the dynasty had a hierarchical chain of command; over time Toghril emerged as the most powerful figure, but there are signs of early rivalry among the relatives.[43] From the earliest mention of the Seljuqs in Transoxiana and Khorasan we find them under

---

[39] Bosworth, *Ghaznavids*, pp. 260–266; Peacock, *Great Seljuk*, pp. 37–39.
[40] Bosworth, *Ghaznavids*, pp. 248, 260; Ibn Ḥawqal, *Configuration*, pp. 437–438.
[41] Cahen, "Malik-nameh," p. 63; Bosworth, *Ghaznavids*, pp. 247, 251–252; Peacock, *Early Seljūq*, pp. 73–81.
[42] Peacock, *Early Seljūq*, p. 68.
[43] Claude Cahen, "The Turkish Invasion: The Selchükids," in *A History of the Crusades*, ed. Kenneth Setton (Philadelphia: University of Pennsylvania Press, 1955), pp. 142–143; Peacock, *Early Seljūq*, pp. 63–68.

several rulers, and this structure did not change as their power increased. After the victory in Dandanaqan Chaghri went to Balkh and the neighboring region of Tukharistan, Toghril to Nishapur, and Musa Yabghu with Ibrahim Inal to Marw.[44]

Toghril held the westernmost territories, and he had a major asset in the services of Ibrahim Inal, an exceptionally competent commander and administrator. Toghril stands out as an organizer who was capable as a commander but perhaps even more gifted in utilizing the efforts of others. When he began to campaign to the west he was following in the footsteps of the "Iraqi" Oghuz, who had taken Rayy. Toghril's first expedition was probably an attempt to bring them under control and to take Rayy, which provided both pasture and access to western Iran. He sent Ibrahim Inal ahead and many of the Oghuz fled into the regions of Diyar Bakr and Mosul.[45] Further expansion in the west continued in the same way, with Toghril sometimes undertaking campaigns on his own and more frequently entrusting them to other commanders, among whom Ibrahim Inal continued prominent.[46] As he moved into central Iran, Toghril expanded his power by joining local power struggles, lending out Seljuq contingents to allies. Kurdish and Turkmen contingents were often found within the same armies, sometimes under Seljuq command, and sometimes under Kurdish leaders.[47] The Iraqi Oghuz continued to campaign in western regions, joined by new Oghuz groups coming in from the steppe. Toghril made use of the confusion they caused, taking advantage of their conquests without accepting full responsibility for their actions.[48]

There were, however, disadvantages to the division of authority with which the Seljuqs furthered their conquests. Military commanders, Iraqi Oghuz, and junior members of the dynasty made separate alliances with local powers and felt ownership in areas they had conquered. Indeed, it was not always clear for whom regions were being taken. In Hulwan on the Iraq-Kurdistan border for instance, the *khuṭba* was read in the name of Ibrahim Inal, and the one surviving coin struck by Ibrahim contains symbols denoting sovereignty.[49] It is hardly surprising to find Toghril soon at odds with some of his most important commanders. In 1049–1050, he asked Ibrahim Inal to hand over Hamadan and several forts in

---

[44] Bosworth, "Political and Dynastic," pp. 21–22. For a chart of the relationships, see Peacock, *Great Seljuk*, p. 53.

[45] Ibn al-Athīr, *Annals*, pp. 15–20.   [46] Ibn al-Athīr, *Annals*, pp. 49–52, 58.

[47] Ibn al-Athīr, *Annals*, pp. 58–60, 63–65, 87, 90.

[48] Bosworth, "Political and Dynastic," p. 42; Ibn al-Athīr, *Annals*, pp. 19–20, 21–23, 50; Ripper, *Die Marwāniden*, p. 188.

[49] Ibn al-Athīr, *Annals*, p. 61; Peacock, *Early Seljūq*, p. 68.

Jibal; Ibrahim refused, and Toghril had to subdue him with force.[50] Ibrahim's actions were not thought to merit serious punishment and he continued to be prominent.

For about fifteen years Toghril suffered only minor setbacks. However, the situation changed when he seized what appeared to be his greatest opportunity and took Baghdad from the Buyids. The Seljuq advance had brought disorder to Iraq and the Jazira. Bands of Kurdish and Arab brigands were pillaging the countryside, while the Bedouin 'Uqaylid, Khafaja and Mazyadid dynasties, discussed in Chapter 3, fought in support of one or another local faction. Within Baghdad, tensions between Sunni and Shi'i added to the disorder and the Turkish slave soldiery began to riot. At the end of 1055 the caliph invited Toghril to enter Baghdad, agreeing to include his name in the *khuṭba*.[51] This event raised Toghril's personal status but his involvement in the area precipitated a crisis that nearly cost him his rule. Toghril's troops were attacked by the population of Baghdad, and they repaid the insult with interest. The atmosphere of the city, already poisonous, worsened. After a few days Toghril tried to prevent his troops from looting, but they continued their destruction and eventually he forced some of his Oghuz followers to leave. The thirteen months that he and his army spent in Iraq were disastrous not only for the population but for the Turkmen army as well and caused serious disaffection within it.[52]

The Buyid commander of Baghdad, al-Basasiri, had taken refuge in the Jazira and taken Mosul. Toghril could not afford to lose the Jazira and he set out to retake it. By the end of the year the province was again under Seljuqid suzerainty, Ibrahim Inal was appointed to Mosul, and in January 1058, Toghril met the caliph and was crowned "king of east and west." However, Toghril was losing support among his followers. In order to hold Iraq and neighboring regions he had given high positions to a number of local rulers: the Mazyadid Dubays, Quraysh of the 'Uqaylids, and the Khuzistani emir Hazarasp b. Bankir. Ibrahim Inal and other relatives were openly angry over the favor shown to Arab rulers.[53] Within a few months Ibrahim was in open revolt and had won over a number of Toghril's soldiers. Toghril called on Chaghri's sons for help and together they defeated Ibrahim in July 1059; this time he was put

[50] Ibn al-Athīr, *Annals*, p. 73.
[51] Ibn al-Athīr, *Annals*, pp. 91–92, 98; Peacock, *Great Seljuk*, pp. 49–50; M. Canard, "al-Basāsīrī," *EI* 2nd. ed.
[52] Ibn al-Athīr, *Annals*, 100–107; Lambton, *Continuity and Change*, p. 165; Peacock, *Early Seljūq*, pp. 96–97.
[53] Ibn al-Athīr, *Annals*, pp. 108–112, 114; M. Canard, "al-Basāsīrī," *EI* 2nd ed.

to death along with his closest allies.[54] Once Ibrahim Inal had been defeated, Toghril was able to pursue his goal of a marriage alliance with the caliph, which he achieved just before his death on 4 September 1063.

The Assessment of Toghril's Reign

In both medieval sources and modern histories of the Seljuqs, Toghril has often been portrayed as the creator of the mature Seljuqid state in which Perso-Islamic principles of rule became paramount. After the first years of conquest, Toghril's interests and those of his nomadic Oghuz followers were thought to have diverged, with the Turkmen eager to continue plundering, while the ruler attempted to promote discipline in the army and a stable administration. This interpretation of Toghril's reign reflects a general paradigm of nomad conquest dynasties and their relations to the sedentary population. The destruction accompanying a nomad conquest was interpreted as hostility to agriculture and city life and a failure to recognize their economic importance. According to this view leaders were educated in the needs of settled society by the Persian viziers in their employ, but their nomad followers remained attached to steppe traditions. Toghril was seen as quick to adapt, while his relatives Chaghri and Ibrahim Inal remained closer to the habits of their Oghuz followers. Toghril was thought to have lost popularity after the takeover of Baghdad because he prevented the Oghuz from looting which, as nomads, they considered a traditional right. Ibrahim Inal's rebellion after Toghril's sojourn in Baghdad has been attributed partly to this tension; he has been portrayed as exploiting the dissatisfaction of the Oghuz troops with Toghril's imposition of personal power and discipline.[55]

Recent scholarship has challenged this interpretation. When the Seljuqs arrived in Khorasan, they were familiar with agricultural regions; from the beginning they sought out cities and tried to get access to tax revenue. The evidence moreover does not suggest that Toghril differed from other Seljuq leaders in his attitude towards plunder, or indeed that looting declined as the Seljuqs adjusted to rule over a settled society. All three early leaders – Toghril, Chaghri and Ibrahim Inal – sometimes allowed plunder and sometimes forbade it; this was true of Toghril both on his first arrival and near the end of his life.

---

[54] *Annals*, pp. 118, 124; Ibrahim Kafesoğlu, *A History of the Seljuks: Ibrahim Kafesoğlu's Interpretation and the Resulting Controversy*, trans. Gary Leiser (Carbondale: Southern Illinois University Press, 1988), p. 44; Peacock, *Great Seljuk*, p. 51.

[55] C. E. Bosworth, "Political and Dynastic," pp. 43–45; Cahen, "The Turkish Invasion," pp. 143–145.

What does emerge from the narrative suggests two competing needs common to both settled and nomad leaders: the army had to be supplied, while the central area of power had to be preserved from harm. On the first conquest of Nishapur, Toghril reportedly ordered Chaghri and Ibrahim Inal to prevent looting, while Chaghri argued in favor of it. Nishapur was the central city of Toghril's allotted territory, and when Chaghri returned to his own center, Marw, he forbade pillage and began to restore agriculture.[56] During the difficult campaign in Kurdistan, Ibrahim Inal allowed his troops to pillage, but in 1057, when he was appointed governor of Mosul, he immediately forbade the practice. This was shortly before the revolt he led against Toghril, supposedly in support of the Oghuz tradition of plunder.[57] Toghril, campaigning in the Jazira a few months earlier, had an army which had suffered months of privation in Iraq. On his way north against al-Basasiri, Toghril allowed plunder both along the way and in the region of Mosul. He had no choice, he said, because his troops were hungry.[58]

We should not view Oghuz troops as nomads whose depredations came from nomad tradition. These men had spent years serving as auxiliaries, and such troops – nomad or not – were rewarded largely with booty. This usage had begun early in Islamic history and was not limited to the Middle East.[59] It was standard to allow at least a day of looting in a newly taken city. The question was how much to allow, and how to keep troops faithful and under control without destroying the lands being conquered. We should note that while plundering by Seljuq troops decreased under the reigns of Alp Arslan and Malik Shah when the army was more efficiently paid, it increased again later when order broke down and contestants could no longer afford to pay and feed their armies.[60] We should likewise recognize that Seljuq campaigns in nomad territories such as Kurdistan were sometimes more destructive than those in urban and agricultural regions, perhaps because they were competing for the same resources – pasture and livestock.[61]

Toghril has also been credited with beginning to replace the Turkmen in his army with mamluks, which were seen as more disciplined and

[56] Bosworth, "Political and Dynastic," pp. 20–21; Bosworth, *Ghaznavids*, p. 244.
[57] Ibn al-Athīr, *Annals*, pp. 58–65, 112.
[58] Ibn al-Athīr, *Annals*, pp. 102, 107–109; Gregory Bar Hebraeus, *The Chronography of Gregory Abû'l Faraj, the Son of Aaron, the Hebrew Physician, Commonly Known as Bar Hebraeus: Being the First Part of His Political History of the World*, trans. E. A. Wallis Budge, 2 vols. (London: Oxford University Press 1932), vol. I, pp. 209–210, 213.
[59] For an example from the same period, see Julie Scott Meisami, *Persian Historiography to the End of the Twelfth Century* (Edinburgh: Edinburgh University Press, 1999), pp. 96–98.
[60] David Durand-Guédy, *Iranian Elites and Turkish Rulers: A History of Iṣfahān in the Saljūq Period* (London; New York: Routledge, 2010), pp. 213–216.
[61] Durand-Guédy, *Iranian Elites*, p. 68.

reliable. Current scholars, however, suggest that Toghril and his successor Alp Arslan continued to value Turkmen troops and did not attempt to deny their close relationship to the dynasty. Although both added some mamluks to the army, the Turkmen remained in the majority throughout their reigns, and their support was thus crucial for the dynasty.[62]

The Reigns of Alp Arslan and Malikshah

By the time of Toghril's death the Seljuqid realm stretched from the border of Anatolia through eastern Khorasan and Khorezm. Because Toghril had remained childless and his brother Chaghri had died before him, the sultanate went to Chaghri's descendants, bringing together the eastern and western sections. Under two sultans, Alp Arslan b. Chaghri (1063–1072) and his son Malikshah (1072–1092), the Seljuqs continued to expand their realm. From the beginning, the administration was set up on Perso-Islamic lines and run largely by bureaucrats of Khorasanian origin. The most prominent of these was the vizier Nizam al-Mulk, a man of enormous ability and ambition who served under both Alp Arslan and Malikshah. These two reigns have been seen as a classical age, comparing favorably to the earlier Buyids and the later Mongols. However, we should not overestimate the power – or the orderly nature – of this state. The Seljuq sultans were never free of internal challenges and they could not overcome all of them. Succession to the throne always brought struggles with relatives, some of whom continued to wield regional power. Many local dynasties remained intact, usually pursuing their own ends.

When Alp Arslan came to the throne in 1063 he faced a serious challenge from a senior cousin, Arslan Isra'il's son Qutalmish, who had played a major role in the conquest of Azerbaijan and Armenia where he remained powerful.[63] These regions were rich in pasture and agricultural land, and many Oghuz had collected there, forming a valuable reserve of manpower. Qutalmish gathered a Turkmen army and headed against Rayy but was defeated by Alp Arslan.[64]

In central Iran and Baghdad Alp Arslan had few challenges to his authority, but elsewhere he had to work to maintain control. In Fars he was able to maintain at best a tenuous hold, and only in the western regions. Alp

---

[62] David Durand-Guédy, "Goodbye to the Türkmens? The Military Role of Nomads in Iran after the Saljūq Conquest," in *Nomad Military Power in Iran and Adjacent Areas in the Islamic Period*, ed. Kurt Franz and Wolfgang Holzwarth (Wiesbaden: Reichert, 2015), pp. 111–113; Peacock, *Early Seljūq*, pp. 68–71.

[63] Peacock, *Early Seljūq*, pp. 66, 70.

[64] Bosworth, "Political and Dynastic," pp. 54, 58; David Ayalon, *Eunuchs, Caliphs and Sultans: A Study in Power Relationships* (Jerusalem: Magnes Press, The Hebrew University, 1999), p. 145.

Arslan's powerful brother Qavurt governed Kerman and aimed at extending his power into Fars.[65] Azerbaijan, Armenia and Anatolia presented both opportunity and challenge: they were closely connected to Syria and the Jazira, which were important to the Seljuqs as rulers of Baghdad. In these areas the Seljuq sultans faced a complicated and unstable situation with two major enemies – the Fatimids and the Byzantines – along with Bedouin and Kurdish dynasties. Within this mix Seljuq princes and Turkmen emirs often pursued their own ends, leading Turkmen troops sometimes in the service of others and sometimes on their own account.[66] After his victory over Qutalmish in 1063, Alp Arslan headed to Azerbaijan, where Qutalmish's sons remained active.[67] In 1069–1070 he set off against the Fatimids, but learning that the Byzantines were approaching with a large army, he headed instead against them and defeated them soundly at the famous battle of Manzikert in August 1071. This battle cost the Byzantine emperor his throne and opened Anatolia to further Turkmen migration.[68] Earlier scholars interpreted Seljuq expansion in the west as a ploy by the dynasty to keep the Oghuz troops happily occupied outside the center of the realm where they were not wanted. However, Andrew Peacock has argued persuasively that the westward advance was a deliberate policy of the sultans, aimed at acquiring pastures needed for their nomad followers.[69]

Alp Arslan was murdered in November–December 1072. His son Malikshah, then about eighteen, was challenged by his uncle Qavurt b. Chaghri but prevailed with the help of the 'Uqaylid and Mazyadid rulers leading armies of Arabs and Kurds.[70] The twenty-year reign of Malikshah is considered the apogee of Seljuqid rule. Several former vassal states became fully incorporated and the realm expanded to reach its greatest extent. Malik Shah's governance was more fully Perso-Islamic and less dependent on Turkmen troops than those of his predecessors. Unlike Toghril and Alp-Arslan, who had divided their time among several different cities, he spent more than half of his reign at Isfahan (though still camped outside); the city now became a true capital.[71] By the end of his reign the mamluk corps had reportedly grown to 50,000, dominating the standing army.[72]

---

[65] K. A. Luther, "Alp Arslān," *EIr*.

[66] Heidemann, *Die Renaissance*, pp. 103–125; Ripper, *Die Marwāniden*, pp. 192–195.

[67] Paul A. Blaum, "Children of the Arrow: The Strange Saga of the Iraqi Turkmens," *The International Journal of Kurdish Studies* 15, no. 1–2 (2001), pp. 155–158; Luther, "Alp Arslān," *EIr*.

[68] Ripper, *Die Marwāniden*, 195–202; Luther, "Alp Arslān," *EIr*.

[69] Peacock, *Early Seljūq*, pp. 143–150.   [70] Bosworth, "Political and Dynastic," p. 88–89.

[71] Durand-Guédy, *Iranian Elites*, pp. 78–79.

[72] Bosworth, "Political and Dynastic," pp. 88, 99.

While Malik Shah's reign saw the growth of the standing army and the incorporation of new territories, it also witnessed the rise of powerful independent emirs, many of them Turkmen. Although the Oghuz had ceased to make up the bulk of the central army, they had not lost their military importance. New Turkmen groups had continued to migrate into the central Islamic region, and by this time they constituted a significant proportion of the nomad population of Seljuqid lands, particularly in the pastures stretching across the northern regions. Turkmen occupied pasturelands stretching across the northern Middle East. There were populations in the regions of Balkh, through northern Khorasan to Marw, the desert and steppe regions from Marw and Sarakhs to the eastern Caspian shore, in Jurjan, and what is now Kurdistan, from Hamadan through northern Jazira.[73] Many moved west to Azerbaijan and Armenia, which offered both excellent pasture and the opportunity to attack Christian territories. In this region the Turkmen soon began to displace the Kurdish nomads who had earlier dominated, and by the end of the Seljuqid period, Azerbaijan had begun a process of Turkification.[74] Nomads continued to migrate into Anatolia, where they soon became an important presence as the Byzantines lost territory.

During Malik Shah's reign emirs increased their power as Azerbaijan, Syria and the Jazira became increasingly independent. Some military commanders – both mamluk and Turkmen – achieved significant autonomy and greater power within the state, especially in border regions. Malik Shah's method of expansion worked to the advantage of ambitious emirs. In 1086 he undertook a major campaign in Georgia and Azerbaijan, then in the Jazira and into northern Syria.[75] From this period also he began to appoint Seljuqid officials over the major cities of the Jazira. The 'Uqaylids lost much of their land, and some dynasties, like the Marwanids, were eliminated. A significant portion of the actual fighting in Malik Shah's expansion was undertaken by local commanders with the help of Seljuqid troops, many of them Turkmen.[76] Central Syria and Anatolia were likewise taken over by princes and commanders who were at best marginally under central authority.[77]

---

[73] Ann K. S. Lambton, "The Internal Structure of the Saljuq Empire," in *The Cambridge History of Iran*, ed. J. A. Boyle (Cambridge: Cambridge University Press, 1968), p. 246; David Durand-Guédy, "The Türkmen-Saljūq Relationship in Twelfth-Century Iran: New Elements Based on a Contrastive Analysis of Three inšā'documents," *Eurasian Studies* IX, no. 1–2 (2011).

[74] Ripper, *Die Marwāniden*, pp. 268; C. E. Bosworth, "Azerbaijan IV: Islamic History to 1941," *EIr*.

[75] C. E. Bosworth, "Malik-Shāh,"*EI* 2nd ed; Bosworth, "Political and Dynastic," p. 98.

[76] Heidemann, *Die Renaissance*, pp. 132–138; Ripper, *Die Marwāniden*, pp. 222–238.

[77] Ibn al-Athīr, *Annals*, pp. 172, 190, 192–193, 197; Merçil, "History," p. 159.

In Anatolia the main actors were two sons of Qutalmish, Sulayman and Mansur, who profited from disarray within the Byzantine state to gather territory in western Anatolia and aimed for independence. Malikshah sent an army which killed Mansur but did not subdue Sulayman, who adopted the title of sultan. After Sulayman's death in 1086 Anatolia remained under the control of his sons and local Turkmen.[78] By the end of Malik Shah's reign, emirs had become a major force, many with troops and territory.

The Fragmentation of Seljuqid Rule

The unity of the Seljuqid sultanate ended with the deaths of two men in 1092: the vizier Nizam al-Mulk was murdered in October, and Malikshah died, probably of poison, in November. Upon Malikshah's death his powerful widow, the Qarakhanid Terken Khatun, obtained a patent from the caliph for her four-year-old son Mahmud. However, the mamluks attached to Nizam al-Mulk quickly enthroned Berk-Yaruq, a son from another wife. Another contender was Malikshah's brother Tutush, governor of Syria, who had the support of a Turkmen army and alliances with numerous Turkmen emirs and local rulers.[79]

Although Berk-Yaruq defeated his rivals, he was never able to consolidate power over the whole of Malikshah's realm. Individual emirs, leading their own armies, were an important element in internal struggles and began to control more of the administration.[80] Several established independent power over large districts, which they passed down to their descendants. One example is the Turkmen commander Artuq, who had campaigned on the Arabian Peninsula for Malikshah and then served his brother Tutush in Syria.[81] Within ten years of Malikshah's death, Artuq's children had established their power in Diyar Bakr.

A Turkic institution, the *atabeg* ("father-lord") facilitated the rise of independent territorial power among emirs. Immature members of the dynasty appointed to governorships were provided with senior emirs as *atabegs*. The *atabeg* was often married to a prince's mother when she became a widow, thus cementing his attachment to the dynasty. The princes themselves became increasingly marginal in the process. It is

---

[78] Claude Cahen, *The Formation of Turkey: The Seljukid Sultanate of Rūm: Eleventh to Fourteenth Century*, trans. P. M. Holt (Harlow, England; New York: Longman, 2001), pp. 8–10; Ibn al-Athīr, *Annals*, pp. 216–220, 223–226.

[79] Bosworth, "Political and Dynastic," pp. 102–108; Ibn al-Athīr, *Annals*, pp. 258–277; Durand-Guédy, *Iranian Elites*, pp. 153–157.

[80] Durand-Guédy, *Iranian Elites*, pp. 207, 213–216; Lambton, *Continuity and Change*, pp. 43–48.

[81] Kafesoğlu, *History of the Seljuks*, pp. 51–52; Ripper, *Die Marwāniden*, pp. 221–228.

not surprising to find that several Seljuqid successor states were founded by *atabegs*.[82] In the 1140s both Fars and Azerbaijan became essentially independent under *atabegs*: Fars under the Turkmen Salghurids, and Azerbaijan under the Eldigüzids, were founded by a *mamluk* emir.

Seljuqid Rule in Khorasan and Anatolia

In 1097 Berk-Yaruq appointed his younger brother Sanjar, then twelve years old, as governor of Khorasan. The province remained under Sanjar's control for almost sixty years, and after 1118 he became the recognized head of the Seljuqid state, with the Seljuq ruler in central Iran seen as his subordinate. Around this time a nomadic dynasty, the Qara Khitay, arrived in Turkestan from the borders of China, causing a new wave of Turkmen immigration. Sanjar led an army against them in 1141 and suffered a devastating defeat. As his campaigns in Transoxiana exhausted his treasury, he turned to taxation. The Oghuz nomads on the borders were among the groups pressed for taxes. Those in the region of Balkh were additionally burdened with a harsh governor, and they rebelled. Nonetheless, Sanjar undertook two punitive expeditions against them, and he was defeated in both. He was captured in 1153 by the Oghuz who carried him with them for several years while they rampaged through Khorasan. Sanjar succeeded in escaping after three years but died thereafter.[83] This was the end of effective Seljuq rule in Khorasan.

For the next twenty years the province remained a battleground for competing powers. This was a period of great hardship to which the Oghuz contributed liberally. They were still without a paramount ruler and probably still migrating into Khorasan.[84] The destruction visited on Khorasan and the general confusion at the end of Seljuq rule changed the relationship between the Turkmens and the Seljuq family, as well as the attitude of the general population. There had been criticism before, but now we find some poets exhorting rulers to fight the Oghuz and explicitly linking them with the devil.[85]

In Anatolia on the other hand, Seljuqid rule expanded and continued into the Mongol period. This region remained a boiling cauldron, with Crusader states, new crusading armies, Byzantine rivalries, Turkmen

---

[82] Lambton, *Continuity and Change*, pp. 229–233; C. Cahen, "Atabak," *EI* 2nd ed.

[83] Bosworth, "Sandjar," *EI* 2nd ed.

[84] Bosworth, "Political and Dynastic," pp. 185–187; A. K. S. Lambton, "Aspects of Saljūq-Ghuzz Settlement in Persia," in *Islamic Civilization, 950–1150*, ed. D. S. Richards (Oxford: Cassirer, 1973), pp. 111–113.

[85] Durand-Guédy, "Türkmen-Saljūq Relationship," p. 43; Peacock, *Great Seljuk*, pp. 121–123. Andrew Peacock takes a less negative view, suggesting that Oghuz destructiveness has been exaggerated.

powers, and autonomous tribes constantly embroiled in war. In addition to its extensive pastures, Anatolia had good agricultural land and important trade routes, and thus offered opportunities for local state building. Over the course of the century new Turkmen principalities developed. One of the earliest and most powerful of these was the state created by the descendants of Qutalmish, active in the area since its first conquest. During the twelfth century their state, known as the Rum Seljuqs, became the greatest power in eastern and central Anatolia, presiding over a period of prosperity and growth of urban life. The Turkmen remained an important element in the population, in close relationship with the dynasty and with the cities to which they provided livestock products.[86] Persian remained the language of administration, but in architecture Anatolia developed new regional styles including Turkic animal themes and traces of Central Asian influence. The prosperity and longevity of the Rum Seljuqs revived Seljuq prestige and made the dynasty a continued source of legitimacy, particularly in Anatolia.

Government and Political Culture

As Turks the Seljuqs inherited a strong political culture, but one in which they did not hold first place; they never adopted the titles *khan* and *khaghan*, as the Qarakhanids had done. When the Seljuqs took over the Middle East, they accepted a tradition which also denied them sovereignty, and in their formal legitimation they adhered solidly to Islamic norms. Like other dynasties, they justified their rule through a patent from the caliph, adopting the title of sultan. The Seljuqid *dīwān* was modeled on that of the Samanids and Ghaznavids, and at the beginning the highest offices went to bureaucrats of Khorasanian descent. These men brought their heritage with them and the language of administration under the great Seljuqs was thus Persian rather than the Arabic used by earlier Muslim dynasties in central Iran. Bureaucrats were instrumental in cultural patronage, and it is not surprising to find that the Persian language continued to gain strength in poetry, belles lettres and history. It was at this time that New Persian became established in the central Iranian lands.

The Seljuqid administration was divided: on one side the court (*dargāh*) and the military with personnel made up of Turks – Oghuz and Mamluk; and on the other, the bureaucracy (*dīwān*) whose personnel was composed of Persians and Arabs. There was thus an ethnic division of

---

[86] A. C. S. Peacock, "Court and Nomadic Life in Saljuq Anatolia," in *Turko-Mongol Rulers, Cities and City Life*, ed. David Durand-Guédy (Leiden: Brill, 2013).

offices underlining the separate identity of the dynasty and its military
servitors. This system remained in place for centuries and became
a marker of successive nomad conquest dynasties. In the Islamic world
the separation of ethnic spheres was seen as natural and indeed necessary
for two reasons: First, Turks were seen as superior fighters and military
might was necessary for the maintenance of order; second, a ruler coming
from outside could remain impartial towards the factions of the society he
ruled, while a ruler from the local population would favor one side.[87]

In Seljuqid government as it actually functioned, the distinction
between Turk and Persian, civil and military, was less stark.
Theoretically, the sultan was head of the army, the vizier headed the
bureaucracy, and a high official maintained communication between
the two spheres. However, since the vizier handled financial affairs, the
offices responsible for the recruitment, payment and equipment of the
standing army came under his jurisdiction. Furthermore, most viziers had
their own military followings and participated in campaigns. The viziers
of the early sultans, al-Kunduri and Nizam al-Mulk, had slave armies
large enough to provide significant military force.[88] The more powerful
emirs within the army sometimes had their own *dīwāns* and could thus
wield power in the civil administration. As with most pre-modern governments, the prerogatives of a given office depended largely on the
person holding it.

Despite their Islamic legitimation, the Seljuqs did not totally abandon
their steppe identity. Alp Arslan showed the importance of the Central
Asian heritage of the dynasty in his early campaign into Transoxiana,
where he elicited expressions of submission from neighboring Turkmens
and Qipchaqs and visited the grave of his ancestor Seljuq b. Duqaq in
Jand. He also married his heir apparent, Malik Shah, to a Qarakhanid
princess.[89] The dynasty retained some institutions and customs from its
steppe past and from its period of service with the Qarakhanids. The
Oghuz appear to have preserved the oral tradition connecting the royal
house with the figure of a wolf, the mythical progenitor of the Türk
Khaghans. Some of the iconography used in documents and coins went
back to steppe imperial traditions. At the head of official documents, the

[87] Carole Hillenbrand, "Islamic Orthodoxy or Realpolitik? Al-Ghazālī's Views on
Government," *Iran* 26 (1988), pp. 83–84; Roy P. Mottahedeh, *Loyalty and Leadership in
an Early Islamic Society* (Princeton, NJ: Princeton University Press, 1980), pp. 177–179.
[88] Lambton, "Internal Structure," pp. 257–264; Carla L. Klausner, *The Seljuk Vezirate:
A Study of Civil Administration, 1055–1194* (Cambridge, MA: Distributed for the Center
for Middle Eastern Studies of Harvard University by Harvard University Press, 1973),
pp. 39–41, 58.
[89] Luther, "Alp Arslān," *EIr*.

Seljuqs placed the emblem of the sultan or *toghra*, which in the early period was the image of a bow and arrow and mace. From the Seljuqs this practice spread to other dynasties, developing gradually into a calligraphic exercise best known from the Ottoman Empire. The bow and arrow also appeared on Seljuqid coins, as it did in Qarakhanid coinage.[90] Like the early Qarakhanids, Seljuq rulers usually camped in tents among the army outside the city while at the same time sponsoring construction within it. This began with Toghril, who underwrote major building projects in Rayy, Baghdad and Isfahan, but lived in camp outside.[91]

In social habits, the dynasty retained its Turkish traditions for some time. At the time of Toghril's marriage to the daughter of the caliph he and his emirs sang to Turkish music and danced in the Turkish fashion, going down on their knees and rising again, and the spoken language of the court remained Turkish.[92] Despite their enthusiasm for correct Islamic observance, the early sultans continued the levirate: the practice of marrying widows of one's brother or father (excepting one's own mother), a habit contrary to Islamic law.[93] The Seljuq sultans spent much of their time feasting, drinking and hunting, all of which accorded with Turkic custom, but these pastimes also conformed to the royal practice of other courts in the central Islamic lands (and indeed elsewhere).[94]

One of the steppe traits shown by the Seljuq dynasty was the prestige and power accorded to dynastic women, and the Turks continued to give high status to women after their arrival in the Middle East. Marriage alliances were an important part of politics; the Seljuqs intermarried with many of the surrounding and vassal powers.[95] Although women moved to their husband's family when they married, royal women retained the prestige attached to their birth and passed it on to their children. Many had their own landed estates, grants of tax revenue

[90] Peacock, *Great Seljuk*, pp. 126–129.
[91] David Durand-Guédy, "Ruling from the Outside: A New Perspective on Early Turkish Kingship in Iran," in *Every Inch a King: Comparative Studies on Kings and Kingship in the Ancient and Medieval Worlds*, ed. Lynette Mitchell and Charles Melville (Leiden: Brill, 2013); *Iranian Elites*, p. 90; Kafesoğlu, *History of the Seljuks*, p. 39; Merçil, "History," p. 153.
[92] Faruk Sümer, *Oğuzlar (Türkmenler): tarihleri, boy teşkilatı, destanları*, 4. baskı. ed. (Istanbul: Türk Dünyası Araştırmaları Vakfı, 1999), pp. 121, 126; Bar Hebraeus, *Chronography*, vol. I, p. 215.
[93] Bosworth, "Political and Dynastic," p. 79; Ibn al-Athīr, *Annals*, p. 129.
[94] Peacock, *Great Seljuk*, pp. 172–177.
[95] Cahen, "Malik-nameh," p. 54; Heidemann, *Die Renaissance*, p. 293; Ibn al-Athīr, *Annals*, p. 155; Carole Hillenbrand, "Women in the Seljuq Period," in *Women in Iran from the Rise of Islam to 1800*, ed. Guity Nashat and Lois Beck (Urbana and Chicago: University of Illinois Press, 2003), p. 108.

(*iqtā'*) from the government, a personal administration and a military following.[96]

Women could wield significant power, particularly during succession struggles. A prime example is that of Malik Shah's Qarakhanid wife Terken Khatun, in her efforts to enthrone her son Berk-Yaruq. Safiya Khatun, the sister of Alp Arslan who was married successively to two 'Uqaylid rulers, provides another illustration. During the struggle after Malik Shah's death, she marched on Mosul with her son and took the city for her husband Ibrahim; when Malik Shah's brother Tutush killed Ibrahim, he appointed her and her son as his deputies in the city.[97] In order to enhance their power ambitious women sometimes married men who could increase their standing, and they might even initiate the match. While trying to keep her son on the throne, Terken Khatun proposed marriage to two members of the dynasty who controlled large armies of Turkmen.[98] The Arabs and Persians involved with the Seljuqs did not always approve the freedom of women; the caliph refused to allow Terken Khatun to act as sole regent for her infant son, and Nizam al-Mulk's famous mirror for princes, the *Siyāsat-nāma,* contains a chapter on the importance of denying power to women and avoiding their influence.[99]

Turks and Turkmen

By the eleventh century, Turks had become familiar as neighbors in the steppe and as military slaves; by the end of Seljuq rule, they were also internal nomads and independent dynastic founders. The Turkmen who migrated into the Middle East have remained an important population up to the present. Their military role has been well chronicled, but the histories provide less information on social and economic conditions. The political organization of the Turkmen in the Seljuqid period remains a puzzle. We know something about Oghuz social structure from the work of the Qarakhanid Mahmud al-Kashghari. He lists the major Oghuz tribes, identifying the Seljuq dynasty as belonging to the Qınıq tribe.[100] However the Seljuqs' tribal name is not mentioned in most other sources, and we do not know that the leaders entered as chiefs of the tribe. Moreover, almost none of the tribal names mentioned by al-Kashghari appear in historical sources chronicling the first century of Seljuqid rule.

---

[96] Lambton, *Continuity and Change,* pp. 35, 110, 259.
[97] Ibn al-Athīr, *Annals,* pp. 266–267.   [98] Peacock, *Great Seljuk,* p. 179.
[99] Ibn al-Athīr, *Annals,* p. 262; Niẓām al-Mulk, *The Book of Government: or, Rules for Kings: the Siyar al-muluk or Siyasat-nama of Nizam al-Mulk,* trans. Hubert Darke, 2nd ed. (London; Boston: Routledge & K. Paul, 1978), pp. 179–186.
[100] al-Kāshgharī, *Compendium of the Turkic Dialects* 1, pp. 101–102.

After the migration into the Middle East, first the Iraqi Oghuz and later a variety of emirs acted largely independently, but no tribal names are attached to such groups until the twelfth century.[101] Two decrees issued by Sultan Sanjar in the twelfth century mention Turkmen leaders but give them the same titles accorded to regular regional officials, and make no use of the standard words for tribes or clans in describing their subdivisions.[102] Andrew Peacock has suggested that tribes may not have been important within the Oghuz and that al-Kashghari, who wrote in Baghdad about 1077, might have exaggerated the importance of tribes in an attempt to make the Seljuqs appear more like Arabs, and thus more legitimate.[103]

It is also possible, as suggested above, that the Seljuqs who entered the Middle East were leaders of armies based not on tribes but on personal followings, thus outside the tribal system. Later, in the twelfth century, a number of Turkmen tribes listed in al-Kashghari did become active: the Salghur in Fars, the Iva'i in Armenia and the Jazira, and the Afshar in Khuzistan are all clearly attested. It is possible that tribes or sections of tribes came into the region during the migrations of the twelfth century; another possible explanation is that as central control broke down, tribal organization developed more strongly.[104] The question has not been thoroughly investigated, and the paucity of detailed sources may make it impossible to find a full explanation.

Throughout their rule, Seljuqid sultans considered the Turkmen as their kin, placing high value on their services and on their economic contribution. The Seljuqid rulers did not distance themselves from the Turkmen or attempt usually to keep them away from cities.[105] Both before and during the Seljuqid period, livestock products are mentioned for several regions with nomad populations; these were among the trade goods contributing to the wealth of towns.[106] Trade expanded under the Seljuqs and was an important part of the economy promoted by the dynasty, and the camels provided by the Turkmen were important to this effort.[107]Most scholars suggest that the Seljuqid period was one of general prosperity, and the regions in which Turkmens were concentrated flourished at least until the disturbances at the end of the dynasty.[108]

---

[101] Claude Cahen, "Les tribus turques d'Asie Occidentale pendant la période seljukide," *Wiener Zeitschrift für die Kunde des Morgenlandes* 51, no. 1–2 (1948).
[102] Durand-Guédy, "Türkmen-Saljūq Relationship," p. 29.
[103] Peacock, *Great Seljuk*, p. 28.   [104] Cahen, "Les tribus."
[105] Peacock, "Court"; Durand-Guédy, "Türkmen-Saljūq Relationship."
[106] Lambton, "Aspects of Saljūq-Ghuzz Settlement in Persia," pp. 116–117, 122–123.
[107] Peacock, *Great Seljuk*, pp. 297–302; Durand-Guédy, "Türkmen-Saljūq Relationship," p. 37.
[108] Heidemann, *Die Renaissance*, pp. 145–146, 150–153; Lambton, *Continuity and Change*, pp. 158–160, 169.

Nomads were considered part of the general population and were taxed accordingly; the pasture tax was considered one of the basic, canonical taxes. Oghuz and others also paid dues to support local officials, some of which went to the central government. When the state was in need, they suffered from higher taxes along with the rest of the population.[109] Our most detailed information on the position of the Turkmen comes from two decrees appointing officials to Turkmen groups in the period of Sanjar, mentioned above. Although the military role is referred to in these documents, the terms used for the Turkmen are those commonly applied to peasants as well: *ra'aya* and *khalq*. Their economic contribution to the realm is mentioned, and while they are seen as a potential threat to the government they are also portrayed as vulnerable to abuse. An official appointed by the government was responsible for allotting pasture and water sources, and it appears that such officials might have been Turkmen.[110]

Although Turkic slave soldiers are often discussed in contrast to the Oghuz, both Turkmen and mamluks were often referred to simply as Turks, and it is sometimes impossible to tell the two apart in the historical sources.[111] Thus some commonality of origin was recognized. Opinions about the Turks among the population were often strong but not universally favorable, and it is not surprising to find *hadīth* brought in to strengthen one or another position. Mahmud al-Kashghari, who aimed to encourage the spread of the Turkish language, quoted a Prophetic *hadīth*: "Learn the tongue of the Turks, for their reign will be long," connecting this tradition to the emergence of the Oghuz themselves.[112] Less friendly observers preferred the apocryphal *hadīth* referring to the Turks: "If they love you they eat you, if they are angry with you they kill you."[113] The theologian al-Ghazali, who enjoyed the patronage of the Seljuqs but had reservations about their followers, struck a middle note in his defense of the new system of governance: the Turks, despite their overbearing pride and many other faults, had the crucial quality of military power, which gave them the ability to guard the caliphate and hence Islam. The *ghāzī* activities of the Turkmen on the Byzantine frontier were thus an important factor in their favor.[114]

---

[109] Lambton, "Internal Structure," pp. 245–249; Niẓām al-Mulk, *The Book of Government*, p. 24.

[110] Durand-Guédy, "Türkmen-Saljūq Relationship," pp. 28–29, 31–35, 44, 46.

[111] Durand-Guédy, *Iranian Elites*, pp. 213–216.

[112] al-Kāshgharī, *Compendium of the Turkic Dialects* 1, p. 70.

[113] Haarmann, "Ideology and History," p. 180.

[114] Hillenbrand, "Islamic Orthodoxy," pp. 83–86.

While they might accept the Turks as rulers, the settled elites considered themselves culturally superior. The ragged Oghuz who entered Khorasan and had the effrontery to take it over were met with ridicule as well as fear. These were people from a lower order of civilization who could not understand the niceties of city life. One story described Toghril and his followers in Nishapur after their victory and final takeover: Toghril ate an almond cake and said, "This is excellent *tutmach* (probably a noodle dish) but there is no garlic in it." His followers, even more ignorant, mistook camphor for salt and complained of its bitterness, without recognizing that it was another substance altogether.[115]

In the Iranian world, Turks had long been neighbors both inside and outside the border, and they were seen as part of the natural order of society. By the time of the Seljuqid invasion, the Turks and the Persians – "*Turk wa Tājīk*" – were regarded as two complementary parts of government and society. As New Persian literature developed in Khorasan and Transoxiana, the images and even the words of the Turks were brought into it. Turks were seen as having two basic qualities: military skill and personal beauty. Young Turkic slaves of both sexes were often portrayed in poetry as love objects, personifying beauty. We can cite one couplet to illustrate the combination of characteristics associated with the Turks:

> My idol is an archer bearing arrows of two kinds
> With which in two ways he pierces hearts, in peace and war.
> In time of peace my heart he pierces with the arrow of his eyelashes,
> In time of war the heart of the enemy with arrows of *khadang* [actual arrows].[116]

The ambivalent attitude towards the Turks, at once necessary soldiers and uncouth nomads, recalls the feelings expressed towards the Bedouin which I described in earlier chapters. The Turks were different in two ways: First, they were strangers speaking a separate language and without either the kinship acknowledged to the Bedouin or their literary contribution. Second, the Turks, unlike the Bedouin, had a social structure and political tradition which encouraged state formation. They were not only soldiers but also rulers over much of the Middle East, and they remained so up to the modern period.

[115] Ibn al-Athīr, *Annals*, p. 40.
[116] Tourkhan Gandjeï, "Turkish in Pre-Mongol Persian Poetry," *Bulletin of the School of Oriental and African Studies* 49, no. 1 (1986), pp. 67–71.

Conclusion

It is not clear how many Oghuz entered the Middle East over the course of the Seljuqid period. After the initial migrations there appear to have been two additional movements into the region in the twelfth century, so that by the end of the century Turkmen constituted a significant population of pastoral nomads throughout the northern regions, particularly in Anatolia and Azerbaijan. Within the central Islamic lands, the Seljuq rulers did not claim sovereign titles and followed the practice of other secondary dynasties in subordinating themselves formally to the caliphs while using the title of sultan for themselves. Nonetheless, they created a new dynastic tradition and a new source of legitimation which lasted beyond the Great Seljuq sultans. The Rum Sultanate, stemming from the branch of Arslan Isra'il, lasted into the Mongol period. Other dynasties, led by Atabegs, ruled in several regions, benefitting from Seljuqid dynastic prestige well after the end of a unified state. An example is the Salghurid dynasty of Fars, which retained control over the province as a tributary of successive powers up to 1270. Former servitors of the Seljuqs established states in the Jazira, Azerbaijan and northern Syria. Although there was little overt reference to the steppe imperial tradition in Seljuqid administration, the steppe nomads were now established in the Middle East both as a ruling class and as an important source of military manpower.

The Seljuqs did not attempt to establish Turkic as a language of literature or administration, and in the religious sphere they sponsored standardization and orthodox revival through their promotion of the madrasa. However, they did effect a significant cultural change in bringing the use of New Persian west as the language of the court and administration, and as a literary language suitable for poetry, belles lettres and history. This went along with the use of a dual administration, dividing offices, theoretically at least, into a Persian civil sphere and a Turkic military one. While the Turco-Iranian synthesis had begun under the Samanids and Ghaznavids, it now became the court culture of most of the Iranian regions.

5   Mongol Conquest and Rule

The Seljuqs had arrived in the Middle East as fugitives; the Mongols came as a conquering army, building a vast empire based on the steppe imperial tradition. They began with a ferocious conquest, then created a new imperial ideal encompassing the Eurasian steppe, the Silk Road and China. For a while, much of the Middle East became a mere province in a world empire that was governed through political institutions developed and tested outside the Islamic world, most particularly in Inner Asia and China. At the same time, the Mongols were quick to recognize local expertise and to ally with regional powers. Within a few months of their arrival in the eastern Islamic lands, they were incorporating Iranians into their armies. The bureaucrats of eastern Iran were soon brought into service and, as in the case of the Seljuqs, Iranian traditions found fertile ground in Mongol court culture. Acculturation went both ways; as the Mongols adapted to the Islamic world, their Muslim subjects in turn adopted some elements of the steppe tradition. The Mongol Empire lost its unity just as the conquest of Iran was completed, but its component parts remained under the rule of Chinggis Khan's descendants, and in some cases continued to expand. Thus, what we might call the Mongol enterprise remained an important world force for centuries.

Mongol rule had a profound cultural impact on the central Islamic lands. The most developed steppe institutions were political and military, and these left a lasting imprint. Like the earlier steppe rulers, the Mongols fostered trade and with it the exchange of goods and ideas over a wide area, from the rivers and forests of the Russian territory to China and the Middle East. They further intensified cultural borrowing by their distribution of personnel and goods throughout their empire. Iran and China became closely connected, as khans in the central Islamic world brought in a stream of Chinese and Central Asians and experimented with new systems of governance and likewise with new foods and plants. Over time the Islamic and steppe imperial traditions became intertwined and together spread to encompass the western section of the Mongol

Empire. The influx of foreign ideas and styles created a period of remarkable efflorescence in Perso-Islamic culture in numerous fields, opening and widening the horizons of the Middle East.

The Formation of the Mongol Empire

The Mongol Empire was the greatest moment in the imperial tradition of the steppe. It arose in the old center of the Türk Khaghanate and incorporated many Turkic institutions. The central steppe territories had remained politically active and connected to neighboring powers from China to western Turkestan. Between the Tarim River Basin and the northern Tien Shan mountains the major power was the Uighur state which had preserved the traditions of the Turkic empire within an increasingly sedentary society. During the Uighurs' rule, Turkic became a literary language, sophisticated enough to use in religious texts and in administration. In the Mongolian steppe, probably the strongest power was the Kereyid khanate in the upper Orkhon region, whose ruling house had likewise remained attached to Turkic traditions and had developed a rudimentary administration. In eastern Mongolia, tribal confederations were smaller and less organized. Among them were the Mongols and the Tatars, whose rulers claimed the title khan.[1]

According to tradition, Temüjin – who became Chinggis Khan – was born into the Mongol tribe, probably about 1167. The account of his youth is a tale of hardship: a widow with her children abandoned by erstwhile followers. The young man gathered a band of personal followers from outside his own tribe who owed their loyalty exclusively to him; these men later formed the center of his army and administration. In the early 1180s he collected his affianced bride, Börte, and attached himself to the leader of the Kereyids, Toghril, known as Ong Khan, who had authority over much of the plateau, including the Mongol tribe. Over the next twenty years Ong Khan and Temüjin collaborated to defeat their rivals, applying unusual violence and sometimes massacring members of defeated tribes. Both seem to have been attempting to introduce a new level of central power, and Temüchin, in particular, worked to undermine the power of tribes, breaking with established custom to impose a new level of discipline in military campaigns.[2] As Temüchin gained strength

---

[1] Isenbike Togan, *Flexibility and Limitation in Steppe Formations: The Kerait Khanate and Chinggis Khan* (Leiden: Brill, 1998), pp. 75–77, 117–118; Thomas T. Allsen, "The Rise of the Mongolian Empire and Mongolian Rule in North China," in *Cambridge History of China*, vol. 6, ed. Herbert Franke and Denis Twitchett (Cambridge: Cambridge University Press, 1994), pp. 323–326, 331–332.

[2] Togan, *Flexibility*, pp. 86, 90–91, 99, 102–103.

and ambition the two men began to disagree, and in 1203 Temüjin fought and defeated Ong Khan. He treated his victory as legitimate succession to the rule of an expanded confederation and appropriated Kereit prestige for his emerging state, in part by marrying into the dynasty.[3] In a campaign lasting from May 1204 into 1205 he broke the power of the remaining tribes and became master of the Mongolian plateau.[4]

In 1206 Temüjin convoked a khuriltai – a gathering of representatives from his own and subject tribes – at the source of the Onon River and adopted a new title: Chinggis Khan. He set up his emerging empire as the continuation of the imperial tradition of the Türk Khaghanate. Both the Orkhon River valley, which had been the central imperial territory of the khaghanate, and the Turkic concept of God-given fortune attached to the person of the ruler were now taken over by the Mongols.[5] Chinggis Khan had a Uighur scribe from the Naiman adapt the Uighur alphabet for the Mongolian language and teach it to his sons. He had already rewarded his personal followers with formal offices. Much of his administration was modeled on the Kereit adaptation of earlier traditions: he ordered his army on a decimal system from units of ten men up to regiments of 10,000, known as *tümens*, a system which went back to the Hsiung-nu. He also formed a central guard corps, the *keshig*, which he put under his most loyal followers.[6] Most tribes were broken up and divided among contingents commanded by outside commanders, many from his following.[7] These institutions became part of Mongol administration and survived among subject states well beyond the end of Chinggisid rule. After his enthronement, Chinggis quickly expanded his realm in several directions. He sent his eldest son Jochi to campaign on the northern and western frontiers, while from 1211 to 1215 he mounted campaigns in north China and Manchuria.[8]

Islamic Central Asia was known to the Mongols, since they traded with the cities of Khorezm, and Chinggis Khan had had several Muslim merchants among his early followers. Two new and aggressive powers had arisen in the region. In Khorezm, a new dynasty of Khwarazmshahs

---

[3] Igor de Rachewiltz, *The Secret History of the Mongols: A Mongolian Epic Chronicle of the Thirteenth Century* (Leiden: Brill, 2006), pp. 108–109.

[4] Paul Ratchnevsky, *Genghis Khan, His Life and Legacy*, trans. Thomas Nivison Haining (Oxford; Cambridge, MA: B. Blackwell, 1992), pp. 52–88; Allsen, "Rise," pp. 338–342; Togan, *Flexibility*, p. 135.

[5] Thomas T. Allsen, "Spiritual Geography and Political Legitimacy in the Eastern Steppe," in *Ideology and the Formation of Early States*, ed. Henri J. M. Claessen and Jarich G. Oosten (Leiden: Brill, 1996), pp. 124–125.

[6] Rachewiltz, *Secret History*, commentary, pp. 410, 464–465, 689; Togan, *Flexibility*, p. 75.

[7] Togan, *Flexibility*, pp. 86, 90–91, 102–103; Allsen, "Rise," pp. 346–347.

[8] Paul D. Buell, "Early Mongol Expansion in Western Siberia and Turkestan (1207–1219): A Reconstruction," *Central Asiatic Journal* 36, no. 1–2 (1992), pp. 4–16.

had gathered an army of Turkmen from the steppe and taken over much of Transoxiana and northern Khorasan. For about a century the Qara Khitay, mentioned in Chapter 4, ruled a realm extending from the western Tarim River Basin to Transoxiana, and the Uighurs had become their vassals. As Chinggis Khan began to expand his empire, the Uighur ruler submitted to him voluntarily in 1211 and the Qarluq chiefs of the Ili valley soon followed suit.[9]

In 1216 Mongol armies began to campaign in the west and by the end of 1218 the Qara Khitay realm was under Mongol control. The Khwarazmshah Sultan Muhammad now faced the Mongols directly, and relations soon deteriorated. When a Mongol caravan reached Otrar on the Jaxartes River it was detained by the governor, who executed its merchants and seized their goods, probably with Sultan Muhammad's encouragement. Chinggis Khan sent an envoy to protest; Sultan Muhammad had him killed. This incident provided the justification for a western campaign, begun in the summer of 1219.[10]

The Mongol Campaign in the Middle East

The Mongol conquest is remembered equally for its destructiveness and for its extraordinary success. Sultan Muhammad Khwarazmshah retreated and left the defense of Transoxiana, Khorezm and Khorasan to the garrison troops of its cities.[11] Chinggis Khan divided his forces and attacked Transoxiana simultaneously with four separate armies.[12] The main army under Chinggis and his youngest son Tolui headed against Bukhara, where they arrived in February 1220. After three days of fighting the population opened the city gates, but since there was continued resistance by the garrison troops in the citadel, the Mongols continued to attack and much of the city was destroyed by fire. They then marched against Samarqand, which also submitted after a few days. A section of the army under Chinggis Khan's followers Jebe and Sübedei pursued Sultan Muhammad who fled west and took refuge on an island in the Caspian, where he died in the winter of 1220–1221. Jebe and Sübedei continued through the Caucasus.

Chinggis Khan's conquests were carried out with a display of force and selective violence that made the Mongols appear to many as a manifestation

---

[9] Thomas T. Allsen, "The Yüan Dynasty and the Uighurs of Turfan in the 13th century," in *China among Equals*, ed. Morris Rossabi (Berkeley: University of California Press, 1983), pp. 246–247.

[10] V. V. Bartol'd, *Turkestan down to the Mongol Invasion*, trans. Mrs. T. Minorsky (London: Luzac, 1968), pp. 393–399.

[11] 'Alā' al-Dīn 'Aṭā-Malik Juwaynī, *The History of the World-Conqueror*, trans. John Andrew Boyle (Manchester: Manchester University Press, 1958), pp. 373–378.

[12] Buell, "Early Mongol," p. 27.

of God's will and gave Chinggis extraordinary charisma. The destructiveness of his campaign was not a result of ignorance or antipathy to agriculture and city life, on the contrary, by the time they arrived in Transoxiana, Chinggis Khan and his followers were well acquainted with settled populations. The Mongols had campaigned extensively in China and had begun to occupy its cities. The western army, moreover, contained some sedentary troops; there was a large corps of Chinese siege engineers and a significant number of Central Asian troops under their own rulers including a *tümen* (10,000) of Uighur troops and contingents from the Qarluq, some of whom were Muslim.[13]

The conquests also stood out for their systematic exploitation of conquered populations. When city populations submitted, they were spared, subjected to a tax and assigned a Mongol official. Usually, the garrison troops in the citadel resisted and were often backed by the population for a few days. In these cities the population was taken out of the town, which the army then looted. The walls and fortresses were destroyed, the garrison was massacred, and the Mongols conscripted military levies and craftsmen before allowing people to return. The cities whose inhabitants showed determined resistance or rebelled after conquest suffered even more theatrical punishment. The population was divided up among the soldiers and killed, and only the religious classes and people considered useful to the Mongols were spared. The Mongol interest in trade and production was apparent in this: craftsmen were spared and immediately put to use, some in the army and others as skilled labor in specialized Mongol workshops.[14]

Local manpower gathered from conquered cities became part of the conquering armies. In the first months, levies were used to gather and carry stones, dig trenches or set up siege machines; they were also pushed before the army in the assault on city walls.[15] Quite soon, however, the levies became more integrated into the Mongol army, and within a year or so, levies and Iranian volunteers could be used as regular soldiers, sometimes making up a significant proportion of expeditionary forces.[16]

[13] John A. Boyle, "Dynastic and Political History of the Īl-Khāns" in *Cambridge History of Iran* (Cambridge: Cambridge University Press, 1968), p. 307; Michal Biran, *Chinggis Khan* (Oxford: Oneworld, 2007), p. 56.

[14] Thomas T. Allsen, *Commodity and Exchange in the Mongol Empire: A Cultural History of Islamic Textiles* (Cambridge; New York: Cambridge University Press, 1997), pp. 31–36.

[15] Juwaynī, *World Conqueror*, pp. 106, 117, 126; Muḥammad ibn Aḥmad Nasawī, *Histoire du sultan Djelal ed-Din Mankobirti, prince du Kharezm, par Mohammed en-Nesawi: texte Arabe publié d'après le manuscrit de la Bibliotèque Nationale* trans. O. Houdas, 2 vols., vol. 2 (Paris: E. Leroux, 1891–1895), pp. 89, 91.

[16] Juwaynī, *World Conqueror*, p. 118; Minhāj Sirāj Jūzjānī, *Ṭabakāt al-Nāṣirī: A General History of the Muhammadan Dynasties of Asia, including Hindustan; from A. H. 194 (810 A. D.) to A. H. 658 (1260 A.D.) and the Irruption of the Infidel Mughals into Islam*, trans.

The conquest of Transoxiana was swift, and the Mongols encountered relatively little resistance. In Khorasan, however, the population was more active. A number joined the Mongol army but many others fought back, and as a result the Mongol campaigns there were longer and more devastating. The high level of resistance was probably due partly to local politics and partly to an understandable miscalculation of Mongol strength. Khorasan had been a battleground for decades – indeed for much of the time since Sultan Sanjar's capture by the Oghuz in 1153 – and it was deeply divided. For the beleaguered population, the Mongols were one army among many within a struggle that was both local and inter-regional. The flight of the Khorezmshah and the approach of the Mongols brought out latent rivalries and allowed new opportunities for those currently out of power. When Sultan Muhammad's sons returned to Khorezm from the Caspian provinces, some people welcomed their return, but others decided to side with the Mongols. Accounts of campaigns in Khorasan often mention "renegades" among the Mongol armies; some of these were soldiers from the Khorezmshah's army, and others were Khorasanian soldiers under local rulers.[17]

Both uncertainty about the future and local disagreements led many cities to resist the Mongols and others to rebel against them after they had submitted, or to attack each other. The results were disastrous, and some cities such as Nishapur, Marw and Herat were devastated several times, both by Mongols and by other Iranians. The Khwarazmshah's son Jalal al-Din Mangubirni, who had escaped from Khorezm and regrouped near Ghazna, twice succeeded in defeating Mongol forces. The news of his victories ignited insurrections throughout Khorasan. In 1221 Chinggis defeated Jalal al-Din, who retreated and spent the next three years south of the Indus, but some cities continued to trust in his future. Anti-Mongol agitation started in Marw and was put down with great ferocity. The resistance movement nonetheless spread to other cities. The Mongols probably did not restore complete control until late summer 1222.[18] When we examine events in Khorasan then, we see that the course of the Mongol conquest was influenced by the actions of the population. Political factions and city notables formed different assessments of Mongol strength, and these combined with local enmities sharpened by years of conflict to create a festival of violence that was part conquest and part civil war.

H. G. Raverty (New Delhi: Oriental Books Reprint Corp.; exclusively distributed by Munshiram Manoharlal, 1970), p. 1068–1069; Nasawī, *Histoire du sultan*, vol. 2, p. 87.

[17] See, for example, *Histoire du sultan*, vol. 2, pp. 75, 90, 120; Jūzjānī, *Ṭabakāt*, pp. 1007, 1039, 1068.

[18] Juwaynī, *World Conqueror*, pp. 163–168; Bartol'd, *Turkestan*, p. 448.

At the end of 1222, Chinggis Khan moved to Transoxiana and in early 1223 the main army departed for the east. Transoxiana was incorporated into the empire, under an Inner Asian official appointed as *darugha* (military governor) of Samarqand and Bukhara. He began to restore the region, importing Chinese, Khitan and Tangut to help with agriculture because of severe depopulation; a Chinese Taoist who visited Samarqand in 1221 stated that its population was reduced to one-fourth of its previous population.[19] The conquest of the city was not the only cause of its depopulation; this was due in part to successive levies of soldiers, and probably also to an earlier rebellion against the Khwarazmshah in 1212 that resulted in a retaliatory massacre.[20]

The Mongols have often been characterized as a "nation at arms," but the army was not the whole of society; nor were nomads the whole of the army. Members of the army were recruited from the larger population – distinguished by a different hairstyle. They were trained in tactics and forbidden to change from one regiment to another. Members of tribes had been deliberately distributed among different decimally ordered regiments, the most important of which were led by members of Chinggis's personal following who were loyal exclusively to him. The army itself was divided into three parts: left wing, right wing and center, and each was under the stable command of a high commander. The *keshig* – the imperial guard – served both as bodyguard and as an institution to control and train future commanders and officials.[21] What was most extraordinary about the Mongol army was its strict discipline, remarked upon by many observers. Punishments for desertion or disobedience were draconian, and soldiers thus could be depended on not only to obey, but to remain loyal through defeats, a crucial strength particularly in the Khorasan campaigns.[22]

Another strength of the army was its mixed composition of nomad and settled soldiers. Starting with troops from the settled populations of Central Asia, the Mongols added levies from the conquered cities, which were brought in not just at the conquest but also through later conscription. There were likewise local soldiers who joined voluntarily, probably both nomad and settled. Together, these troops sometimes formed a significant proportion of the army, particularly in the later

[19] Paul D. Buell, "Sino-Khitan Administration in Mongol Bukhara," *Journal of Asian History* 13, no. 2 (1979): pp. 122–125, 134–141; Igor de Rachewiltz, "Yeh-lü A-hai (ca. 1151– ca. 1223), Yeh-lü T'u-hua (d. 1231)," in *In the Service of the Khan: Eminent Personalities of the Early Mongol-Yüan Period*, ed. Igor de Rachewiltz, Hok-lam Chan, Hsiao Ch'i-ch'ing and Peter W. Geier (Wiesbaden: Harrassowitz, 1993), pp. 118–119.
[20] Juwaynī, *World Conqueror*, p. 122; Bosworth, "Political and Dynastic," p. 194.
[21] Timothy May, *The Mongol Art of War: Chinggis Khan and the Mongol Military System* (Barnsley, England: Pen & Sword Military, 2007), pp. 27–34.
[22] May, *Mongol Art of War*, pp. 47–49.

MS. DIEZ A. FOL. 72
SEITE 13

Figure 5.1 Mongolian Archer on Horseback. Iran. Miniature by Muhammad ibn Mahmudshah al-Khayyam, ca. 1420–1425. Brush and ink on paper. Staatsbibliotek zu Berlin, Preussischer Kulturbesitz, Orientalabteilung, Saray-Albums (Diez-Albums), fol. 72, p. 13.

campaigns. Although nomads are famous for their skill in mounted archery, other skills were also useful, particularly in siege warfare, and it may well have been advantageous to have some troops who did not require the amount of pasturage needed for nomad troops. While the core of the army was Mongolian light cavalry, Chinggis Khan's army should not be considered purely a "nomad army." This was a mixed force and an exceptional one, an army of a size and quality rarely found in the history of nomads.

The Middle East in the Early Mongol Empire

The conquered regions of the Middle East now formed one edge of an empire centered in Mongolia, and administration was designed to benefit the empire as a whole. Chinggis Khan died in August 1227. His sons by his principal wife Börte became the progenitors of the four branches of the dynasty, and most of the empire came to belong to their descendants. Their individual territories are designated by the term *ulus*, signifying both land and population. The Russian steppes formed the *ulus* of the eldest son Jochi, while the Semirechie and Turkestan went to the second son Chaghadai, and the Altai was the *ulus* of the third son Ögedei. As the youngest son, Tolui kept the heartland of Mongolia and served as regent on his father's death. Ögedei was enthroned as supreme khan – *khaghan* – by the Mongol princes at a *khuriltay* in the fall of 1229.

Transoxiana was joined with the other sedentary regions of the Silk Road. The regional governor repaired irrigation systems, restored agriculture, and introduced a tax reform abolishing most extraordinary taxes, at least in theory. Contemporary observers and numismatic evidence suggest that by 1260 Central Asia had nearly regained its earlier prosperity.[23] The situation was very different in Iran, where Chinggis Khan had installed officials only in a few eastern cities.[24] Local rulers in Iran, eastern Anatolia, and Syria found it wise to offer submission and many traveled to the central court in person.[25] One who did not submit was the Khwarazmshah's son Jalal al-Din Mangubirni, who left India to campaign throughout the Middle East. The level of pillage he allowed his army soon turned both rulers and populations against him. In 1230 a new Mongol expedition arrived in Iran to deal with Jalal al-Din and impose control. Jalal al-Din retreated and was subsequently killed by Kurds in the summer of 1231. The Georgians and Armenians were subdued and most of the major cities of Central Iran surrendered with minimal resistance. Azerbaijan, with its excellent pasture, became the center of Mongol administration over western Iran.

Under Ögedei and his successors, Güyüg (1246–1248) and Möngke (1251–1259) the administration was systematized, and mechanisms were developed to maximize the exploitation of conquered lands and peoples. The Mongol Empire was a mix of brilliantly conceived organization and administrative chaos. The largest settled regions were not included in the individual *uluses* of Chinggis Khan's sons. Chinggis Khan had appointed *darughas* – military governors – in many cities and had created administrations in northern China and Transoxiana. Ögedei Khan transformed

[23] Buell, "Sino-Khitan Administration," pp. 139–147; Thomas T. Allsen, "Maḥmūd Yalavač (?–1254); Masʿūd Beg (?–1289); ʿAlī Beg (?–1280); Buir (fl. 1206–1260)," in *In the Service of the Khan*, pp. 122–127.

[24] Paul D. Buell, "Tribe, 'Qan' and 'ulus' in Early Mongol China: Some Prolegomena to Yüan History," unpublished PhD dissertation, University of Washington (1977), p. 154.

[25] Juwaynī, *World Conqueror*, p. 250.

these into jointly managed secretariats under civilian governors, a system that was later extended into Iran. The *khaghan*'s officials in the secretariats were accompanied by representatives of the Jochid, Chaghadayid and Toluid houses. In this way the *khaghan* maintained his claim on the settled territories while acknowledging the interests of other branches of the family. In the armies sent on major campaigns, the lines of all four brothers were likewise represented, and since some soldiers remained as regional guard troops, each area of the empire had armies representing the four dynastic branches. Troop contingents known as *tamma,* usually conscripted from a variety of armies, were stationed in border regions, both to protect the boundaries and to aid in further expansion. These armies remained in place over decades and often became important regional power centers.[26] The dispersal of personnel from each branch of the family throughout the empire helped to create a common interest and culture, but it also made the internal administration of each *ulus* difficult.

Ögedei Khan carried out a census of the conquered regions and reorganized the official post – a system of stopping places and horses kept for official business throughout the empire – and in 1235 he began the construction of the capital city Kharakhorum in the Orkhon Valley near the old capital of the Türk Khaghanate. The government collected two standard taxes from the settled population – a tax on agricultural produce (*qalan*) and a poll tax (*qupchur*) – along with a tax on trade (*tamgha*). Throughout the empire, nomads – including Mongols – were assessed at a rate of one animal per hundred.[27] In many places, however, taxes were less systematized. Both local commanders and Chinggisid princes were eager to increase their personal income, and the population suffered from dues levied by innumerable people connected to the government or to the Mongol elite.

The great khan Möngke (1251–1259) brought the Mongol Empire to the height of its unified power. He undertook a series of reforms designed to rationalize taxes while maximizing resources for the central government. In Iran the poll tax became a progressive one, from one dinar for the poor to seven dinars for wealthy men. In 1252 Möngke organized a new census, covering many areas that had not been counted before. One major purpose was the mobilization of troops; the subject population was

---

[26] Timothy May, "The Mongol Conquest Strategy in the Middle East," in *The Mongols' Middle East*, ed. C. P Melville and Bruno De Nicola (Leiden: Brill, 2016), pp. 15–22.

[27] Thomas T. Allsen, *Mongol Imperialism: The Policies of the Grand Qan Möngke in China, Russia, and the Islamic Lands, 1251–1259* (Berkeley: University of California Press, 1987), pp. 159–162, 169; Igor de Rachewiltz, "Yeh-lü Ch'u Ts'ai (1189–1243); Yeh-lü Chu? (1221–1285)," in *In the Service of the Khan*, pp. 150–151.

divided into decimal units from ten to 10,000, of which a portion served as soldiers and others provided for the army's needs. Thus, settled soldiers became a permanent part of the Mongol army.

Despite efforts by the *khaghans*, it proved impossible to prevent widespread confusion and abuse, partly due to problems at the center. Accession to the office of *khaghan* was based on consensus among the major Chinggisid princes, and this was not easy to reach; thus, there were long periods of interregnum during which the widow of the former khan served as regent. During these times, princes and emirs expanded their power within the satellite administrations at the expense of the government and the population. In the twenty-four years between the death of Chinggis Khan and the enthronement of Möngke Khan in 1251, the Mongol Empire was without a khan for ten years, enough time to undo much of the systematization achieved by the *khaghans*.

Early Mongol Governance in the Middle East

Mongol armies in the Middle East centered in two areas which provided winter and summer pastures within a convenient distance. In the west, the summer pastures lay in the mountainous regions of Ala Taq, north of Lake Van, and the area southwest of Sultaniyya. As winter pastures the Mongols used the low-lying regions of Arran, Mughan, the Jaghatu River, south of Lake Urmiya, and later the environs of Baghdad.[28] In the east, the largest winter pastures were in Jurjan, the regions around Sarakhs, and Marw. The administrative center was in the summer pasture at Radkan, near Tus.[29]

From the time of the expedition of 1230, Mongolian troops and commanders were active throughout Iran, not as a cohesive bloc, but as one contentious group among many. Mongol officials soon began to compete against each other and allied with regional Iranian rulers. Mongol governors hired Persian bureaucrats, thus involving another group famous for its infighting. One can take as an example the politics of Khorasan, about which we are well informed. Here rival camps arose in the northern region and the split within the Mongol administration combined with existing power struggles among the local rulers of Khorasan and Mazandaran to divide both Mongols and Persians into rival camps. Ögedei summoned the combatants to appear before the court in Kharakhorum, where provincial enmities became part of contentious court politics lasting

---

[28] Rashīd-al-Dīn, *Rashiduddin Fazlullah's Jami'u't-tawarikh: Compendium of Chronicles*, trans. W. M. Thackston (Cambridge, MA: Harvard University, Dept. of Near Eastern Languages and Civilizations, 1998), pp. 518–520, 551, 629.

[29] Rashīd-al-Dīn, *Compendium*, pp. 518, 594–595, 598, 605, 609.

throughout Ögedei's reign.[30] Mongol and Iranian politics thus became closely intertwined, and the two peoples soon began to influence each other. We have usually credited the Persian bureaucrats, who wrote the histories, with introducing the Mongols to settled culture. However, local Iranian rulers, working in alliance with Mongols at all levels, probably also exerted cultural influence. On their side, Iranians became familiar with Mongol traditions and some took pride in their knowledge.[31]

During the reign of Ögedei the Mongols began to restore agriculture in Iran, though not as successfully as they did in Transoxiana. Mongol commanders played a significant part in this process, often in cooperation with Iranian officials. Ögedei ordered that Herat be repaired after the devastating punishments it had suffered, and the task was overseen by the Mongol governor. In 1239–1240, the Mongol governor of Khorasan restored buildings, markets and irrigation in the center of his administration – the region of Tus and Radkan. The Mongol commanders beneath him also built mansions and parks. The next governor, Arghun Agha, continued the development of Tus, and improved his winter pasture area, rebuilding the village of Arzanqābād near Marw, where he had a palace, and adding further parks and mansions for his followers.[32] There can be no doubt that the Mongols were still largely nomadic and that they regarded themselves as a steppe power. The building of these centers therefore suggests that the construction of imperial centers with developed agriculture and fixed palaces for the Mongol elite was not seen as a denial of nomadic identity.

The Founding of the Ilkhanid Dynasty

Möngke Khan began his reign in a weak position as the son of Chinggis Khan's youngest son Tolui, and because he had come to power through a coup against the line of Ögedei Khan. He therefore cemented the power of his line by sending out two major military expeditions in which the chief commanders were his own younger brothers: Khubilay, who was sent to China; and Hülegü, who was sent to consolidate Mongol rule over the Middle East. Hülegü set out in 651/1253 and arrived at Samarqand in 653/1255. He brought with him a large army that became part of the Mongol population of Iran and is therefore worth discussing. From the army belonging to the Toluids, Hülegü was granted two out of each ten

---

[30] Juwaynī, *World Conqueror*, pp. 488–489, 492–505.
[31] Jean Aubin, *Émirs mongols et vizirs persans dans les remous de l'acculturation*, Studia Iranica. Cahier 15 (Paris; Leuven, Belgique: Association pour l'avancement des études iraniennes; Diffusion Peeters Press, 1995), pp. 26–27.
[32] Juwaynī, *World Conqueror*, pp. 501, 510.

soldiers. He then marched through Ögedeyid territories and added soldiers and commanders from that branch. In addition, he was accompanied by large contingents of Oirats and Qunqirat, two tribes whose leading lineages married into the dynasty and had thus managed to retain their cohesion.[33]

By the time of Hülegü's arrival, new taxes were in force and local rulers were ordered to provide supplies and to accompany the army. It is not surprising, therefore, that some people who had previously shown obedience should balk at the new conditions. The caliph likewise refused the Mongol demands, so in January 1258 three Mongol armies converged on Baghdad along with local armies, including Armenians, Georgians, and the Atabegs of Shiraz and Mosul. The assault began on January 29 and the caliph surrendered on February 10. The inhabitants of Baghdad were systematically slaughtered and the city sacked for seven days, apparently at Möngke's orders; the scene echoed the massacres of the first Mongol conquest. On February 20, the caliph was killed, probably by being rolled in a carpet and kicked, since the shedding of blood on the ground was forbidden by Mongol custom. This moment was a momentous one for the Islamic world, and Hülegü had reportedly been warned that disaster might befall him if the caliph were killed; however, no calamity occurred.

In the autumn of 1258, Hülegü invaded Syria with the experienced commander Ked-Bugha as advance guard. The subjugation of Syria and Egypt appeared to pose little challenge, since the Ayyubid dynasty was in disarray and the Mamluk regime in Egypt was in its infancy. By the beginning of the summer the Mongol army had taken the northern cities and reached Gaza, where Hülegü learned of the developing struggle over the succession to Möngke and turned back, leaving behind a small part of the army under Ked-bugha.[34] In the meantime, the situation in Egypt had changed with the accession of the mamluk Qutuz to the throne in 1259. Qutuz gathered a significant force and when the armies joined battle at 'Ayn Jalut in Galilee on September 3, 1260, Ked-Bugha was killed, and his troops fled.[35] The Mamluks' victory provided instant prestige to their nascent state. In 1261 the new sultan Baybars welcomed a fugitive 'Abbasid, thus acquiring a shadow caliph, and from this time on the Mamluks presented their rule as a bulwark of Islam against the infidels.

---

[33] Michael Hope, *Power, Politics, and Tradition in the Mongol Empire and the Īlkhānate of Iran* (Oxford: Oxford University Press, 2016), pp. 92–100.

[34] Reuven Amitai-Preiss, *Mongols and Mamluks: The Mamluk-Īlkhānid War, 1260–1281* (Cambridge: Cambridge University Press, 1995), pp. 16–28; R. Stephen Humphreys, *From Saladin to the Mongols: The Ayyubids of Damascus, 1193–1260* (Albany: State University of New York Press, 1977), pp. 330–363.

[35] Amitai-Preiss, *Mongols and Mamluks*, pp. 39–45.

The Middle East was now divided into two sections: a primarily Iranian region governed by pagan Mongols, and an Arab one ruled by Muslim slave soldiers of Turkic descent, in the name of a shadow caliph.

Möngke's death on August 12, 1259 marked the end of the unified Mongol Empire; the Chinggisid princes were unable to reach consensus on a new *khaghan*. When Khubilai had himself enthroned as khan, Hülegü was the only important ruler to recognize him, and he was rewarded in 1262 when Khubilai's envoys formally invested him with the title Ilkhan and with official power over the Mongol Middle East. The two khanates maintained close relations, with frequent exchanges of personnel.[36]

Hülegü soon came into conflict with Berke, the Jochid ruler of the Golden Horde, and hostilities broke out in 1261–1262 over the rule of northwestern Iran. Berke had converted to Islam and was now allied with the Mamluks. The Mongols had for some time been in contact with the pope and European rulers, and Hülegü sent a mission in 660/1262 to King Louis, proposing cooperation.[37] These two opposing alliances lasted through much of the Ilkhanid period. The Golden Horde periodically raided through the Caucasus; since the Mongol capital was in Azerbaijan, and the vulnerable winter pastures lay to the north, this was a significant threat. The Mamluks and Ilkhans likewise remained enemies. The Ilkhans undertook several expeditions to Syria, none of which resulted in long-term rule, while the Mamluks raided and sometimes occupied Mongol vassal powers in Anatolia and Armenia. In the east, the Ilkhans were soon in conflict with the Chaghadayid Khanate, which gradually took over the eastern part of Afghanistan and threatened the Ilkhans' Khorasanian territories.

The Ilkhans ruled directly over most of northern Iran and Iraq but left eastern Anatolia and parts of Iran under the control of vassal dynasties. The most powerful of these were the Sultanate of Rum (1077–1307), described in Chapter 4; the originally Ghurid Kartids in Herat (1245–1381); the Qara-Khitay Qutluq-Khanid dynasty of Kerman (1222 to 1305/1306); and the Turkmen Salghurids of Fars (1148–1280). The dynasties of Fars and Kerman both married princesses into the Ilkhanid dynasty and became active in central politics, bringing the dynasty also into local rivalries.[38]

---

[36] Thomas T. Allsen, "Changing Forms of Legitimation in Mongol Iran," in *Rulers from the Steppe: State Formation and the Eurasian Periphery*, ed. Gary Seaman and Daniel Marks (Los Angeles: Ethnographics Press, 1991), pp. 226–232; "Notes on Chinese Titles in Mongol Iran," *Mongolian Studies* 14 (1991), pp. 27–39.

[37] Jean Richard, "D'Älǧigidäi à Ġazan: la continuité d'une politique franque chez les Mongols d'Iran," in *L'Iran face à la domination mongole*, ed. Denise Aigle (1997), pp. 62–63.

[38] George Lane, *Early Mongol Rule in Thirteenth-Century Iran: A Persian Renaissance* (London; New York: RoutledgeCurzon, 2003), pp. 96–175.

The Rule of the Ilkhans

Much of the Middle East was now an independent khanate ruled by pagan Mongols. The Islamic caliphate and the unified Mongol Empire had ended within a year and a half of each other: the caliphate on February 20, 1258, and the unified empire with Möngke's death on August 11, 1259. However, Chinggisids continued to rule much of Eurasia, and the traditions of both empires continued to command loyalty. Islamic and Mongol traditions became increasingly intertwined as Mongols, both within and outside the Middle East, converted to Islam, and Mongol political institutions became part of the governance of Ilkhanid lands. Like the Seljuqs, Mongol rulers in the Middle East had adopted much of the administrative apparatus of earlier Middle Eastern dynasties. Their administration was also to some extent a dual one, with a Mongol military and an Iranian civil administration. The two branches were not well differentiated, however; Mongol officials sometimes oversaw the *dīwān* and some Persian viziers held authority over both members of the dynasty and Mongol emirs. Towards the end of the dynasty, a few powerful Persian viziers even became members of the Mongol *keshig*.[39]

The transition from province to khanate was not without strain. The satellite administration in Iran was now disbanded, and the region came directly under the Ilkhan. However, at the time of the conquest rights over the income of some districts and populations in Iran had been granted to members of other Chinggisid branches, and these could not be easily revoked. Moreover, Mongol *tamma* troops and governors had been established in Iran since the reign of Ögedei and had acquired regional power and local alliances. The major Mongol officials and commanders, known as *noyans,* often held inherited rights to high position. Royal women had their own entourage (*ordo*), including armed retainers, and they had independent sources of income in taxes, trade and workshops.[40] The inclusion of women and *noyans* in state deliberations was formalized in the ceremonies surrounding the accession of a new ruler.[41]

Within the new khanate, both *noyans* and members of the dynasty were determined to retain their inherited rights. As soon as central control weakened, they seized what they considered theirs, making it difficult for the central government to collect the money it needed. Members of the dynasty and the Mongol elite were involved in administration alongside

[39] Peter Jackson, *The Mongols and the Islamic World from Conquest to Conversion* (New Haven, CT: Yale University Press, 2017), pp. 282–285.
[40] Bruno De Nicola, *Women in Mongol Iran: The Khātūns, 1206–1335* (Edinburgh: Edinburgh University Press, 2017), pp. 132, 151–152, 159.
[41] *Women,* pp. 95, 98; Rashīd-al-Dīn, *Compendium,* pp. 548, 562, 580.

Iranian bureaucrats and the combination of two groups involved in factional fighting made politics particularly murderous: a remarkable percentage of Persian viziers and Mongol commanders died violent deaths.[42] This was not an easy realm to rule.

Despite the difficulties that the Ilkhans faced both within their realm and with their neighbors, the reigns of the first two Ilkhans, Hülegü (1260–1265) and Abaqa (1265–1282), are considered times of relative order and prosperity. Abaqa died of delirium tremens on April 1, 1282, and the three reigns which followed mark a period of increasing internal strife. His brother and successor, Tegüder Aḥmad, reigned for only two years. From the beginning his position was undercut by the power of Abaqa's son Arghun, who inherited a portion of his father's troops and property, and who succeeded in taking the throne in 1284. Over the course of Arghun's reign (1284–1291) the rivalries and ambition of his *noyans*, in alliance with princes, royal women, viziers and members of local dynasties, came to dominate political life. Arghun was succeeded by his brother Geikhatu (1291–1295), who has been remembered as a profligate khan. To do him justice, there was already a financial crisis in the state and some of his generosity may have been an attempt to retain the loyalty of his followers.[43] Soon Geikhatu's *noyans* began to conspire against him and he was seized and killed on 6 Jumada I 694/March 24, 1295. The thirteen years of confusion following Abaqa's death had brought the Ilkhanid economy to a crisis.

It was under these conditions that Geikhatu's son Ghazan achieved power. He had been governor of the crucial province of Khorasan and had the help of the powerful emir Nawruz, the son of Arghun Agha, who had governed Iran under Möngke Khan. Nawruz had inherited great wealth in land and flocks centered in Radkan and had dominated the region for much of Ghazan's governorship.[44] Ghazan's reign is remembered for three major actions: he converted the Ilkhanate to Islam, he instituted major administrative reforms, and he weakened the power of the Mongol *noyans* and members of the dynasty. On Ghazan's death in 1304 his brother Öljeitü succeeded to the throne and enjoyed an unusually comfortable position, since Ghazan had destroyed the power of noyans and princes and had left no male offspring. After Öljeitü's death in 1316, his twelve-year-old son, Abu Saʿid, was enthroned without opposition,

---

[42] David Morgan, "Mongol or Persian: The Government of Īlkhānid Iran," *Harvard Middle Eastern and Islamic Review* 3, no. 1–2 (1996), pp. 62–76; Judith Pfeiffer, "Conversion to Islam among the Ilkhans in Muslim Narrative Traditions: The Case of Aḥmad Tegüder," unpublished PhD dissertation, University of Chicago (2003), pp. 226–227; Aubin, *Émirs mongols*, p. 82; Jackson, *The Mongols*, pp. 294–296.
[43] Rashīd-al-Dīn, *Compendium*, p. 741.   [44] Aubin, *Émirs mongols*, p. 53.

though actual power in the beginning lay with his chief noyan, Amir Choban. The Ilkhanate continued to defend itself successfully, but when Abu Sa'id died in 1335, he left no child or other suitable successor, and the Ilkhanate soon came to an end.

For many years the accepted view of the Ilkhanate was that of nomad rulers gradually educated by their Persian viziers to value and support Perso-Islamic civilization and its agricultural base. According to this formulation, it was the khan who was most likely to promote assimilation and respect for the settled economy, while a significant proportion of his Mongol followers opposed both. The turning point of the dynasty was seen as 1295, when Ghazan Khan restored Islam as the official religion and instituted reforms considered the first recognition of the needs of the settled population. This formulation flows naturally from the contemporary histories, most of which were written by bureaucrats in the service of the Ilkhans. The most influential was that of Ghazan's and Öljeitü's vizier, Rashid al-Din, who carried out Ghazan's reforms. However, in recent years scholars have increasingly questioned this analysis of assimilation, as they have done for the Seljuqs. There are two questions to ask: first, whether acculturation began with the ruler and was resisted by the *noyans*; and second, whether Ghazan's reforms represented a turn towards the agricultural sector and away from a policy favoring nomads.

Ghazan's adoption of Islam was long considered a sign of the Ilkhanid dynasty's adjustment to the Perso-Islamic culture of its subjects, and a prelude to his reforms. Ghazan converted at the urging of Amir Nawruz shortly before he came to power, and he soon proclaimed Islam the religion of the realm.[45] Charles Melville has shown, however, that conversion among the Mongol army elite was widespread by the time of Ghazan's accession; it is therefore possible that most of the army was already Muslim. Thus, Ghazan probably converted as much to gain support within the army as to appeal to the settled population.[46] We should remember that when Hülegü arrived, much of Iran had already been under Mongol administration for several decades. As previously mentioned, the Mongol army and administrators had been closely in touch with Iranians, and within a few years of Chinggis Khan's first attack, the soldiers levied from Iranian cities were fighting alongside Mongol soldiers. Both before and during Ilkhanid rule, Mongol emirs

---

[45] Boyle, "Dynastic," pp. 378–380.
[46] Charles Melville, "Pādshāh-i Islām: The Conversion of Sultan Maḥmūd Ghāzān Khān," *Pembroke Papers* 1 (1990), pp. 159–177; Pfeiffer, "Conversion," pp. 85–99.

allied with local Iranian rulers and bureaucrats.[47] Thus acculturation occurred at many levels and had begun before the establishment of the Ilkhanate.

The second question is whether agriculture in Iran had been suffering due to the Mongols' failure to understand its importance, and whether Ghazan's reforms represent a repudiation of earlier attitudes favoring nomad exploitation of settled populations. Scholars have usually concentrated on the need to protect agriculture, but it is possible that the problem was not only the disruption of the settled economy, but also the impoverishment of the lower segments of society, both settled and nomad. The plight of Mongol soldiers contributed to a crisis during the reign of Geikhatu, which Ghazan had to address before he could bring the realm to order.

Rashid al-Din, who tends to paint a bleak picture of earlier Ilkhanid rulers to highlight Ghazan's achievements, nonetheless describes the impoverishment of the army as beginning only when the old order broke down. He states that under Hülegü and Abaqa, when Mongol customs were still in effect, although Mongol soldiers did not receive wages or provisions, an annual tax of livestock and nomad products was reserved for poorer soldiers.[48] Later, however, the Mongol troops had become increasingly impoverished. He cites a number of abuses to explain the plight of the ordinary peasant and nomad. In addition to noting general corruption and the resulting over-taxation – a problem for settled and nomad alike – he rails against the hordes of messengers (*elchis*) engaged in both government and private business, who covered the land like a plague of locusts. Assuming the right to help themselves to supplies, messengers seized goods by force, depleting both livestock and harvests. This plague increased with the growing weakness of the central government.[49] The falconers and leopard keepers who provided animals and birds for court hunts behaved in much the same way.[50] While the higher Mongol commanders were able to extort larger subsidies from the ruler, soldiers at a lower level achieved no such favor.[51] Some apparently

---

[47] Beatrice F. Manz, "Nomads and Regional Armies in the Middle East," in *Nomad Military Power in Iran and Adjacent Areas in the Islamic Period*, ed. Kurt Franz and Wolfgang Holzwarth (Wiesbaden: Reichert, 2015), pp. 11–22.

[48] Rashīd-al-Dīn, *Compendium*, pp. 730, 736.

[49] Rashīd-al-Dīn, *Compendium*, pp. 704–705, 714–718, 759–761. Similar abuses are reported earlier. See Jackson, *The Mongols*, p. 301.

[50] Rashīd-al-Dīn, *Compendium*, pp. 751–755.

[51] A. P. Martinez, "Some Notes on the Īl-Xānid Army," *Archivum Eurasiae Medii Aeivi* VI (1986), pp. 206–213; Aḥmad ibn Yaḥyā ibn Faḍl Allāh al-'Umarī, *Das mongolische Weltreich. Al-'Umarī's Darstellung der mongolischen Reiche in seinem Werk Masālik al-abṣār fī mamālik al-amṣār*, trans. Klaus Lech, Asiatische Forschungen, Bd. 22 (Wiesbaden: Harrassowitz, 1968), p. 154.

had become so impoverished that they sold their children into bondage.[52] It is possible that the impoverishment of Mongol soldiers was also due to wider social changes in the transition from tribe to army, since the 1290s saw a similar problem in China, where some soldiers were likewise driven by poverty to sell their children into slavery.[53]

When troops had to prepare for a campaign without sufficient supplies, they stole each other's horses to eat and pillaged agricultural populations. This was a problem that Ghazan experienced in Khorasan in 1291–1293.[54] Ghazan thus faced an immediate crisis which threatened both the Mongol army and the agricultural population. This problem was one impetus for reforms aimed at providing a secure fiscal base for the army and protection for settled populations. To support the army, grants of land were to be distributed to Mongol soldiers according to rank down to commanders of ten; these were to be farmed, probably by slaves or subjects, as was the case under Khubilai in China.[55] Land and other taxes were to be collected according to fixed rates written on plaques attached to the walls of buildings; nomads could write them on steles erected wherever they thought best.[56] Numerous extraordinary taxes were repealed, and envoys and military were not allowed to demand lodging at will. Other measures promoted restoration of abandoned land and systematized currency, weights and measures. Ghazan's measures share similarities with many of Khubilai Khan's programs in China, and we should note that Bolad Ch'eng Hsiang, a high official who had served under Khubilai, was at court.[57] Thus these reforms represent not only an adjustment to local conditions, but a broader movement towards change.

In the last decades several scholars have questioned whether Ghazan's reforms were fully carried out, since there is little evidence beyond Rashid al-Din's account and some abuses apparently continued.[58] Nonetheless,

[52] Rashīd-al-Dīn, *Compendium*, pp. 735–736.
[53] Ch'i-ch'ing Hsiao, *The Military Establishment of the Yuan Dynasty* (Cambridge, MA: Council on East Asian Studies, Harvard University: distributed by Harvard University Press, 1978), pp. 29–30.
[54] Rashīd-al-Dīn, *Compendium*, pp. 604–613.
[55] al-'Umarī, *Das Mongolische Weltreich*, p. 155; Hsiao, *Military Establishment*, pp. 20–22, 46.
[56] Rashīd-al-Dīn, *Compendium*, p. 711.
[57] Thomas T. Allsen, "Biography of a Cultural Broker, Bolad Ch'eng-Hsiang in China and Iran," in *The Court of the Il-khans 1290–1340*, ed. Julian Raby and Teresa Fitzherbert (Oxford: Oxford University Press, 1996), pp. 7–22.
[58] David O. Morgan, "Rašīd al-Dīn and Gazan Khan," in *L'Iran face à la domination mongole*, ed. Denise Aigle, Bibliotèque Iranienne (Tehran: Institut Français de Recherche en Iran, 1997), pp. 185–186; Reuven Amitai, "Continuity and Change in the Mongol Army of the Ilkhanate," in *The Mongols' Middle East*, ed. C. P. Melville and Bruno De Nicola (Leiden: Brill, 2016), p. 44.

there does appear to have been some change for the better, particularly in Öljeitü's reign. This happy outcome may be due also to Ghazan's success in curbing the power of the Mongol elite, in particular the great *noyans*. He had likewise taken steps to diminish the influence of dynastic women, in part by interfering in the inheritance of their *ordos*, some of which now passed to male members of the dynasty instead. Indeed, it is notable that women become less conspicuous from the time of his reign.[59] The depredations of the high elite – both Mongol and Iranian – are a major theme in Rashid al-Din's discussion of the reforms.

Nomadism and Tribalism in the Mongol Period

The Mongol period brought a significant nomad population into the Middle East. There were three separate conquests – in 1219–1220, 1230 and 1255 – each bringing new troops, many accompanied by their families. It appears that most Mongols remained nomadic. The Ilkhanid rulers regularly traveled between winter and summer pastures, accompanied by their *ordos* in which soldiers, chancellery and bazar were housed in a moving tent city. Within the army likewise, seasonal pastures were allotted to each *tümen* (10,000).[60] Observers and Mongol historians attest to the continuance of pastoral nomadism in the Mongol army.[61] Most of these nomads were in the northern regions, from Anatolia to Khorasan, with the greatest concentration around the two centers of power, Khorasan and Azerbaijan. In addition to the main army there were *tamma* troops garrisoning several regions, particularly eastern Khorasan and the regions to the south of it, partly under Ilkhanid and partly under Chaghadayid control. Some *tamma* troops had become largely independent under their own leaders and were feared for their plundering expeditions; the most notable were the Negüderi active in Sistan, Kerman and Fars.[62] Fars and central Iran also had a sizeable nomad population, largely Iranian and Turkmen.[63]

---

[59] De Nicola, *Women*, pp. 159–164.

[60] Charles Melville, "The Itineraries of Sultan Öljeitü," *Iran* 28 (1990), pp. 55, 58, 60; John Masson Smith, "Mongol Nomadism and Middle Eastern Geography: Qīshlāqs and Tümens," in *The Mongol Empire and Its Legacy*, ed. Reuven Amitai-Preiss and David O. Morgan (Leiden: Brill, 2000), pp. 41–42, 51–52.

[61] Reuven Amitai, "Did the Mongols in the Middle East Remain Pastoral Nomads?" in *Seminar at Max Planck Institute, Halle, Germany* (Internet: Academia.edu), pp. 10–13.

[62] Beatrice F. Manz, *The Rise and Rule of Tamerlane*, Cambridge studies in Islamic civilization (Cambridge: Cambridge University Press, 1989), pp. 159–161.

[63] Denise Aigle, *Le Fārs sous la domination mongole: politique et fiscalité, XIIIe-XIVe s*, Studia Iranica, Cahier 31 (Paris: Association pour l'avancement des études iraniennes, 2005), pp. 77–80.

In the regions outside Mongol control, nomads also remained important. Syria contained a significant nomad population, within which Turkmen were increasingly predominant. The Mamluk sultan Baybars (1260–1272) installed Bedouin, Kurds and Turkmen as military settlers in many areas of Syria, with the task of guarding the country against enemies, serving in the official postal service (*barīd*) and supplying horses to the government. From the beginning of the Mamluk state, nomads, including Mongols, Kurds, and Turkmen had found a place in the army, though they could not hold high rank.[64] Other nomads served as auxiliaries and received land in return.

The Mamuk borders with Anatolia and the Jazira became the domain of Turkmen nomad confederations encouraged to raid neighbors, and when possible, to acquire new land. In 1298 the sultan granted the region of Marʿash on the Armenian border to the Turkmen who later formed the Dhuʾl Qadr confederation; they were subject to the governor of Aleppo and participated in campaigns against the Armenians and the Mongols.[65] The frontier with the Jazira was the territory of Bedouin tribes and the Turkmen Döger.[66] While the Mamluks made use of the nomads, their attitude towards them was highly ambivalent. Turkmen were sometimes courted and favored, due in part to a perceived kinship between them and the early Mamluk sultans, who prided themselves on their Turkic Qipchaq origin. On the other hand, they were characterized as rebels, thieves and irreligious people.[67]

Over this period Anatolia became a major repository of nomad population. Immigration had begun during the Seljuq period, and the Mongol occupation of Azerbaijan pushed more Turkmen west. The Mongol victory over the Rum Seljuqs at Köse Dagh in 1243 brought most of eastern Anatolia under Mongol suzerainty, although at first, rule remained largely indirect. There were three major spurts of immigration, in the 1230s, 1260s and late 1270s.[68] The Oghuz Turkmen were the

---

[64] David Ayalon, "The Auxiliary Forces of the Mamluk Sultanate," *Der Islam* 65 (1988), pp. 15–20; Robert Irwin, *The Middle East in the Middle Ages: The Early Mamluk Sultanate, 1250–1382* (London: Croom Helm, 1986), pp. 50–53.

[65] Margaret L. Venzke, "The Case of a Dulgadir-Mamluk Iqṭāʿ: A Re-Assessment of the Dulgadir Principality and Its Position within the Ottoman-Mamluk Rivalry," *Journal of the Economic and Social History of the Orient* 43, no. 3 (2000): pp. 407–408.

[66] Gerhard Väth, *Die Geschichte der artuqidischen Fürstentümer in Syrien und der Ġazīraʾl Furātīya (496–812/1002–1409)* (Berlin: K. Schwarz, 1987), pp. 167–168; F. Sümer, "Döger," *EI* 2nd ed.

[67] Barbara Kellner Heinkele, "The Turcomans and Bilād aš-Šām in the Mamluk Period," in *Land Tenure and Social Transformation in the Middle East*, ed. Tarif Khalidi (Beirut: American University of Beirut, 1984), p. 169; Ayalon, "The Auxiliary Forces of the Mamluk Sultanate," p. 16.

[68] Rudi Paul Lindner, *Nomads and Ottomans in Medieval Anatolia* (Bloomington: Research Institute for Inner Asian Studies, Indiana University, 1983); Sara Nur Yıldız, "Mongol Rule in Thirteenth-century Seljuk Anatolia: The Politics of Conquest and History

largest group among the nomad population, but there were also Qipchaqs, related to the ruling class of the early Mamluk state; Mongols; and Khorezmian nomads, some previously under the Khorezmshahs.[69] Their political culture was formed by the nature of their arrival: most came not as a conquest army, but as semi-independent groups of frontier fighters. The Muslim-Christian border region, known in Turkic as *uj*, had characteristics associated with other frontiers – adaptability to local conditions and impatience with higher authority. After the Seljukids of Rum lost power in 1306, Mongol governors ruled eastern Anatolia from two regions: Diyar Bakr to the south, an important center for winter pastures; and the summer pastures in the region of Mush and Akhlat.[70] Control was partial, however. Local independence and the fluidity of politics led to the rise and fall of innumerable small principalities – or *beyliks* – mostly founded by powerful commanders who were able to gain independence and recruit soldiers from the nomadic tribes.[71]

The active trade routes, extensive pastures and good agricultural land of Anatolia provided a strong power base for the Mongol commanders appointed to govern it. Several Mongolian lineages became established there and were active over generations. In 1314, Abu Saìd's emir Choban was appointed to the governorship, and his family remained powerful in the region for the next ten years. Several other great emirs succeeded to this post, most notably Shaykh Hasan Jalayir, founder of the Jalayirid dynasty.[72] These families founded the western successor states to the Ilkhans, and in the centuries thereafter, the nomads of Anatolia provided leadership, troops, or both for many of the dynasties who ruled the Middle East after the Mongols.

For the Mongols as for the Seljuqids, the question of tribalism is complex. Among the Turkmen, tribes appear to have gained importance in the Mongol period. As I wrote in Chapter 4, there is little evidence of

Writing, 1243–1282," unpublished PhD dissertation, University of Chicago (2006), pp. 161–162, 256, 264–265.

[69] Speros Vryonis, *The Decline of Medieval Hellenism in Asia Minor and the Process of Islamization from the Eleventh through the Fifteenth Century* (Berkeley: University of California Press, 1971), pp. 245–246; Ilhan Şahin, "The Oguz Turks in Anatolia," in *The Turks*, ed. C. Cem Oguz et al. (Ankara: Yeni Türkiye Publications, 2002), p. 419; Tuncer Baykara, "Society and Economy among the Anatolian Seljuks and Beyliks," in *The Turks*, ed. C. Cem Oguz et al., pp. 611–613.

[70] F. Sümer, "Ḳarā-Ḳoyunlu," *EI* 2nd ed.

[71] Ilham Erdem, "Eastern Anatolian Turkish States," in *The Turks*, ed. C. Cem Oguz et al., pp. 477–506; Salim Koca, "Anatolian Turkish Beyliks," in *The Turks*, ed. C. Cem Oguz et al., pp. 507–553.

[72] Charles Melville, "Anatolia under the Mongols," in *Cambridge History of Turkey*, ed. Kate Fleet (Cambridge: Cambridge University Press, 2009), pp. 89–92.

tribal organization among the Turkmen of the early Seljuqid period. The traditional tribal names of the Oghuz do appear in the twelfth and thirteenth centuries, held by several regional dynasties including the Salghurids and Döger, and a branch of the Döger tribe was powerful near Edessa.[73] In the fourteenth century more tribes with traditional Oghuz names are mentioned on the Syrian-Egyptian border, and with the collapse of the Ilkhanids they appear in eastern Anatolia as part of rising confederations.[74]

Among the Turco-Mongolian population tribal power was uneven. Chinggis Khan had created a decimal army and divided most tribes among several different regiments, thus largely removing tribes as centers of power. Within the central Ilkhanid territories, tribalism seems not to have played a significant role in politics. Many of the great *noyans* of the Ilkhanid period bear tribal names, but these appear to denote a descent line rather than a larger corporate group, and their power depended in large part on dynastic favor, which was often cemented by intermarriage.[75] The only tribe which was clearly an active political entity was the Oirat, whose leader had married Chinggis Khan's daughter. Subsequent marriages cemented its power, and a significant segment of the tribe came west in the army of Hülegü and was still under its own leadership. It remained as a large cohesive tribe in the region of Diyar Bakr beyond the period of the Ilkhanate.[76]

Over time, however, the new troop contingents formed by the Mongols became power centers in themselves. Mongol soldiers were closely connected to their regiments, which they were not permitted to leave.[77] Rashid al-Din mentions several *tümens* whose command was either inherited by descendants of the original commander or reassigned by a khan.[78] Both regiments and royal camps (*ordos*) could remain intact over generations, sometimes passed on within one family and sometimes re-assigned. This is attested for the *ordos* of Ilkhanid dynastic women; the *ordo* of Hülegü's wife Dokuz Khatun, who died in 1265, can be traced through numerous other women into the fourteenth century.[79] *Ordos* consisted of servants, livestock, and soldiers, and the regiments also presumably owned considerable livestock, since we know that pasturages

[73] F. Sümer, "Döger," *EI* 2nd ed.

[74] Cahen, "Les tribus"; John E. Woods, *The Aqquyunlu: Clan, Confederation, Empire*, rev. and expanded ed. (Salt Lake City: University of Utah Press, 1999), pp. 25–28.

[75] See, for example, Patrick Wing, *The Jalayirids: Dynastic State Formation in the Mongol Middle East* (Edinburgh: Edinburgh University Press, 2016), pp. 42–58.

[76] Anne F. Broadbridge, "Marriage, Family and Politics: The Ilkhanid-Oirat Connection," *Journal of the Royal Asiatic Society* 26, no. 1–2 (2016).

[77] May, *Mongol Art of War*, p. 31.   [78] Rashīd-al-Dīn, *Compendium*, pp. 42, 91.

[79] De Nicola, *Women*, pp. 156–157.

were assigned to them. It seems probable that membership in the *ordos* and in troop contingents was hereditary, independently of ownership or leadership. The army of Arghun Agha passed to his son Nawruz; this was known as the Jawun-i Qurban and remained intact into the fifteenth century. In the fourteenth century we find two armies, the *tümen* of Kebek Khan and the Boroldai *tümen,* which are specifically identified as the descendants of the followers of Kebeg and the troops of Boroldai, both dating from the early fourteenth century, and without clear leadership.[80] Thus an *ordo* or a regiment could over time develop into a new corporate entity, not originally based on kinship, but maintained through heredity. Some maintained leadership from within, and thus they should be seen as tribes.

Outside of the most central Ilkhanid territories, new tribes quite soon began developing out of the regiments formed by the Mongol state. In a situation of constantly shifting power relationships and frequent disruption, nomads required leaders who could protect or seize pasture rights and deal with neighboring powers. In Kerman and Fars, two Mongol tribes named after earlier commanders, the Jurma'i and the Ughani, were active in the early fourteenth century.[81] In Anatolia, the families of earlier commanders had remained powerful, and at the end of the Ilkhanate we find important political groups named after earlier Mongol commanders. One was the Samaghar, named after the commander intermittently posted to the region in the 1260s and led by his descendant. Another was the Barambay, named after the son of the Mongol *noyan* Sütay, who had earlier governed Diyar Bakr. Yet another was named Jawunghar, the Mongolian term for the advance guard.[82] The same process took place in the eastern borders of the Ilkhanate and in the Chaghadayid khanate, as will be discussed in Chapter 6.

The Economic Impact of the Mongols

It is difficult to form an accurate picture of the economic impact of the Mongols. In 1960 the Soviet scholar I. P. Petrushevsky produced a study of agriculture under the Ilkhans, shaped by Soviet policies dictating a negative assessment of Mongol rule.[83] His argument was based on

---

[80] Manz, *Rise and Rule*, pp. 34, 158.   [81] Jackson, *The Mongols*, pp. 205–206.

[82] Jürgen Paul, "Mongol Aristocrats and Beyliks in Anatolia. A Study of Astarabādī's *Bazm va Razm,*" *Eurasian Studies* IX, no. 1–2 (2011), pp. 115–117, 127–128; Melville, "Anatolia," pp. 61, 67, 77, 82–84. I should note here that Jürgen Paul does not denote these groups as tribes, which he defines as groups organized according to either real or fictive kinship. Since my definition is broader, they fit within it.

[83] I. P. Petrushevskiĭ, *Zemledelie i agrarnye otnosheniia v Irane XIII–XIV vekov* (Leningrad: Izd-vo Akademii nauk SSSR, Leningradskoe otd., 1960). Parts are summarized in

flawed computations and is no longer fully accepted, but no comprehensive study has since taken its place. In general, assessments of Mongol impact have become less negative. Contemporary descriptions show that agriculture suffered badly from the conquests, but some allowance must be made for rhetorical hyperbole and the desire to blame Mongol destructiveness for a decline that had begun earlier.[84] Although both Hülegü and Abaqa inflicted destruction on cities, both were aware of the need to restore the realm.[85] Hülegü began reconstruction almost immediately after taking Baghdad, and Abaqa ordered its agriculture restored.[86]

We must also consider the causes of agricultural problems and ask whether the presence of nomads was naturally destructive. If this were the case, agriculture would have suffered most in the regions surrounding the major pastures and routes, in Azerbaijan and Khorasan. However, these regions appear to have recovered, and some areas close to Mongol camps even flourished, with new towns appearing. In these areas the market for agricultural produce provided by the Mongols may have outweighed the impact of nomad depredations. In other places, however, nomadism was harmful.[87] Fars and Kerman, for instance, suffered considerably from the depredations of semi-independent nomad tribes.[88]

Corruption and over-taxation were also serious problems. I have already discussed the extortion inflicted by emirs and princes. Local governors often bribed Mongol collectors, thus enriching themselves at the expense of the population.[89] The situation could be worse in areas ruled through local powers, where the regional dynasty provided an additional level of corruption. Fars provides a vivid illustration of the difficulties facing the Ilkhanid tax administration. Under several different khans, officials arrived with a reform agenda only to suffer attack and demotion.[90] During the

---

I. P. Petrushevskiĭ, "The Socio-Economic Condition of Iran under the Īl-Khāns," in *The Cambridge History of Iran, vol. V* (Cambridge: Cambridge University Press, 1968), pp. 483–537.

[84] Lambton, *Continuity and Change*, p. 219; Jean Aubin, "Réseau pastoral et réseau caravanier. Les grand' routes du Khurassan à l'époque mongole," *Le Monde iranien et l'Islam* 1 (1971), pp. 107–108; Jean Aubin, "La propriété foncière en Azerbaydjan sous les Mongols," *Le monde iranien et l'Islam* 4 (1976–1977), p. 130.

[85] See, for example, Juwaynī, *World Conqueror*, pp. 616–617; Aḥmad b. Jalāl al-Dīn Faṣīḥ Khwāfī, *Mujmal-i Faṣīḥī*, ed., Muḥammad Farrukh (Mashhad: Bāstān, 1960–1961) II, pp. 334, 337, 340.

[86] Aigle, *Le Fārs*, p. 124.

[87] Jean Aubin, "Réseau pastoral"; Qazvīnī, Ḥamd Allāh Mustawfī, *The Geographical Part of the Nuzhat-al-qulub* (Leiden: Brill; London: Luzac, 1915–1919), pp. 61–66, 68–73, 78–94; Aubin, "La propriété foncière," pp. 112–113.

[88] Jackson, *The Mongols*, p. 206.   [89] Aigle, *Le Fārs*, pp. 152–153.

[90] Ann K. S. Lambton, "Mongol Fiscal Administration in Persia, pt. II," *Studia Islamica* 65 (1987), pp. 100–121; Lane, *Early Mongol Rule*, pp. 133–141; Aigle, *Le Fārs*, pp. 92, 104, 120, 127.

struggle preceding Ghazan's accession, taxes were increased and a levy of 20 percent was raised from livestock in the province, thus bringing the nomadic tribes into disorder.[91]

On the other hand, trade and production were actively promoted by the Mongols and flourished in this period. Tabriz and Sultaniyya became international trading centers where the land routes through Central Asia connected with those of the Golden Horde and the sea trade of the Persian Gulf. The Ilkhans were conscientious in protecting trade routes in both the Black Sea and the Gulf.[92] The leadership engaged directly in international trade through partnerships known as *ortoq*, in which booty and other income was entrusted to merchants in return for a share of profits. Dynastic women were also conspicuously active; many had received shares of land, booty and artisanal manpower from the conquests, which they invested in trade.[93] There was thus a close relationship between the Mongol government and international merchants, who benefitted from significant privileges; a number served the administration, particularly as holders of tax farms.[94] While *ortoqs* stimulated trade, they also led to an atmosphere of speculation and consequently often to indebtedness among members of the dynasty.

The increase in trade promoted the growth of the middle classes. Skilled craftsmen seem to have risen in status, while practical and linguistic skills provided a path to advancement within government. The success of upstarts of lower status is a frequent lament of Ilkhanid bureaucrat historians.[95] However, this was a period of great disparity between rich and poor. I have written above about the plight of ordinary nomads; many peasants likewise suffered severe financial stress, some even abandoning their land in desperation. At the same time, merchants, viziers and some members of the Mongol elite were amassing enormous wealth. We can take as examples the two great historians of the period, Rashid al-Din and Juwayni; Rashid al-Din amassed a huge fortune, and the Juwayni family acquired vast landholdings.[96] The economic hardship seen under the Ilkhans may be no more due to nomad exploitation of settled resources

---

[91] Lambton, "Mongol Fiscal Administration," pp. 109–110.

[92] Jacques Paviot, "Les marchands italiens dans l'Iran mongol," in *L'Iran face à la domination mongole*, ed. Denise Aigle, p. 84; Jean Aubin, "Les princes d' Ormuz du XIIIe au Xve siècle," *Journal Asiatique* 24 (1953), pp. 85, 92–93.

[93] De Nicola, *Women*, pp. 152–154.

[94] Lambton, "Mongol Fiscal Administration," pp. 105–106, 114.

[95] Oliver Watson, "Pottery under the Mongols," in *Beyond the Legacy of Genghis Khan*, ed. Linda Komaroff (Leiden: Brill, 2006), pp. 330–333; Bernard O'Kane, "Persian Poetry on Ilkhanid Art and Architecture," in *Beyond the Legacy of Genghis Khan*, ed. Linda Komaroff (Leiden: Brill, 2006), p. 353; Aubin, "Propriété foncière," p. 129.

[96] Aubin, "Propriété foncière," pp. 93–94.

than to extortion by Iranian and Mongol elites from the general population, settled and nomad alike.

Cultural Impact

The Mongols came into the Middle East as imperial rulers, imposing their own institutions, and the Mongol Empire brought most of Eurasia into one interconnected system with unprecedented levels of travel and exchange. The steppe imperial tradition became intertwined with the Islamic heritage, both through Mongol rule and through the expansion of the Islamic religion. The Mongols also brought with them an expansive world view, encompassing the Eurasian steppe and its neighbors – China, Russia and western Europe. The first Mongol rulers in the Middle East were pagan and treated all religions as equal; their promotion of Buddhism was particularly resented, since it was seen as polytheism. The source of legitimacy was no longer the caliphate, but the family of Chinggis Khan and the authority of the supreme *khaghan*. For some time after the demise of the unified Mongol Empire, legitimate sovereignty remained limited to the descendants of Chinggis Khan. With the end of the caliphate, there was no impediment either to Muslim acceptance of Chinggisid rule, or to Mongol conversion to Islam. There were moreover some commonalities between Islamic and Mongol ideologies, most notably a belief that successful conquest indicated God's favor and thus justified rule. By the mid-fourteenth century the Ilkhanate, the Golden Horde, and the Chaghadayid Khanate were all officially Muslim.

While the Mongol rulers adopted Perso-Islamic chancellery practice, they brought with them new government structures, some of which remained in place well beyond the Ilkhanate. Institutions such as the military governor assigned to a city – *darugha* – and the imperial guard, the *keshig*, lasted into the Safavid dynasty.[97] A more contentious element of Mongol tradition was the *yasa* (Mongolian: *jasakh*), a term usually translated as "law" or "code." There is controversy over whether the *yasa* was a specific set of laws existing as a written document. The precepts preserved deal primarily with military and administrative matters, but in the Middle East by the fourteenth century the term *yasa* had come to signify both law and custom (*yosun*). The *yasa* and *yosun* were considered central to Mongol power, but some tenets contravened requirements of the *shari'a*. The most problematic were a prohibition against washing in

[97] Charles Melville, "The *Keshig* in Iran: The Survival of the Royal Mongol Household," in *Beyond the Legacy of Genghis Khan*, ed. Linda Komaroff (Leiden: Brill, 2006), pp. 135–164.

running water, which interfered with the Muslim ablution, and the rules on how animals should be killed – by cutting the breast and squeezing the vital organs – which went against Muslim dietary law demanding the slitting of the throat. Mongols also practiced the levirate – marrying the wives of their deceased fathers – likewise contrary to Islamic law. Islamic histories recount stories of Muslims punished for infringing on these customs by tyrannical pagan khans, most notably Chinggis Khan's son Chaghadai, but it seems unlikely that Mongol rules were fully enforced on the Muslim population. After the Ilkhanid conversion to Islam, most customs specifically contrary to Islam appear to have been abandoned; in any case, we hear little about them. The *yasa* seems to have been an elastic and changing code, adapting over time to a new society; its edicts are described quite differently by various historians. Whatever the reality of the *yasa*, as an idea and a marker of identity, it continued to be central to Turco-Mongolian government and remained for some Muslims a potent symbol of the alien nature of Mongol governance.[98]

In the realm of cultural production – scientific, literary, and artistic – the Mongol impact was clearly a positive one. The Mongol taste for Chinese and Central Asian culture brought in new influences which initiated a period of extraordinary cultural efflorescence in Iran. The Mongols also showed a predilection for practical scientific knowledge such as astronomy, medicine, pharmacology, agronomy, and geography. When Chinggis Khan conquered the Middle East he brought along Chinese astronomers, one of whom was in charge of an observatory in Samarqand by 1222.[99] Hülegü in turn brought doctors and astronomers from China, and on his conquest of the fortress of Alamut from the Isma'ilis he acquired its famous library and instruments, along with the brilliant scholar Nasir al-Din Tusi (1201–1274) for whom he founded an observatory whose calculations lay behind most later astronomy in the Middle East and Europe.

The later Mongol khans were also patrons of art and architecture. Abandoning the Mongol custom of secret burial, Ghazan built a mausoleum for himself in a *waqf* complex in Tabriz, with religious institutions, an observatory, library, hospital, and a kitchen to feed the poor.[100] In 713/1313–1314 his successor Öljeitü completed a mausoleum in the town of

---

[98] Denise Aigle, "Mongol Law *versus* Islamic Law. Myth and Reality," in *The Mongol Empire between Myth and Reality: Studies in Anthropological History*, ed. Denise Aigle (Leiden: Brill, 2015). For another recent discussion, see David Morgan, "The 'Great yasa of Chinggis Khan' revisited," in *Mongols, Turks and Others*, ed. Reuven Amitai and Michal Biran (Leiden: Brill, 2005), pp. 291–308.

[99] Thomas T. Allsen, *Culture and Conquest in Mongol Eurasia*, Cambridge studies in Islamic civilization (Cambridge: Cambridge University Press, 2001), p. 165.

[100] Birgitt Hoffmann, *Waqf im mongolischen Iran: Rašīduddīns Sorge um Nachruhm und Seelenheil* (Stuttgart: F. Steiner, 2000), p. 112.

Sultaniyya. The complex became a new ceremonial capital, and the mausoleum is considered a masterpiece of Islamic architecture.

The vizier Rashid al-Din was a towering figure in Ilkhanid cultural life.
This great polymath was born in 647 or 648/1249–1251 and probably began
his career at court quite young.[101] He was the author, or compiler, of several
encyclopedic works. His treatise on agronomy is distinguished by its inclusion of numerous plants from outside, particularly from China. His greatest
work was his world history, the *Jāmi' al-tawārīkh*, begun for Ghazan and
completed about 710/1310. It put earlier histories of the Islamic world into
a new frame that encompassed the Mongols, Europeans, Chinese and
others. Rashid al-Din made use of many experts, using Indian and
Buddhist scholars and experts in Chinese and Mongolian traditions. For
centuries afterwards, universal histories included both the regional kings of
Iran and the four branches of the Chinggisid house.[102] The history was
illustrated – a practice new with the Ilkhans – and the paintings show strong
Chinese and Central Asian elements. By the 1330s a new Persian style of
painting had begun, one which developed into the Persian miniature.

In crafting their legitimation, the Ilkhans turned to Iranian traditions,
particularly to the *Shāhnāma*, which their artists produced in magnificent,
illustrated manuscripts. Like earlier nomad dynasties, they identified with
the Turanian king, Afrasiyab.[103] The promotion of Persian traditions in
the Mongol court combined with active cultural borrowing to create new
Persian styles in art, architecture and historiography that were increasingly distinct from Arab culture. The cultural achievements of the
Ilkhans, and the magnificent monuments they erected, contributed to
their lasting prestige within the Perso-Islamic world.

The Mongol Legacy

Mongol rule was a watershed in the history of the Middle East. This is
when the modern ethnic division took shape. The Ilkhanid realm
stretched across most of the northern Middle East and included Iraq
but did not extend into Syria or Egypt. It thus created a separation between
the Arab cultural region of the Mamluk Sultanate, still showing token loyalty

---

[101] Hoffmann, *Waqf*, pp. 59–72.
[102] Charles Melville, "From Adam to Abaqa: Qāḍī Baiḍāwī's rearrangement of history,"
Studia Iranica 30, no. 1 (2001), pp. 71–79.
[103] Tomoko Masuya, "Ilkhanid Courtly Life," in *The Legacy of Genghis Khan: Courtly Art
and Culture in Western Asia, 1256–1353*, ed. Stefano Carboni and Linda Komaroff
(New York; London: Metropolitan Museum of Art; New Haven: Yale University
Press, 2002), pp. 84–85; A. S. Melikian-Chirvani, "Conscience du passé et résistance
culturelle dans l' Iran mongol," in *L'Iran face à la domination mongole*, ed. Denise Aigle
(Tehran: Institut français de recherche en Iran 1997), pp. 145–159.

to the 'Abbasids, and Iran, which was in the Mongol sphere. The Middle East became divided into three major cultural zones, one Arab, one Iranian, and one – in Anatolia – primarily Turkic. In Iran the concept of a separate Iranian realm – *Irān zamīn* – returned to use after centuries in abeyance. This term reflected a new regional and cultural consciousness but did not imply either that a political realm would coincide with the boundaries of *Irān zamīn*, or that it would be ruled by Iranians. Despite strong separate identities and feelings of superiority on each side, Mongols and Iranians intermarried and became closely connected both culturally and politically.[104] Ambitious Iranians had early realized that an understanding of Mongolian culture was an asset, and numerous Turkic and Mongolian words entered the language. While Iranians resented some Mongol practices, they nonetheless accepted many aspects of Mongolian political culture, which remained important for centuries after the fall of the Ilkhans.

The vast extent of Chinggis Khan's conquests and the spectacular punishments he visited on rebellious cities gave him an almost unmatched charisma, and the success of his descendants in expanding and ruling a world empire cemented the prestige of his dynasty. The Mongols were cursed by many historians, but they commanded respect. The Mongol heritage was treasured and elaborated despite the breakup of the empire and the changing identity in the western Mongol realms as the elite converted to Islam and adopted Turkic as their spoken language. The population of Mongolia and the army of Chinggis Khan had been made up of both Turkic and Mongolian speakers sharing a political culture. Over time, Turkic won out as the language of speech, while loyalty to Mongol tradition remained, and by the end of the dynasty, the ruling class of the western Mongol world is best characterized as Turco-Mongolian. While they mixed with the eastern Turks, they remained separate from the Oghuz/Turkmen in language and political culture. From this period into the nineteenth century, the Turks provided much of the military manpower of the Middle East, as well as most of its ruling dynasties.

By destroying the central caliphate, the Mongols inaugurated a new era in which it was possible to assert full sovereign rule over separate regions of the Islamic world. This act made possible the empires of the early modern period – the Ottomans, Safavids, Mughals and Uzbeks – each of which fostered a unique cultural complex, while sharing many elements of the mixed culture that developed under the Mongols.

---

[104] al-'Umarī, *Das Mongolische Weltreich*, p. 159; Yali Xue Tatiana Zerjal et al., "The Genetic Legacy of the Mongols," *American Journal of Human Genetics* 72 (2003), pp. 717–721.

6 After the Mongols: Timurids, Turkmen and Ottomans

The collapse of the Ilkhanate in 1336 did not mark the end of Mongol influence in the Middle East. Through the northern regions of Iran and eastern Anatolia, Turco-Mongolian personnel and their armies remained active and powerful. Nor did the end of the Ilkhanate signal the decline of the Mongol enterprise as a whole. The Chinggisid dynasty continued to reign through much of Eurasia – in China until 1368 and for centuries more both in the Chaghadayid territories, and in the Golden Horde as well as other Jochid khanates to the north. By this time the Islamic and Mongol traditions had ceased to be separate. Through much of the steppe, the nomads were Muslim and acquainted with Persian culture. The Middle East was part of a wide world in which the figure of Chinggis Khan and the memory of the unified Mongol Empire retained over-whelming prestige. By destroying the caliphate, the Mongols had made it possible for sovereign Mongol states to adopt Islam and for the religion to spread to vast new territories. In this world, however, legitimate sover-eignty was limited to the descendants of Chinggis Khan, and in the fourteenth century this tradition in its turn became a problem for rulers, calling for new forms of steppe legitimation.

Within the Islamic Mongol world, with which we are concerned here, separate identities had begun to form reflecting regional and historical variations, different levels of involvement with the Mongol enterprise, and different paths within it. The Mongols had ruled from two regions: the pastures of northwestern Khorasan and the highlands of Azerbaijan. After the fall of the Ilkhans several centers of power emerged, with increasing separation between the eastern and the western regions. In the east, Ilkhanid successor states bordered the Chaghadayid realm, which was strongly attached to the Chinggisid tradition. Azerbaijan, in contrast, was drawn into the politics of Arab Iraq, Syria and especially Anatolia. Over time, therefore, these two regions developed separate political cultures. The western regions, with a large Turkmen population, moved to a more tribal structure and a legitimation built on an earlier steppe tradition. In the east, both organization and legitimation remained Chinggisid.

The later fourteenth century saw the creation of new domains. The towering figure of the period was the Turco-Mongolian conqueror Temür, known in the West as Tamerlane. Temür rose to power near Samarqand in 1370 and set out first to take over the western half of the Chaghadayid khanate, then to recreate the Mongol Empire symbolically, and finally to dominate both the Islamic and the Mongol worlds. To the north he was challenged by the equally ambitious Jochid ruler, Tokhtamish, who reunited much of the Jochid *ulus* and harried the borders of Temür's realm.

In the west, the political picture was more complicated. In Anatolia the Oghuz population outnumbered the Turco-Mongolian nomads, and separate principalities sprang up through the region. The Ottoman dynasty had begun to develop by 1300, and through the fourteenth century it gradually expanded, moving into eastern Anatolia towards the end of the century under the leadership of Yildirim (Thunderbolt) Bayazid. The Mamluk sultanate attempted to control the areas bordering northern Syria, often through client confederations of Turkmen tribes. Several major tribal confederations arose in eastern Anatolia and later expanded into Iran, most notably the Qaraquyunlu and the Aqquyunlu – the Black and White Sheep.

Rulers of the fourteenth century were not only conquerors; they were also major cultural patrons. The brilliant achievements of the Ilkhans had made them a model for their Turkic successors, who created a highly sophisticated artistic culture in architecture, literature and the arts of the book. In historiography and political ideology, they produced a synthesis of Turkic, Mongolian and Perso-Islamic traditions that remained influential for centuries thereafter.

Western Iran after the Ilkhans

When the Ilkhan Abu Saʻid died without an heir in 1335, Iran became the scene of a struggle among local rulers, viziers, and Mongol emirs promoting a bewildering variety of puppet khans connected to the Ilkhans. It is probably no coincidence that the two powers who emerged as the major rivals for rule in the western Ilkhanid territories, the Jalayirid and the Chobanid families, had both served as governors of Anatolia, which had become an important locus of power and sometimes independence.[1] Several Turco-Mongolian groups in eastern Anatolia – the Oirat tribe or confederation, led by ʻAli Padshah, the followers of the former governor Shaykh Hasan Jalayir, and the descendants of the powerful emir

---

[1] Charles Melville, "Čobān," *EIr*; Wing, *Jalayirids*, pp. 63, 69–70.

Choban Suldus – headed east to assert their power.[2] Shaykh Hasan Jalayir, grandson of Arghun Khan, soon promoted a Chinggisid khan. In 1338 the descendants of Choban made a bid for power, using Abu Saʻid's sister Sati Beg – Choban's widow – as candidate for Khan.[3]

For twenty years after the death of Abu Saʻid the Chobanids had the upper hand, ruling Persian Iraq and Azerbaijan, while the Jalayirids held Diyar Bakr, Arab Iraq and Khuzistan, with their center at Baghdad. Over time, however, the Jalayirids gained a major advantage by winning control over the Oirat troops, who were now apparently without internal leadership.[4] In 1357 the khan of the Golden Horde invaded Azerbaijan, leaving the Chobanids badly weakened. The next year, Shaykh Hasan Jalayir's son and successor, Shaykh Uways, was able to take the region. By the time of his death in 1374, Shaykh Uways had expanded his realm through northern Iran to Rayy and was recognized as suzereign by the Iranian dynasties of the Caucasus, Fars and central Iran. Thus, for about thirty years the Jalayirids were the dominant power over much of the former Ilkhanate.[5]

By now the exclusivity of the Chinggisid claim to sovereignty was weakening in much of Iran. The Chobanids had begun to claim Iranian descent for some of their puppet khans and, twenty years after Abu Saʻid's death, it was possible for Shaykh Uways Jalayir to abandon the use of a khan and mint coins in his own name.[6] Nonetheless, the Mongol heritage was still central to dynastic legitimation. Shaykh Uways claimed legitimacy as the reviver of Chinggisid custom and as the true successor to Abu Saʻid, emphasizing continuities in genealogy, ideology and administration. The style of his coinage echoed that of the Ilkhans and some coins even used the Uighur script, which the Ilkhans had retained for some formal documents.[7] The Jalayirids likewise kept the political structure of the Ilkhanate, in which tribal powers remained largely submerged. Emirs might hold great power, but the sources do not identify them by tribe; nor did the dynasty itself claim legitimacy from its Jalayir identity.[8]

The regions further from the Ilkhanid center and under looser rule seem to have returned to a more decentralized system, permitting the resurgence of tribal groups, some of which were formed from the remnants of Mongol armies. The regions of Quhistan, Mazandaran and northwestern Khorasan were controlled by a variety of minor local dynasties and Mongol emirs, some leading inherited regiments. These included the descendants of the former governor Arghun Agha, whose

---

[2] Woods, *Aqquyunlu*, p. 29.   [3] Melville, "Čobān" *EIr*; Wing, *Jalayirids*, pp. 64–68.
[4] Wing, *Jalayirids*, pp. 83–94.   [5] Wing, *Jalayirids*, pp. 103–115.
[6] Wing, *Jalayirids*, p. 129; Boyle, "Dynastic," p. 416.   [7] Wing, *Jalayirids*, pp. 130–134.
[8] Wing, *Jalayirids*, pp. 195–197.

following, known as the Jawun-i Qurban, was centered in the pastures of Tus and Radkan. In eastern Iran, loyalty to the Chinggid legacy was still strong. Thus in 1336 the regional ruling elite – Turco-Mongolian emirs and tribal leaders; local rulers, both Iranian and Turkic; bureaucrats; and Sufi shaykhs – gathered to enthrone Taghay Temür, a descendant of Chinggis Khan's brother Jochi Qasar.[9] Despite several campaigns to the west, however, Taghay Temür never expanded his power beyond Khorasan.

Further to the east and west, in eastern Khorasan and Transoxiana on the one side, and in Anatolia to the other, tribal and local powers were yet more important. It was here that the largest successor states arose and soon came to dispute the rule of the entire region. We will begin with the history of Anatolia, which had become perhaps the greatest reserve of pastoral nomadism in the region.

Anatolia after the Ilkhanids

With the loss of Ilkhanid control, power devolved on the *beyliks* which had sprung up after the dissolution of the Rum Sultanate. Most of these combined nomad Turkmen and Turco-Mongolians with settled population and many were ruled by Turkmen. One of the driving motives for political activity was the desire to control access to the great summer and winter pastures of the region, often quite far apart from each other. These pastures were contested among confederations and by individual tribes acting under their own leaders. The situation was complicated by the Turkmen tribes of northern Syria, who also depended on Anatolia for summer pastures. Under such pressure, tribes whose pastures were endangered looked to the leaders of *beyliks* and confederations for help, sometimes paying dues for the use of pasture. Another important goal was the control of the trade routes which crisscrossed Anatolia, providing income to rulers through tolls and protection money, while also offering their nomad followers a market for their livestock and perhaps for their services as guides.[10] The local historian 'Aziz ibn Ardashir Astarabadi, writing in 1397–1398, paints a vivid picture of tribes, local rulers and confederations struggling for survival and preeminence.[11]

---

[9] Jean Aubin, "Le qurlitai de Sultân-Maydân (1336)," *Journal Asiatique* CCLXXIX (1991), pp. 180–192.

[10] Woods, *Aqquyunlu*, pp. 29–30, 56, 62, 80; Sara Nur Yıldız, "Post-Mongol Pastoral Polities in Eastern Anatolia during the Late Middle Ages," in *At the Crossroads of Empires: 14th–15th Century Eastern Anatolia. Proceedings of the International Symposium held in Istanbul, 4th–6th May, 2007*, ed. Deniz Beyazit (Paris: De Boccard, 2012), pp. 30, 33, 38.

[11] See, for example, Paul, "Mongol Aristocrats."

It is impossible here to list all the *beyliks* and nomad coalitions of Anatolia, so I will limit my discussion to a handful of the most important ones. One of the longest lasting was that of the Turkmen Karamanids, who held the Konya Nigde region in central Anatolia.[12] From the middle of the thirteenth century, the Karamanids had maintained some level of independence and for their armies they could call upon a variety of pastoralist tribes. One Mongol governor remained after the fall of the Ilkhans: Eretna, whose lands lay to the west of the major Mongol strongholds. He turned for patronage to the Mamluk sultan and formed a principality stretching at its height from Samsun on the Black Sea to Nigde and Konya, which he contested with the Karamanids.[13] After Amir Eretna died in 1352, his capital region of Sivas came under the control of a judge of Turkmen descent, Qadi Burhan al-Din.[14] Jürgen Paul has provided an analysis of Burhan al-Din's governance, showing the importance of the Mongol emirs and tribes who provided a significant portion of his military and exerted considerable influence over policy. Several former Mongol contingents led by the descendants of their earlier commanders were now becoming tribes, along with other tribes of uncertain provenance.[15] During their spring migration, the Mongol leaders regularly visited Burhan al-Din in Sivas, exchanged presents with him, and consulted about possible military action. Their wishes and needs were clearly a factor in Burhan al-Din's actions. One of their constant concerns was access to the pastures of Kayseri in central Anatolia, which were part of their normal migration.[16] Burhan al-Din himself claimed Turkmen descent and, especially in his later years, Turkmen tribes were also an important part of his power structure. There are several mentions of formal meetings with Turkmen in summer pasturelands. These lands were an appropriate setting in which to form a network of nomad tribal alliances, without which Burhan al-Din could not retain his regional position.[17]

Another Anatolian power which gained strength with the fall of the Ilkhans was the Turkmen Dhu'l Qadr confederation. In 1298, the Mamluk sultan granted the region of Mar'ash on the Armenian border to the Turkmen who later formed the Dhu'l Qadr, who were subject to the governor of Aleppo.[18] While they remained formally subservient to

---

[12] F. Sümer, "Ḳaramān-oghullarï," *EI* 2nd ed.   [13] Claude Cahen, "Eretna," *EI* 2nd ed.

[14] Claude Cahen, "Eretna," *EI*, 2nd ed.

[15] As I stated in Chapter 6, Paul has defined a tribe as a group based on a real or constructed genealogy tracing members to one ancestor, and thus he does not use the term to describe most of these groups. Paul, "Mongol Aristocrats," pp. 116–131.

[16] Paul, "Mongol Aristocrats," pp. 133–137.

[17] Paul, "Mongol Aristocrats," pp. 148–149.

[18] Venzke, "Dulgadir-Mamluk," pp. 407–408.

the Mamluks, the Dhu'l Qadr soon emerged as a significant power, and one which could not be fully controlled.[19] The Karamanids, Eretnids and Dhu'l Qadr were part of an interlocking political field bounded to the south by the Mamluk sultanate and to the east by the Jalayirids. To the west, they eventually met the rising power of the Ottoman state.

The Ottomans became involved in the politics of eastern Anatolia only in the late fourteenth century, but had their origins much earlier, as a group of nomads whose winter pasture was east of the Sea of Marmara. This area lies on the edge of the steppe region and at the confluence of several routes. The Ottoman career of expansion began during the last three decades of the Ilkhanate. They first appear in the histories in July 1302, when their leader Osman defeated a Byzantine force near Nicomedia/Izmit. At this time their armies were largely nomadic, but also included other populations, both Christian and Muslim.[20] The nomads lived in close proximity and in symbiosis with settled populations; as they departed for their summer migration, they left their goods in the fortress of a local lord, and on their return the women paid its owner in cheese, rugs and sheep.[21]

Over time nomadism declined as a source of wealth for the Ottomans, whose territory was best suited for agriculture, as were the rich areas to the north and west into which they soon began to expand. Over the next thirty years the Ottomans added increasing numbers of foot soldiers to their army and many of their originally nomad subjects appear to have switched to transhumance. By the time that the Ilkhanate ended in 1335, the Ottomans had expanded their territory from the Sea of Marmara to the Black Sea and had begun to create a regular bureaucracy.[22] Under two energetic sultans, Orhan (1324–1362) and Murad I (1362–1389) they absorbed essentially all the Byzantine territories in Anatolia and much of southeastern Anatolia. This movement brought them into contact with the Karamanids who were also expanding – for a while as far as Kayseri – and attracting numerous new tribes to the confederation.[23]

[19] Venzke, "Dulgadir-Mamluk," pp. 409–413.
[20] Cemal Kafadar, *Between Two Worlds: The Construction of the Ottoman State* (Berkeley: University of California Press, 1995), pp. 10–17, 37–57.
[21] Lindner, *Nomads and Ottomans*, p. 25; Kafadar, *Between two Worlds*, pp. 125–129.
[22] Lindner, *Nomads and Ottomans*, pp. 26–37; Lindner, *Explorations in Ottoman Prehistory* (Ann Arbor: University of Michigan Press, 2007), pp. 35–53.
[23] F. Sümer, "Karamān-Oghullarï," *EI* 2nd ed.; Rudi Lindner, "Anatolia, 1300–1451," in *Cambridge History of Turkey*, ed. Kate Fleet (Cambridge: Cambridge University Press, 2009), pp. 114–115.

The Rise of New Anatolian Powers

The fluidity of politics in eastern Anatolia and the Jazira encouraged the emergence of tribal confederations; the situation was similar to that of the Bedouin and Kurdish regions in the tenth and eleventh century, when the rivalry between the Fatimids and 'Abbasids provided new political opportunities for nomad groups. Several major powers attempted to expand their influence in the region, none with complete success, or with great comfort. The Mamluks played a significant part in Anatolian tribal politics over several centuries, attempting to extend their influence and to control nomads migrating across their borders. The Jalayirids, having started their career in eastern Anatolia, still profited from the manpower of the Oirat, who migrated between winter pastures near Mosul and summer grazing grounds in Eastern Anatolia.[24] The Jalayir competed with Ottomans, and later the Timurids. Each outside state sought alliances with tribal leaders, who were thus able to play one against another, and when attacked to find refuge with the enemy of their enemy. Attempts by these neighboring states to attract and incorporate nomads were generally unsuccessful, perhaps because they attempted to suppress tribes as centers of independent power.

The two rising powers we will discuss here, the Qaraqoyunlu and the Aqqoyunlu, were confederations of Turkmen tribes able to move and expand or contract in order to adapt to changing situations. Both eventually developed into bureaucratic states, but unlike the Ottomans they retained a strong tribal structure and nomadic lifestyle. The central tribes of the Qaraqoyunlu are mentioned under the Ilkhans holding winter pastures in the Mosul region and summering in the area of Van. The rise of the confederation began during the rule of Bayram Khwaja, who by his death in 1380 controlled a confederation covering the region from Mosul to Erzerum. Formally, the Qaraqoyunlu were vassals of the Jalayirids, but they were often rivals as well. When the Jalayirids split after the death of Sultan Husayn in 1382, the Qaraqoyunlu achieved independence.[25] The ruling tribe of the Aqqoyunlu, known as Bayandur, claimed descent from the legendary Oghuz Khan, and was mentioned by Rashid al-Din as one of the leading Oghuz tribes.[26] In the later fourteenth century the leader of the tribe gathered a confederation under his leadership along the northern Mamluk frontier and allied with the ruler of a section of the former Eretnid territories.[27] At this point the Aqqoyunlu were only a minor power in the Anatolian cauldron.

---

[24] Wing, *Jalayirids*, p. 78.   [25] F. Sümer, "Ḳarā-Koyunlu," *EI* 2nd ed.
[26] Rashīd-al-Dīn, *Compendium*, pp. 25, 34.   [27] Woods, *Aqquyunlu*, pp. 25–29, 34–37.

Near the end of the fourteenth century the Ottomans attacked the Karamanids, and hostilities intensified during the reign of the ambitious Sultan Yildirim Bayezid (1389–1402). The entry of the Ottomans into the politics of eastern Anatolia did not, however, impede the growth of the tribal confederations. A centralizing government did not appeal to autonomous nomad populations; thus, tribes dislodged from the Karamanids often moved east to join the Aqqoyunlu or Qaraqoyunlu. The independent attitude of the Turkmen tribal commanders is illustrated in the terms on which the Qaraqoyunlu had agreed to join the Jalayirids in 1382; they demanded that the Turkmen be allowed to fight in their own way, and that they keep the spoils of battle.[28] The nomads of eastern Anatolia had retained their independence from the centralized states on their borders. They were soon to encounter yet another threat, with the rise of the great conqueror Tamerlane.

The Eastern Regions and the Rise of Tamerlane

Like Chinggis Khan, Temür remains a figure larger than life. Although he was not himself a Chinggisid, Temür stood clearly within the Mongol tradition, at once deferring to the figure of Chinggis and attempting to equal him. Over the course of his reign, he defeated every ruler of note within his horizon. For the powers of Iran and Anatolia Temür and his dynasty presented a daunting challenge, first and most acutely in the military realm but later also in terms of dynastic prestige.

Temür rose to power in Transoxiana, within the remains of the Chaghadayid khanate. A few decades before his rise the khanate had divided in two. The western regions – Transoxiana and much of what is now Afghanistan – became largely independent and were known as the Ulus Chaghatay. In 1347 the emir of a powerful nomad group known as the Qara'unas seized power over the Ulus while the eastern region remained under Chinggisid khans.[29] The Qara'unas had originated as *tamma* troops garrisoning eastern Khorasan; since they were not descended from Chinggis, they governed in the name of a Chinggisid puppet khan.[30]

The Ulus Chaghatay was a confederation of tribes, most of which were probably formed from Mongol armies. Chinggis Khan had granted four

---

[28] Wing, *Jalayirids*, pp. 155–156.
[29] Michal Biran, "The Mongols in Central Asia from Chinggis Khan's Invasion to the Rise of Temür: The Ögödeid and Chaghadaid Realms," in *The Cambridge History of Inner Asia: the Chinggisid Age*, ed. Allen J. Frank, Nicola Di Cosmo, Peter B. Golden (Cambridge: Cambridge University Press, 2009), pp. 58–59.
[30] "Mongols in Central Asia," p. 59; Manz, *Rise and Rule*, pp. 43–45, 51, 57, 155, 158.

regiments of a thousand to his son Chaghadai, headed by commanders from the Barlas, Jalayir and Suldus; at the time of Temür's rise, these were among the most powerful tribes of the Ulus. As I wrote in Chapter 5, most regiments in the Mongol army were made up of soldiers from different tribes, and there is no evidence that those assigned to Chaghadai were an exception. It seems most likely therefore that the tribes originated as regiments, probably remaining under the command of the family of the earlier commander and taking the name of his tribe; indeed, this is well attested for the Barlas.[31] Of the other major tribes the Arlat probably descended from troops of Arlat emirs who came to the region somewhat later, while the Yasa'uri originated in the army of the dissident emir Yasa'ur who was active in the early fourteenth century.[32] The sources refer to these groups as large bodies of people (*il, qawm*), able to field troops of their own. Many had been in the region from about the time of Chinggis Khan's death, and in the relatively decentralized Chaghadayid realm they had developed into separate powers.

The Ulus came into being around the time that the new tribal confederations were forming in Anatolia and shared many things in common with them. Its members were nomadic tribes that were politically active and willing to follow a leader as long as he brought them advantage. Attempts at coercion were met with resistance or desertion. However, there were also significant differences between the two areas. In Anatolia, Seljuqid and Mongol traditions held almost equal weight, and by the later fourteenth century tribal rulers could rule in their own names. The Ulus Chaghatay remained strongly attached to the Chinggisid tradition. Its tribes were nomadic, and each held territory suitable for both winter and summer pasture. However, Timurid histories put much less emphasis on migration and on control of pasture than do the Anatolian ones. Summer and winter pastures in the east did not usually require crossing territory belonging to other powers, as tribes in Anatolia were often forced to do. Moreover, there is little evidence of the competition over pasture which was so central to Anatolian politics.[33]

The story of Temür's rise to power has much in common with tales of Chinggis Khan's youth. Both came from the aristocracy, but not from a ruling lineage; both lost their fathers relatively early, gathered personal followings and attached themselves to more powerful leaders. Temür belonged to the Barlas tribe, one of the major tribes of the Ulus

---

[31] The Suldus are not mentioned in Rashid al-Din's list of Chaghadai's troops, but they do appear in the Mongol and Timurid genealogies. Manz, *Rise and Rule*, pp. 156–158, 163–164; Rashīd-al-Dīn, *Compendium*, pp. 279–280.

[32] Manz, *Rise and Rule*, pp. 155–156, 164–165.

[33] Manz, *Rise and Rule*, pp. 27–28, 36–38.

Chaghatay, and began his rise to power in the classic fashion of nomad conquerors, by going outside his own tribe to gather support. He first appears in the histories in 1360, when he allied with the invading eastern Chaghadayid khan to become chief of the Barlas. The next ten years were ones of constant political struggle. Over this period Temür gradually increased his power, supporting various candidates for leadership and gathering a personal following outside his tribe.[34]

In 1370, Temür defeated the Qara'unas leader Amir Husayn and took power over the Ulus Chaghatay. He incorporated the Qara'unas troops into his army and married several of Amir Husayn's wives, including two Chinggisid women. For his capital he chose the prestigious city of Samarqand, where he called a convocation to recognize the rule of his own puppet khan.[35] Titles connoting sovereignty – sultan, padshah and khan – were reserved for the puppet khan, while Temür himself used the title amir, or Amir-i Kabir (Great Commander) adding the epithet *güregen* – royal son-in-law. Like Chinggis Khan, Temür centralized power within his confederation before embarking on his conquests. The tribal leaders of the Ulus soon began turning against his rule, but as tribes rebelled, Temür was able to defeat them and put them under the leadership of personal followers. Unlike Chinggis, who decimated many defeated tribes, Temür treated tribal leaders with care. Nonetheless, over the course of eleven years he transformed his army from a tribal confederation into a decimally organized army of conquest commanded by men from his personal following.[36] Tribal leadership no longer provided a separate power base. Here Temür's confederation differed markedly from those of the western regions.

Temür developed his ambitions within the framework of the Mongol Empire. The first campaigns he undertook were against the Eastern Chaghadayid Khans and Khorezm, both part of the Mongol Empire, and he justified these expeditions through Chinggisid ideology.[37] When in 1375–1377 Tokhtamish, a Chinggisid pretender to the Jochid Blue Horde on Temür's northern border, applied for help, Temür gave him a warm reception and helped him to regain his throne. In 1380 Temür began to look to the south and west. Within Iran he pursued goals both strategic and symbolic, aiming at control over the northern trade routes while laying claim to the inheritance of the Mongol Ilkhanate. In Mazandaran, he defeated the upstart who had supplanted the

---

[34] Manz, *Rise and Rule*, pp. 45–57.   [35] Manz, *Rise and Rule*, pp. 57–58.
[36] Manz, *Rise and Rule*, pp. 58–62.
[37] John E. Woods, "Timur's Genealogy," in *Intellectual Studies on Islam: Essays Written in Honor of Martin B. Dickson*, ed. Michael Mazzaoui and Vera B. Moreen (Salt Lake City: University of Utah Press, 1990), pp. 101–104.

Chinggisid dynasty of Taghay Temür and installed Taghay Temür's son Lughman, allowing him the imperial title padshah, carried by the Ilkhans. In northwestern Iran he took the city Sultaniyya, symbolically important as the Ilkhanid necropolis.

With three Chinggisid khans as protégés, Temür aimed at a symbolic restoration of the Mongol Empire, with himself at its center. He increased his personal charisma by imitating Chinggis Khan's actions. In fact, his conquest of cities and his punishment of those that rebelled were eerily reminiscent of Chinggis Khan's campaigns. In cities conquered after a rebellion the population was taken out and divided into categories, with craftsmen and ulama spared, and systematic massacres in which soldiers were given a quota of heads to present to their commanders. In an additional and very effective touch, Temür's army often built minarets with the severed heads of rebellious populations; as they decomposed, they glowed in the night.[38] For his court etiquette, Temür imitated that of the Mongol *khaghans*.

However, Temür was not the only person who remembered Mongol history, and while he campaigned in Iran, his former protégé Tokhtamish was seizing control of the fragmented Golden Horde. Tokhtamish renewed the earlier Jochid alliance with the Mamluks and invaded Azerbaijan in 1385–1386.[39] Over the next ten years Temür expanded and consolidated his power in Iran, but his greatest effort was concentrated on his duel with Tokhtamish, who as a descendant of Chinggis could legally claim the title of khan. After several inconclusive campaigns into the steppe, in 1395 Temür was able to inflict a decisive defeat on Tokhtamish; he then ravaged the winter pastures and trading cities of the western steppe and installed his own pretender over the Golden Horde.[40] With this campaign, Temür achieved primacy within the western Mongol world.

Temür's steppe campaign of 1395 marks a turning point in his career. Despite his hard-won success he made no effort to incorporate the steppe into his realm. He did not install a permanent administration over the Golden Horde, although in Iran and Central Asia he had already begun to appoint his sons as governors in the major provinces. The regions Temür chose to put under his administration included the territory of the Ilkhans and that of the western Chaghadayids; although it contained much

---

[38] Jean Aubin, "Comment Tamerlan prenait les villes," *Studia Islamica* 19 (1963).

[39] Beatrice F. Manz, "Mongol History Rewritten and Relived," in *Figures Mythiques des mondes musulmans, special issue of Revue des mondes musulmans et de la Méditerranée*, ed. Denise Aigle (Aix en Provence: Édisud, 2001), pp. 138–140.

[40] M. G. Safargaliev, *Raspad Zolotoĭ Ordy*, Uchenye zapiski (Saransk: Mordovskoe knizhoe izd-vo, 1960), p. 172.

territory suitable for nomadism, the larger part of the economy was agricultural and urban. The definition of his realm did not mark the end of Temür's campaigns. By the 1390s, Temür had acquired an additional ambition – primacy within the Islamic world – and in 1398 he set out against the Delhi sultanate of India. The new ambition did not push out the old; Temür was still determined recreate the Mongol Empire symbolically. At the time of his Indian campaign, he was already planning to attack China where the Ming dynasty had overthrown the Mongol Yüan.[41]

The Clash over Anatolia

Within the central Islamic world, Temür faced two great rivals for prestige: the Ottoman Empire under Yildirim Bayezid (1389–1402) and the Mamluk sultanate. Both states were closely involved with the powers of eastern Anatolia, to which Temür now turned his attention. All the actors in this struggle were connected in one way or another to the heritage of the steppe, and their clash tells us a great deal about competing identities and ideologies within the Middle Eastern nomad traditions. In the welter of claims and counterclaims, insults and counter-insults the sources record, we see how alive the history of earlier nomad dynasties remained, and how important the distinctions among Turks and Mongols of different backgrounds still were.

After taking Baghdad from Sultan Ahmad Jalayir in 1393, Temür sent an embassy to the Mamluk sultan Barquq (r. 1382–1399) laying claim to the Ilkhanid territories. The response was unequivocally negative. The sultan murdered Temür's envoys and when Sultan Ahmad arrived in Cairo seeking refuge, Barquq received him with conspicuous honor, parading him around as a new protégé and vassal.[42] Temür's response was to send a yet haughtier letter, a direct copy of the demand for submission that Hülegü Khan had sent to the Ayyubids and the Mamluk sultan Qutuz in 1259–1260:

Know that we are the soldiers of God, created from his wrath, given dominion over those on whom His anger has descended ... We do not feel tenderness for the one who complains, nor do we have mercy on the tear[s] of the one who weeps, for verily God has torn mercy from our hearts ....

---

[41] Beatrice F. Manz, "Temür and the Problem of a Conqueror's Legacy," *Journal of the Royal Asiatic Society* series 3 vol. 8, no. 1 (1998), p. 25.

[42] Patrick Wing, "Between Iraq and a Hard Place: Sulṭān Aḥmad Jalāyir's Time as a Refugee in the Mamluk Sultanate," in *Mamluk Cairo, A Crossroads for Embassies: Studies on Diplomacy and Diplomatics*, ed. Frédéric Bauden and Malika Dekkiche (Leiden: Brill, 2019), pp. 164–166.

Our hearts are like mountains and our numbers like sand ... He who makes peace with us is saved, and he who fights us regrets it ...[43]

In response, Sultan Barquq also returned to past models, sending a letter claiming guardianship of Islam and suggesting that Temür was an infidel.[44] From this time on the Mamluks were open enemies.

In 1394–1395 Temür sought an alliance with the Ottoman sultan Bayezid, who was then occupied in the western Ottoman regions.[45] Temür's letter to Bayezid initiated a correspondence which lasted until his invasion of Anatolia in 1402. The language of their letters, both in praise and in blame, gives insight into the fault lines within the nomad heritage. Temür's first letter was written in the hopes of detaching Bayezid from the Mamluks. The title used for Bayezid, "Ghazi Bayezid Khan," acknowledged both Bayezid's Islamic merit and his status within the Turco-Mongolian world. Sultan Barquq on the other hand, was a nobody – a Circassian slave page, who had overthrown and killed his master and imprisoned the 'Abbasid shadow caliph.[46] This passage refers to the fact that Barquq came from a new line of Mamluk sultans, Circassians from the Caucasus who had taken over the sultanate from the Qipchaq Turks who had held it earlier. Temür was pointing out that Barquq was not only a slave and an outsider, but one who had killed a ruler who although a slave was at least a Turk.

Temür's alliance with Bayezid did not last long. As Bayezid turned his attention east, he wrote to Barquq requesting a diploma from the Abbasid shadow caliph recognizing him as the heir to the Seljukids of Rum.[47] Meanwhile Temür again headed west to attack Sultan Ahmad Jalayir (now back in Baghdad) and the Qaraqoyunlu chief, Qara Yusuf. Both took refuge with Bayezid. The correspondence between Temür and Bayezid gained in frequency and declined in civility. Temür boasted of his conquests and the overwhelming size of his army, identifying himself with the Ilkhans; Bayezid answered by stating that his ancestor Ertoghrul had defeated a large army of Mongols and Tatars.[48] Thus the earlier struggles between the Turkmen of Rum and the Chinggisid Mongols were resurrected. As Bayezid continued intransigent, Temür clearly expressed the superiority that the eastern Turco-Mongolians claimed

[43] Anne F. Broadbridge, *Kingship and Ideology in the Islamic and Mongol Worlds* (Cambridge: Cambridge University Press, 2008), p. 182.
[44] Broadbridge, *Kingship*, pp. 174–185.
[45] Zeki Velidi Togan, "Timurs Osteuropapolitik," *Zeitschrift der deutchen morgenländischen Geselschaft* 108 (1958), pp. 279–280; Lindner, "Anatolia, 1300–1451," pp. 129–130.
[46] Togan, "Timurs Osteuropapolitik," pp. 279–281.   [47] Broadbridge, *Kingship*, p. 175.
[48] 'Abd al-Ḥusayn Nawā'ī, ed. *Asnād wa makātibāt-i tārīkhī-i Īrān* (Tehran: Bungāh-i Tarjama va Nashr-i Kitāb, 2536/1977), pp. 97–103.

over the Turkmen. He accused Bayazid of giving himself airs beyond his station; he was after all merely the descendant of a Turkmen boatman, and Turkmen were known to be without judgment.[49] Now Bayazid was sailing the boat of vain ambition into the whirlpool of conceit, and if he did not lower his sail and drop the anchor of repentance, he would find himself buffeted by waves of revenge and would drown in the sea of calamity.[50]

After defeating the Mamluk army in Syria, Temür prepared to attack the Ottomans in the spring of 1402. The two adversaries both led formidable armies. In addition to his own troops, Temür had some Anatolian forces, notably the Aqqoyunlu, who sided with him. Bayazid commanded a highly trained standing army with additional Anatolian Turkmen and Mongol soldiers.[51] Temür also wooed local forces, sending an emissary to the Mongols of Sivas, Kayseri and Malatya with promises of independence under their own khans.[52] When the two armies met near Ankara in July 1402, Temür's strategy bore fruit. Some Mongol and Turkmen troops deserted the Ottomans to join Temür. Bayazid's army suffered decisive defeat, with Bayazid himself taken captive.[53] Although Temür spent a few more months campaigning in Anatolia, he made no attempt to create his own administration there.[54] As he left, he divided the Ottoman realm, now a vassal state, among three of Bayazid's sons, and reestablished many of the beyliks that Bayazid had destroyed.[55]

Temür defeated both the Mamluks and Bayazid, and deported a large body of nomads, but the tribal confederations of Anatolia and Azerbaijan remained largely outside his control. He never succeeded in gaining a firm hold over Azerbaijan; nor did he succeed in weakening the Qaraqoyunlu for long. The Aqqoynlu received the region of Amid (Diyar Bakr) in reward for their service, a grant which helped the branch of Temür's ally Qara 'Uthman to gain preeminence and increase internal control.[56] Eastern Anatolia remained a repository of nomad and tribal power threatening the Timurid hold on Azerbaijan and Baghdad.

[49] Michele Bernardini, *Mémoire et propagande à l'époque timouride*, Studia Iranica. Cahier 37 (Paris: Association pour l'avancement des études iraniennes, 2008), p. 151.
[50] Sharaf al-Dīn 'Alī Yazdī, *Ẓafarnāma* (Tehran: Amīr Kabīr, 1957), vol II, pp. 186–189.
[51] Marie-Mathilde Alexandrescu-Dersca, *La campagne de Timur en Anatolie (1402)* (Bucharest: Imprimeria Nationala, 1942), pp. 57–59, 114–115.
[52] Alexandrescu-Dersca, *La campagne*, p. 55.
[53] Alexandrescu-Dersca, *La campagne*, pp. 68–79.
[54] Alexandrescu-Dersca, *La campagne*, p. 91.
[55] Colin Imber, *The Ottoman Empire, 1300–1650: The Structure of Power*, 2nd ed. (Houndmills, Basingstoke, Hampshire: Palgrave Macmillan, 2009), p. 16.
[56] Woods, *Aqquyunlu*, pp. 41–43.

Temür returned to Samarqand and began to prepare for his most ambitious campaign, ostensibly to retake China from the Ming dynasty. Before setting out he called a convocation or *khuriltay* held in a magnificent tent city. The Spanish ambassador Ruy Gonzales de Clavíjo noted the Chaghatay grazing their flocks as he approached Samarqand, and the supplies gathered for the army included several horses and ten sheep for every soldier. Thus, it appears that the core of Temür's army remained nomadic. By this time Temür was probably in his eighties, and far from well.[57] Several times he had to postpone his departure due to illness, but finally the army set off through the winter steppe. They reached Otrar, a bit beyond the Jaxartes, and there, in February 1405, Temür died.[58]

From Temür to Shahrukh

The army with which Temur achieved his conquests combined settled and nomadic soldiers, like that of Chinggis Khan. The regional dynasties Temür conquered were left in place and required to accompany him on campaigns with their armies. Troops were also raised from the provinces of Iran and joined the Chaghatay army on campaign. Though less prestigious than the central army, the settled troops contributed significantly to the army's power.[59] While nomad horsemen had greater mobility than settled troops and required less grain, they needed more extensive pastures. The combination of nomad and settled troops provided a mix of different skills and allowed campaigns in a variety of terrain. Through much of the Timurid period, the main army appears to have remained Chaghatay, with the power of the tribes suppressed due to the division of their members among different regiments. Tribes, however, were not destroyed, and while they appear rarely in the histories, some did remain in existence. After Temür's death we hear of the Suldus tribe in its old territories and of the Jalayir in new ones, while in the later succession struggle after Shahrukh's death the Arlat appear, providing some support to one of the contestants in their old territories; some Jalayir are likewise mentioned.[60]

---

[57] For Temür's date of birth, see Beatrice F. Manz, "Tamerlane and the Symbolism of Sovereignty," *Iranian Studies* 21, no. 1–2 (1988), pp. 113–114, n33.

[58] Beatrice Forbes Manz, *Power, Politics and Religion in Timurid Iran* (Cambridge: Cambridge University Press, 2007), p. 16.

[59] Manz, *Rise and Rule*, pp. 91–100; Manz, *Power, Politics*, pp. 123–126.

[60] Manz, *Rise and Rule*, pp. 132–136; Manz, *Power, Politics*, p. 269n.; Abū Bakr Ṭihrānī Iṣfahānī, *Kitāb-i Diyārbakriyya*, eds. N. Lugal and F. Sümer (Ankara: Türk tarih Kurumu Basımevi, 1962–1964), p. 350.

Temür created a sovereign realm which combined Turco-Mongolian with Perso-Islamic norms and could be ruled effectively with the resources he commanded. He set up systematic administration only in areas which had primarily settled population and had been under the control of the Ilkhans or the Chaghadayids. Most regional powers remained in place under him, serving in his armies. Cities were looted and heavily taxed at the time of conquest and those which resisted sometimes suffered exemplary punishments, but on departing Temür often left behind a part of the army to restore buildings and agriculture.[61] We should note that nomad populations were not given preferential treatment. Like the Seljukids and Mongols, Temür was often brutal towards the nomads he encountered whose livestock and pasture he wanted for his army. Although local nomads were often recruited for regional campaigns, they remained auxiliaries.[62]

Temür's death led to a protracted struggle in which the eventual winner was his youngest surviving son Shahrukh (r. 1409–1447), who was governor of Khorasan and made Herat the new capital. The Timurids are sometimes seen as an example of Ibn Khaldun's pattern of nomad dynasties, with Temür portrayed as adhering to steppe traditions, gradually abandoned by his successors as they adopted Perso-Islamic norms. This characterization can be disputed. Temür himself was a strong patron of Perso-Islamic culture; it was at his court and under his supervision that many of his sons and grandsons received the education that made them knowledgeable patrons of art and scholarship. Chaghatay emirs likewise patronized both religion and Persianate culture from the very beginning of the dynasty.[63]

The theoretical divide between the Turco-Mongolian and Perso-Islamic traditions was expressed in the two competing codes: the Islamic *shariʿa* and the Mongol *yasa*, discussed in Chapter 5. Shahrukh, renowned for his piety, is reported to have repealed the *yasa* and discontinued the *yarghu* court associated with it. However, such accounts are contained in works by members of the religious classes and are not echoed in the dynastic histories, where Shahrukh's devotion to Islam is presented as a continuation of his father's policies.[64] Throughout Shahrukh's reign and those of his successors, Temür's original followers – the Chaghatay nomads – remained the backbone of the army and an important element in civil administration.

[61] Manz, *Rise and Rule*, p. 116.   [62] Manz, *Rise and Rule*, pp. 100–106.
[63] Manz, *Rise and Rule*, pp. 109–110.
[64] Maria Subtelny, *Timurids in Transition: Turko-Persian Politics and Acculturation in Medieval Iran*, vol. 19, Brill's Inner Asian library (Leiden; Boston: Brill, 2007), pp. 25–27; Manz, "Mongol History," p. 144.

Timurid administration was based theoretically on the dual system, but as under earlier dynasties, the distinction between the Turkic military and Arab or Persian civil spheres was often blurred. Turco-Mongolian emirs were active in many aspects of administration, including the Persian *dīwān*. Many built garden palaces for themselves in the suburbs and sponsored building programs within the cities along with Persian notables.[65] On the other side, some Persian viziers led troops in battle, as did some Iranian city notables.[66]

Shahrukh had a very different mission from that of Temür; he aimed to retain, not enlarge, the realm that Temür had left. Two regions remained outside Shahrukh's grasp: the western border from Baghdad to Azerbaijan and the northeastern regions stretching to Issyk Kul. Both were inhabited primarily by nomadic tribes and had not been solidly under Timurid rule. The Eastern Chaghadayids remained a problem, requiring several campaigns, but the greater threat emerged in the middle of Shahrukh's reign with the rise of a nomad confederation under the Jochid Abu'l Khayr Khan, who took over much of the Qipchaq steppe and for a while also Khorezm. In the west, Shahrukh struggled throughout his reign to maintain a hold over Azerbaijan. The region was of great symbolic importance since he continued to claim the legacy of the Ilkhanate. Although he repeatedly defeated the western tribal confederations, he could not dislodge them, and effective Timurid power usually stopped at Sultaniyya.

Through most of the fifteenth century, first the Qaraqoyunlu and then the Aqqoyunlu expanded their power at the expense of their neighbors. We cannot attribute their success entirely to military prowess, since when they engaged in full-scale battles with the Ottomans, Mamluks or Timurids, they usually lost. What distinguished them was their ability to absorb military defeat and repeated succession struggles without suffering permanent collapse. Unlike other rulers whom Temür had defeated, Qara Yusuf Qaraqoyunlu quickly recovered and was well prepared to take advantage of the struggle on Temür's death. He seized Azerbaijan in 1408, then in 1411 took Baghdad from the Jalayirids. Shahrukh undertook three major expeditions to Azerbaijan and each time defeated the Qarqoyunlu armies, but the best he could attain was a largely fictional suzerainty over Qaraqoyunlu leaders appointed as "governor." The periodic defeats of the Qaraqoyunlu worked to the advantage of the Aqqoyunlu, as the two confederations contested the

[65] Manz, *Power, Politics*, pp. 80–110, 164–177.
[66] Manz, *Power, Politics*, pp. 147–150, 157–165.

pastures and trade routes of eastern Anatolia from Erzerum to Diyar Bakr throughout Shahrukh's reign.

Despite the control of important cities and the development of sophisticated administrations, both the Aqqoyunlu and the Qaraqoyunlu retained their tribal structure. For the Aqqoyunlu, who sponsored several dynastic histories, we have a picture of the conduct of government. The sultan enhanced his power through the use of a personal military following, recruited from both tribal nomads and non-tribal populations. This was regularly paid, and not organized on tribal lines. The chiefs within the confederation had similar retinues on a smaller scale. Women held a relatively high position and could be important political players. The ruler consulted regularly with a council of family, chief officers and tribal leaders, and seems to have been bound by its decisions. Regionally, the Aqqoyunlu governed through princely appanages with a fixed share of local revenue; princes were accompanied by an army made up of members of different tribes.[67] This system of government limited the power of the ruler and made centralization difficult, but it allowed the nomad confederations of eastern Anatolia to survive under often chaotic circumstances, and to make use of new opportunities when they arose.

New Ideologies and New Genealogies

Struggles over territory were accompanied by rivalry within the ideological sphere; the various dynasties of steppe provenance competed for prestige both as Muslims and as inheritors of the steppe imperial tradition. The Timurids claimed superiority over those outside the Mongol heritage and likewise over steppe peoples less adept in high culture. To them, the Turkmen and Mamluks lacked pedigree and imperial background, an attitude we have seen displayed in Temür's correspondence with Bayazid and the Mamluk sultan. On the other hand, some groups within the Mongol world were thought to lack culture and discipline. The Timurids, claiming the term Chaghatay for their own followers, called the eastern Chaghadayids either Moghuls or "Chete," robbers. The term "Uzbek," which at this time referred to the nomads of the eastern Qipchaq steppe, was sometimes used as a term for those considered uncultured.[68]

---

[67] Woods, *Aqquyunlu*, pp. 14–19.
[68] Beatrice F. Manz, "The Development and Meaning of Čagatay Identity," in *Muslims in Central Asia: Expressions of Identity and Change*, ed. Jo-Ann Gross (Durham: Duke University Press, 1992), pp. 37–39; "Multi-ethnic Empires and the Formulation of Identity," *Ethnic and Racial Studies* 26, no. 1 (2003), pp. 85–87.

The early fifteenth century produced a new spate of historical writing and a variety of founding narratives. Once again, a divide emerges between the eastern and western regions. Temür had used two strategies to make up for his modest official position. He had fostered a heroic image of himself as a second Chinggis Khan, favored by destiny and endowed with exceptional powers. Towards the end of his career, he had also begun to refer to the status of his Barlas ancestor Qarachar Noyan, who had served both Chinggis Khan and Chaghadai.[69] Shahrukh retained and elaborated both aspects of Temür's legitimation, which he reworked to fashion Temür as a dynastic founder in his own right. The Chinggisid puppet khans were no longer considered useful, and Temür was posthumously awarded their sovereign titles. At the same time, the Timurids embellished the genealogy of the Barlas, connecting the Timurids to Chinggis Khan through a common ancestor. They thus retained their Mongol legitimacy while glorifying a more immediate Muslim dynastic founder.

The powers of Anatolia used another set of myths to counter Timurid prestige. To compete with the charisma of Chinggis Khan, Turkmen dynasties turned to the legendary Turk Oghuz Khan, who became the subject of an elaborate myth incorporating the ancestors of these dynasties and furthermore providing them with Islamic roots, since according to legend Oghuz refused his mother's milk until she agreed to convert to monotheism.[70] This legend had been incorporated into steppe history in the Mongol period and was included by Rashid al-Din in the *Jāmiʿ al-tawārīkh*, where Oghuz Khan appears also as a great conqueror who had taken over much of the Middle East. It was now adopted by three major Turkmen rulers of the fifteenth century: Qara ʿUthman Aqqoyunlu (1379–1435), the Ottoman sultan Murad II (1421–1444 and 1446–1451) and Jahanshah Qaraqoyunlu (1438–1467).[71] Thus the Turkic-speaking nomad dynasties of the Middle East were divided into two distinct groups each claiming steppe heritage through a different ancestral myth.

Another difference between legitimation in Anatolia and Iran was the amount of emphasis put on nomadism, which was part of the ideology of the western powers but does not appear in Timurid sources. The Anatolian approach is neatly illustrated by the strategy of Qara Yusuf

---

[69] Manz, "Mongol History," pp. 139–141; Woods, "Timur's Genealogy," pp. 99–100.

[70] Devin A. DeWeese, *Islamization and Native Religion in the Golden Horde: Baba Tükles and Conversion to Islam in Historical and Epic Tradition* (University Park: Pennsylvania State University Press, 1994), pp. 85–86.

[71] Stefan Kamola, "History and legend in the Jāmiʿ al-tawārīkh: Abraham, Alexander and Oghuz Khan," *Journal of the Royal Asiatic Society* 25, no. 4 (2015), pp. 557–569.

Qaraqoyunlu when he wrested Azerbaijan from Temür's son Amiranshah in 1408. Instead of taking power over the region in his own name, he persuaded the Jalayirid ruler to recognize his son Pir Budaq b. Qara Yusuf as an adopted son, and established Pir Budaq in Tabriz as heir to the Jalayir dynasty, which posed as successor to the Ilkhanids. Qara Yusuf himself returned to the pastures of his followers. According to a later historian, he explained his actions through his Turkmen descent: "I am from the Turkmen people. My summer residence is Alataq and my winter residence is Diyarbakr and the banks of the Euphrates. The throne of the sultanate does not belong to us."[72] We may understand this as the means by which Qara Yusuf was able to retain hold of two areas and populations attached to incompatible political traditions. His adoption of Jalayirid/Ilkhanid tradition served to challenge Shahrukh's claim to the Ilkhanid realm, including Azerbaijan; at the same time, he maintained his appeal to nomads who wished to retain their freedom.

For both the Aqqoyunlu and the Qaraqoyunlu, the need to control pastures and the routes between them was central to political life. As the confederations expanded, they took major cities, established courts, and patronized high culture on the pattern of earlier dynasties, both settled and nomadic. Nonetheless they had to accept the autonomy of the tribal leadership. The emphasis on freedom and the primacy of nomadism distinguished them from the centralized states surrounding them and helped to attract tribes away from the Mamluks and the advancing Ottomans, both of whom could also claim Turkic ancestry. Qara 'Uthman Aqqoyunlu (1403–1435) was reported to have said that the Turkmen should not become sedentary, since their sovereignty lay in their nomadic way of life. In his book of advice (*Pandnāma*) the nomad confederation and warband were included with the peasantry as part of the classic circle of justice.[73]

It seems odd to find a similar emphasis on nomadism in Ottoman histories of the fifteenth century, since by 1400 the Ottoman state had adopted an administration and military based primarily on sedentary populations. Nonetheless the myth developed about Orhan's ancestor Ertoghrul connected him firmly to a nomad lifestyle. Tales about him bring up both summer and winter pastures and the importance of live-stock in his entourage.[74] These stories may have originated during the interregnum after Bayazid's death, when his son Muhammad Çelebi

---

[72] Wing, *Jalayirids*, pp. 170–174.   [73] Woods, *Aqquyunlu*, pp. 17, 56.
[74] Lindner, *Explorations*, pp. 18–23; Kafadar, *Between two Worlds*, pp. 94–103; Dimitris J. Kastritsis, "The Ottoman Interregnum (1402–1413): Politics and Narratives of Dynastic Succession" unpublished PhD dissertation, Harvard University, 2005, pp. 35–47, 261–262.

made use of Turkmen and Tatar forces from northeastern Anatolia in his campaigns against his brothers.[75]

The Timurids on the other hand, although many of their followers were nomad, distinguished themselves from the Tajiks primarily as Turks – people with an imperial steppe background and military prowess, which the Tajiks were thought to lack. While the Anatolian confederations sought to differentiate themselves from their more settled neighbors, the Timurids faced the opposite challenge. To the north and east they bordered on territory that was both more solidly nomadic and more tribal: the decentralized Chaghadayid khanate and the rising Uzbek confederation. Thus, in distinguishing themselves from their neighbors, it made sense to stress their superiority in culture and organization.

During the fifteenth century, religious movements arose challenging existing rulers. In response, Turkic leaders sought to claim personal religious charisma and to connect their heritage to the Islamic world. The Oghuz legend, with its incorporation of Islam, neatly provided dual legitimation to the Turkmen. The Timurids developed a new version of the Mongol genealogical myth, which was carved on Temür's tombstone. Temür's ancestry was taken back to Chinggis Khan's mythical ancestress Alan Go'a, said to have been impregnated by a shaft of light; this light was now identified as the spirit of 'Ali b. Abu Talib. Another inventive genealogy connected the Timurids to the genealogical tree of the Yasawi Sufi order, taking them back to 'Ali again, now via Muhammad al-Hanafiyya.[76]

Turkmen, Ottomans and Timurids through the Fifteenth Century

Shahrukh's death unleashed a bitter struggle, and his successor Abu Sa'id (1451–1469) was never able to extend his power securely over the whole of the Timurid realm. In 1452 Jahanshah Qaraqoyunlu took advantage of Timurid strife to annex almost all of western Iran. He now adopted the titles sultan and *khaghan*, commensurate with his new status as ruler over much of the former Ilkhanate.[77] The Qaraqoyunlu did not retain their new position for long; in 1467 The Aqqoyunlu, under a new ruler, Uzun Hasan (r. 1452–1478), defeated and killed Jahanshah and the

---

[75] H. Inalçik, "Meḥemmed I," *EI* 2nd ed.

[76] Kazuo Morimoto, "An Enigmatic Genealogical Chart of the Timurids: A Testimony to the Dynasty's Claim to Yasavi-'Alid Legitimacy?" *Oriens* 44 (2016), pp. 159–172.

[77] Woods, *Aqquyunlu*, p. 78; Hans Robert Roemer, *Persien auf dem Weg in die Neuzeit: iranische Geschichte von 1350–1750* (Beirut: Orient-Institut der Deutschen Morgenländischen Gesellschaft, 1989), pp. 194–195.

Qaraqoyunlu fragmented. Uzun Hasan annexed most of their tribes and took over both Baghdad and Azerbaijan. By the end of 1469 he had incorporated all the Qaraqoyunlu territories in Iran.[78] Moving into Iran, Uzun Hasan brought many of the tribesmen of Anatolia east, where they formed a new nomad population under their own leaders. It was at this time that several tribes active through the nineteenth century arrived in Iran, the Qajars, Bayat and Afshar among them.[79]

In twelve years Uzun Hasan had risen from contestant for power over a confederation to ruler of an empire. The transition did not occur without strain. Establishing a capital in Tabriz, he became heir to the administrative tradition of the Ilkhanids, Jalayirids, and Timurids. He aimed at centralization; he appears to have attempted to standardize procedures over the disparate parts of his realm and is reported to have produced a compilation of laws later used by the Ottomans. This may have been a collection and systematization of earlier customs.[80] Uzun Hasan's attempt to promote central control alienated many of the nomad elite, and perhaps for that reason Hasan did not change his military organization, which remained largely tribal.[81] After his death in 1477, his son Ya'qub (1478–1490) gained the throne. Again attempting to centralize, Ya'qub instituted a further tax reform in the name of Islamic orthodoxy and tried to recall the tax-exempt land grants (*soyurghals*) given out to Turkmen emirs and some members of the 'ulama. Both classes objected, and the attempt was given up. To curtail the power of Bayandur princes, Ya'qub abandoned the practice of handing out princely appanages, granting provincial governorships instead to tribal emirs.[82] Thus Turkmen rule brought a new level of nomad population and tribal power to Iran, making both provincial governance and the maintenance of a fighting force dependent on relations with the tribes.

During the first part of his reign, Uzun Hasan had managed to hold his own against the expanding Ottomans. The Ottoman realm was reunified under Murad II (1421–1444 and 1446–1451), and both Murad and his successor Mehmed Fatih (1444–1446, 1451–1481) pursued campaigns

[78] Hans Robert Roemer, "The Safavid Period," in *The Cambridge History of Iran: The Timurid and Safavid Periods*, ed. Laurence Lockhart and Peter Jackson (Cambridge: Cambridge University Press, 1986), p. 116; Woods, *Aqquyunlu*, pp. 84, 96–100.

[79] Woods, *Aqquyunlu*, pp. 108–110; Vladimir Minorsky, "A Civil and Military Review in Fārs in 881/1476," *Bulletin of the School of Oriental and African Studies* X (1940–1942), pp. 172–176.

[80] Woods, *Aqquyunlu*, pp. 102–106, 109; Vladimir Minorsky, "The Aq-Qounlu and Land Reforms," *Bulletin of the School of Oriental and African Studies* XVII (1955), pp. 449–450.

[81] Woods, *Aqquyunlu*, p. 110.

[82] Minorsky, "The Aq-Qoyunlu," pp. 451–458; Woods, *Aqquyunlu*, pp. 132–135, 144–145.

of expansion and centralization which culminated in an imperial state. The Ottoman armies soon took over much of southern Anatolia. The Karamanid Beylik, however, remained independent. The combination of nomadic lifestyle, tribal organization and daunting terrain made this a particularly difficult region for outside powers to conquer, and for some time the Ottomans and Aqqoyunlu competed for influence over Karamanid politics.[83] In 1472 Uzun Hasan marched west against the Ottomans, initiating a war which ended in a major Ottoman victory in 1473, due in part to the Ottomans' use of firearms, which the Aqqoyunlu did not yet possess. This defeat struck a serious blow to Uzun Hasan's prestige and when he died in 1477 the Aqqoyunlu confederation again fractured. His son Ya'qub succeeded in gaining power, but expansion ended and unity proved impossible to maintain. Nonetheless, despite Ottoman might and the disarray among the Aqqoyunlu, at the time of Mehmed's death in 1481, the Ottomans had not established power beyond Karaman, the Eretna sultanate and Trabzon.[84] The Ottoman Empire was now a centralized bureaucratic state, and the tribal society of the eastern Anatolian frontier was not an easy fit.

The Aqqoyunlu's neighbors to the east were in no better position to profit from Aqqoyunlu civil wars. The Timurid realm was divided, with Abu Sa'id's successors ruling in Transoxiana while Khorasan came under the control of his cousin, Sultan Husayn-i Bayqara (r. 1470–1506). Sultan Husayn never enjoyed much military might and made little attempt to increase his territory, but within the small region he held he presided over a period of agricultural prosperity and cultural splendor. From this time on the Timurids posed no threat to their neighbors and retained their prestige through cultural rather than military accomplishment.

Despite its decline in power, the Timurid dynasty retained many of the characteristics it had held under Temür. Although increasingly dependent on intensive agriculture, the Timurids under Sultan Husayn continued to act within the framework of the Mongol Empire, while increasing their prestige as a center for Islamic scholarship and piety. Both the *shari'a* and the *yasa* were still invoked. We get a glimpse into the meaning of Turco-Mongolian and Islamic tradition in the vivid memoirs composed by one of the last of the Timurid princes, the founder of the Mughal dynasty, Zahir al-Din Babur. Babur was a grandson of Abu Sa'id and descended from Chinggis Khan on his mother's side. Family

---

[83] Inalçik, "Meḥemmed II," *EI* 2nd ed.; Imber, *The Ottoman Empire, 1300–1650*, pp. 28–33.
[84] Woods, *Aqquyunlu*, pp. 114–129; Venzke, "Dulgadir-Mamluk," pp. 428–429.

and marriage relationships linked him to both of the Timurids' steppe neighbors – the Jochid Uzbeks and the eastern Chaghadayid Khans.[85] Throughout his memoir he comments on the character of princes and emirs, their morals, religious observance, and military prowess, associated with Turco-Mongolian background and habits. In Herat, visiting the sons of Sultan Husayn, he is at once admiring and suspicious of their sophistication and the luxury of their court, which, in its use of gold and silver utensils, supposedly went against the *yasa*. As warriors he found them sadly wanting.[86] On the other hand, when Babur visited his maternal relations, the Eastern Chaghadayid khans, he noted their praiseworthy loyalty to the Chinggisid tradition but also their lack of polish. When he attempted to regain his position in Ferghana with the help of Eastern Chaghadayid troops, he blamed his failure in part on their lack of discipline and of loyalty, although it appears that Mongol military tactics and Moghul troops were important factors in the success of his Indian campaign.[87]

The Timurid dynasty fell at the beginning of the sixteenth century, with the Uzbek conquest of Transoxiana in 1501 and of Khorasan in 1507. Babur, pushed out of Transoxiana by the Uzbeks, took his armies eventually to India and founded the Mughal dynasty, also known as the later Timurids. Here the legacies of Chinggis Khan and Temür continued to be valued. Despite its relatively short duration, the Timurid dynasty played a crucial part in creating a synthesis of Turco-Mongolian and Perso-Islamic tradition. The figure of Temür was fully developed as a dynastic founder – at once a second Chinggis Khan and an Islamic sovereign – and was combined with the cultural brilliance of Herat under Shahrukh and especially Sultan Husayn-i Bayqara. Together these achievements made the Timurid dynasty a cultural icon and a source of legitimacy for the dynasties that followed.

Cultural Patronage and the Steppe Legacy

Dynasties of nomad provenance played a central role in the cultural life of the Middle East in the post-Mongol period. Rulers were eager to inherit Mongol prestige and they therefore continued court patronage in the

---

[85] Maria E. Subtelny, "Bābur's Rival Relations: A Story of Kinship and Conflict in 15th–16th Century Central Asia," *Der Islam* 66, no. 1 (1989).

[86] Ẓahīr al-Dīn Muḥammad Babur, *Baburnama: Chaghatay Turkish Text with Abdul-Rahim Khankhanan's Persian Translation*, trans. W. M. Thackston, Sources of Oriental Languages and Literatures (Cambridge, MA: Harvard University: Department of Near Eastern Languages and Civilizations, 1993), vol. 2, pp. 389–392.

[87] Babur, *Baburnama*, vol. 1, pp. 131, 201–202, 220–221, 568–570, 685–690.

traditions set by the Ilkhans, who had brought in practices and goods from the east along with new art forms. The successor dynasties created an art of synthesis in which Chinese and Central Asian themes combined with Islamic traditions. The Mongol heritage became something which could be considered indigenous and became immensely popular. One major strength of Ilkhanid patronage was the writing of history, notably the great world chronicle of Rashid al-Din, the *Jāmiʿ al-tawārīkh*, which I discussed in Chapter 5. The successors to the Ilkhanids continued the new tradition, and made the late fourteenth and fifteenth century a high point for historiography. In 1360, soon after taking Azerbaijan, Shaykh Uways Jalayir had a universal history written for him, the *Tārīkh-i Shaykh Uways*, modeled on the *Jāmiʿal-tawārīkh*, but bringing the story up to the present. Here the Ilkhans and the Jalayirids follow earlier states in the Islamic world; at the same time, their history is seen within the frame of a continuing Mongol Empire, whose history continues outside the central Islamic lands.[88] The Timurid rulers were even more active in the patronage of historical works. At the court of Shahrukh, the historian Hafiz-i Abru collected the histories of earlier times, including Rashid al-Din, adding the history of Temür's and Shahrukh's period. Later Timurid historians, notably Mirkhwand and the hugely popular Khwandamir, who began his career under Husayn-i Bayqara, carried the project of universal history into their own time.[89] The Turkmen dynasties also commissioned histories; most of these were more limited in scope and presented their patrons as heirs to the Oghuz tradition, thus also recognizing the steppe as relevant to their history but not embracing the Mongol worldview.[90]

Another innovation of the Mongols was the development of the Persian miniature, illustrating historical and literary works. After the fall of the Ilkhans, a few courts in Iran – the Inju'ids and Muzaffarids in Shiraz, and the Jalayirids in Tabriz and Baghdad continued to produce miniatures.[91] As new conquerors took over these cities, they employed many of the same people; the Timurid prince Iskandar Sultan presided over a brilliant court in Shiraz, while the Qaraqoyunlu continued the artistic traditions of

---

[88] C. A. Storey and Yuri Bregel, *Persidskaia literatura, bio-bibliograficheskiĭ obzor*, 3 vols. (Moscow: Nauka, 1972), p. 337.

[89] John E. Woods, "The Rise of Tīmūrīd Historiography," *Journal of Near Eastern Studies* 46, no. 2 (1987).

[90] C. P. Melville, "Between Tabriz and Herat: Persian Historical Writing in the 15th Century," in *Iran und iranisch geprägte Kulturen*, ed. Ralph Kauz, Birgitt Hoffmann, and Markus Ritter (Wiesbaden: Reichert, 2008), pp. 30–33.

[91] Linda Komaroff and Stefano Carboni, *The Legacy of Genghis Khan: Courtly Art and Culture in Western Asia, 1256–1353* (New York: Metropolitan Museum of Art; New Haven, CT: Yale University Press, 2002), pp. 47, 60, 108, 223–225.

Tabriz. When Shahrukh took Tabriz in the winter of 1420–1421, one of his prizes was the famous calligrapher Ja'far Tabrizi, who finished his illustrious career in Herat.[92] During the reigns of Shahrukh and Husayn Bayqara, Herat became a brilliant center for cultural production. Its styles of miniature painting and calligraphy became the model for contemporaries and for later dynasties. Two sons of Uzun Hasan Aqqoyunlu are also famous for their patronage of painting: Khalil, who presided over a court in Shiraz during his father's reign, and Ya'qub b. Hasan who ruled during the last years of the united Qaraqoyunlu.[93]

The works of the Aqqoyunlu and the Timurids exerted enormous influence on later dynasties – the Uzbeks, Mughals, Safavids and Ottomans. Both fell at the height of their cultural brilliance, with the death of Sultan Ya'qub Aqqoyunlu in 1490 and that of the Timurid Sultan Husayn Bayqara in 1506. The painters, calligraphers, poets, and historians who had flourished at their courts had to find new employment, and the courts of erstwhile rivals were delighted to receive them. These prestigious figures thus became arbiters of taste for a new generation of rulers, preserving and disseminating a synthesis of Chinese, Inner Asian and Perso-Islamic culture.

The Rise of Turkic as a Language of High Culture

Although written Turkic literature in the Islamic world began well before the Mongol period, it was the post-Mongol age, and particularly the fifteenth century, which established Turkic, written in the Arabic alphabet, as a language of high culture. The earliest and fastest development was in Anatolia, where Turkic had begun to supplant Persian by the late fifteenth century. We have a few fragments of Anatolian Turkic poetry from the thirteenth century, and by the early fourteenth century Turkic mystical and folk poetry was quite well established; the famous Anatolian poet Yunus Emre, whose lyrics are still widely read, died in 1320.[94] The numerous local courts of the fourteenth and fifteenth centuries were connected to the wider cultural world and offered opportunities for ambitious scholars and writers. In the early fifteenth century, the rulers

---

[92] Nazan Ölçer, "The Anatolian Seljuks," in *Turks: A Journey of a Thousand Years*, ed. David Roxburgh (London: Royal Academy of Arts, 2005), pp. 118–119; W. M. Thackston, *Album Prefaces and Other Documents on the History of Calligraphers and Painters* (Leiden: Brill, 2001), pp. 8, 13.

[93] B. W. Robinson, *Fifteenth-Century Persian Painting: Problems and Issues* (New York: New York University Press, 1991), pp. 3–44.

[94] Alessio Bombaci, *Histoire de la littérature turque* (Paris: C. Klincksieck, 1968), pp. 177, 225–242.

of Aydin, situated on the Aegean, patronized writings in Arabic, Persian and Turkic.[95]

The self-consciously Turkic/Seljuqid identity of many rulers and elites led to an upsurge of literature in their language. Verse romances were very popular, as were epics recounting the exploits of Turkic fighters for the faith, such as the *Dede Korkut*, which was probably written in its current form under the Aqqoyunlu.[96] While battles for the faith might provide the moral justification for such works, their heroes spent easily as much time in romantic adventures and lengthy feasts, in which they consumed mountains of meat washed down with seas of wine and fermented mare's milk. These tales could also incorporate variations of the Oghuz legend.[97] During the centralizing reign of Murad II (1421–1444 and 1446–1451) the first Ottoman chronicles appeared, one or two already in Turkish.[98] From this time on Ottoman Turkish remained established as a language of high culture. In the Aqqoyunlu and Qaraqoyunlu courts Persian remained the main literary language, but Turkic poetry found an audience, especially with the Aqqoyunlu.[99]

The other western region important for the development of Turkic literature was the Mamluk sultanate. Despite their determined stand against the Mongols, the Mamluks took pride in their Turkic identity. Throughout the Qipchaq period they patronized works in and about Turkic, including translations of religious and military works, dictionaries and grammars of Qipchaq Turkic, and verse romances. Indeed, several of the earliest monuments of Islamic Turkic literature have come down to us through their hands, including the unique copy of al-Kashghari's treatise on the Turks and their language, the *Dīwān lughāt al-Turk*, and one of the few early copies of the Qarakhanid mirror for princes, the *Qutagtu Bilig*. Early versions of the legends comprising *Dede Korkut* are also to be found in Mamluk literature.[100]

---

[95] Sara Nur Yıldız, "Aydınid Court Literature in the Formation of an Islamic Identity in Fourteenth-Century Western Anatolia," in *Islamic Literature and Intellectual Life in Fourteenth- and Fifteenth-Century Anatolia*, ed. A. C. S. Peacock and Sara Nur Yıldız (Würzburg: Ergon Verlag, 2016), pp. 197–213.

[96] Jo-Ann Conrad, "Dede Korkut: Reintegrating the Historic, the Heroic, and the Marvelous," *Turcica* 33 (2001), pp. 244–250.

[97] Bombaci, *Histoire de la littérature turque*, pp. 185–199, 249–251; Woods, *Aqquyunlu*, pp. 179–182.

[98] Bombaci, *Histoire de la littérature turque*, pp. 252, 264–265; Barbara Flemming, "Old Anatolian Turkish Poetry and Its Relationship to the Persian Tradition," in *Turkic-Iranian Contact Areas: Historical and Linguistic Aspects*, ed. Lars Johanson and Christine Bulut (Wiesbaden: Harrassowitz, 2006), pp. 49–52.

[99] Bombaci, *Histoire de la littérature turque*, pp. 183–185.

[100] al-Kāshgharī, *Compendium of the Turkic Dialects* 1, pp. 10–24; Fikret Turan, "The Mamluks and Their Acceptance of Oghuz Turkic as a Literary Language: Political Maneuver or Cultural Aspiration?" in *Einheit und Vielfalt in der türkischen Welt:*

When the Cherkes replaced the Qipchaq mamluks as sultans, they found themselves in an anomalous situation: as non-Turks amid a host of Turkic rulers. Mamluks were associated with Turkic identity; indeed, the Mamluk ruling class was known to the population as the *dawlat al-turkiyya*. Determined to keep the Qipchaqs out of power, the Cherkes sultans did not continue patronage of the Qipchaq language but instead attached themselves to the Turkmen heritage, changed their names for Oghuz ones, and encouraged literary works in Oghuz.[101]

In the east it was the Timurids who developed Turkic into a language of court literature. Poetry in Turkic gained popularity starting in Temür's reign and reached its apogee during the reign of Husayn-i Bayqara, in the poetry of the brilliant bureaucrat and poet Mir 'Ali Shir Nava'i, whose lyrics are still celebrated in the Uzbek republic. Nava'i (who also wrote in Persian) celebrated the superiority of Turks and the Turkic language in a composition entitled *Muḥākamat al-lughatayn* – The Contest of Two Languages. Persian, he wrote, was full of Turkic vocabulary:

The Persian language would be lost without Turkish expressions, for the Turks have created many words to express nuances and gradations of meanings which cannot be understood until explained by a knowledgeable person.[102]

By the late fifteenth century, some Turkic rulers were also writing in Turkic; this was the language in which the Timurid prince Babur wrote his memoirs. Poetry in Turkic was more widespread. Sultan Husayn Bayqara was the most famous of the prince poets of that period, but the Qaraqoyunlu ruler Jahanshah (d. 1467) also wrote sophisticated religious poetry, and the last Aqqoyunlu, Ya'qub, left behind some Turkic verses.[103] Several of the last Mamluk sultans did likewise.[104] Turkic was now an established written language, just as Turks were an integral part of the population.

Conclusion

When the Ilkhans fell, Mongol Khans still ruled over much of the former empire, and throughout its territory only descendants of Chinggis Khan

Materialien der 5. Deutschen Turkologenkonferenz Universität Mainz, 4.–7. Oktober 2002, ed. Hendrik Boeschoten and Heidi Stein (Wiesbaden: Harrassowitz, 2007), p. 41; Jo-Ann Conrad, "Dede Korkut," p. 247.

[101] Turan, "The Mamluks," pp. 40–44.

[102] Mīr 'Alī Shīr Nawā'ī, *Muḥākamāt al-lughatayn*, trans. Robert Devereux (Leiden: Brill, 1966), pp. 5–6.

[103] Bombaci, *Histoire de la littérature turque*, pp. 183–185.

[104] János Eckmann, "Die kiptschakische Literatur," in *Philologiae Turcicae Fundamenta*, vol. II, ed. Jean Deny (Aquis Mattiacis: Steiner, 1964), pp. 299–300.

had the right to claim sovereign power. Over the fourteenth century, however, tribal leaders gained strength. Chinggisid rule was not finished, but it was deeply fragmented and in many places had given way to either settled or tribal powers. Within the central Islamic lands actual Chinggisid rule ended with the Ilkhans, though power remained largely in the hands of nomads or rulers of nomad provenance. Nomads remained a significant proportion of the population and, for most states, a majority within the military.

In earlier centuries, nomads had arrived in the Middle East from Central Asia, and as migration succeeded migration, many moved into Anatolia. After the fall of the Ilkhans, the movement of nomad populations went the other way, from Anatolia into Iraq and Iran. The conquest of Iran by the Qaraqoyunlu and the Aqqoyunlu transformed its ethnic and political geography. Under the Seljukids and Mongols, most Turkic and Mongol nomads had congregated in the northern pastures; now Turkmen became numerous also in southern Iran. There was a change likewise in the social and political organization of many nomads. The Seljukids, Ilkhans and Timurids had all used non-tribal armies and for much of their rule had suppressed tribes as power centers. In Anatolia, a decentralized system developed during the fourteenth century, in which tribes again became central to military and political activity. The Turkmen dynasties brought this system into Iran, making tribalism an important element in both military and provincial administration.

The Mongol destruction of the caliphate had opened the way both to the conversion of Mongol rulers and to the creation of independent sovereign states in the Middle East. It was no longer necessary to retain the capital in Baghdad, with its depleted agricultural resources, or to pay lip service to an undivided Islamic empire. The new regional states were all in some way connected to the steppe heritage and continued to use it. Most also sought to connect themselves with the memory of the Ilkhanate, which held prestige as a part of the Mongol Empire and for its brilliant cultural achievements, imitated by its successors.

The court culture of the fourteenth and fifteenth centuries was highly sophisticated, but it did not return to the classical pre-Mongol models. New forms and motifs remained along with a broader world view. Turkic written in the Arabic alphabet joined Arabic and Persian as a language of high culture. By the end of the fifteenth century, Turks had become indigenous to the Middle East, and the imperial traditions of the steppe had become intertwined with those of the Arabs and the Persians.

7   The Rise of Nomad Tribes, 1500–1800

The early sixteenth century brought with it a political revolution in the creation of the "Gunpowder Empires." In 1501, Shah Isma'il I declared himself Shah and founded the Safavid state, ruling most of Iran. From 1500 to 1507 the Uzbeks took over the Timurid territories, founding the Chinggisid Uzbek Khanate; in 1516–1517, the Ottomans under Selim I conquered Anatolia up to Kurdistan, and the whole of the Mamluk state. Finally, in 1526 the Timurid prince Babur took Delhi and founded the Mughal Empire. These were the states – Safavid, Ottoman, Uzbek, and Mughal – which brought the central Islamic lands into the modern era.

In the history of nomads, the turn of the sixteenth century also marks a turning point. The last three chapters have covered the Middle Periods of Islamic history, in which nomads from the Eurasian steppe entered the Middle East and gained control over almost the whole of it. This was a great period for the power of nomads, but not for that of tribes; in the Seljuqid, Ilkhanid and Timurid states, tribalism was largely suppressed in military and political organization. The exceptions to this were the tribal confederations of Anatolia, which were forming at the end of the period. In the new order that arose in the sixteenth century, nomads held sway over somewhat less territory, but tribalism was more widespread, and tribes became a major political force.

The Ottoman and Safavid states, with which we will concern ourselves here, had widely different policies towards both nomadism and tribalism. The Safavids arose out of the Aqqoyunlu confederation and embraced both tribes and nomads. Turkmen and Mongol nomads formed the core of the Safavid army, gaining tribal pastures and regional holdings throughout Iran and much of what is now Afghanistan. The Ottomans continued their efforts to create a centralized army and state, a system in which tribes and nomads had a less central role. However, with Ottoman expansion into new nomad territories, actual government in the border regions was a matter of negotiation with local powers, including nomads.

The Turkmen nomads of eastern Anatolia and northern Syria remained autonomous and receptive to outside alliances. In Arabia and Syria, the Bedouin were likewise active, with new tribes migrating north from the Arabian Peninsula to dominate the Syrian desert, much of Iraq, and parts of the Jazira.

In the sixteenth century the Ottoman and Safavid Empires were able – with some lapses – to maintain control over tribal leaders. Over the course of the seventeenth century the balance changed, and the eighteenth century saw an age of decentralization with local powers, including nomads, largely autonomous through much of the Middle East. The fall of the Safavid dynasty in 1722 was followed by the spectacular conquests of the tribal leader Nadir Shah Afshar, who briefly conquered all of Iran and much of Afghanistan. After his death, the chiefs under him returned to their own regions to found new states. In the Ottoman Empire, the Wahhabi movement mobilized nomads to take over much of the Arabian Peninsula and sparked new tribal migrations to the north and west. This was the situation in the Middle East at the dawn of the nineteenth century.

The Rise of the Safavids

The Safavid dynasty was of Iranian – probably Kurdish – extraction and had its beginnings as a Sufi order located at Ardabil near the eastern border of Azerbaijan, in a region favorable for both agriculture and pastoralism. Its rise was intimately connected to the Turkmen nomads of Anatolia and Azerbaijan. To understand Safavid history, we must return to the fifteenth century and to Aqqoyunlu rule. At about the time that the Timurid ruler Shahrukh died in 1447, the Safavid order became involved in the rivalry between the Qaraqoyunlu and the Aqqoyunlu, each of which supported a different candidate for the leadership of the order. The younger claimant, Shaykh Junayd, sought help – and soldiers – from powers in Anatolia and eventually found a useful ally in the Aqqoyunlu ruler Uzun Hasan, whose sister he married. Over the next years he led his followers in a series of campaigns in eastern Anatolia and the Caspian region of Shirwan under the banner of holy war.[1] On Junayd's death in battle in 1460, Haydar, his infant son by his Aqoyunlu wife, was recognized as heir. Haydar continued to develop the Safavid religious-military organization, introducing the distinctive scarlet headdress ($t\bar{a}j$) which

---

[1] Adel Allouche, *The Origins and Development of the Ottoman-Ṣafavid Conflict (906–962/1500–1555)* (Berlin: Schwarz, 1983), pp. 41–47.

became the identifying mark of Safavid devotees, and won them the epithet Qizilbash – red head – by which they later became known.[2]

A number of early Iranian religious beliefs had survived in the Middle East and combined with Sufi and Shi'ite ideas to create a set of doctrines usually characterized as *ghuluww* (extremism). These included the doctrine of a living *mahdi* – a messiah. Such beliefs found a following in Anatolia and parts of Syria, and among the populations they attracted were many members of the Turkmen tribes.[3] Scholarship on the early Safavid movement is in flux. Most writers have portrayed the following of Junayd and Haydar as a radical Shi'ite order whose leader was at once a religious leader and commander over a sizeable Turkmen army of believers.[4] According to the Aqqoyunlu historian Khunji Isfahani, Junayd's followers openly called Junayd God and continued to consider him living after his physical death.[5] However, both the extreme Shi'ite views of Junayd and Haydar and the centrality of the Turkmen in their armies have recently been called into question, and some see the early Safavid following as an army of *ghāzīs* from a variety of backgrounds.[6]

Over the course of Haydar's career, Uzun Hasan Aqqoyunlu took over western and central Iran. Despite Haydar's marriage alliance with the dynasty, Safavid and Aqqoyunlu interests soon began to diverge, and in 1488 Haydar was killed fighting the Aqqoyunlu.[7] As the Aqqoyunlu descended into civil war, Haydar's youngest son Isma'il took refuge in Lahijan in the Caspian mountains where he was protected and given a religious education by the elders of the Safavid order.[8] In 1499, at the age of twelve, Isma'il left Lahijan for Ardabil with seven powerful members of his entourage and a few hundred followers. Numerous Qizilbash devotees had remained loyal to the order throughout Azerbaijan, eastern

---

[2] Shahzad Bashir, "The Origins and Rhetorical Evolution of the Term Qizilbāsh in Persianate Literature," *Journal of the Economic and Social History of the Orient* 57, no. 3 (2014).

[3] Kathryn Babayan, *Mystics, Monarchs, and Messiahs: Cultural Landscapes of Early Modern Iran* (Cambridge, MA: Distributed for the Center for Middle Eastern Studies of Harvard University by Harvard University Press, 2002), pp. XV–XXIV.

[4] Allouche, *Origins*, pp. 30–39.

[5] Ali Anooshahr, *Turkestan and the Rise of Eurasian Empires: A Study of Politics and Invented Traditions* (Oxford: Oxford University Press, 2018), p. 78.

[6] Anooshahr, *Turkestan and the Rise of Eurasian Empires*, pp. 56–83; Ayfer Karakaya-Stump, "Subjects of the Sultan, Disciples of the Shah: Formation and Transformation of the Kiszilbash/Alevi Communities in Ottoman Anatolia" (Cambridge, MA: Harvard University, 2008), pp. 172–181.

[7] Allouche, *Origins*, pp. 50–53; Michel M. Mazzaoui, *The Origins of the Ṣafawids: Šīʿism, Ṣūfism and the Ġulāt* (Wiesbaden: F. Steiner, 1972), pp. 75–77.

[8] Jean Aubin, "Révolution chiite et conservatisme. Les soufis de Lâhejân, 1500–1514 (Études Safavides II)," *Moyen Orient et Océan Indien. Middle East and Indian Ocean XVIe–XIXe siècles* 1 (1984), pp. 2–8.

Anatolia and Syria; now Isma'il set out to gather them around himself. In the spring of 1500, he moved through the pasturelands of northern Azerbaijan. Having started out with only a few hundred soldiers, by the end of the summer he had an army of about 7,000.[9] After several successful battles, he entered Tabriz in the summer of 1501 and was crowned as Shah. By 1510 he had conquered Baghdad and most of Iran.

Isma'il now stood both at the head of a Sufi order which was at the same time a largely nomadic army, and at the head of an evolving state. The Qizilbash were organized into large political and religious communities called *oymaq*. Although many *oymaqs* included numerous named subgroups, the term is usually translated as tribe, and I shall follow that practice here. Some *oymaqs*, like the Qajar, the Afshar and the Dhu'l Qadr, came from existing tribes or confederations which had converted to the Safavid cause. Others, like the Tekkelu, Rumlu and Shamlu, seem to have been new, based probably on regional populations. While most Qizilbash seem to have been Turkmen, some sedentary villagers or townsmen were included within the *oymaqs*. After Shah Isma'il's accession, membership in the Safavid order was limited to members of the *oymaqs*; the newly conquered populations were excluded.[10]

The Qizilbash had a strong communal culture centered on absolute loyalty to their leader. Isma'il enjoyed great personal charisma as a poet, warrior, and king. In his poetry, written in Turkish, he presented himself as the reincarnation of earlier prophets and kings, while many of his followers considered him one with God.[11] At this time it is clear that *ghuluww* mysticism and apocalyptic thought were central to the movement.[12] Despite his claim to divinity, the shah did not keep aloof from his followers; he passed on booty and wealth and took part in large communal feasts with heavy public drinking.[13] Isma'il created a new religious office, that of *khalīfa al-khulafā* – chief deputy. Below him were numerous other *khalīfas*, one to each of the tribal sections, and to villages and districts even beyond his actual realm, since the Safavids retained numerous adherents in Anatolia.[14]

---

[9] Jean Aubin, "L'avènement des Safavides reconsidéré," *Moyen Orient et Océan Indien. Middle East and Indian Ocean XVIe–XIXe siècles* 5 (1988), pp. 9–15; Masashi Haneda, *Le châh et les Qizilbāš: le système militaire safavide* (Berlin: K. Schwarz, 1987), pp. 63–64.

[10] Martin Dickson, "Sháh Ṭahmásb and the Úzbeks (The Duel for Khurásán with 'Ubayd Khán: 930–46/1524–1540)," unpublished PhD dissertation, Princeton University (1958), pp. 6–8, 266–267; Woods, *Aqquyunlu*, pp. 13, 164.

[11] Babayan, *Mystics, Monarchs*, pp. xxviii–xxxii.

[12] Colin P. Mitchell, *The Practice of Politics in Safavid Iran: Power, Religion and Rhetoric* (London: I. B. Tauris, 2009), pp. 19–38.

[13] Aubin, "L'avènement," pp. 43–53, 62–63.

[14] Willem Floor, "The *Khalīfeh al-Kholafa* of the Safavid Sufi Order," *Zeitschrift der deutchen morgenländischen Gesellschaft* 153, no. 1 (2003): pp. 52–53.

It is tempting to regard Ismaʻil's early campaigns as a triumphal progress towards the creation of the Safavid state. However, his military activity was part of a civil war within the Aqqoyunlu confederation, and he can be seen as one of several ambitious leaders who aimed for preeminence.[15] After the death of the last Aqqoyunlu ruler in 1514, the Safavids took over some of the Aqqoyunlu confederate tribes along with many of their habits and institutions. In Ismaʻil's early years, the Qizilbash of Anatolia and Syria were a significant source of support; Turkmen nomads continued to join his following, partly through attraction, and partly due to local famine accompanied by Ottoman persecution.[16] It was the rise of the Ottoman sultan Selim I and the defeat at Chaldiran which prevented expansion or consolidation in the western regions, and centered the Safavid state within Iran.

Nomads and Tribes in Safavid Administration

Like the Aqqoyunlu rulers, Ismaʻil incorporated tribal structure into his administration. This was a realistic policy given the strength of tribal leadership and Ismaʻil's reliance on Turkmen manpower. As I showed in Chapter 6, both Uzun Hasan Aqqoyunlu and his son Yaʻqub had met resistance to their centralizing policies. In 1496, four years before Ismaʻil declared himself shah, the briefly enthroned Aqqoyunlu sultan Ahmad attempted to create an Ottoman-style administration, with a ban on wine, the recall of benefices, and the abandonment of tribal law; after only six months of rule, he was overthrown. These experiences served as a warning to other leaders.[17] Ismaʻil's decision to incorporate tribal structure and to include new populations within it through the *oymaqs* presents a striking contrast to the policies of Chinggis Khan and Temür, who used their personal following as the top command in a decimally organized army, preventing tribes from developing as centers of power.

Both the Safavid army and provincial administration were organized along tribal lines. The *oymaqs* had recognized leaders and contributed contingents to the army. In the early Safavid period almost all military commanders were identified by tribal names and led troops from their own *oymaqs*; in an account of an army review in 1530 we find 15–18,000 soldiers from each of the two largest *oymaqs*, 6–9,000 each from several others. Tribes had a recognized place in either the left or the right wing of the army, which they appear to have retained through most of the Safavid period.[18] The system of provincial government was closely connected to

---

[15] Woods, *Aqquyunlu*, pp. 163–166.   [16] Roemer, "The Safavid Period," pp. 218–219.
[17] Woods, *Aqquyunlu*, pp. 158–159.   [18] Haneda, *Le châh*, pp. 46–50, 104–110.

the military structure and also organized tribally. Qizilbash emirs were appointed to governorships, providing troops for local defense, while land grants and provincial holdings provided upkeep for their soldiers. In the early Safavid period the Qizilbash appointed as governors over provinces were often chiefs of their *oymaq*; if they were not, the governorship usually brought with it the appointment to lead the tribe as well.[19] *Oymaqs* were allotted specific territories known as *ulka*, which provided income and pasture.[20] Until the reign of Shah 'Abbas almost all regions of the realm were governed by tribal leaders.[21]

At this time governors of provinces usually appointed subordinate officials, held judicial power, and retained much of the income of the province.[22] When the shah or his delegates set out on a major campaign they called on the governors to join the army with their contingents.[23] Some governorships came to be considered the property of a specific tribe; the Dhu'l Qadr retained Fars for several generations, the Qajars were governors of Ganja and parts of Azerbaijan, while the Afshar held on to the governorships of Kerman and Kuh-Giluya with neighboring regions.[24] However, despite the close connection between *oymaqs* and provincial rule, tribal territories and provincial governorships were not identical. Qizilbash and other officials were given land grants as a source of income, and these were not necessarily in the province governed by the chief of the tribe. Thus, the regional power of individual tribes was diluted.[25]

Up to the middle of the Safavid period, tribal chiefs were convened at important junctures to decide the affairs of state, and they considered this part of their function.[26] The shahs attached the Qizilbash elite to the

---

[19] Klaus Röhrborn, *Provinzen und Zentralgewalt Persiens im 16. und 17. Jahrhunder* (Berlin: de Gruyter, 1966), p. 25.

[20] Vladimir Minorsky, *Tadhkirat al-mulūk: a manual of Ṣafavid administration (circa 1137/ 1725), Persian text in facsimile (B.M. Or. 9496)*, E. J. W. Gibb memorial series (London: Luzac, 1980), pp. 14–15, 27, 86; Aubin, "L'avènement," p. 29; Dickson, "Shāh Ṭahmásb," pp. 6–8, 13.

[21] Röhrborn, *Provinzen*, pp. 18–19, 24, 29.

[22] Röhrborn, *Provinzen*, pp. 24–27, 54–55, 61.

[23] Röhrborn, *Provinzen*, pp. 44–48; Dickson, "Shāh Ṭahmásb," pp. 13, 65–66, 93, 134.

[24] Röhrborn, *Provinzen*, pp. 4, 10, 31.

[25] Röhrborn, *Provinzen*, p. 54; Minorsky, *Tadhkirat al-mulūk*, pp. 27–28, 85–87; Maria Szuppe, *Entre Timourides, Uzbeks et Safavides: questions d'histoire politique et sociale de Hérat dans la première moitié du XVIe siècle* (Paris: Association pour l'avancement des études iraniennes, 1992), p. 37; Maria Szuppe, "Kinship Ties between the Safavids and the Qizilbash Amirs in Late Sixteenth-Century Iran: A Case Study of the Political Career of Members of the Sharaf al-Din Oghli Tekelu Family," in *Safavid Persia: The History and Politics of an Islamic Society*, ed. Charles Melville (London: I. B. Tauris, 1996), p. 87.

[26] Haneda, *Le châh*, pp. 94–97, 207; Röhrborn, *Provinzen*, p. 31.

dynasty through marriage alliances often stretching over several generations. Thus, many of the major *oymaq* amirs were close relatives of the shah.[27] While the ruler had the power to appoint both provincial governors and the chiefs of *oymaqs*, candidates unacceptable to the tribe would be rejected. The chiefs themselves were likewise forced to consider the wishes of their subordinates, who held both territories and troops of their own.[28] The more powerful tribes could thus promote their own interests, and in the absence of a strong ruler the central offices of the state became a prize to be fought over among them.

The Persian narrative sources give little information on the level of nomadism among the Qizilbash, but there is mention of pastures assigned to them. European observers noted the presence of nomads throughout the Safavid dominions, including many Turkmen. We have an account of Shah Tahmasp's army in 1538 which characterizes his troops as nomads, while also mentioning the distinctive red hat. A source from the reign of Shah Sultan Husayn (1694–1722), the *Tuḥfat-i Shāhī*, contains a list of nomad tribes *(īlāt)*, some with summer and winter pastures, and this includes several of the Qizilbash oymaqs.[29] The Qizilbash were not the only nomads within Safavid territories. As Ismaʻil took over new territories, he incorporated independent dynasties and tribal powers into the Safavid system as vassals; their rulers were given the title *walī*. Four large areas remained under the rule of *walīs* almost to the end of the dynasty: Georgia, Kurdistan, Luristan with the Bakhtiyari territories, and Khuzistan, then often called ʻArabistan.[30] These last three were regions with a strong nomadic presence whose location along the Ottoman border gave them a position of strength. In Khuzistan the Mushaʻshaʻ dynasty stood at the head of a coalition of Arab tribes, usually loyal to the Safavids in a turbulent region. The Lurs to their north had maintained relative autonomy and were ruled by a local dynasty from the Mongol period. Within the Lur the Bakhtiyari tribe began its rise to power.[31] The Kurds occupied the most open and contested border between the Ottomans and the Safavids, and they increased their strength considerably.

[27] Szuppe, "Kinship Ties"; Andrew J. Newman, *Safavid Iran: Rebirth of a Persian Empire* (London: I. B. Tauris, 2006), pp. 15, 29, 40, 45, 54.

[28] Röhrborn, *Provinzen*, p. 25; Szuppe, "Kinship Ties," pp. 81–85, 89.

[29] Daniel T. Potts, *Nomadism in Iran, From Antiquity to the Modern Era* (Oxford: Oxford University Press, 2014), pp. 228–247; Marina Kunke, *Nomadenstämme in Persien im 18. und 19. Jahrhundert* (Berlin: K. Schwarz, 1991), pp. 132–144.

[30] Röhrborn, *Provinzen*, pp. 73–88.

[31] Minorsky, *Tadhkirat al-mulūk*, pp. 44, 112; Rudi Matthee, *Persia in Crisis: Safavid Decline and the Fall of Isfahan* (London: I. B. Tauris, 2012), pp. 143, 227.

Safavid Shahs and the Qizilbash

Although Isma'il chose to institutionalize the tribal system, the dangers of Qizilbash power were clear from an early date. When he became shah in 1501, Isma'il proclaimed Twelver Shi'ism as the official religion of the realm, thus implicitly setting up a separate religious hierarchy outside Qizilbash control. In 1508 he pushed out the Sufi elders who had counseled him in Lahijan and continued to occupy high positions and began to delegate significant power to his highest Iranian bureaucrats, who over time became more powerful and grew more distant from the early religious and martial enthusiasm.[32] The central post of *wakīl* – deputy to the shah – went to an Iranian, as did for a while the position of *amīr al-umarā*. While the office of *wakīl* was a central one, in the hands of an Iranian who had no independent military force, it remained vulnerable to the Turkmen emirs. The two Iranians who gained significant power in this position under Isma'il both came to bad ends due to the machinations of the Qizilbash.[33] Isma'il also acted to curtail the power of some of the most powerful *oymaqs* and their leaders by stripping them of their positions and replacing them with members of less powerful tribes.[34] However, he depended too heavily on the Qizilbash organization to risk destroying it.

If the Turkmen tribal elite had objected only to the concentration of power in the hands of an Iranian, Safavid politics might have remained relatively simple. However, most were equally unwilling to allow preeminence to one of their own. In the absence of a strong shah, tribal rivalries quickly became murderous. Shah Isma'il's death in 1524, leaving the throne to his ten-year-old son Tahmasp, precipitated the first major tribal contest, within which Tahmasp was little more than a pawn. Safavid succession struggles were numerous, complicated and bloody, and they left the realm vulnerable to outside threats from the Ottomans and the Uzbeks on their borders. Instead of detailing each succession struggle individually, I will present here a simplified account of the contest at Shah Isma'il's death to serve as an example of *oymaq* politics.

During most of Isma'il's reign, the Ustajlu had been the most powerful of the *oymaqs*, holding the important office of *qurchibashi*, commander of the Shah's guard regiment. Two other *oymaqs* also had very significant power: the Shamlu and the Tekkelu. At Tahmasp's accession his tutor, Div Sultan of the Rumlu tribe, claimed the position of regent and gathered support from most emirs of the Rumlu, Tekkelu and Dhu'l Qadr, who were all eager to weaken the hold of the Ustajlu. Undistracted by

---

[32] Mitchell, *Practice of Politics*, pp. 19–52.   [33] Aubin, "L'avènement," pp. 115–118.
[34] Roger Savory, *Iran under the Safavids* (Cambridge: Cambridge University Press, 1980), pp. 50–51.

threats on the border and Uzbek depredations in Khorasan, the great *oymaq* emirs devoted themselves wholeheartedly to the internal struggle for power.[35] The first round went to Div Sultan and his allies, notably the Tekkelu. They successfully pushed most of the Ustajlu out of Tabriz, killed two leading Ustajlu emirs and expropriated some of the Ustajlu lands (*tiyuls*).[36]

The tide turned in 1531, however, when the Shamlu and most of the other *oymaqs* united against the Tekkelu, joined by Shah Tahmasp, who was eager to assert some personal power. The Tekkelu lost many of their positions and large numbers were killed; the Shamlu and returning Ustajlu now shared power, with their emirs as regents.[37] Neither external nor internal peace resulted. While the Tekkelu were being attacked, one of their emirs took refuge with the Ottomans, whom he encouraged against the Safavids. In 1533–1534 the Ottoman army took Bitlis, Tabriz, and all of Arab Iraq. In 1535 the Uzbeks mounted a major invasion of Khorasan, bringing Herat into chaos. Shah Tahmasp was now approaching twenty, and he began to assert his power. In 1533 he put Sultan Husayn Shamlu to death; this is considered his emergence as a true ruler. In 1536 he assembled his armies, marched to Khorasan, and pushed out the Uzbeks.[38]

After this it is not surprising to find Shah Tahmasp eager to curb the military power of the Qizilbash. He set out to create new centers of power to balance the might of the *oymaqs*. The Shah's personal corps, the *qurchi*, was expanded to approximately 5,000 troops. These soldiers owed allegiance to their commander rather than the chiefs of their tribes, and in 1533 leadership was taken away from tribal chiefs. Tahmasp also campaigned in the Caucasus and brought back captives to serve as soldiers. These were known as *ghulām* – translated as page or slave – but they could hold significant power and retained ties to their families and native regions.[39] With these measures, Tahmasp succeeded in concentrating power in his own hands, but he did not destroy the tribal system or disengage it from military and provincial administration. Instead, he added new power centers which joined the struggle for control at his death in 1576. There were even more contestants this time, with Georgian *ghulāms* and dynastic women along with the major *oymaqs*. The contest lasted almost uninterrupted through the reigns of

[35] Dickson, "Sháh Ṭahmásb," pp. 18, 52–66; Haneda, *Le châh,* pp. 170, 178–179.
[36] Savory, *Iran under the Safavids,* pp. 52–54; Dickson, "Sháh Ṭahmásb," pp. 67–68.
[37] Dickson, "Sháh Ṭahmásb," pp. 197–201.
[38] Savory, *Iran under the Safavids,* pp. 55–56, 61; Dickson, "Sháh Ṭahmásb," pp. 200–202, 265–295, 340–357.
[39] Haneda, *Le châh,* pp. 168–180; Savory, *Iran under the Safavids,* pp. 64–66.

Tahmasp's two successors, Isma'il II (1576) and Muhammad Khudabanda (1578–1588). In 1587–1588 Murshid Quli Khan Ustajlu took advantage of an Uzbek invasion to engineer the abdication of Shah Muhammad and the enthronement of Muhammad's son 'Abbas, making himself *wakil*.[40]

The reign of Shah 'Abbas is considered the defining moment of the Safavid dynasty and early modern Iran. He is remembered for his patronage of art and trade and likewise for his centralizing policies, which he pursued with ruthless cruelty. By the time he was enthroned, 'Abbas was sixteen years old; in his world that meant he had reached the age of self-assertion, and he moved quickly first against his *wakil*, and then against other tribal powers.

Shah 'Abbas is credited with the decisive shift of the Safavid power structure away from tribal power towards central control on three fronts: political, religious and economic. He used several stratagems – the movement of populations, the introduction of new military personnel, and the transformation of state land into crown land. The artillery corps and the *qurchi* regiment became a larger proportion of the total army.[41] In times of need, 'Abbas continued to call upon loyal elements to come to his aid under the rubrick of Shahsevan (those who love the shah) and he gave this title also to some of the nomads fleeing to his kingdom from Ottoman repression.[42] 'Abbas's best-known initiative was the promotion of *ghulāms*, mostly of Caucasian Christian provenance. By the end of his reign, many of the great provinces were governed by *ghulāms*, while others had *qurchi* governors – governorships no longer belonged to the same tribe over generations.[43] However the *ghulāms* and their families could also become powerful; an example is the Georgian Allahverdi Khan, who commanded a large army and became master of much of southern Iran where he passed power on to his own children.[44]

Tahmasp had attempted to weaken tribal structures and 'Abbas carried this policy further. In a number of cases, he put *ghulāms* in charge of tribal sections when "there was no suitable tribal leader available."[45] Tribes were also broken up by the practice of forced migration. Nomads were sometimes moved in order to install them as a military population in a threatened region; as smaller groups, away from their place of origin,

---

[40] Savory, *Iran under the Safavids*, pp. 70–75.
[41] Minorsky, *Tadhkirat al-mulūk*, pp. 32–33; Haneda, *Le châh*, pp. 184–197.
[42] Tapper, *Frontier Nomads*, pp. 36–37, 49–51, 83–87.
[43] Röhrborn, *Provinzen*, pp. 29–33; Haneda, *Le châh*, pp. 206–207.
[44] Rudi Matthee, "Relations between the Center and the Periphery in Safavid Iran: The Western Borderlands v. the Eastern Frontier Zone," *The Historian* (2015), pp. 435–436.
[45] Röhrborn, *Provinzen*, p. 31; Minorsky, *Tadhkirat al-mulūk*, pp. 16–18.

they were expected to remain loyal to the Safavids. Some populations were transferred as punishment for misdeeds.[46] In 1596–1597 Shah 'Abbas ordered a massacre of the Tekkelu *oymaq*, which he blamed for offenses that included participation in a recent uprising in Mazandaran. He ordered that every Tekkelu found anywhere should be killed by the governor of the province concerned.[47]

One of the most important changes introduced by Shah 'Abbas was the conversion of large quantities of state land into crown land. It was state lands which provided *tiyuls*, grants of land with income granted to commanders and governors. Crown lands on the other hand belonged to the dynasty; thus the income they produced financed the sovereign directly. They were garrisoned by court regiments rather than by the Qizilbash *oymaq* troops and were put under a vizier rather than a governor.[48] On the religious front, likewise, 'Abbas continued earlier policies to reduce Qizilbash influence. Shah Tahmasp had twice performed public repentance in which he ceremoniously dropped practices against the shari'a, including the consumption of wine, an important part of Qizilbash feasting. Abbas distanced the government further from the Qizilbash, ensconcing the Twelver Shi'ite 'ulama in positions of power.[49]

The dynasty's moves against Qizilbash power continued after the death of Shah 'Abbas in 1666. Crown lands grew at the expense of state lands as the *tiyuls* of commanders were expropriated. However the Safavid shahs continued to depend on the Qizilbash organization, which still provided new military recruits from Anatolia where the Safavids retained a loyal following.[50] Although they turned many provinces into crown lands, the Safavid shahs retained the older system on the borders where the state was most threatened, and indeed settled nomad tribes in these areas.[51] We can see the dilemma facing the Safavids in another move which served to weaken the Turkmen tribes: the signing of a treaty with the Ottomans at

[46] Hirotake Maeda, "The Forced Migrations and Reorganization of the Regional Order in the Caucasus by Safavid Iran: Preconditions and Developments Described by Fazli Khuzani," in *Reconstruction and Interaction of Slavic Eurasia and Its Neighboring Worlds, in Slavic Eurasian Studies*, ed. Ieda Osamu and Uyama Tomohiko (Hokkaido: Research Center, Hokkaido University, 2006), pp. 247–252; John R. Perry, "Forced Migration in Iran during the Seventeenth and Eighteenth Centuries," *Iranian Studies* 8 (1975), pp. 205–208.

[47] Perry, "Forced Migration," pp. 206–208; Szuppe, "Kinship Ties," pp. 94–95.

[48] Roemer, "The Safavid Period," p. 269; Bert Fragner, "Social and Internal Economic Affairs," in *Cambridge History of Iran. The Timurid and Safavid Periods*, ed. Peter Jackson and Laurence Lockhart (Cambridge: Cambridge University Press, 1986), pp. 522–523.

[49] Mitchell, *Practice of Politics*, pp. 69, 110; Babayan, *Mystics, Monarchs*, pp. 351–352, 362–364.

[50] Floor, "Khalifeh al-Kholafa," pp. 70–73; Karakaya-Stump, "Subjects of the Sultan," pp. 182–183.

[51] Matthee, *Persia in Crisis*, pp. 27–47, 142.

Zuhab in 1639. With this agreement the Safavids gave up several western regions and implicitly acknowledged Ottoman military superiority. The consequent reduction in military forces did indeed diminish the role that the Qizilbash played in politics, but it did so at the expense of Safavid power in general.[52]

Shah 'Abbas achieved great success during his reign, but he set the dynasty on a course which bought centralization at the price of weakness, and by moving nomad groups to the borders he actually contributed to the resurgence of local tribal power. The new crown lands were ruthlessly exploited through governors and tax farmers whose tenure was kept short to prevent the formation of new power centers. Unlike the *oymaq* chiefs who had held hereditary *tiyuls* and therefore had a long-term interest in the land, the new officials often bought their office and had to recoup their expenses quickly.[53] Many scholars have presented the Safavid move against tribal power and towards centralization as a success, citing the reduced power of the Qizilbash. However, we need to distinguish the position of the major Qizilbash *oymaqs* as a force within the state from the strength of nomads and tribes in general.[54] The history of the eighteenth century clearly shows the fragility of Safavid centralization and the continued power of pastoralists in Iran.

After the reign of Shah 'Abbas, the largest Safavid *oymaqs* did play a smaller part; the Ustajlu, Rumlu, and Turkman largely disappear from the histories, as do the Dhu'l Qadr and the Mawsillu, who had previously held significant regional power, while the Tekkelu and Shamlu appear to have survived in a reduced position.[55] Two of the original Qizilbash *oymaq*s, the Qajars and the Afshars, gained strength in the later Safavid period. The Afshars became strongly ensconced around Mashhad in Khorasan and in Kerman, while the Qajars retained some territory in Azerbaijan, as well as Mazandaran and Marw. Both tribes undoubtedly benefited from their position on the borders of the realm. Other nomadic powers which had never been part of the Qizilbash increased their standing. The Luts retained their autonomy, and we see the rise of the Bakhtiyari section, whose leaders had become governors under Shah Tahmasp.[56] In return for an annual payment in mules, Bakhtiyari governors had the right to collect taxes in Dizful and Shushtar. In the later

---

[52] Matthee, *Persia in Crisis*, pp. 117–118.
[53] Matthee, *Persia in Crisis*, p. 149; John Foran, "The Long Fall of the Safavid Dynasty: Moving beyond the Standard View," *International Journal of Middle East Studies* 24 (1992), pp. 286–287.
[54] See Matthee, "Relations."
[55] John R. Perry, *Karīm Khān Zand: A History of Iran, 1747–1779* (Chicago, IL: University of Chicago Press, 1979), p. 19.
[56] Matthee, *Persia in Crisis*, p. 149.

Safavid period they were the major suppliers of nomad products to the capital city of Isfahan, and they were a valuable source of soldiers in the final struggles of the dynasty.[57]

Nomadic groups on the borders also began both to raid and to enter into the politics of the Safavid state. Two groups of tribal and partially nomadic people on disputed borders – the Kurds on the Ottoman border, and the Afghans on the borders of the Mughal Empire – expanded and organized under the Safavids. By the seventeenth century they had developed an indigenous literature and identity, along with stronger internal political structures. During the last three decades of Safavid rule raids by these peoples were constant and destructive, reaching well inside the borders.

Ottomans and Nomads

While the Safavids incorporated both tribalism and nomadism into their government structure, the Ottomans pursued the opposite course, at least to the extent that they were able to do so. In Chapter 6 we ended the Ottoman narrative in 1481, at the death of Mehmet II – the conqueror of Constantinople and creator of a more imperial, centralized state. Nomads continued to make up a significant proportion of the empire's population in the European province of Rumelia and in Anatolia, but they were increasingly incorporated into provincial governance, and were subject to taxation and conscription. At the same time the Ottomans continued to move eastward to take over territories in which nomads were more numerous, more independent and more powerful.

In 1485, Mehmed's successor Beyezid II (1481–1512) began a struggle with the Mamluks for the control of eastern Anatolia. The greatest problem was the Qizilbash, who owed their primary allegiance to the Safavids; obedience to the Ottomans was thus provisional at best. It was Selim I (1512–1520) who really expanded the nomad presence within the Ottoman Empire, though he was no friend to pastoralists. After defeating Isma'il at Chaldiran in 1514, Selim pushed the Safavids out of most of eastern Anatolia, then in 1516–1517 he took over the Mamluk sultanate and won the allegiance of most of the Kurdish principalities on the Iranian border. His successor, Suleiman Kanuni (1520–1566), added Baghdad and Iraq and pushed the border into Azerbaijan, though these territories remained contested. The government set out to incorporate its new nomad subjects into the state but did not find the task an easy one. In

---

[57] Gene R. Garthwaite, *Khans and Shahs: A Documentary Analysis of the Bakhtiyari in Iran* (Cambridge: Cambridge University Press, 1983), pp. 49–51.

1522 the Dhu'l Qadr confederation was disbanded, leading to six years of rebellion in their territory. Selim deliberately repressed the Qizilbash; all known members were registered, a number were massacred, and some others imprisoned. Large numbers crossed into Azerbaijan to serve the Safavids, while many of those who remained in Anatolia and Diyar Bakr still considered themselves under the authority of the Safavid *khalīfa*.[58]

The Ottomans brought most of their new nomad populations into their administrative system. Syria, eastern Anatolia and much of the Kurdish region were surveyed shortly after the conquest and organized under the existing *timar/sanjak* system. Egypt, Baghdad, Basra and most of the Arabian Peninsula remained outside. The *timar* was an institution similar to the *iqta*': grants of land revenue in return for service. *Timar* holders had to appear on campaign with armed cavalries calculated according to the size of their holding. *Timars* were organized into sub-provinces, known as *sanjaks*, and put under military officials. In conquered territories, the Ottomans distributed land to their own servitors but also granted military status – including the right to hold a *timar* – to the local elites, including pastoralists; this was done in Karaman, the territories of the Dhu'l Qadr, and the smaller Kurdish principalities, as well as parts of Syria.[59] In population registers nomads were distinguished from settled populations, each subject to a different set of taxes. While settled communities remained within one *sanjak*, nomads who migrated between summer and winter pastures often crossed borders.

Although the Ottoman administration was theoretically consistent, in practice it conformed to local conditions. Syria was within the *timar* system, but government control faded out as one progressed into the desert. Some nomad tribes appear not to have been assigned to a *timar*, owing their taxes directly to the governor or the central government – if they paid at all. Others were simply not included in the registers. The Bedouin regions of 'Ajlun in Transjordan, parts of Hawran, and Tadmur in northern Syria appear not to have been directly under Ottoman fiscal control.[60]

For most nomad regions the sixteenth century was a period of increasing incorporation and control, much of which was reversed in the following centuries.[61] The seventeenth century was a time of stress for the

---

[58] Roemer, "The Safavid Period," pp. 221–223; Floor, "*Khalifeh al-Kholafa*," pp. 64, 71–72.

[59] Halil Inalcik, "Tīmār," *EI* 2nd ed.; Bruce Masters, "Egypt and Syria under the Ottomans," in *The New Cambridge History of Islam, vol. 2. The Western Islamic World Eleventh to Eighteenth Centuries*, ed. Maribel Fierro (Cambridge: Cambridge University Press, 2010), pp. 415–416.

[60] Wolf D. Hütteroth, "Ottoman Administration of the Desert Frontier in the Sixteenth Century," *Asian and African Studies* 19 (1985).

[61] Masters, "Egypt and Syria under the Ottomans," pp. 411–421; Bernard Haykel, "Western Arabia and Yemen during the Ottoman Period," in *New Cambridge History of Islam, vol. 2. The Western Islamic World Eleventh to Eighteenth Centuries*, ed. Maribel Fierro (Cambridge:

Ottomans. Control over the desert and the Jazira was threatened by the migration of Bedouin confederations from the Arabian Peninsula. The most important was the 'Anaza, which had become preeminent in the Najd region of the Arabian Peninsula in the sixteenth century, but in the seventeenth century was challenged by new arrivals. From the middle of the century, groups of the 'Anaza began to move into the Syrian desert where they replaced the Mawali tribe, which had accepted Ottoman payment and kept peace in the Syrian desert.[62] As the 'Anaza moved into their new territories, they competed for pasture and the control of trade routes, causing increased disorder among the tribes and the movement of nomads into both eastern and central Anatolia.

The Ottomans attempted to increase their control over nomads, sometimes openly and violently, and sometimes more subtly. Ottoman policies encouraged the expansion of settled agriculture, and farmers began to take over marginal lands including nomad pasture. However, the 1590s saw the onset of the Little Ice Age with exceptional cold and drought, affecting both agriculture and pastoralism. The change in climate may have contributed to the outbreak of the destructive Jelali Rebellion in Anatolia, which lasted from 1596–1610. These factors, along with the increase in population due to competition over pasture in northern Syria, brought a wave of nomad movement from eastern Anatolia westwards into central Anatolia, and a dramatic increase in nomad pillaging of farmland, particularly in the marginal lands at the edge of the steppe, some of which had been their pastures. This situation is reported through much of Anatolia, the Jazira and northern Syria.[63]

In reaction, the Ottomans attempted policies of forcible settlement, military conscription and heavy taxation, causing more westward movement. Anatolian population and agriculture were slow to recover, with much land remaining in nomad hands, and at the end of the seventeenth century the government began a concerted program of nomad settlement, moving nomads to new lands and demanding that they cultivate them. At about the same time, a new policy of conscripting populations seen as unsettled – including both nomads and brigands – to man garrison fortresses served to suppress pastoral migration.[64] Another Ottoman policy, less coercive, but more constant and pervasive, was the move to

Cambridge University Press 2010), pp. 441–445; Tom Sinclair, "The Ottoman Arrangements for the Tribal Principalities of the Lake Van Region of the Sixteenth Century," *International Journal of Turkish Studies* 9, no. 1–2 (2003), pp. 140–143.

[62] Uwaidah M. al Juhany, *Najd before the Salafi Reform Movement* (Reading, UK: Ithaca Press, 2002), pp. 65, 69.

[63] Sam White, *The Climate of Rebellion in the Early Modern Ottoman Empire* (Cambridge: Cambridge University Press, 2011), pp. 42–43, 70–72, 130–132, 229–242.

[64] Reşat Kasaba, *A Moveable Empire: Ottoman Nomads, Migrants, and Refugees* (Seattle: University of Washington Press, 2009), pp. 53–54, 65–68; Halil Inalcik, "The Yürüks,

register and control summer and winter pastures. Although it was recognized that nomad groups might have to cross *sanjak* lines in their migrations, the government preferred to keep them within one administrative area and above all tried to avoid variation in the use of pasture. These limitations sometimes caused hardship for pastoralists and for the leaders attempting to maintain control within nomad regions.[65] Over time, the policy undoubtedly favored sedentarization, and at the end of the seventeenth century the Ottomans made several direct attempts to settle nomads on the land.[66]

Tribes and Nomads along the Ottoman-Iranian Border

While the Ottomans pushed for sedentarization in internal regions, nomadism continued strong along the eastern frontier. In the centuries that followed the rise of the Safavids and the Ottoman conquest of Syria, the border between the two states shifted back and forth over the same region, creating a space for autonomous tribal powers of pastoral or mixed economy. In their contests over the valuable Gulf port of Basra, the region of Baghdad, and the northern Euphrates region, the two powers depended heavily on local tribes. The border region stretched from the Caucasus to the Persian Gulf, through largely mountainous territory to marsh and desert towards the south. Kurds and Turkmen were the primary border population in the north; in the middle the Iranian Lurs populated the central Zagros region, while Arab tribes controlled significant sections of the southern Jazira and Mesopotamia. In the south, Khuzistan, also known as 'Arabistan, had a mixed population, with some Lurs and Turkmen Afshar, and a larger population of Arab tribes. State control over the frontier region was partial at best. On the Safavid side, the territory was organized in semi-autonomous *wilāyats*, ruled by largely hereditary local leaders. The five *wilāyats* which remained to the late Safavid period were all along this frontier: 'Arabistan, Lur, the Bakhtiyari territory, Kurdistan and Georgia.[67] On the Ottoman side likewise, the state had little actual control and depended heavily on tribal leaders who switched allegiance at will.[68]

Their Origins, Expansion and Economic Role," in *Oriental Carpet and Textile Studies*, ed. R. Pinner and H. Inalcik (London: HALI, 1986), pp. 46–48.

[65] Inalcik, "The Yürüks," pp. 49–50; Rhoads Murphy, "Some Features of Nomadism in the Ottoman Empire: A Survey Based on Tribal Census and Judicial Appeal Documentation from Archives in Istanbul and Damascus," *Journal of Turkish Studies* 8 (1984), pp. 195–196.

[66] Kasaba, *Moveable Empire*, pp. 72–76.   [67] Matthee, *Persia in Crisis*, pp. 143–144.

[68] Rudi Matthee, "The Safavid-Ottoman Frontier: Iraq-i Arab as Seen by the Safavids," in *Ottoman Borderlands: Issues, Personalities and Political Changes*, ed. Kemal Karpat and

Several groups expanded their power in this period. It was particularly decisive for the Kurds, who had formed several states before, but now developed a consciousness of themselves as a people. By this time the name seems to have come to denote the Kurds more or less as we understand them today – as the tribal people of what is now Kurdistan. The first source written by a Kurd and dealing specifically with Kurdish history is the *Sharafnāma*, written in the late sixteenth century by Sharaf al-Din Khan Bitlisi (d. 1603–1604). The *Sharafnāma* first gives a history of Kurdish dynasties, and then proceeds to a broader history of Muslim dynasties, in which the author includes his own lifetime from personal experience. In this work the term Kurd appears for the ethnic group, and there is a clear sense of a common culture and history.[69]

The Kurdish region was important to the Ottomans as a buffer separating the Safavids from their Qizilbash followers in Anatolia. The Ottomans incorporated a number of principalities, some of which enjoyed the trappings of independence: minting their own coins and pronouncing the *khuṭba* in the name of the local ruler. Despite a sense of common identity, the Kurds seem to have had little desire for a central Kurdish power. Most of the region was organized as *hükümet* – vassal states – but it was also incorporated into the *sanjak* system, with leading families as *sanjak beys*, holding the right of appointment of some subordinate officials. Tribes remained intact, but the migration patterns were restricted to the *sanjak*. The rearrangement of migration patterns caused some predictable hardship.[70]

The Ottomans were prevented from using coercive techniques against the Kurds by the presence of the Safavids on the western border. In general, the Ottomans were the greater power, but some Kurdish principalities chose a Safavid alliance, especially during the rule of strong shahs such as Shah 'Abbas. When campaigning in Safavid territory, the Ottoman army depended on Kurdish support for local information, transport, diplomacy and auxiliary troops. Both the Safavids and the Ottomans used Kurdish spies to provide information about the other side; some Kurds worked as double agents, informing on both sides.[71]

Robert W. Zens (Madison: University of Wisconsin Press, 2003); Rudi Matthee, "Between Arabs, Turks and Iranians: The Town of Basra, 1600–1700," *Bulletin of the School of Oriental and African Studies* 69, no. 1 (2006).

[69] Stephan Connermann, "Volk, Ethnie oder Stamm? Die Kurden aus mamlükischer Sicht," *Asien und Africa. Beiträge des Zentrums für asiatische und afrikanische Studien der Christian-Albrechts-Universität zu Kiel* 8 (2004), pp. 27–28.

[70] Sinclair, "Ottoman Arrangements"; Bruinessen, *Agha, Shaikh, and State*, pp. 168, 171.

[71] Mustafa Dehqan and Genç Vural, "Kurds as Spies: Information-Gathering on the 16th-Century Ottoman-Safavid Frontier," *Acta Orientalia Academiae Scientiarum Hungaricae* 71, no. 2 (2018), pp. 197–216.

Their choice of affiliation and the usefulness of their services gave Kurdish princes and tribal leaders new leverage, which they used to increase their autonomy at the level of tribe and principality. It is likely also that nomadism increased in the area, due to the scorched-earth tactics the Safavids used against the Ottoman advance.[72] Throughout the period of this chapter, the Kurds remained a border population, self-consciously separate from the powers on their borders, proud of their martial prowess, but divided in allegiance.

Decentralization in the Eighteenth Century

As we have seen, border powers gained strength in the seventeenth century. Both the Safavid and the Ottoman governments undertook attempts at centralization, but the end of the century found their central governments in a weakened position. There was a rise in autonomous regional powers, including nomad tribes, some taking power in their own name and many others serving in the armies of new warlords. The most spectacular of these last was the Turkmen leader Nadir Shah Afshar, who seized power in Iran after the end of the Safavid dynasty.

By the end of the seventeenth century the weakness of the Safavids had become clear. The army was incapable of defending the government from either internal or external threats. Neither the military nor the tribes settled on the border were receiving the money owed to them and they could not be relied on to fight when asked. There were raids from the mountain Lezghis of the Caucasus, from the Turkmen on the northeastern frontier, the Uzbeks, and the nomadic Baluch on the southeastern frontier. Subject peoples rebelled, particularly those in border regions: the people of Kerman, the Afghans of Qandahar, the nomads of Khuzistan, and the Lur of southern central Iran. When the Ghilzay Afghans took Isfahan in 1722, their victory was due less to their strength than to the weakness of the Safavids.[73]

The Afghans were a partially nomadic group that had long inhabited the border between Iran and the Subcontinent. Over several centuries they had increased their territory, while the rivalry between the Safavid and Mughal states had given them a strategic position and involved their leaders in the politics of both states. In 1722 the Ghilzay Afghans invaded

---

[72] Rhoads Murphy, "The Resumption of Ottoman-Safavid Border Conflict, 1603–1638: Effects of Border Destabilization on the Evolution of Tribe-State Relations," in *Shifts and Drifts in Nomad-Sedentary Relations*, ed. Stefan Leder and Bernard Streck (Wiesbaden: Reichert, 2005), pp. 307–323.

[73] Matthee, *Persia in Crisis*, pp. 206–41. For a divergent view, see Newman, *Safavid Iran*, pp. 104–106, 116.

and took Isfahan. They followed their victory with a campaign through much of Iran, but their armies met continued resistance. Unfortunately for Iran, the fall of the Safavids left behind several evenly matched powers, whose leaders fought for control through the rest of the century. A number of Baluch and Afghan groups were active in Iran, and several internal tribes also aimed for preeminence, most notably the Qajars, centered primarily in Mazandaran and Astarabad, the Afshars of Khorasan, and the Lur tribes between Isfahan, Khuzistan and Shiraz.

After the fall of Isfahan to the Afghans, most opponents gathered around the Safavid prince Tahmasp, son of the last reigning Safavid monarch, who found support among several nomad groups – Bakhtiyari, Shahsevan and Qajar.[74] After 1726, Nadir Afshar, whose tribe was centered in western Khorasan, emerged as Shah Tahmasp's most important ally. For the next six years he campaigned alongside Tahmasp, while the balance of power between them gradually changed. In 1729 they retook Isfahan from the Ghilzay Afghans. In 1732 Nadir Shah deposed Tahmasp, and in 1736 he felt secure enough to claim the title of shah for himself.[75]

Nadir Shah was a man in a hurry. After deposing Tahmasp he campaigned against the Ottomans and took Baghdad, then headed to Azerbaijan and the Caucasus. In 1736 he moved southeast, conquering Qandahar, then Delhi in March 1738. From there he proceeded to take Kabul, then Sind. By the fall of 1740 he was attacking Bukhara and Khiva. Like the earlier conqueror Tamerlane, Nadir did not attempt to retain his most distant conquests; neither India nor Central Asia became part of his realm.[76] Unlike Temür, however, he failed to consolidate his gains to form a working state.

Nadir's army was both modern and traditional. He expanded the guard regiment and created an effective artillery corps with modern firearms. He mustered an extraordinarily large army, considering the condition of his realm. In addition to peasants and the tribal groups within Iran, he enlisted Afghans, Baluch, Uzbeks, Turkmen, and also Lezghis from the Caucasus. Nonetheless, the basic structure of his army resembled that of the Safavids. The cavalry still made up most of the army and remained tribally organized. Indeed, Nadir used group rivalries within the army to promote greater zeal in battle.[77]

---

[74] Newman, *Safavid Iran*, pp. 124–125.

[75] Peter Avery, "Nādir Shāh and the Afsharid Legacy," in *Cambridge History of Iran, vol. 7. From Nadir Shah to the Islamic Republic*, ed. Gavin Hambly, Peter Avery, Charles Melville (Cambridge: Cambridge University Press, 1991), pp. 29–31.

[76] "Nādir Shāh and the Afsharid Legacy," pp. 31–42.

[77] Michael Axworthy, "The Army of Nader Shah," *Iranian Studies* 40, no. 5 (2007), pp. 639–643.

Nadir's conquests were ruthless and ruinously expensive. He himself came from a nomad background and gave prominence to nomadic tribes in his army, but his reign brought hardship to nomads, just as it did to the settled population. His campaigns were interrupted by frequent resistance movements, especially among pastoralists. In October 1732 the Bakhtiyari rebelled; at the end of 1733 Nadir had to raise the siege of Baghdad to put down an uprising in Khuzistan led by Muhammad Khan Baluch.[78] Rebellions were put down with violence, the leaders were usually killed along with large numbers of tribesmen, and tribes were often further punished with the deportation of several thousand households to Khorasan. Here they were resettled, and many conscripted into the army.[79] This practice served to break up recalcitrant tribes while gaining manpower for the army and population for Khorasan.

By 1744 the population was showing acute disaffection and Nadir Shah was displaying signs of insanity, becoming a danger to his associates as well as his subjects.[80] In 1747 he was murdered by several of his closest followers. Whereas many of the populations that Shah ʿAbbas relocated had remained in their new territories, at Nadir's death there was a general exodus as his commanders left to start fighting on their own account. Though for a few years he had united much of the nomad population within his armies, Nadir left Iran poorer and more fragmented that he had found it.

In many ways Nadir Shah was a transitional figure, combining Safavid rule through tribal powers with the expansive conquests associated with the nomads of the steppe. In the realm of ideology he likewise marks a combination of traditions. The four great regional empires which had taken over the central Islamic lands were all connected to the Turkic and Mongolian steppe heritage, which continued to influence their worldview.[81] Shah Ismaʿil had risen to power and led his early conquests as a messianic figure, and his successors inherited some of his religious charisma. With the distancing of the Qizilbash, however, the Safavids sought out elements of legitimation from the steppe tradition, and they had turned not to Chinggis Khan but to the Muslim Tamerlane. Under Shah ʿAbbas, historians claimed that Temür had paid his respects to the early

---

[78] Michael Axworthy, *The Sword of Persia: Nader Shah, from Tribal Warrior to Conquering Tyrant* (London: I. B. Tauris 2006), pp. 107–111, 127–130, 142–143.

[79] Perry, "Forced Migration," pp. 208–210.

[80] Axworthy, *Sword of Persia*, pp. 258–263.

[81] Cornell H. Fleischer, *Bureaucrat and Intellectual in the Ottoman Empire: The Historian Mustafa Âli (1541–1600)* (Princeton, NJ: Princeton University Press, 1986), pp. 275–279, 283–286.

Safavid shaykhs, and indeed had granted them *waqf* land in almost all areas of his dominion – thus legitimating Safavid rule over the former Timurid realm.[82] Throughout the seventeenth century, legends of Temür's connection to the Safavids proliferated: we have an account of a prophetic dream narrated by the Imam 'Ali to the head of the Safavid order, and of the rediscovery of Temür's sword, supposedly given to Shah 'Abbas's successor, Shah Safi.[83]

Nadir Shah used both religious and Turco-Mongolian sources of legitimation, emphasizing ties with the Safavid house, and likewise with Tamerlane.[84] Just as Temür had imitated the actions of Chinggis Khan, Nadir recalled Temür's career in his choice of regions to conquer and the brutality of his methods. He claimed Iraq as a territory that had belonged to Temür; he also named his grandsons after members of the Timurid house. A dynastic chronicle recounts a story offering supernatural evidence that Nadir should be seen as Temür's successor. While camped near the fortress of Kalat, where Temür had achieved a significant victory, Nadir awoke at night and noticed a glow on the mountainside. Seeking this out he discovered a hidden treasure and an inscription identifying it as having belonged to Temür and stating that he who arrived there would be the *Ṣāḥib Qirān* (Lord of the Fortunate Conjunction), a title that had been held earlier by Temür.[85]

Nadir Shah introduced a major innovation in his attempt to reformulate Turkic identity, erasing the distinction between the western Turks and those who shared the legacy of the Mongol Empire. The term "Turkmen" had previously denoted the Oghuz; now Nadir used the term to denote all Turks as inheritors of sovereignty. To justify his stance and claim a common heritage with the Ottomans, he invoked the history of Chinggis Khan:

In the time of Chingiz Khan, the leaders of the Turkman tribes, who had left the land of Turan and migrated to Iran and Anatolia, were said to be all of one stock and one lineage. At that time, the exalted ancestor of the dynasty of the ever-increasing state [the Ottoman Empire] headed to Anatolia and our ancestor settled in the provinces of Iran. Since these lineages are interwoven and

---

[82] Maria Szuppe, "L'évolution de l'image de Timour et des Timourides dans l'historiographie safavide, XVIe–XVIIIe siècles," in *L'héritage timouride Iran – Asie centrale – Inde XVe–XVIIIe siècles*, ed. Maria Szuppe, *Cahiers d'Asie centrale* ¾ (Tashkent; Aix-en-Provence, 1997), pp. 315–322; Sholeh Alysia Quinn, *Historical Writing during the Reign of Shah 'Abbas: Ideology, Imitation, and Legitimacy in Safavid Chronicles* (Salt Lake City: University of Utah Press, 2000), pp. 45, 85.

[83] Quinn, *Historical Writing*, pp. 87–89; Szuppe, "L'évolution," pp. 322–324.

[84] Ernest Tucker, *Nadir Shah's Quest for Legitimacy in Post-Safavid Iran* (Gainesville: University Press of Florida, 2006), p. 13; Axworthy, *Sword of Persia*, p. 281.

[85] Tucker, *Nadir Shah's Quest*, pp. 9–10, 13, 37–38, 68–75.

interconnected, it is hoped that when his royal highness learns of them, he will give royal consent to the establishment of peace between [us].[86]

In a letter presented to the Ottomans after his assumption of the title of shah in 1736 Nadir claimed legitimacy simply as a Turk, stating that "kingship is the ancestral right of the exalted Turkmen tribe."[87] Thus the rulers of the regional states – the Chinggisid khans of Khiva, the Timurid/Chinggisid Mughals, the Ottomans, and Nadir himself, all had equal legitimacy.

The Middle East in the Later Eighteenth Century

The second half of the eighteenth century saw the rise of new nomad powers in both Iran and the Ottoman Empire, as decentralization increased throughout the Middle East. Iran remained a battleground for fifteen years after Nadir Shah's death. Nadir Shah had moved populations within Iran and brought in troops from outside. Many of these, together with mountain and pastoral populations, remained politically active after his death. Several autonomous political regions emerged: Khorasan, where the Afshar dynasty survived as a minor power; northern Iran from Astarabad to Qazwin, dominated by the Qajars; and central and southern Iran, inhabited by the Lurs and eastern Kurds with the Bakhtiyari confederation as the major force. Struggles for power were closely intertwined as leaders tried both to assert control over their own regions and tribes, and to extend rule outward.

The first winner was Karim Khan of the small Zand tribe on the Luri-Kurdish border. In 1751 he became the preeminent leader among the Lurs, and by 1762 had taken most of southern and central Iran. Karim Khan had begun as the weakest of the contenders for power, and his success may have been due in part to the fact that the two most powerful groups, the Bakhtiyari and the Qajars, were split into warring factions more willing to ally with outside powers than with their internal rivals. Karim Khan made Shiraz his capital, and from 1762 until his death in 1779 he controlled a large part of Iran, from Khuzistan to Azerbaijan. He did not aspire to formal sovereignty, however, and for much of his reign ruled in the name of a Safavid puppet khan, presenting himself as "wakīl" – deputy.[88] The eastern territories – Sistan, Kerman and Khorasan – remained outside his domain, and the Caspian regions under the Qajars, though formally within the realm, never fully submitted to his rule.[89] Though he used considerable violence, Karim Khan allowed autonomy to the tribal powers under him, exerting control by

---

[86] Tucker, *Nadir Shah's Quest*, p. 37.   [87] Tucker, *Nadir Shah's Quest*, p. 39.
[88] Tucker, *Nadir Shah's Quest*, p. 110.
[89] John Perry, "The Zand Dynasty," in *The Cambridge History of Iran*, vol. 7, ed. Gavin Hambly et al. (Cambridge: Cambridge University Press), pp. 85, 95–96.

keeping members of the leadership as hostages at court and through occasional force. He did not develop a large, organized bureaucracy, but did promote trade, agriculture and city life, building up his capital at Shiraz. His reign provided a short respite for the population of Iran in the middle of a difficult century, but it did not transform political structures.[90] At Karim Khan's death, hostilities broke out again, as various members of the dynasty fought each other and other tribes gained power, most notably the Qajars, who eventually founded the dynasty which ruled Iran through the nineteenth century.

The second half of the eighteenth century was also a difficult period for the Ottoman Empire, which lost effective control of several regions, while nomad groups gained autonomy and importance. In Palestine, the Bedouin Zaydani family rose to power, particularly under the shaykh Zahir al-'Umar (1690–1775) who from about 1750 to his death expanded his power through northern Palestine, dominating the trade route to Damascus and the regions which had traditionally financed the pilgrimage caravans. He thus put the Hajj in jeopardy. He also conquered the port city of Acre, gaining control within the cotton trade.[91]

The most consequential event for the nomads of the Ottoman lands was the founding of the Wahhabi state on the Arabian Peninsula. In 1744–1745 the religious reformer Muhammad ibn 'Abd al-Wahhab allied with Muhammad al-Sa'ud, the *amīr* of the town of Diriyya in the Najd. Al-Sa'ud supported a *jihād* to spread the new doctrine, and in return became the secular leader of the community. Those who joined the community agreed to obey both the religious and the political leadership and to fight for the cause. Those who did not agree were subject to raiding.[92] The leadership of the Sa'udi state was settled, and the movement spread first to villages and towns; the nomads were slower to join and never became part of the ruling elite. However, by the 1780s nomad tribes had begun to enlist in campaigns of expansion which provided income for the Sa'udi state and enriched those who participated. Religious enthusiasm was likewise a factor, and some tribes converted to the Wahhabi doctrine. Unlike earlier confederations on the Peninsula, the Sa'udis imposed a regular tax – the *zakāt* – on the tribes under them and replaced many of the tribal leaders; nonetheless the social and political structure remained tribal and was not fundamentally changed.[93]

---

[90] Perry, "The Zand Dynasty," pp. 95–102.

[91] Eugene Rogan, *The Arabs: A History* (New York: Basic Books, 2009), pp. 45–49.

[92] Madawi al-Rasheed, *A History of Saudi Arabia* (Cambridge: Cambridge University Press, 2010), pp. 14–18.

[93] al-Rasheed, *A History*, p. 19; Alexei Vassiliev, *The History of Saudi Arabia* (London: Saqi Books, 1998), pp. 89–93, 112–126.

By the end of the eighteenth century the Wahhabis had taken the Holy Cities and destroyed much of the Ottoman hold on the Arabian Peninsula, and their impact was felt well beyond. Although some nomads accepted their leadership, others did not. Various sections of the great Shammar confederation chose different sides, and those who did not want to join the Wahhabis began to migrate first into Iraq and then into the Jazira. By the end of the century, they were strongly established in their new regions and largely autonomous.[94] Tribes from the Arab Peninsula also entered southern Iraq and the province of Baghdad, strengthening nomad power at the expense of the Mamluk emirs who ruled the province largely independent of Ottoman control. Despite numerous attacks on the tribes, the government was unable to dislodge them or to provide security on the routes by themselves.[95] Much of Iraq's hinterland was effectively under tribal and largely nomad control.

Social and Economic Conditions

In the early modern period, covered in this chapter, European travelers' accounts and trade documents begin to provide a fuller view of the life of nomads, revealing some of the everyday realities which are omitted in historical chronicles. In addition, for the Ottoman Empire rich government archives have survived that have not yet been fully exploited. Thus we can draw some general conclusions, though with the reservation that conditions differed from region to region. It is clear that in both the Safavid and the Ottoman domains, nomads made up a significant part of the population. For Safavid Iran we have no firm figures; scholars estimate the nomad population of Iran at the end of the Safavid period at 30 percent of the total, though some estimates are higher.[96] In the Ottoman Empire, tax records begin in the 1520s and note the percentage of population that was considered nomadic. In western and central Anatolia nomads were estimated at 16 to 17 percent; in southeastern Anatolia about 70 percent were registered as nomadic. For the Syrian and Iraqi provinces, we have figures from the latter part of the sixteenth century, showing about 36 percent for

---

[94] Bruce Masters, "Semi-autonomous Forces in the Arab Provinces," in *The Cambridge History of Turkey, vol. 3. The Later Ottoman Empire, 1603–1839*, ed. Suraiya N. Faroqhi (Cambridge: Cambridge University Press, 2006), p. 190; M. al-Rasheed, "Shammar," *EI* 2nd ed.

[95] Hala Mundhir Fattah, *The Politics of Regional Trade in Iraq, Arabia, and the Gulf, 1745–1900* (Albany: State University of New York Press, 1997), pp. 28–41.

[96] Willem M. Floor, *The Economy of Safavid Persia*, Iran-Turan Bd. 1 (Wiesbaden: Reichert, 2000), p. 8; Matthee, *Persia in Crisis*, p. 6; Kunke, *Nomadenstämme* p. 18.

Baghdad and Aleppo provinces, and about 32 percent for Basra.[97] Thus some Ottoman regions may have equaled or even surpassed the Safavid ratio of nomad to settled population.

Not surprisingly, nomads played a particularly crucial role in transport and trade – both regional and long distance. Camels were the most important animal for transport; they were used not only in caravans, but also often in delivering taxes paid in kind. Given that the annual pilgrimage caravans passing through the Syrian and Arabian deserts required up to 40,000 camels, we should recognize the huge numbers needed for trade and pilgrimage together. Nomads also played an important part in guiding caravans and in maintaining security on the roads.[98] The official pilgrimage caravans, crucial to the prestige of the Ottoman state, were heavily dependent on nomad services and cooperation. First of all, pilgrims required water when passing through the deserts of Syria and Arabia, and the Bedouins had to be persuaded to share this scarce resource with them. Second, supplies needed by pilgrims as they passed through barren terrain were usually transported by Bedouin and deposited in storehouses along the road. And finally, pilgrims always required an escort. In return for these services, tribes received remuneration, usually regular subsidies, and to ensure loyalty their shaykhs were often given insignia and titles.[99] The provisioning of the capital with sheep for meat and dairy products also depended in part on nomads. Most sheep came from the northern and western regions, but Anatolia was also an important source and was sometimes called upon for as many as 60,000 sheep at a time.[100]

In border and desert regions not fully incorporated into Ottoman government, administration was often in the hands of the tribal shaykhs who were responsible for maintaining order and imposing the law over their tribesmen. Tribes controlled recognized areas, known as their *dira*, within which they collected taxes and provided security. The tax they collected was called *khuwwa*; this is often translated as "protection money" but literally means brotherliness and implied some commonality of interest and identity. Tribes also collected tolls from travelers passing through their regions; these were also called *khuwwa*. *Khuwwa* should not be understood simply as a tax of the nomad on the settled. It was also paid

[97] Ömer Lûtfi Barkan, "Research on the Ottoman Fiscal Surveys," in *Studies in the Economic History of the Middle East from the Rise of Islam to the Present Day*, ed. Michael A. Cook (London: Oxford University Press, 1970), pp. 169–171.
[98] Halil Inalcik and Donald Quataert, *An Economic and Social History of the Ottoman Empire, 1300–1914* (Cambridge: Cambridge University Press, 1994), p. 39; Suraiya Faroqhi, *Pilgrims and Sultans: The Hajj under the Ottomans, 1517–1683* (London: I. B. Tauris 1996), p. 46.
[99] Faroqhi, *Pilgrims and Sultans*, pp. 6, 34, 43, 48, 54–56.
[100] White, *The Climate of Rebellion*, pp. 27–41, 48.

by weaker tribes to stronger ones, both of which might be nomads. Over time, smaller tribes within the *dīra* of powerful confederations such as the 'Anaza might become a part of the larger entity, with a genealogical link provided by a putative ancestor.[101] When governments expanded into such regions and attempted to monopolize the collection of taxes, nomads often retaliated by raiding.[102]

Nomads developed a reciprocal relationship with cities and towns in their regions. They required a market, while many cities depended directly on neighboring pastoral populations for meat and dairy products and sometimes for materials needed in the production of trade goods, notably wool and leather. Isfahan, Mosul, and Baghdad for instance had close market relations with nearby nomadic populations. Since cities could impose a tax on the sale of livestock, trade with nomads provided considerable income.[103] The presence of pastoralists thus could stimulate the development of regional trade centers. It is notable that when Nadir Shah moved nomads into Khorasan to develop the region, he created trading towns for them.[104] Several kinds of goods important to international trade depended on livestock products; for instance, Kerman traded in goat hair products, and in Anatolia wool carpets were a growing industry. We see tribal shaykhs active therefore in numerous aspects of trade, which was central to their livelihood. When no suitable market towns were available to them, shaykhs sometimes founded new settlements.[105] Some invested in trade themselves, acting as merchants while leaving the everyday care of herds to shepherds.[106] At a lower level, ordinary nomads sometimes participated independently in the economy as day laborers, both in manufacture and for public works. They had the advantage of being more mobile than peasants and could thus move seasonally.[107] In the Safavid realm, the Bakhtiyari were conscripted by Shah 'Abbas as laborers to link together two rivers near Isfahan; this work went on for years.[108]

---

[101] Juhany, *Najd*, pp. 69–70.

[102] Dina Rizk Khoury, *State and Provincial Society in the Ottoman Empire: Mosul, 1540–1834* (Cambridge: Cambridge University Press, 1997), pp. 23, 39; Fattah, *Politics*, pp. 31–32; F. H. Stewart, "Khuwwa," *EI* 2nd ed.

[103] Khoury, *State and Provincial Society*, p. 31; Fattah, *Politics*, p. 35; Minorsky, *Tadhkirat al-mulūk*, p. 179.

[104] Khoury, *State and Provincial Society*, pp. 27–34; Avery, "Nādir Shāh and the Afsharid Legacy," p. 52.

[105] Fattah, *Politics*, pp. 25–26, 186–187.

[106] Matthee, *Persia in Crisis*, p. 159; Inalcik and Quataert, *Economic and Social History*, pp. 38–39.

[107] Kasaba, *Moveable Empire*, pp. 32–34; Inalcik, "The Yürüks," pp. 52–54; Inalcik and Quataert, *Economic and Social History*, p. 40.

[108] Arash Khazeni, *Tribes & Empire on the Margins of Nineteenth-Century Iran* (Seattle: University of Washington Press, 2009), p. 24.

While nomads were an integral part of the economy in several regions, this does not mean that there was no friction with settled populations. The Ottoman local records contain complaints from each group against the other. Villages wrote to protest animals straying into fields during migrations or pastured in their fields without permission. Settled populations who herded animals complained of the theft of their livestock. There were numerous instances of nomads collecting extra taxes for protection and of attacks on villages or caravans. The nomads likewise lodged complaints: they had animals seized while on migration even though they had paid the full tax; they were sometimes charged exorbitant pasture dues, even on government land to which they had rights; and when they reclaimed abandoned lands, the original owners sometimes returned to seize them. In adjudicating between the two groups the Ottoman government tried to remain evenhanded.[109]

The maintenance of security on trade and pilgrimage routes was a constant source of tension. When pilgrimage authorities failed to fulfill their obligations to the Bedouin, or when contracts went to the enemies of nearby tribes, Bedouin responded by raiding. Small-scale raids could be tolerated, but the authorities sometimes met larger attacks with bloody reprisals. In the seventeenth century relations worsened, and twice, in 1632, and again from 1683 to 1699, there was serious violence in the desert from both sides.[110] At times trade and travel were largely blocked by inimical tribal forces attacking caravans, particularly in Syria and Iraq. We see various causes for breakdowns in order. Periods of hardship among nomads due to weather conditions or the immigration of new populations such as the 'Anaza often caused fighting over scarce resources and attacks on travelers. Grievances over high taxation, military conscription, or other ill-treatment also resulted in raiding. The Ottoman-Safavid border in Khuzistan was almost always a region of conflict, in which travel was difficult and dangerous.[111]

In administrative structures nomads held an anomalous place. Many nomad populations were required to serve in the military, and thus were taxed at a somewhat lower rate than peasants. There were two standard nomad taxes which had existed at least since the Mongol period: a herd tax calculated on the number of animals, and pasture dues. Dues for pasture might also be collected privately, by the owners of land useful for

---

[109] Murphy, "Some Features," pp. 194–195; Kasaba, *Moveable Empire*, p. 30; Khoury, *State and Provincial Society*, p. 61; Moshe Sharon, "The Political Role of the Bedouins in Palestine in the Sixteenth and Seventeenth Centuries," in *Studies on Palestine during the Ottoman Period*, ed. Moshe Ma'oz (Jerusalem: Magnes Press, 1975), pp. 15, 20.

[110] Faroqhi, *Pilgrims and Sultans*, pp. 65–69.

[111] Sharon, "Political Role," pp. 15–22; Matthee, "Between Arabs, Turks," pp. 58, 72–74.

nomads.[112] Some nomad populations were required to provide particular products. In the Ottoman Empire we find groups delivering arrows or butter to the state, and in Iran the Bakhtiyari Lurs paid an annual tribute in mules.[113] There is some scholarly controversy over Ottoman policies towards nomads in the sixteenth and seventeenth centuries, particularly on the issue of tax. A few taxes were added on nomads in general, while tax incentives were organized to encourage settling. Some scholars consider the taxes levied on nomads as a serious burden that was designed to encourage settlement; others believe taxes were reasonable.[114]

In most of the Ottoman Empire, the proportion of nomad to settled population seems to have declined over the period under discussion. Figures for the sixteenth century have been analyzed and show that while both the nomad and the settled population was growing, the overall percentage of nomads within the population of the whole of Anatolia declined somewhat.[115] For much of Anatolia this trend appears to have been reversed with the Jelali rebellion and climate extremes at the end of the century.[116] In the Arabian Peninsula, the Syrian desert and the Safavid-Ottoman border, nomads continued numerous, autonomous and active in military affairs. In Iran, as I have stated above, nomadism seems to have increased, especially at the beginning and the end of this period. Thus, from the Ottoman borders through Iran, nomadic tribes formed a central part of the political and social fabric at the end of the eighteenth century.

Military Developments

In the three centuries from 1500 to 1800, the global military balance shifted in favor of European powers while the military power of Iran declined in relation to that of the Ottomans. We need to consider what role nomadism played in this development. Since Europe vastly improved its military technology in the seventeenth and eighteenth centuries, firearms have been cited as a major factor and nomad disdain for new technology has been seen as one cause for Safavid inferiority to the Ottomans. However, recent scholarship has brought this analysis into question. In a region like Europe, with a high population density and

---

[112] Lindner, *Nomads and Ottomans*, pp. 56–59; Kasaba, *Moveable Empire*, p. 27; Inalcik and Quataert, *Economic and Social History*, p. 36; Murphy, "Some Features," p. 193; Fragner, "Social and Internal Economic Affairs," pp. 538–539.

[113] Inalcik, "The Yürüks," p. 54; Garthwaite, *Khans and Shahs*, p. 49.

[114] Lindner, *Nomads and Ottomans*, pp. 56–62, 82–84; Murphy, "Some Features," p. 193; Khoury, *State and Provincial Society*, p. 31.

[115] Barkan, "Ottoman Fiscal Surveys," p. 169. Note these figures include Karaman, Zulkadiriye and other regions of central and eastern Anatolia.

[116] White, *The Climate of Rebellion*, pp. 238–243.

increasing use of infantry, firearms quickly led to a military revolution. In the Middle East, where the terrain was more difficult and distances often very large, cannon had fewer advantages. Armies did profit from heavy artillery in sieges but sacrificed mobility and lost time in reaching their destination.[117]

Handguns were also used in the Middle East, but the early ones had serious drawbacks. Early muskets were loaded through the barrel, the soldier first measuring out the powder, and then loading wadding, powder and pellet and ramming them down. It was difficult to do all this on horseback, and most horsemen dismounted to use their guns. In Europe, massed firepower worked well against armies of infantry and heavy cavalry. In the Middle East gunmen usually faced mounted archers, some of whom could discharge up to six arrows a minute while charging, circling or retreating. This made reloading a dangerous affair. Middle Eastern light cavalry moreover used the compound bow of the Mongols which had a longer range and far greater accuracy than muskets. Even with the improved muskets of the eighteenth century, soldiers shooting at a target 33 yards wide at 67 yards scored only 46 percent of the time. The experienced archers of the mamluk army on the other hand were expected to be able to hit a target of 38 inches at 75 yards.[118] Once the charge was over and the armies engaged in hand-to-hand combat, the musket was less useful than the saber.

Nonetheless, Middle Eastern powers were eager to acquire and use firearms. One advantage they offered was that they required much less training than did mounted archery.[119] The ruler could conscript townsmen and peasants with no previous military experience, train them, and have an army responsible directly to him. The Ottomans, whose military efforts were focused primarily against Europe, were the first to develop firearms and over time increased infantry at the expense of cavalry. Two decisive Ottoman victories are attributed to their superior firepower: the Battle of Chaldiran in 1514, when the Ottomans defeated Shah Isma' il; and their victory over the mamluks at Marj Dabiq in 1516, which sealed the conquest of Egypt and Syria.[120]

Nomad armies of mounted archers did sometimes look down on artillery and firearms as dirty and demeaning. Nonetheless, the Safavid armies were using artillery within a year of coming to power, although they never

---

[117] Kenneth Warren Chase, *Firearms: A Global History to 1700* (Cambridge: Cambridge University Press, 2003), p. 23; Rhoads Murphy, *Ottoman Warfare, 1500–1700* (New Brunswick, NJ: Rutgers University Press, 1999), p. 66.

[118] Chase, *Firearms*, pp. 24, 73–74.

[119] Geoffrey Parker, *The Military Revolution: Military Innovation and the Rise of the West, 1500–1800* (Cambridge: Cambridge University Press, 1988), p. 17.

[120] Chase, *Firearms*, pp. 104–105; Savory, *Iran under the Safavids*, pp. 41–43.

integrated it as fully into their army as the Ottomans.[121] We find firearms prominent in the army of Nadir Shah, where they were also used by cavalry units, and the largely nomadic powers that contested Iran after Nadir Shah's fall also had firepower.[122] By the late sixteenth century many Bedouin owned firearms, and by the mid-seventeenth century the Kurds on the Safavid-Ottoman border seem to have had them as well.[123]

However, while firearms were decisive in some battles, they did not win the wars. What was most decisive in war was organization, logistics and discipline; it was excellence in these that gave the Ottomans a permanent advantage over the Safavids. Ottoman soldiers were well nourished and well equipped, and they were motivated through substantial and predictable rewards.[124] The Iranian armies – based first on tribal contingents, later on a variety of competing forces, and not regularly paid – were much less reliable. Thus, we cannot ascribe the decline of Middle Eastern armies primarily to inferior firepower. If the presence of nomad populations in regional armies had a negative effect, it was not because they refused to use firearms but because tribal autonomy made some difficult to control.

Despite the problem of discipline, nomads remained an important part of the military. In Iran and Afghanistan, they constituted a significant proportion of the army through the eighteenth century. In the Ottoman Empire nomads lost importance in the central army, but they remained useful in the waging of war on both fronts. They provided livestock products to feed the army, supplied animals for transport, and often organized the transport itself. They were used for intelligence, and had a role also in the deployment of artillery because they could scout out the routes ahead of the army and could also cover the army in retreat; it was local Kurds, for instance, who made it possible for the Ottomans to retreat and regroup safely after their failure to take Baghdad in 1620.[125] For Ottoman campaigns, the use of nomad troops often tipped the scales in their favor.[126] Thus while the management of nomadic tribes was a headache for many states, interstate competition – in other words, war – was still difficult without them.

---

[121] Chase, *Firearms*, p. 117; Matthee, *Persia in Crisis*, p. 112; "Unwalled Cities and Restless Nomads: Firearms and Artillery in Safavid Iran," in *Safavid Persia*, ed. Charles Melville (London: I. B. Tauris, 1996), 391.

[122] Axworthy, "Army," pp. 635–641; Perry, *Karīm Khān Zand*, pp. 68, 87.

[123] Faroqhi, *Pilgrims and Sultans*, p. 69; Matthee, "Unwalled Cities," pp. 405–407; Matthee, *Persia in Crisis*, pp. 144, 217–218.

[124] Murphy, *Ottoman Warfare*, pp. 85–98, 166.

[125] Murphy, *Ottoman Warfare*, pp. 74, 82, 109; Murphy, "Resumption," pp. 316–317.

[126] Murphy, *Ottoman Warfare*, pp. 67–71, 191.

Conclusion

The Middle Periods have been seen as the age of the steppe traditions, which were still relevant in most of the Middle East through much of the fifteenth century. Nomads were a significant portion of the population in many regions and were particularly powerful in Anatolia where Turkmen tribal confederations became expansive powers. With the conquest of Iran first by the Qaraqoyunlu and then the Aqqoyunlu, both new nomads and a stronger tribal structure were imported into Iran, initiating a new era of tribal organization in both provincial government and the military. At the turn of the sixteenth century this process was completed by Isma'il's creation of the Safavid state, which brought a continued influx of Anatolian nomads. The conquests of the Ottoman sultan Selim I blocked Safavid expansion west and created a long borderland stretching from the Gulf to the Caucasus. Over the next centuries the Ottomans faced successive Iranian states across a buffer zone made up of primarily nomadic and tribal populations largely outside the control of either state. Here both nomad and tribal power was strengthened by the need for local allies on the part of the rival powers. One should note that while this was a border region for both states, for the Middle East it was a central area straddling major trade routes.

The Mongols and Timurids had suppressed tribalism while retaining their steppe nomad origin both as a source of legitimacy and as a bond with the armies that served them. The Ottomans and Safavids referred sometimes to Turkic traditions – the Oghuz in the Ottoman case, and Tamerlane in the Safavid – but their primary legitimation was within the religious tradition of the Middle East. Both used nomads in their military, but were likewise threatened by them, in large part probably because of the strength of tribal powers. Even the Safavids, who created the Qizilbash oymaqs, soon attempted to dilute their power and their ideological importance. Despite continued reliance on nomad troops, the sense of a common origin with the dynasty declined. In the ideological sphere, we see here the end of the Turco-Mongolian age. Nadir Shah's attempt to revive the steppe heritage in a unified Turkic identity did not last beyond his lifetime.

In the political and economic sphere, nomads remained more important. The Ottomans succeeded in suppressing nomad powers through their central territories, including much of Anatolia, but tribes and nomads remained integral to society and politics in Kurdistan, Syria, Iraq and the Arabian Peninsula. In Iran, despite the efforts of the Safavid shahs, nomads remained integrated into both the military and provincial system and dominated the region.

The nineteenth and twentieth centuries were a decisive period for nomads in the Middle East. At the end of the eighteenth century, nomad pastoralists had lost numbers and influence in the central Ottoman lands, but their tribes still wielded considerable power in the eastern borderlands, much of Syria, and the Arabian Peninsula. In Iran they remained a significant proportion of the population and furnished the majority of military personnel. By the late twentieth century, there were fewer nomads; those who remained contributed to the regional economy but could wield no force and had little influence. Over the centuries discussed in this book we have seen periodical fluctuations in nomad numbers and strength, but the changes described in this chapter are likely to be permanent.

The most fundamental causes of this change were the modernization of the Middle East and the encroachment of European powers. In the eastern Ottoman lands, the nineteenth century begins with decentralization and apparently an increase in nomad population. However, while the Ottomans were losing power in relation to Europe, internally this was a period of consolidation and systematization, with the imposition of increasing control over nomadic tribes. The Ottoman government, recognizing its military and economic inferiority to Europe, began a series of modernizing reforms in the late eighteenth century. These culminated in the Tanzimat reforms introduced in 1839 by Sultan Abdul-Mejid (1839–1861). The new order militated against the regional accommodations of city, town, and nomad which had developed throughout the eighteenth century.

The Middle East was also undergoing a revolution in transport, with the introduction first of steam navigation and then of the railroad. Increasing integration into the world economy encouraged tribal shaykhs to invest in agriculture at the expense of pastoralism. By the end of the nineteenth century, it is clear that many nomads had begun to settle and to practice agriculture. In Iran, westernizing reform movements started later and went less deep. Throughout the nineteenth century most nomad tribes remained intact and in control of significant territory, while tribal contingents remained the greater part of the army. However, the new economic order affected Iranian nomads just as it did those of the Ottoman Empire. As tribal shaykhs became more fully involved in the global economy, their interests sometimes became increasingly distant from those of their followers.

Earlier travelers to the Middle East had provided some general description of pastoral nomads and tribal populations. By 1800 the European powers had become actively involved in the Middle East and there was an interest in the science of ethnography among academics and administrative personnel. The Arabian tribes attracted particular attention; they inhabited strategic regions and the Bedouin offered a rich and romantic culture for study. For this reason, we have both documents and detailed reports by travelers and scholars who attempted to document the nomadic lifestyle, providing us a fuller understanding of tribal structure and the relationship between nomads and settled communities.

European involvement in the Middle East often worked against the interests of nomads in encouraging government controls and mechanized transportation. At the same time the British, deeply involved in the Gulf, offered alternative partnerships to neighboring pastoralists. The disruptions of the early twentieth century, with the Constitutional Revolution in Iran and World War I throughout the region, brought a resurgence of nomad activity and strength. In both Iran and the Ottoman Empire nomad tribes were often pulled into the struggle and offered a choice of allies. This period was the last great moment of nomad power, but it created a new order in which nomads have played a lesser part.

The Ottoman Lands in the Early Nineteenth Century

The beginning of the nineteenth century was a time of strength for the nomads and tribes in the eastern Ottoman territories. In the Kurdish regions new emirates achieved considerable autonomy and took part in the politics of Iran and the eastern Ottoman lands. The northern Syrian desert, formally under the governors of Damascus and Aleppo, was largely controlled by Arab tribes among whom the 'Anaza was paramount. In most of the Hawran, which cultivated rain-watered grain, Bedouin shaykhs shared power with local rulers while farther south and east, in the Balqa region, Bedouin tribes were dominant.[1] The province of

[1] Eugene Rogan, *Frontiers of the State in the Late Ottoman Empire: Transjordan, 1850–1921* (Cambridge: Cambridge University Press, 1999).

Baghdad, still under the control of Mamluk governors, was largely autonomous. Its eastern and southern regions were governed in uneasy cooperation with local tribes, while the south was closely involved with the politics of the Persian Gulf and the Arabian Peninsula. At the outset of the nineteenth century most of the Arabian Peninsula was under the control of the first Sa'udi state, which was still expanding.

Even with the fuller information we have on this period, it is not always clear which tribes we should count among the nomads. Almost all of the important Arab tribes included several economic strategies – camel nomadism, sheep and goat herding, and agriculture. In most of the Arabian Peninsula, villagers and town dwellers also held strong tribal affiliations, particularly among the elite, and those who did not have a tribal genealogy were considered inferior.[2] Some tribes are noted as having a primarily Bedouin lifestyle; these include the Shammar, 'Anaza and Tayy in the Jazira and Syrian desert, with the Bedouin Shammar also important in the Najd.[3]

The economies of nomad, town, and village were closely related, and one might talk of a spectrum of economic strategies. Villagers usually raised some livestock in nearby pastures, and the urban elite sometimes owned large flocks, for which they hired herders.[4] Many nomads, even Bedouin, planted crops in seasonal pastures, and some ordinary nomads also worked in the fields as day labor during harvest.[5] Bedouin shaykhs often owned date palm plantations; sometimes they collected a share of the harvest from farmers and sometimes they cultivated plantations directly through tribal labor and slaves. Some owned additional agricultural land which they managed like other large landowners, giving the land out to be cultivated by sharecroppers to whom they provided seed and implements.[6]

We can see the functioning of the *khuwwa* system in more detail during this period. The extent to which it provided actual protection within the tribal *dīras* varied widely. In some places there does seem to have been a sense of common community and interest across different populations. In Transjordan for instance, the Bani Sakhr tribe stationed a member of the tribe in each village as a "brother" to take responsibility for protection

---

[2] Juhany, *Najd*, pp. 95–97; Rogan, *Frontiers of the State*, pp. 7–8.
[3] Tom Nieuwenhuis, *Politics and Society in Early Modern Iraq: Mamlūk Pashas, Tribal Shaykhs and Local Rule between 1802 and 1831* (The Hague: Martinus Nijhoff, 1982), pp. 122–132.
[4] Khoury, *State and Provincial Society*, pp. 60–61; Madawi al-Rasheed, *Politics in an Arabian Oasis: The Rashidi Tribal Dynasty* (London: I. B. Tauris, 1991), pp. 15–17.
[5] Norman N. Lewis, *Nomads and Settlers in Syria and Jordan, 1800–1980* (Cambridge: Cambridge University Press, 1987), p. 5; Juhany, *Najd*, p. 75.
[6] Rasheed, *Politics*, pp. 16, 76, 95–96; Lewis, *Nomads and Settlers*, pp. 31, 158.

and to adjudicate disputes according to Bedouin law.[7] It seems likely that relations between nomad and settled were closer in regions distant from the larger urban centers, where populations went back and forth between pastoralism and agriculture. In Syria, the relatively close relations between Bedouin and town in Transjordan, mentioned above, contrasts with the more conflictual relationship found for instance in the Aleppo region.

While the system of *khuwwa* worked under favorable conditions, both villages and caravans often found that the payments were extorted by force and did not ensure protection. This practice was undoubtedly caused in part by the overbearing behavior of powerful Bedouin tribes, with a custom of raiding both nomad and settled. To some extent, however, it was the normal functioning of states which did not possess a monopoly of force. Similar complaints were voiced about the Ottoman authorities, who arrived to collect taxes with an armed force and likewise sometimes failed to protect the population.[8]

For provincial governors the control of the tribal populations was a constant challenge. Although governors could certainly inflict punishment, they did not have the military force to maintain control over the desert routes or to collect taxes in the more remote desert and steppe regions. They could ally with the strongest tribes and bolster the power of their shaykhs with subsidies and titles. Ottoman officials also often involved themselves in tribal succession struggles, attempting to install rulers who would be reliable allies. Another option was the time-honored practice of fomenting strife among the tribes in order to weaken them all. As we have seen in earlier periods, this strategy usually worked only in the short term and at the expense of the population, which suffered the hardships of constant strife. Despite this, it remained a common practice in the nineteenth century.

The actions of the governor of Aleppo dealing with the 'Anaza provide a good example of the limitations of government control and the variety of motivations that animated governors' decisions. The Fid'an section of the 'Anaza was the major tribe in the summer pastures near Aleppo. During the 1811 migration, they ruined forty villages and destroyed the harvest. However, instead of inflicting punishment, the next year the governor of Aleppo attempted to use the 'Anaza troops against other problem groups, both the janissaries and rebel governors. By 1816 the 'Anaza were raiding west of Aleppo, where they seized a caravan and had to be bought off. In

---

[7] Rogan, *Frontiers of the State*, pp. 26, 33–35.
[8] *Frontiers of the State*, pp. 21, 41–42; Frederick F. Anscombe, *The Ottoman Gulf: The Creation of Kuwait, Saudi Arabia and Qatar* (New York: Columbia University Press, 1997), pp. 58–59, 62.

1818 there were skirmishes with the governor's troops, which ended in a negotiated peace.[9] The relationship with the 'Anaza was both too equal and too useful to compromise by excessive use of force.

The first decades of the nineteenth century were a tumultuous time. The Sa'udi-Wahhabi state achieved a series of spectacular victories, gaining control over most of the Arabian Peninsula. When the Wahhabis reached the limits of expansion, they lost the loyalty of their allies and they were overthrown in 1818 through the power of the Ottoman governor Muhammad 'Ali, by then essentially independent in Egypt. Muhammad 'Ali also controlled the Holy Cities as governor of the Hijaz, and for a decade, from 1831 to 1841, he extended his power over most of Syria. During this time, however, the Ottomans did manage to reassert control over several other border regions. In 1831, with the help of Kurds and other local tribes, they overthrew the Mamluk governor of Baghdad and put the province under direct Ottoman rule. In a series of expeditions from the 1830s to the 1850s, Ottoman troops managed to destroy the independent Kurdish emirates of eastern Anatolia and institute more direct rule. In 1841 the Hijaz and the Holy Cities returned to Ottoman rule under the restored Hashemite Sharif dynasty which had held it earlier.

Two developments of the 1830s had less immediate effect but brought greater long-term change. One of these was the introduction of steamship transport in the Gulf and along the Tigris and Euphrates Rivers. Steam power had relatively little impact at the beginning, since the tribes along the rivers could collect *khuwwa* from boats as well as caravans, but over time the efficiency of new transport and the British power behind it led to a shift in trade routes from land to water, cutting into the Bedouin economy.[10] The other crucial event was the beginning of the modernizing Tanzimat reforms in 1839 with the *Khatt-i sherif* of Gülkhane, the first of a series of decrees aiming to institute a more European form of governance. These reforms introduced a major shift in the understanding of government and society. All classes were to be treated alike, and fixed taxes would be collected by government agents.

The Implementation of the Tanzimat

The Tanzimat laws were promulgated over a period of several decades and implemented gradually, especially in the more remote border provinces. One aim was to decrease the independence of tribes and to increase agriculture at the expense of pastoralism. New land laws culminating in

---

[9] Lewis, *Nomads and Settlers*, pp. 9–10.   [10] Fattah, *Politics*, pp. 124–127, 137–138.

the Land Law of 1858 required registration of land based on written proof of ownership, which rarely existed. This provision made it difficult to preserve the collective ownership and the practice of seasonal land use rights on which pastoralism depended.

The implementation of the Tanzimat was neither smooth nor steady. Among the early measures was the introduction of a census and military conscription. Governors in Syria and Iraq began to implement the census over the 1840s and 1850s, while extending government administration into the frontier through military campaigns. In 1845 the governor of Aleppo fortified the steppe frontier, attacked the Bedouin and ordered the restoration of villages and uncultivated fields. In 1852 there was a major settlement program in the summer pastures of the Fid'an tribe of the 'Anaza near Aleppo. Tribesmen were given land with tax exemptions, and their shaykhs were paid as irregular cavalry. This worked for a while, but some groups returned to nomadism when the tax exemptions ended.[11] During the same period, the Ottoman government in Damascus began military campaigns into northern Transjordan, but actual control proved difficult.[12] Local tribes continued to collect *khuwwa*, and the district soon returned to the control of tribes and village headmen. In Baghdad, attempts to impose a census and conscription began with the creation of the regional army in the 1840s, but the negative reaction limited the implementation to the central regions; in the late 1850s an attempt to impose conscription on the southern tribes led to insurrection.[13]

Expeditions in the 1860s had more permanent results and at this time the Ottomans began to install garrisons in tribal and nomadic regions.[14] In 1867 the Damascus government successfully asserted control over the tribes in the hinterlands of Hims and Hama, and incorporated the northern regions of 'Ajlun in Transjordan.[15] In 1868 the governor of Aleppo created the Governorate of the Desert, establishing military posts stretching northeast from Damascus, at Dayr al-Zawr, Palmyra, Sukhna and Qaryatayn. Actual control was still difficult to attain, however. The river tribes of mixed livelihoods were forced to pay taxes, but the more fully nomadic Shammar and 'Anaza rebelled and did not accept the government camel tax until the end of the century.[16] In the 1870s, the energetic governor of Baghdad, Midhat Pasha, began to extend control over the

---

[11] Lewis, *Nomads and Settlers*, pp. 42–45.   [12] Rogan, *Frontiers of the State*, pp. 45–48.
[13] Ebubekir Ceylan, *The Ottoman Origins of Modern Iraq: Political Reform, Modernization and Development in the Nineteenth-Century Middle East* (London: I. B. Tauris, 2011), pp. 58–64, 76.
[14] Fattah, *Politics*, p. 187.
[15] Rogan, *Frontiers of the State*, p. 48; Lewis, *Nomads and Settlers*, pp. 124–125.
[16] Lewis, *Nomads and Settlers*, pp. 30–33.

outlying districts, established a line of military posts along the Euphrates, and implemented conscription among the tribes with only partial success. The advance of Ottoman control continued to meet with resistance from settled and nomad alike. Military conscription was particularly unpopular; even in the early twentieth century, it could not be safely imposed on all regions. In the desert regions of southern Transjordan, conscription and disarmament were still out of the question for the tribes.[17]

While resistance led the Ottoman government to desist in its efforts to impose conscription, in the matter of taxation it was more successful. However, even after the imposition of government taxation, the nomad tribes were reluctant to give up their collection of *khuwwa*, which they considered their right. The tribes often continued to collect in places where they retained sufficient strength, or when troops withdrew they might resume collection. The result was that peasants sometimes found themselves paying both the government tax and the *khuwwa*.[18]

Despite some successes, the Ottomans did not have the manpower to enforce their rule continuously. One expedient they used was to adapt the old system of recognizing paramount tribal shaykhs within a more centralized system. This system could be used to undercut the authority of tribal shaykhs. Shaykhs sometimes received tax farms for their own districts or were appointed as subgovernors (*kaymakam*). They thus became part of the administration; they were responsible for delivering the taxes set by the regional government and could be dismissed. The government sometimes demanded extortionate taxes, making the shaykh unpopular with the tribe. *Dīras* might be divided into several tax farms, diluting the central tribal authority.[19] With greater incorporation of tribal areas into the government tribesmen increasingly turned to government authorities to solve disputes and some shaykhs began to lose their role as judges and arbitrators.[20] With government patrols, their military role was reduced and the possibility of collecting *khuwwa* destroyed; they then lost the ability to redistribute wealth, which had been a cornerstone of tribal authority. Taken together these changes gradually undermined the internal position of the tribal shaykhs whose lands were more fully incorporated.

The restructuring of land ownership brought even greater changes. The Provincial Land Law promulgated in 1858 was designed in part to promote the extension of agricultural land and the sedentarization of nomads. It had a profound impact on the tribes, most particularly the

[17] Rogan, *Frontiers of the State*, pp. 186, 214.
[18] Lewis, *Nomads and Settlers*, pp. 29, 32, 37–38, 125.
[19] Ceylan, *Ottoman Origins*, pp. 128, 142–144, 162–163.
[20] Ceylan, *Ottoman Origins*, p. 106; Rogan, *Frontiers of the State*, pp. 181–183.

sections that practiced nomadism. Land was now to be surveyed, classified and registered in the name of individuals. To prove a claim to land, customary usage rights were no longer sufficient – only three forms of acquisition were recognized: inheritance, purchase or grant by a government authority. Very few tribal people, nomad or peasant, could prove ownership of the land they used, almost all of which was collective and regulated by the tribal shaykhs.[21] Some *dīra* lands were forcibly taken by the state and given to new settlers, and some tribal claims were refused. In other cases, however, the government used incentives to get tribes to accept the division of the *dīra* into individual landholdings.

The smaller and more sedentary tribes were more likely to divide the land broadly, while in the richer tribes, and especially those for whom pastoralism was the major economy, the leading shaykhs were able to register large amounts of land in their own names.[22] The creation of new categories of saleable land produced a lively market. Some lands went into the hands of city elites, but much remained with the shaykhs. Landowning was not new to tribal shaykhs, but as their personal holdings increased, the pastoral economy became less important to them. The Middle East was now part of the world economy and had begun to export grain and other agricultural produce; indeed, even before the land law some tribal shaykhs had been major dealers in grain. Now many found greater advantage in agriculture, which produced higher profits than pastoralism, and they began to encourage tribesmen to settle.[23] As a smaller portion of their power and prestige came from the tribe itself, the interests of the shaykhs were less closely allied with those of ordinary members of the tribe.

Over the course of the nineteenth century the tribes of Syria and Iraq lost autonomy, and sedentarization significantly increased. Change, however, came slowly. Ottoman centralization provoked resistance, with frequent rebellions and Bedouin raids, and southern Transjordan and the northern Syrian desert retained considerable independence. Even in the early twentieth century, some tribes continued to collect *khuwwa*. With the market for camels still quite strong, the Bedouin economy remained profitable.[24]

---

[21] Ceylan, *Ottoman Origins*, pp. 160–161; Stanford J. Shaw and Ezel Kural Shaw, *History of the Ottoman Empire and Modern Turkey* (Cambridge: Cambridge University Press, 1977), p. 114.

[22] Rogan, *Frontiers of the State*, pp. 88–89.

[23] Lewis, *Nomads and Settlers*, pp. 127–130; Fattah, *Politics*, pp. 156–157; Ceylan, *Ottoman Origins*, p. 164.

[24] Lewis, *Nomads and Settlers*, 34–35, 37, 156.

The Arabian Peninsula followed a separate trajectory and experienced much less direct pressure from the Ottoman government. It remained only marginally within the Ottoman Empire, with its tribes essentially intact. The Ottomans could neither manage to exert full control nor leave the region entirely to its own devices. The Hijaz remained under dual rule until World War I, with Ottoman officials responsible for commercial, political and foreign relations. The Hashemite Sharifs managed the two Holy Cities and the tribal confederations which surrounded them. It was thus their responsibility to safeguard the route of the pilgrimage.[25]

After its defeat in 1818 the Wahhabi state had managed to find a refuge in Riyadh and hold power until 1890 as a vassal of a new tribal power, the Rashidi dynasty (1836–1921) of the Shammar confederation. The Shammar were one of the largest and most powerful of the Bedouin confederations, but like others, also included sheep and goat nomads and sedentary populations. The Rashidi dynasty was a sedentary lineage which had established itself in the oasis of Hail in 1836 and had gained recognition from the Shammar tribe; this was the first time that all the Shammar of the Peninsula had formally recognized a single leader.[26] Up to the end of the century, the dynasty remained in control of central Arabia, from the Najd to Jabal Shammar, benefitting from the control of the caravan trade that passed through, from the collection of *khuwwa* and from subsidies provided first by the Egyptians and later by the Ottomans. For control over the tribes, they maintained a small private army of slaves and settled soldiers while using Shammar tribal troops for occasional campaigns. This was a classic tribal state in which rulers used their authority to allot pasture and redistribute resources, along with superior access to information, to maintain their power. The Ottoman government generally favored the Rashidi state but gave some subsidies also to outside tribal leaders.[27] The Arabian Peninsula therefore did not undergo the social, economic and political transformation that the later nineteenth century brought to the other Ottoman lands.

Iran under the Qajars

In Iran the position of nomads remained much stronger. The Qajar state founded by Agha Muhammad Qajar in the 1790s began as a tribal confederation in a region divided among numerous competing powers. In the early nineteenth century the Qajar shahs succeeded in building up a court and bureaucracy in Tehran and in establishing provincial governorships

---

[25] Madawi al-Rasheed, *A History of Saudi Arabia*, pp. 30–31.
[26] Rasheed, *Politics*, pp. 39, 45–46, 75.   [27] Rasheed, *Politics*, pp. 69–82, 93.

under Qajar princes, but they had inherited a region with little effective bureaucracy and their armies were made up largely of tribal contingents. In attempting to increase their power and to bring the population more fully under control they were hampered by new geopolitical realities, with England dominating the Gulf and the Russians advancing in the Caucasus. There was no possibility of territorial expansion; instead, the Qajars were soon embroiled in expensive defensive wars which brought them neither prestige nor income. The possibilities for economic growth were limited by European domination of the market in textiles, which the Iranians exported, and in arms, which they needed. Though the shahs were able to improve both security and the economy, they did not have the power to extend their control directly into Iranian society.

A major source of weakness for the dynasty was its inability to create an effective army independent of nomadic tribal manpower. From the beginning of the century the shahs attempted to bring nomads more fully under control, using many of the same techniques as the Ottomans. However, they did not apparently try to settle nomads. Indeed, their policy seems to have been both to retain nomads within Iran and to preserve pastoralism.[28] Nomadic tribesmen remained necessary to the state as a military resource, as a source of crucial livestock products and for the taxes they paid, and they were powerful in most regions of Iran. The territories of the Qajar tribe in Azerbaijan and Mazandaran remained central to the Qajar army and administration. The Shahsevan confederation occupied the region stretching from Western Azerbaijan towards Qazwin. It had become an organized force under Nadir Shah but in the nineteenth century its leadership became less centralized, and it did not constitute a major power for much of this period.[29] Farther to the west, the Kurdish border states were generally under Ottoman more than Qajar influence. Turkmen Afshar tribes were present in both Khorasan and Azerbaijan along with a number of other tribal groups, some of which had been resettled during the turbulent political period of the eighteenth century.[30]

South and central Iran also supported large populations of nomads – Iranian, Arab and Turkmen. The region from Isfahan to Khuzistan was the territory of the Bakhtiyari, mentioned in Chapter 7. The Shiraz countryside was dominated by the Qashqa'i confederation, whose tribes migrated between winter pastures south and west of Shiraz and summer

[28] See, for example, Lois Beck, *The Qashqa'i of Iran* (New Haven, CT: Yale University Press, 1986), pp. 72–76; Tapper, *Frontier Nomads*, pp. 151–167.
[29] Tapper, *Frontier Nomads*, pp. 21–26, 35–37.
[30] Ervand Abrahamian, *Iran between Two Revolutions* (Princeton, NJ: Princeton University Press, 1982), p. 15.

pastures north and northeast of the city.[31] East of the Qashqa'i territories were several originally independent tribes of mixed ethnicity, later formed into the Khamsa confederation.[32] The Gulf littoral was populated primarily by Arab tribes, among whom the most prominent confederation was the Banu Ka'b of Muhammara (now Khorramshahr) east of Basra, who combined pastoralism with agriculture.[33] In the east, Iran suffered from raiding by two largely nomadic tribal confederations straddling its borders: the Baluch to the southeast, and in the northeast, the Yomut and Göklen Turkmen. The Turkmen were particularly feared and disliked because of their sale of Persian captives in the slave markets of Bukhara.[34]

As the century progressed, the tribes of Iran became increasingly involved with outside powers. Some of the Shahsevan migrated between Russian and Iranian territory and were thus under Russian control for part of the year. The British had set up client states along the shores of the Gulf and increasingly negotiated independently with tribes in Iranian territories, including the Bakhtiyari, the Banu Ka'b and the tribes of the Khamsa confederation.

Shahs and Nomads in the Nineteenth Century

Agha Muhammad's successors, starting with Fath 'Ali Shah (r. 1797–1834) are credited with moving against tribal power and increasing internal security.[35] Like the Ottomans, the shahs attempted to bring tribes under control by formalizing rule over confederations, making tribal leaders agents of the government to be appointed by the shah. In 1818–1819, Fath 'Ali Shah bestowed the title of *ilkhani* on the Qashqa'i chief Jani Khan, making him responsible for the tribal populations of Fars.[36] In 1839 Muhammad Shah (1834–1848) created the somewhat lower position of *ilbeg* for the Shahsevan, appointing an *ilbeg* to each of the major divisions of the confederation.[37] The position of *ilkhani* was introduced to the Bakhtiyari in the 1860s.[38] For both the Qashqa'i and the Bakhtiyari the office *ilbegi* was also used, not infrequently held by the

---

[31] Pierre Oberling, *The Qashqāī nomads of Fārs* (The Hague: Mouton, 1974), p. 15.

[32] Beck, *Qashqa'i*, pp. 4, 79.

[33] See Willem Floor, "The Rise and Fall of the Banū Ka'b. A Borderer State in Southern Khuzestan," *Iran* 44 (2006).

[34] Afsaneh Najmabadi, *The Story of the Daughters of Quchan: Gender and National Memory in Iranian History* (Syracuse, NY: Syracuse University Press, 1998), pp. 53–57.

[35] Oberling, *Qashqāī*, pp. 48–49; Abbas Amanat, *Pivot of the Universe: Nasir al-Din Shah Qajar and the Iranian Monarchy, 1831–1896* (Berkeley: University of California Press, 1997), p. 3.

[36] Beck, *Qashqa'i*, pp. 52, 83.   [37] Tapper, *Frontier Nomads*, p. 180.

[38] Garthwaite, *Khans and Shahs*, p. 9.

brother or son of the *ilkhani*. These two offices remained within the same lineages into the twentieth century, thus creating a stable aristocratic stratum. In 1861–1862 Nasir al-Din Shah (1848–1896) decided to balance tribal politics in Fars by creating a new confederation of five formerly independent tribes, given the name Khamsa (five). They were put under the leadership of a man from a Persian merchant family of Shiraz, 'Ali Muhammad Khan, who held the hereditary title of Qawam al-Mulk. 'Ali Muhammad Khan's family was familiar with these tribes, from whom it had recruited military forces to protect its commercial empire. The creation of the Khamsa confederation was encouraged by the British, who were concerned with the safety of the southern routes.[39]

The *ilkhani*s and *ilbegi*s were invested by the government as leaders of their confederations and could therefore be dismissed, though official dismissal did not always prevent tribesmen from continuing to obey a leader they trusted. *Ilkhani*s were held responsible for collecting tribal taxes due to the government, for maintaining order within their districts, and particularly for maintaining security on the routes.[40] Their position gave them independent sources of revenue since they collected taxes also for their own use and levied tolls both on tribesmen and on commercial traffic along the roads they controlled. Two important routes went through tribal territories in the south: the Shiraz-Bushehr route through Qashqa'i lands and the Shiraz-Abadan route through the Khamsa territory.[41] Tribal management of the routes was a continuous source of friction with the Iranian government and later in the century also with the British, since raiding along them was a standard way for tribal populations to express discontent or to weaken their rivals.[42]

While strong *ilkhani* leadership worked to increase security, it also threatened to encroach on the power of provincial governors and of the shah himself. Furthermore, the *ilkhani*s, as powerful members of the elite, became involved in the politics of the dynasty. Like the Ottomans, the Qajars tried to limit the strength of tribal confederations by undermining or eliminating the leaders they had appointed when they became too powerful, and by fomenting strife within the tribal leadership. I will give one example here: In 1832 the Qashqa'i *Ilkhani* Muhammad 'Ali was so powerful that it was said he could make all of Fars rotate around his index finger, and he felt free to make demands on the governor of Fars. When

---

[39] Beck, *Qashqa'i*, pp. 79–83; Vanessa Martin, *The Qajar Pact: Bargaining, Protest and the State in Nineteenth-Century Persia* (London: I. B. Tauris, 2005), pp. 48–53.

[40] Garthwaite, *Khans and Shahs*, pp. 82–83; Beck, *Qashqa'i*, pp. 80–83; Oberling, *Qashqāī*, p. 23; Tapper, *Frontier Nomads*, p. 183.

[41] Garthwaite, *Khans and Shahs*, pp. 105, 107; Oberling, *Qashqāī*, pp. 83–84.

[42] Oberling, *Qashqāī*, p. 92; Garthwaite, *Khans and Shahs*, p. 130.

the governor failed to fulfill his requests he moved many of his tribesmen to the province of Kerman, where they were welcomed for the tax income they would bring. Under pressure from the shah the governor was forced to give in and the tribe returned.[43] However, when a powerful ally of the *ilkhani* in Azerbaijan died, the governor of Fars took his revenge; the *ilkhani* was arrested, his estates in Shiraz plundered, and Qashqa'i graves dug up. The *ilkhani* was later released and reinstated, only to be arrested again a year or two later and moved to Tehran where he was kept hostage for thirteen years.[44]

The tribal leaders did not depend entirely on the collective strength of their followers for their position; they were also major landowners. The Bakhtiyari *ilkhani* family held estates providing significant income, while the Qashqa'i had a magnificent building in Shiraz and also large land-holdings. The leading families of tribal confederations led their tribes not as first among equals, but as a wealthy elite that was able to deal with the provincial powers, the Qajar dynasty, and foreign states using the manpower and economy of their followers as only one of their sources of strength.[45] In the first decade of the twentieth century, the Bakhtiyari acquired a new source of wealth when the British D'Arcy concession struck oil in their territories. Although the Bakhtiyari leaders were persuaded to settle for a small percentage of profits, their royalties and further sale of land to the concession provided significant new income.[46] A description of Hajji Quli Sardar As'ad and other Bakhtiyari leaders by the British official Sir Mortimer Durand shows his surprise at finding a leader of nomads who could deal with him in his own cultural sphere:

[He had] a fine new house with many curious prints and pictures on the walls; and his little son, a bright pleasant boy of twelve, came and read to us a little story out of an English book ... the chiefs were very well read. It was curious to hear them talking of Stanley's travels in Africa, and the war in the Transvaal, and bacteriology, and all sorts of unexpected things. The Sipahdar told us he had a son who was being educated in Paris.[47]

The ordinary nomads did not share all the advantages of their leaders. Although in general the tax burden on nomads was lighter than that of peasants, it was nonetheless oppressive and observers noted the poverty of some nomads.[48]

---

[43] Oberling, *Qashqāī*, p. 49.   [44] Beck, *Qashqa'i*, pp. 72–76.
[45] Beck, *Qashqa'i*, pp. 86–87.   [46] Khazeni, *Tribes and Empire*, pp. 112–157.
[47] Potts, *Nomadism*, pp. 328–329.
[48] Oberling, *Qashqāī*, p. 60; Tapper, *Frontier Nomads*, pp. 188, 243.

The Qajar Military

Nomads were an essential part of the Qajar military. Despite considerable effort and the use of outside advisors and officers, the Qajars were never able to create a standing army that was strong enough to enforce the will of the state, let alone to defend its territory. Most of the cavalry, which formed the core of the army, was recruited from nomadic populations. Like earlier rulers in Azerbaijan, the shah called together tribal leaders at the Persian new year in March and gave orders for the recruitment of troops.[49] Facing the expansionist Russian Empire on his border, Fath 'Ali Shah's son 'Abbas Mirza, governor of Azerbaijan, followed the lead of the Ottomans and created a new standing army, the *nizām-jadīd*, which was equipped with modern uniforms and trained by European officers. This move aimed to make the state less dependent on tribal levies. Used against the Russians in 1812, the unit suffered a humiliating defeat. There were several further attempts at army reform over the century, but the quality of the standing army remained low; it was poorly equipped and even more poorly paid. Many soldiers had to turn to outside work to survive, and mutinies were not infrequent.[50] Training for most of the troops concentrated on parade drill, the goal being to produce a respectable army for reviews. Weapons practice was limited to the tribal infantry who had already been trained in the use of firearms.[51]

The tribal cavalry regiments were considered a more effective force. These were salaried forces provided in return for tax exemptions and were led by tribal commanders.[52] Most troops came from the north, but both the Bakhtiyari and the Qashqa'i contributed regiments led by members of the *ilkhani* families. Command of these contingents gave the younger members of the family valuable experience and connections with the dynasty and elites outside their territory.[53] The armies serving the Shahs were only a part of the military forces present in Iran. Princes assigned to governorships were expected to raise armies from their regions, and they often recruited tribesmen.[54] The *ilkhani* families had their own tribal contingents, and in some cases at least, the chiefs of

---

[49] Tapper, *Frontier Nomads*, p. 185; Stephanie Cronin, *Armies and State-Building in the Modern Middle East: Politics, Nationalism and Military Reform* (London: I. B. Tauris, 2014), p. 46; Potts, *Nomadism*, p. 297.

[50] Cronin, *Armies*, pp. 55–62; Martin, *Qajar Pact*, pp. 134–143.

[51] Reza Ra'iss Tousi, "The Persian Army, 1880–1907," *Middle Eastern Studies* 24, no. 2 (1988), pp. 210–212.

[52] Tousi, "The Persian Army, 1880–1907," p. 217; Cronin, *Armies*, p. 63; Garthwaite, *Khans and Shahs*, pp. 64–65.

[53] Garthwaite, *Khans and Shahs*, pp. 64–65, 79–81; Oberling, *Qashqāī*, pp. 48, 70.

[54] Beck, *Qashqa'i*, p. 75.

subordinate tribes likewise had private forces at their disposal.[55] What made nomad troops useful – and at the same time potentially dangerous – was their access to modern firearms. Despite attempts by the shahs to limit arms sales, the tribes were able to buy guns from the British in the south or from the Russians in the north, and observers considered the tribal confederations significantly better armed than the standing army.[56] By the later nineteenth century, breech-loading firearms suitable for mounted cavalry were available, and their use was a significant advantage.

Nomads in the Constitutional Revolution and World War I

After the death of Nasir al-Din Shah in 1896, the Qajars' hold on power outside the capital weakened, and tribal confederations became ascendant in the provinces. Britain and Russia were deeply involved in Iranian affairs, and their power was formalized in the Anglo-Russian agreement of 1907. This treaty divided Iran into three zones: the north under the influence of Russia, the southeast under British influence, and the rest a neutral zone. The British negotiated independently with the confederations of the south; they were closely allied with the powerful Shaykh Khaz'al who headed the Arab Banu Ka'b confederation centered on the border between Iran and Iraq. The Bakhtiyari also dealt directly with British officials in their negotiations over the oil concession and the Bakhtiyari road, which was built across the Zagros through Bakhtiyari lands. Fars was officially part of the neutral zone, but it lay along the trade routes to the Gulf and thus also attracted British interference.

The outbreak of the Constitutional Revolution in 1906 brought the confederations into national politics. The country was divided between those advocating a constitution and a parliament, and supporters of the Shahs. As usual in periods of strife, tribal rivalries became aligned with issues of national and international politics. These dynamics can be seen clearly in the history of Fars. The strongest leader of the Qashqa'i during this period was Isma'il Khan Sawlat al-Dawla, who was able to muster 2 or 3,000 soldiers, at least for part of the year. Nevertheless, although he held the position of *ilkhani* for most of the period from 1904 to 1933, Sawlat al-Dawla was never able to control all members of the confederation. The tribes of Fars were split both on the constitutional issue and on their relations with the British. Sawlat al-Dawla was an enemy of the British, and he quickly sided with the constitutionalists against the shah,

---

[55] Garthwaite, *Khans and Shahs*, pp. 80–81; Oberling, *Qashqāī*, p. 23; Tapper, *Frontier Nomads*, pp. 239–243.
[56] Potts, *Nomadism*, p. 323; Tousi, "The Persian Army, 1880–1907," pp. 215, 218.

allying with revolutionary clubs in Shiraz and the ulama of Fars and Najaf. The rival Khamsa were close allies of the British and now sided with the shah. With the victory of the constitutionalists and the creation of a parliament (*majlis*), the major tribal confederations were ensured representation, with seats for the Bakhtiyari, Qashqa'i, Khamsa, Shahsevan and Turkmen.[57]

The Bakhtiyari became involved later but played a decisive role and for a while gained national power. The main mover was the same Hajji 'Ali Quli Sardar As'ad who so surprised Durand with his sophistication. He had served as commander of the Bakhtiyari contingent within the prime minister's guard, then moved back and forth between the Bakhtiari territories, service in Tehran, and residence in Europe. In 1909 when Muhammad 'Ali Shah dissolved the *majlis*, 'Ali Quli was in Paris but returned to Iran and allied with Shaykh Khaz'al who provided funds for a campaign. After gathering troops among the Bakhtiyari he and his brother moved towards Tehran. As constitutionalist troops from the north joined the Bakhtiyari, support for the shah crumbled and the revolutionaries took the capital without violence, replaced Muhammad 'Ali Shah with his young son Ahmad, and restored the *majlis*.[58] In the governments that followed, the Bakhtiyari elite played a leading part. 'Ali Quli Sardar As'ad, for instance, served first as minister of the interior, then as minister of war and as Majlis deputy, while his brother Najaf Quli Khan Samsam al-Saltana was appointed as governor of Isfahan and later served as prime minister. There were also Bakhtiyari governors in several major cities, and Bakhtiyari troops remained garrisoned in the city until the autumn of 1913.

Not surprisingly, the ascent of the Bakhtiyari brought a reaction among the other tribes. Aiming to curb Bakhtiyari power, the Qashqa'i even allied with their rivals, the Khamsa, and Ismail Khan Sawlat al-Dawla created a brief alliance with Shaykh Khaz'al of Muhammara and the leader of the Lurs.[59] As the government in Tehran suffered one crisis after another, the countryside outside Tehran increasingly came under the control of the tribal confederations. This situation brought disorder and problems for both nomad and settled. Rivalry among confederations was one problem; another was increasingly assertive leadership at the sub-tribal level, which made it impossible for the *ilkhani*s to assert control over their subordinates or to prevent raids along the routes. Both tribal power and general disorder in Iran lasted through World War I. Iran began the

---

[57] Beck, *Qashqa'i*, pp. 100–106.

[58] 'A. A. Sa'īdī Sīrjānī, "Baktīārī; Ḥājī 'Alīqolī Khan Sardār As'ad," *EIr*; Khazeni, *Tribes and Empire*, pp. 176–182.

[59] Oberling, *Qashqāī*, p. 91; Beck, *Qashqa'i*, p. 107.

twentieth century much as it had found itself before the Qajar dynasty, with a central government unable to assert power over its nominal realm and the countryside largely under the control of local powers, many of them largely nomadic.

The Early Twentieth Century in the Arab Lands

During World War I the Ottoman Empire sided with the Axis powers and became a significant theater in the war, which brought disruption and suffering to nomad and settled populations but also offered opportunities for self-assertion. Over the course of the nineteenth century the British had gained influence over parts of the empire, concentrating their attention on Egypt and the Persian Gulf. When World War I broke out local leaders had to decide which power to support. The two best-known movements involving nomads were the creation of the new Sa'udi state and the Arab Revolt of 1916. Both began in the Arabian Peninsula, which had preserved significant autonomy and a large Bedouin population. Both initiatives, however, were led by people from the settled population and owed part of their success to financial backing from European powers.

The twentieth century transformed the Arabian Peninsula. At the turn of the century the Ottomans began to build a modern infrastructure; the telegraph was extended to the Hijaz in 1900 and the Hijaz railway reached Medina in 1908, posing a threat to Bedouin income from the pilgrimage. As a result, there were attempts to destroy the railroad tracks, which the Ottomans countered with force but also with subsidies and gifts.[60] The beginning of the century also saw the rise of the second Sa'udi state, created by 'Abd al'Aziz Al-Sa'ud (Ibn Sa'ud). The Sa'udis had lost Riyadh in 1890 and had taken refuge in Kuwait; from here Ibn Sa'ud launched a successful surprise attack on Riyadh in 1902 with a force of only forty to sixty men. Over the next several years he took several commercial towns from the Rashidis. All this he achieved with an army made up largely of townsmen. In 1913 he took the coastal region of Hasa, a strategic region for the trade of the Peninsula, particularly for the Shammar tribe. At this point the Ottomans, generally favoring the Rashidi, came to an agreement also with Ibn Sa'ud, recognizing him as a vassal.[61] Meanwhile the British India Office was searching for allies against the Ottomans, and in 1915 they signed an agreement with Ibn Sa'ud as ruler of Najd, Hasa, and other territories, giving him a lump sum of 20,000 pounds and promising a regular subsidy along with shipments

[60] Rasheed, *Politics*, p. 209.   [61] Rasheed, *A History*, pp. 38–39.

of machine guns and rifles. In return he was not to correspond with other foreign powers or attack local leaders under British protection.[62]

While this was happening the British Commissioner in Cairo was pursuing a different course, wooing the Hashimite ruler of the Hijaz, Sharif Husayn, and encouraging him to rebel against the Ottomans. As recompense he was promised an independent Arab kingdom after the war, which would include Mesopotamia and most of Syria. The British offered money, guns and grain in return. This was the famous Husayn-McMahon correspondence. Although Sharif Husayn's religious prestige made him well-positioned to lead a revolt, he was less well off from a military standpoint. The Ottoman government had about 12,000 troops garrisoned in the cities of the Hijaz. The Sharif, responsible for the countryside and the tribal confederations, had an insignificant regular army and depended on volunteers from the tribal confederations.[63] The history of the Arab Revolt illustrates both the strengths and – even more clearly – the limitations of Arab tribal armies.

Sharif Husayn remained the acknowledged leader, but the active fighting was carried out by his four sons; the most central was Faysal about whom we are well informed because the famous T. E. Lawrence – Lawrence of Arabia – was attached to his camp. Sharif Husayn had spent time in exile in Istanbul, and his sons were educated there. At the same time, they were well schooled in the tribal politics necessary to assemble a fighting force in the Hijaz.[64] On June 2, 1916, Faysal and his brother 'Ali set out to gather tribal forces and on June 9 they cut the railroad track and the telegraph lines, then defeated the Ottoman garrison of Mecca. Over the months that followed they took Jeddah, Ta'if and several Red Sea ports with the help of British forces. However, their position soon deteriorated, and their forces began to disperse.[65] While Sharif Husayn and his sons were motivated by wider ambitions, their tribal followers had primarily local concerns: rivalries with other tribes, fear of Ottoman encroachment and the threat the railway posed to their livelihood. They also required payment. Faysal had nothing to give and had to disguise the fact by having a locked chest filled with stones conspicuously guarded by his slaves and carried into his tent every night.[66]

---

[62] Rasheed, *A History*, pp. 39–40.
[63] William Ochsenwald, *Religion, Society and the State in Arabia: The Hijaz under Ottoman Control, 1840–1908* (Columbus: Ohio State University Press, 1984), pp. 154–158; Eugene Rogan, *The Fall of the Ottomans: The Great War in the Middle East* (New York: Basic Books, 2015), p. 302; Ali A. Allawi, *Faisal I of Iraq* (New Haven, CT: Yale University Press, 2014), p. 73.
[64] Allawi, *Faisal*, pp. 10–17.
[65] Allawi, *Faisal*, pp. 69–70, 74–75; Rogan, *The Fall*, pp. 299–301.
[66] Allawi, *Faisal*, p. 72.

Over the next months the Hashemites managed to improve their central army and to recoup their losses. For the army they recruited both officers and soldiers from Arabs who had been Ottoman prisoners of war, creating a small but dependable regular army. The British furnished the funds needed to reward tribes, and crucial support in holding the Hashemite positions.[67] The progress of the Arab Revolt often seemed to the British maddeningly slow and fitful: the princes spent much of their time in meals and audiences, drinking coffee, exchanging news and mediating disputes, but this activity was the necessary prelude to gathering and keeping their armies. Since most tribal volunteers only fought near to their own terrain, a campaign in a new area required a new army; one coalition was used for the central Hijaz, another had to be formed for the northern Hijaz, and yet another for the campaign into Syria. While the forces of the Arab Revolt are often referred to as Bedouin, in the Hijaz the majority came from largely sedentary tribes, and at the beginning the camel riders made up at most 10 percent. As the campaign moved north through more fully nomadic territory, the Bedouin became an increasingly important part of the army.[68] Over time the Arab Revolt turned largely to guerrilla tactics; one of their major assignments was to attack the Hijaz Railroad, providing diversion for the Egyptian Expeditionary force under Allenby. This task was well suited to the nomad and semi-nomad tribes of the region, who were long accustomed to raiding travel routes. The Arab Revolt thus fulfilled British needs and raised Faysal to prominence as a successful leader. As it turned out, however, the revolt did not win the expected rewards for either the Hashemites or the tribes they led. The Hashemites were not given the territories they had been promised, and the war brought changes, both technological and political, which gradually undermined nomad power.

Nomads in the Middle East after World War I

After the first two decades of the twentieth century nomad tribes gradually lost much of their influence. Neither the new states which arose at this period, nor the European colonial powers wished to incorporate nomads as earlier states had done. Part of this change was due to advances in military

---

[67] Allawi, *Faisal*, p. 82; Rogan, *The Fall*, pp. 303–307.

[68] Allawi, *Faisal*, pp. 77–80; Joseph Kostiner, "The Hashimite Tribal Confederacy of the Arab Revolt, 1916–1917," in *National and International Politics in the Middle East: Essays in Honour of Elie Kedourie*, ed. Edward Ingram (London: F. Cass, 1986), p. 13. See also Max Freiherr von Oppenheim, *Die Beduinen*, vol. 2, 3 (Leipzig: Otto Harrassowitz, 1939–1952), vol. 2, pp. 232, 277, 293, vol. 3, p. 88.

218   Nomads in the Modern Middle East

technology that allowed states to assert control over difficult regions. Perhaps the most important weapon was the airplane, which was highly effective against nomad troops and camps. Neither desert nor mountain could now offer secure protection. Equally significant was the growing reach of state infrastructure, which made it possible for the central government to control the countryside and to collect taxes, while new roads and railways replaced old trade routes and deprived nomads of much of their earlier income. Thus, nomadic populations were weakened in part by force, and in part by the changes inherent in modernization.

In the Arabian Peninsula the 1920s brought the rise of the Sa'udi state. While the Hashemites were leading the Arab Revolt, Ibn Sa'ud had been expanding his power. In 1921 he inflicted a decisive defeat on the Rashidis, and in 1925 completed his conquest of the Hashemite kingdom, becoming the sultan of Najd and king of the Hijaz. Like many other states of the period, the Sa'udis used the nomads but eventually helped to weaken them. Ibn Sa'ud belonged to a sedentary lineage and the core of his army came from village and agricultural populations; throughout his career, these were the people he could count on.[69] Wahhabi doctrine promoted a generally negative view of nomadism, portraying nomads as ignorant and unobservant – they had to be brought into the fold before they could be considered true Muslims.[70] Nonetheless, Ibn Sa'ud needed Bedouin troops and, like the Rashidis and the Hashemites, he spent considerable time on tribal politics.

Under Ibn Sa'ud a new movement developed which tapped the manpower of the nomadic tribes: the Ikhwan ("brothers"), who became active about 1912. It was customary to send preachers from the Wahhabi villages to proselytize among the neighboring tribes. These preachers had considerable success, even among the Bedouin. Tribal converts were encouraged to abandon nomadism and perform the *hijra* – that is, to move into a truly Islamic, and settled, community. This policy was a direct reference to the Prophet Muhammad's *hijra* from Mecca to Medina and was also a recreation of the *hijra* policy of the early Muslim rulers discussed in Chapter 2, which encouraged men to leave their tribes and settle as soldiers in the new garrison cities. Converts who answered this call at the time of Ibn Sa'ud were known as Ikhwan, and they settled in new towns

---

[69] Abdulaziz H. al-Fahad, "The *'Imama vs.* the *'Iqal: Hadari*-Bedouin Conflict and the Formation of the Saudi State," in *Counter-Narratives: History, Contemporary Society, and Politics in Saudi Arabia and Yemen*, ed. Madawi al-Rasheed and Robert Vitalis (New York: Palgrave Macmillan, 2004), pp. 43, 49–50.

[70] David Commins, *The Mission and the Kingdom: Wahhabi Power behind the Saudi Throne* (London: I. B. Tauris, 2016), pp. 80–81; al-Fahad, "'Imama," pp. 42–45.

called *hijra* (plural *hujar*) where they were expected to take up sedentary occupations but also be ready at all times to be called up for war.
The Ikhwan soon attempted to enforce the Wahhabi doctrine on
populations who were not fully compliant. The first *hijra* was set up
in 1913 and other settlements quickly developed thereafter, so that
by 1930 most tribes had settlements associated with them.[71]

Ibn Sa'ud quickly began to make use of the Ikhwan, providing them
stipends and incorporating them into his armies. Scholars are not entirely
in agreement about their military importance, but they were certainly
a major force during Ibn Sa'ud's rise to power, pushing for expansion and
sometimes for forcible conversion.[72] However the Ikhwan were a two-
edged sword, and the inner edge was almost as sharp as the outer. The
atrocities they committed against nomads and Shi'ites created ill-will,
threatening Ibn Sa'ud's reputation, and they brought disorder both into
the state administration and into the management of tribal grazing
grounds. Their refusal to accept the borders agreed upon between Ibn
Sa'ud and the British in 1925 and their continued raiding into Syria and
Iraq also threatened relations with the European powers. There were
crises in 1916, 1919, and 1925–1926, and from 1927 to 1930 on the
Ikhwan were fully in revolt, finally defeated only with the help of British
air power.[73]

It is difficult to assess how the Ikhwan related to nomadism or to
the issue of tribal power. On one hand, they gave up their animals to
take up a settled life, and the importance of this step was emphasized
both by the Ikhwan themselves, who often attacked nomads as infidels, and by Ibn Sa'ud.[74] On the other hand, the boundaries between
the Ikhwan in the *hujar* and their Wahhabi fellow-tribesmen outside
were not always clear. It is notable that among the complaints from
the Ikhwan were the taxation of nomadic tribes and limitations on
grazing land.[75] The relation of the Ikhwan movement to tribal power
is also ambiguous. The Ikhwan were to move away from the tribe
into the *hujar*. Meanwhile, tribal leaders were strongly invited to
move to Riyadh for proper indoctrination, where they were brought
into the central tribal council, and had to depend on the government

---

[71] Rasheed, *A History*, pp. 57–58; John S. Habib, *Ibn Sa'ud's Warriors of Islam: The Ikhwan
of Najd and Their Role in the Creation of the Sa'udi Kingdom, 1910–1930* (Leiden: Brill,
1978), pp. 47–59.
[72] Joseph Kostiner, "On Instruments and Their Designers: The Ikhwan of Najd and the
Emergence of the Saudi State," *Middle Eastern Studies* 21, no. 3 (1985), pp. 306–307.
[73] Kostiner, "On Instruments," pp. 305, 309, 311–315; Rasheed, *A History*, pp. 62–68;
Habib, *Ibn Sa'ud's Warriors*, pp. 79–86.
[74] Commins, *Mission*, pp. 85–87; Kostiner, "On Instruments," pp. 308–309.
[75] Commins, *Mission*, pp. 88–89.

for gifts to distribute.[76] On the other hand, most *hujar* were settled by a particular tribe and remained associated with it; Ikhwan settled in the *hujar* therefore retained loyalty to their tribal leaders. Chief among these was Faysal al-Duwish, head of the Mutayr tribe, who fought against the creation of frontiers which cut off migration routes, restricted raiding, and denied tribes access to grazing and wells.[77]

In general, scholars have interpreted the Ikhwan rebellion as a movement to preserve tribal power; thus, Ibn Sa'ud's victory over the Ikhwan should be seen as a victory for a centralized, non-tribal state.[78] By 1925 he had abolished the tribal *diras* and outlawed the practice of intertribal raids. From the 1920s and increasingly after the defeat of the Ikhwan, the nomad tribes were made dependent on subsidies from the central government and lost much of their independence.[79]

In Iraq and Syria nomads and tribes also lost influence, while the government gradually gained decisive power. After the war it became clear that the British did not plan to honor their promises of Arab independence, and that the French did not intend to give up Syria. The French and British Mandates imposed foreign and more intrusive rule which brought resistance from their new subjects. Nomads were involved, but they were not the leaders in the larger movements. The Iraqi Revolt of 1920, remembered as a decisive moment in Iraqi national consciousness, was begun by nationalists and depended on the military manpower of the tribes of the middle and southern Euphrates who practiced agriculture along with sheep and goat pastoralism.[80] Some Bedouin of the northern regions, notably the Shammar Jarba who occupied much of the Jazira, were active at the beginning of the revolt, but they were quickly put down by the British.[81] The revolt in central and southern Iraq lasted several more months, but the use of the British air force, with the destruction of villages and other settlements, extinguished the uprising before the end of the year.[82] While many tribes resisted, some shaykhs played a different

---

[76] Habib, *Ibn Sa'ud's Warriors*, pp. 30, 48–52.   [77] Commins, *Mission*, pp. 88–89.

[78] Rasheed, *A History*, p. 6; al-Fahad, "'Imama," p. 36; Kostiner, "On Instruments," p. 307.

[79] Ugo Fabietti, "State Policies and Bedouin Adaptation in Saudi Arabia, 1900–1980," in *The Transformation of Nomadic Society in the Arab East*, ed. Martha Mundy and Basim Musallam (Cambridge: Cambridge University Press, 2000), pp. 84–85.

[80] Amal Vinogradov, "The 1920 Revolt in Iraq Reconsidered: The Role of Tribes in National Politics," *International Journal of Middle East Studies* 3, no. 2 (1972).

[81] Charles Tripp, *A History of Iraq* (Cambridge: Cambridge University Press, 2007), pp. 39–40; John Frederick Williamson, "A Political History of the Shammar Jarba Tribe of al-Jazirah: 1800–1958," unpublished PhD dissertation, Indiana University (1974), pp. 154–155.

[82] Vinogradov, "1920 Revolt," pp. 136–138.

game, allying themselves with successive powers, choosing them according to their chances of success and their willingness to pay for service. The prime example of this was Shaykh Nuri al-Sha'lan of the Ruwalla Bedouin: he first served the Ottomans, then joined Faysal in the Arab revolt, and after that he went back and forth between the British and the French, finally receiving a stipend from the French for safeguarding caravans in the desert.[83]

Although nomads who resisted could be defeated, nomads did pose a challenge to both the British and the French mandates, just as the new order posed a challenge for them. The new boundaries drawn in the north between the Turkish Republic, French Syria, and British Iraq and in the south with the rising Sa'udi state, often divided tribes and compromised migration routes. For the nomads these boundaries meant that they might be blocked from moving to seasonal pastures and face the loss of their livestock. If they did migrate, they faced the possibility of paying taxes to two separate states.[84] For government authorities, the presence of state borders meant that tribal shaykhs could escape across them after conducting raids.

The Mandate powers adopted many of the earlier Ottoman policies. Like the Ottomans, the French and British encouraged nomads to engage in agriculture. They also attempted to register arable land in the name of individuals, leading to further concentration of land in the hands of tribal shaykhs. We find ever more tribal shaykhs engaging in agriculture on a large scale, often in tandem with merchants from the city.[85] The Mandate powers identified a leader for each tribe, paid him a regular subsidy, and held him responsible for maintaining order and delivering taxes; in some cases, they allowed the collection of *khuwwa*.[86] In their response towards raiding, however, the British and French pursued a new and different policy. The Ottomans had not attempted to prevent

---

[83] Dawn Chatty, *From Camel to Truck: the Bedouin in the Modern World* (New York: Vantage Press, 1986), pp. 18–19; Allawi, *Faisal*, p. 449.

[84] Williamson, "A Political History," pp. 171–173; Tariq Tall, "The Politics of Rural Policy in East Jordan, 1920–1989," in *The Transformation of Nomadic Society in the Middle East*, ed. Martha Mundi and Basim Musallam (Cambridge: Cambridge University Press, 2000), p. 93.

[85] Chatty, *From Camel*, pp. 40–41, 69–70; Tripp, *A History*, pp. 43, 51, 180; Christian Velud, "French Mandate Policy in the Syrian Steppe," in *The Transformation of Nomadic Society in the Arab East*, ed. Martha Mundi and Basim Musallam (Cambridge: Cambridge University Press), p. 75; Philip S. Khoury, *Syria and the French Mandate: The Politics of Arab Nationalism 1920–1945* (Princeton, NJ: Princeton University Press, 1987), p. 187.

[86] Velud, "French Mandate Policy," pp. 64–67; Philip S. Khoury, "The Tribal Shaykh, French Tribal Policy, and the Nationalist Movement in Syria between Two World Wars," *Middle Eastern Studies* 18, no. 2 (1982), pp. 185–186; Tripp, *A History*, p. 38; Williamson, "A Political History," pp. 153–154, 167, 180.

intertribal conflict and were willing to put up with disorder for the sake of preventing tribal alliances. In contrast, the French and the British were eager to end raiding and inserted themselves in the process of tribal negotiation, bringing tribes together with Mandate officials. They collaborated on two major conferences in 1925 and 1927. In 1926 raiding became illegal in British Iraq, sometimes punished by air raids, and in 1927 the French and British established a tribal court to settle claims.[87] Over the long run the reduction in raiding did much to weaken tribal leaders as a political force, since military leadership had been an important part of their authority over their tribes.

Although increasing sedentarization of nomads during the interwar period was due in part to Mandate policy, much was also the result of economic and technological development. World War I had ushered in the age of oil and of motor transport. Over the course of a few decades the truck and car made the caravan a thing of the past and largely destroyed the market for camels. Thus, the Bedouin, who had been the most prestigious and powerful of the nomads, lost much of their economic base – the sale of camels and horses and the guidance of caravans. Some became settled or turned to other occupations, often in transport or the military. Others replaced camels with herds of sheep and goats, still earning a living, but no longer able to retreat into the distant desert and retain their independence.[88] The war and the development of the machine gun likewise marked the end of cavalry as a fighting force, weakening the market for horses and the usefulness of mounted soldiers. Many tribal shaykhs now became fully part of the urban elite, with their main residence in town and only occasional visits in the tribe. Some became members of the Syrian Chamber of Delegates, thus becoming representatives more than leaders of tribes.[89] The nomads of Iraq and Syria did not cease all military activity, and we find them still engaging in occasional raids throughout the first half of the century. However, they were no longer central to the politics of the region as a whole.

Nomads in Pahlavi Iran

In Iran, a similar development took place in the twentieth century, one that was likewise due to both government policy and economic change. At the end of World War I, the central government held almost no power outside of Tehran. The south of the country was dominated by the great tribal confederations, which were under the sway of the British.

---

[87] Chatty, *From Camel*, pp. 34–36, 57–58; Williamson, "A Political History," pp. 164–171.
[88] Chatty, *From Camel*, pp. 40–42.   [89] Khoury, "The Tribal Shaykh," pp. 186–189.

Kurdistan, Azerbaijan and Gilan were largely under the control of separatist movements, and there were revolts among the Kurds and in Khorasan. In 1921 the British encouraged the Cossack Brigade led by the officer Reza Khan to take over Tehran. Reza Khan became minister of war, but from the beginning he was the active power, and in 1925 he was proclaimed shah. His goal was to form a centralized nation state in Iran, with a population as homogeneous and as Persian as he could make it. In this endeavor he had the approval of government officials and modern intellectuals; few people in Iran wanted a continuation of the confusion and lawlessness then prevailing. In his early campaigns against tribal powers Reza Khan had the support of some tribal leadership, and nomads made up part of the army he sent against recalcitrant tribes.[90]

In the mid-1920s, Reza Shah sharpened his campaign against the largely nomadic tribal confederations, particularly against the most powerful – the Qashqa'i and the Bakhtiyari. He put the Qashqa'i under a military governorship and ordered them disarmed. What made central control painful was not simply incorporation, but the oppression and corruption that accompanied it. The treatment of the Qashqa'i was symbolized by one particular outrage: an army captain's demand that Qashqa'i women feed his litter of puppies with their breast milk.[91]

Reza Shah assailed tribal power from a variety of directions. At the beginning he sought to attract the tribal leadership, working to separate them from the lower echelons of the tribe. As in other states, land-registration laws often resulted in the conversion of communal pasture into personal property owned by the khans. This situation was resented by ordinary nomads and peasants within the tribe, creating a division between the top leadership and tribesmen.[92] Reza Shah both exploited and exacerbated these tensions. The tribal leadership spent considerable time in Tehran or provincial cities; Reza now used representation in the central *majlis* to keep them away from tribal territories. In 1923 he engineered the election of Sawlat al-Dawla Qashqa'i to the *majlis* and then restricted him to the capital.[93] Over time, increasing numbers of tribal *ilkhani*s were detained in Tehran or provincial cities. In their absence the middle leadership, chiefs of individual tribes, became more autonomous.[94] Nomadic populations participated increasingly in the national and international economy as day laborers, some, especially the Bakhtiyari, working in the oil industry. Their interests thus began to

[90] Stephanie Cronin, *Tribal Politics in Iran: Rural Conflict and the New State, 1921–1941* (London: Routledge, 2007), pp. 2–5; Beck, *Qashqa'i*, pp. 129–130.
[91] Beck, *Qashqa'i*, p. 132.   [92] Cronin, *Tribal Politics*, pp. 85–86, 94–97.
[93] Beck, *Qashqa'i*, p. 131; Cronin, *Tribal Politics*, p. 25, 43–44.
[94] Cronin, *Tribal Politics*, pp. 70–73, 120, 124.

diverge from those of the khans, and they became more aware of the public sphere. Reza Shah was able to use press campaigns to discredit tribal leaders not only with the general public, but also among some tribespeople as well.[95]

The Bakhtiyari, the most powerful confederation at the end of World War I, was the most vulnerable, due in part to its involvement in central politics. Ironically, the other weakness of the Bakhtiyari leaders was their income as shareholders in the Anglo-Persian Oil Company. The shares they received represented the tribal interest but were held in the name of the leading lineage. Over time, as expenses mounted and the Great Depression set in, members of the family borrowed against their shares, encouraged by the company, which provided loans it knew could not be repaid. Money which was supposed to be passed to the tribal membership as a whole could no longer be given, causing increasing resentment from the subordinate khans.[96] The result was that when the government attacked, the Bakhtiyari leaders could not count on support from the lower echelon of the tribe.

In 1927–1928 Reza Shah began to implement his modernization plan, introducing a census, land registration, and a western dress code. Again, the program was carried out without consideration for the population and it aroused opposition throughout the countryside. The government also began to relocate tribes and to implement forcible settlement of nomads.[97] These moves, together with Reza Shah's dismissal of the head of the Khamsa confederation, brought the southern tribes into rebellion; the Khamsa, Qashqa'i and neighboring tribes raised armies strong enough to attack the aerodrome, cut the routes, and threaten Shiraz. At this time the *ilkhani* Sawlat al-Dawla was under arrest, and the uprising was organized by other members of the lineage along with mid-level tribal leaders. The struggle ended in a stalemate; the Pahlavi army was still not truly effective, while the tribes could not remain stationary around Shiraz when the change of season required migration. The next year several sections of the Bakhtiyari rebelled and scored a number of victories. The government had to give in to some of the tribal demands, releasing imprisoned leaders and removing direct government oversight.[98]

Reza Shah, however, was still determined to bring the nomadic tribes fully under control. The forcible settlement of nomads was implemented from 1932 onwards; nomads were forbidden to migrate in their usual large groups and were to practice agriculture, moving into newly

---

[95] Cronin, *Tribal Politics*, pp. 103–104.   [96] Cronin, *Tribal Politics*, pp. 133–159.
[97] Cronin, *Tribal Politics*, pp. 31–32, 113.   [98] Cronin, *Tribal Politics*, pp. 104, 120–127.

constructed houses. It was impossible to build enough houses in the time allotted and some locations were not habitable for the whole year. Migrations were blocked by the army and sometimes attacked through aerial bombing. These measures resulted in a huge loss of livestock for the nomads, and for the settled population, an acute shortage of meat and dairy products. Both ordinary nomads and peasants suffered destitution.[99] The resulting crisis brought a suspension of the prohibition of migrations in 1933, but due to corruption, migration often required bribery and the fees became a drain on the pastoral economy.[100]

Reza Shah next went against the tribal leadership. An undefined conspiracy known as the "Bakhtiyari plot" served as a pretext for the arrest of many of the Bakhtiyari elite – much of their land was expropriated and a number were executed. Sawlat al-Dawla Qashqa'i was again arrested, along with his son, for supposedly fomenting revolt. He and several other tribal leaders died in prison, presumably after a dose of what was known as "Pahlavi coffee."[101] Tribal representation in the *majlis* was ended. Tribes came under direct military rule and most tribal leaders were forbidden to enter their tribal territories. By the end of the 1930s the nomads were impoverished, without effective leadership, and becoming sedentarized.[102]

It was World War II that rescued the nomads of Iran. Reza Shah was sympathetic to the Germans, and in 1941 the British and Russians forced him to abdicate. On his departure many pastoralists abandoned their houses, bought livestock and re-armed. The tribal leaders, released from prison, returned to the tribal territories and to their former positions. They regained importance also in national politics, though not at the level they had earlier known.

Nomads in the Modern World

While nomads remained active after World War II, their political weight was much reduced. Uprisings could cause inconvenience, but they did not seriously threaten the central government. With the creation of newly independent states – or in the case of Iran, a return to independence – rulers in the Middle East were eager to present themselves as modern and developed. Thus, most governments promoted sedentarization. Usually, foreign advisors and agricultural specialists encouraged more intensive land use and likewise saw nomads as a holdover from the past who were

[99] Cronin, *Tribal Politics*, pp. 88, 167–170, 191–192; Beck, *Qashqa'i*, pp. 137–139.
[100] Cronin, *Tribal Politics*, pp. 35–38, 110.
[101] Cronin, *Tribal Politics*, pp. 165–166, 172–186; Beck, *Qashqa'i*, p. 137.
[102] Cronin, *Tribal Politics*, pp. 34, 156, 166; Beck, *Qashqa'I*, pp. 131, 140–142.

sure to disappear over time.[103] Increasing government control over the allocation of land and maintenance of order led to the loss of important functions for the leadership of tribes, no longer able to lead military raids or to allocate pastures. Many tribal chiefs were now spending more of their time in cities, though some retained the functions of representative and mediator.[104] The result of these changes has been an increase in sedentarization. Many of those who remained nomadic supplemented their income through a range of occupations, including contract herding and various forms of transport and day labor.[105] As I have shown, subsidiary occupations are attested also at an earlier period, so this is not an entirely new phenomenon.

As was the case in the interwar period, the suppression of nomadism was pursued with greater intensity in Iran than in the Arab countries. After the abdication of Reza Shah and the resumption of nomadism in 1941, there was a resurgence of tribal activity which alarmed Reza Shah's son and successor, Muhammad Reza Shah (1941–1979), and he moved strongly against the nomads in the 1960s. Leadership was destroyed at the level of individual tribes, with migration, land allocation, settlement of disputes and military activity again taken over by the government. The national Land Reform Law of 1962 targeted tribal lands in particular. Another and very effective policy against nomadism was the importation of meat and milk products from abroad, which lowered their price and made the pastoral economy less profitable.[106] Muhammad Reza Shah's reign ended with the 1979 revolution and the establishment of the Islamic Republic, which at first showed favor to pastoralists. Meat and dairy imports ended, and nomadism once again increased. Some of the tribal leaders, including those of the Qashqa'i, returned to Iran hoping to resume their former positions, but the Islamic Republic soon turned against them and has kept the nomadic population securely under government control ever since.[107]

Towards the end of the twentieth century the remaining nomads of the Middle East adopted motor transport on their annual migrations. Instead of moving slowly through spring and fall pastures to reach their summer and winter grazing grounds, most nomads now load their animals in

---

[103] Chatty, *From Camel*, pp. xviii–xix; Donald P. Cole, "Where Have the Bedouin Gone?" *Anthropological Quarterly* 76, no. 2 (2003), p. 259.

[104] Chatty, *From Camel*, pp. 58–60.

[105] Lois Beck, "Economic Transformations Among Qashqa'i Nomads, 1962–1978," in *Continuity and Change in Modern Iran*, ed. Michael E. Bonine and Nikki R. Keddie (Albany, NY: State University of New York Press, 1981), pp. 94–96; Chatty, *From Camel*, pp. 108–110; Potts, *Nomadism*, p. 417.

[106] Beck, "Economic Transformation," p. 101.

[107] Tapper, *Frontier Nomads*, pp. 311–314; Potts, *Nomadism*, pp. 414–417.

trucks and accomplish the migration in a few days. With fewer pastures and a longer stay in those that remain, it has become necessary to purchase feed. Nomads therefore remain near the settled community for much of the year.[108] Pastoralism by truck is more profitable and probably easier, but some aspects of earlier migrations are missed. Among the Bedouin, it appears that it is the women, not the men, who have regretted the end of the long migrations, which were times in which much of their labor was cooperative rather than individual. With the loss of the camel, moreover, other satisfying tasks such as weaving have been reduced or eliminated.[109] For the Qashqa'i in Iran, the shortening of the migration season has also affected women and girls, who used to forage along the route for additional foods which added significantly to their diet, and for natural dyes to use in their weaving of rugs.[110] Pastoral nomadism has thus survived in modern form and with a market orientation. The days of long migrations, regional power and military exploits are remembered and retold, but they are no longer lived.

Nomads and Modern Nationalism

The advent of the modern period brought a major change in ideologies of state legitimation. The Middle East entered this period ruled mostly by dynasties of nomad or steppe origin, but emphasis soon shifted from dynastic legitimation to the promotion of unitary state power. Nomad forebears became less important and the challenges of controlling nomad societies less acceptable. The Tanzimat promoted direct government of the whole society and homogenization of the population. Thus, any structures and lifestyles which hindered the penetration of government into society were viewed negatively. Nomads came to be seen as savage and backward people who had to be settled if the region was to become part of the enlightened modern world. The belief that nomadism was a holdover from pre-modern society, something to be phased out as society modernized, was shared with many European thinkers and lasted well into the twentieth century.[111]

In the nineteenth century some nostalgia for nomad origins did survive. The Ottoman sultan Abdul-Hamid (1876–1909) revived the Oghuz

---

[108] Tapper, *Frontier Nomads*, pp. 310, 313; Beck, "Economic Transformation," p. 105; Chatty, *From Camel*, p. 104.

[109] Chatty, *From Camel*, pp. 104–110.   [110] Beck, *Qashqa'i*, pp. 105–106.

[111] Selim Deringil, "'They Live in a State of Nomadism and Savagery:' The Late Ottoman Empire and the Post-Colonial Debate," *Comparative Studies in Society and History* 45, no. 2 (2003), pp. 312, 317, 327; *The Well-Protected Domains: Ideology and the Legitimation of Power in the Ottoman Empire 1876–1909* (London: I. B. Tauris, 1998), pp. 31–32.

genealogy of the Ottomans, which had been celebrated in the fifteenth century but was later ignored. A commemorative ceremony was staged yearly at the shrine of the dynasty's legendary founder, Ertuğrul Gazi, with the "original tribe" of the Ottomans dressed as medieval Central Asian warriors. After the rise of the Turkish Republic in 1923, Mustafa Kemal (Ataturk) discarded the Ottoman heritage and promoted a new Turkish identity. Now Turks were identified not by their nomad and imperial steppe heritage, but linguistically, and also physically through their supposed brachycephalic build – their short, wide skulls. Studies of physical anthropology were commissioned, along with a government project to produce terms of Turkic origin to replace Arabic and Persian words. With the dictates of modern nationalism demanding a local origin, neither the Oghuz Khan legend nor the Türk Khaghanate of Mongolia would serve, and the formation of the Turks was pushed back in time to accommodate the Hittites, who had ruled a powerful empire in central Anatolia from about 1600 to 1180 BC and could thus be identified with modern-day Turkey from well before the time of Islam.[112]

In Iran the westernizing elite of the late nineteenth century came to see nomads as the cause of Iranian decline and eventual subjugation to the west.[113] During the Constitutional Revolution, the rescue of the constitutional government by the Bakhtiyari made them briefly into heroes, but as a new concept of the nation developed, nomads were seen once again as a problem. They spoke a variety of languages and often allied with the British or the Russians.[114] The chaos that followed the Constitutional Revolution and World War I, when the tribal confederations controlled much of the country, reinforced this negative view of nomadism.[115] Under Reza Shah's successor, Muhammad Reza Shah, these ideas continued in force even among the dissident intellectuals. The well-known writer Jalal Al-i Ahmad, in his famous treatise *Gharbzadegi* (*Plagued by the West*), attacked many of the shah's westernizing programs, but likewise vilified the nomads:

In short, no century in our legendary or historical past has gone by without being marred once or twice by the hoofprints of nomadic invaders from the northeast .... Each time we tried to build a house, as soon as we got to the ramparts, some hungry invading tribe would come from the northeast and pull the ladder out from under our feet, destroying everything from the foundation up.[116]

---

[112] M. Şükrü Hanioğlu, *Atatürk: An Intellectual Biography* (Princeton, NJ: Princeton University Press, 2011), pp. 160–175.
[113] Cronin, *Tribal Politics*, p. 17.
[114] Khazeni, *Tribes and Empire*, pp. 170–173; Najmabadi, *Daughters of Quchan*, pp. 35–50.
[115] Cronin, *Tribal Politics*, p. 27.
[116] Jalal Al-e Ahmad, *Plagued by the West (Gharbzadegi)* trans. Paul Sprachman (Delmar, NY: Caravan Books, 1982), pp. 12–13.

The folkloric aspect of nomadism has been seen as less objectionable than the political. The most useful nomads in this regard are the Bedouin, who have been used to promote tourism in the Arab lands and even in Israel. Thus tourism, along with transport, smuggling and day labor, has become one of the occupations taking the place of herding and control of routes. The accoutrements of Bedouin nomadism – the goat-hair tent, camels, hospitality, and the ubiquitous coffee – are now reproduced for the market.[117] In several new states the Bedouin image has been useful as an icon of national culture and identity. Radio programs in Kuwait, newly invented traditions of horse and camel racing in Sa'udi Arabia, and liberal use of the Bedouin tent hospitality in Jordan all serve to present a link to a Bedouin past which no longer presents a threat.[118] There is a parallel here with the use of the Bedouin ideal in the Umayyad and early 'Abbasid periods. If we bemoan the questionable authenticity of the modern Bedouin theme park, we must remember that the same issues confronted scholars of the ninth century who sought out Bedouin for their linguistic and cultural studies.

Conclusion

The decline of nomad power in the modern period is undoubtedly connected with the growing strength of government and the development of new military technology. What is probably even more important is the decrease in the usefulness of nomad pastoralists to settled society and to the state. The development of steamships in the nineteenth century provided transport that was more efficient than the camel caravan, where water travel was possible. The telegraph and railway allowed faster communication and travel even overland, and it is surely not by chance that both were targets of attacks by nomads. The most fateful development was the discovery and use of oil for motorized transport starting in World War I, which soon made the camel caravan obsolete. The market for camels largely disappeared, and so did the nomad responsibility for the security of routes through steppe, mountain and desert. Pastoralists had also served as guides and protectors for caravans on those routes and had controlled and taxed the regions in which they pastured. This system had not been perfect; order among tribes and between tribes and government had often broken down. However, pre-modern governments usually did not have the ability to maintain control over difficult terrain

---

[117] Cole, "Where Have the Bedouin Gone?" pp. 254–256.

[118] Cole, "Where Have the Bedouin Gone?" pp. 256–258; Andrew Shryock, *Nationalism and the Genealogical Imagination* (Berkeley: University of California Press, 1997), pp. 7, 312.

themselves, since they lacked the manpower needed to garrison roads and provide supplies. Thus, even as the governments expanded their reach, they often returned the task of controlling and taxing marginal regions to tribal leaders. In the twentieth century, with the advent of the truck and the building of roads, it became possible for states to assert stable control over territories which had earlier been under nomad protection.

World War I also introduced the machine gun and the airplane, and these ended the use of cavalry that had been at the core of Middle Eastern armies for millennia. As the markets for horses declined and nomads were no longer needed as mounted auxiliaries, the nomads of the Middle East lost several of their major functions within wider society. They were no longer indispensable in war, trade could be carried on largely without them, and the peripheral lands could be kept more or less quiet through direct government control. What remained necessary was the provision of livestock products. Despite state attempts to create a fully sedentary society, it has become clear that in some regions the practice of pastoral nomadism is still the best way to use marginal lands and to supply the population with meat, milk, wool and leather.

9   Conclusion

The central Islamic lands are set in a region of dry climate and difficult terrain; it is doubtful that they could have developed a rich cosmopolitan society without the presence of pastoral nomads. It was the improved camel saddle and the development of camel nomadism that made it possible for caravans to cross the Syrian desert and to connect Mesopotamia to the Syrian coast and the Arabian Peninsula. The mounted nomadism of the steppe likewise created new opportunities: horses, sheep and goats were combined with Bactrian camels, used in trade routes running north-south, from the forests and rivers of northern Russia to the Black Sea and Transoxiana, and east-west, linking China and the Middle East along the Silk Road from the second century BC onwards. Nomads provided most of the animals needed for caravans and were well placed to guide them through territory which they could navigate more easily than the settled population. Their military prowess and mobility also allowed them to protect the routes, a task that pre-modern states could not manage with only settled manpower. This protection was admittedly imperfect – nomad raids often disrupted trade – but even in settled districts the maintenance of security was rarely fully reliable. Finally, the nomads provided invaluable military manpower as mounted archers, and likewise the horses necessary for any state to maintain an army.

The medieval Middle East stands out for its urban development, active trade and artisanal production. We should recognize that these achievements were due in part to nomads, who not only provided the means of transport, but also helped to provision the cities with animal products – milk and meat for consumption, wool and hides for the manufacture of textiles and leather goods – central to the economy. Thus, the Islamic Middle East was built on two complementary economies. While pastoralists and agriculturalists were seen as separate, in marginal territories people moved back and forth between the two lifestyles, depending on both climate and political circumstances. In times of disorder agricultural

land might turn into pasture, and the same could happen due to pro-
longed drought. This change can be seen as a negative outcome, since
agriculture is a more intensive form of land use, but the availability of
pastoral nomadism also provided a means of survival when agriculture
failed.

The Political Dynamics of Nomad-Sedentary Relations

Just as they contributed to a complex economy, pastoral nomads played
a central role in state building within the Middle East, starting before the
rise of Islam. Part of their contribution was military. Nomads were
involved in the development first of chariot warfare and then of mounted
archery. They also made an important political contribution. We see two
different processes in state building involving nomads; the internal
nomads, such as Bedouin, usually developed small, local polities, while
those of the steppe, coming from an imperial tradition, brought their
ideology into the Middle East and created large territorial states often
with imperial pretensions.

The two best-known types of nomads internal to the Middle East were
the Arab Bedouin and the Iranian Kurds. While the Bedouin were often
important in the formation of states, they usually provided military manpower while accepting leadership from the settled population. This was
the case with the Arab conquest and early caliphate, and later with the
Isma'ili Qaramita at the turn of the tenth century and the Jannabi dynasty
which controlled the pilgrimage routes from Bahrayn and Hajar in the
first part of the tenth century, both of which have been discussed in
Chapter 3. We see a similar pattern in the nineteenth and twentieth
centuries with the rise of the Rashidi, Hashemite and Wahhabi/Sa'udi
states in the Arabian Peninsula.

Under certain conditions, however, the Bedouins and Kurds did
develop their own states; this was most likely to happen when their
territories lay between competing powers who pulled nomad groups
into their political contests, strengthening their internal leadership while
also providing tribes the opportunity to play one state against the other.
The contest between the Roman and Sassanian empires in the century
before the advent of Islam led to the rise of two well-known states or
confederations: the Lakhmids and the Ghassanids on either side of the
Syrian desert. In the tenth century a similar situation arose when the
Fatimid caliphate in Egypt competed over Syria with the Abbasids of
Baghdad. The nomad states of this period were largely local; their leaders
rose through service to nearby settled powers. In the north we see two
Bedouin powers, the Numayr (ca. 999–1077) in Mayyafariqin and the

'Uqaylids (990–1096) in Mosul, Nisibis and Anbar. A bit later the Mazyadids (961–1150) controlled significant territory in Iraq; they and the 'Uqaylid dynasty controlled the whole length of the Euphrates and much of the Sawad. Most of these dynasties continued into the Seljuqid period.

A similar situation arose in Anatolia in the late fourteenth and fifteenth centuries, when the Mamluk sultanate, the Timurid state and the Ottomans competed over the region both through direct military action and through local nomad allies, in this case primarily Turkmen. The result was the rise of the *beyliks* of Anatolia, and of the two great tribal confederations which took over Iran – the Aqqoyunlu and the Qaraqoyunlu. The final example of this phenomenon is the rise of nomad and mountain powers along the Ottoman-Safavid border in the sixteenth century, forming a buffer territory of tribes and small states running from the Kurdish principalities in Kurdistan and Azerbaijan, through the Lur and Bakhtiyari territory and the tribal territories of Iraq, to the Arab tribes of Khuzistan. It was not until the late nineteenth century that much of this region came fully under the control of the states that bordered it.

The state building of the steppe nomads was considerably more ambitious and was closely connected to political processes in the Eurasian steppe. The break-up of the Türk Khaghanate after 850, causing the western migration of many Turkic peoples, and later the formation of the Mongol Empire, brought new and politically sophisticated nomad populations into the central Islamic lands. It is not entirely by chance that their descendants provided most of the leadership for Middle Eastern states from the eleventh to the nineteenth centuries. The Seljuqids were not from the ruling clan of the Turks and came in as fugitives, but they soon gained in ambition and turned to conquest; twenty years after coming across the Oxus, Toghril was in control of Baghdad. The Mongols and the Timurids, both arriving as conquering armies, aimed at the creation of empires combining the whole of Iran and Iraq – in the Mongol case, also Anatolia.

It is notable that all three of these powers came in with armies that were not tribally organized. Our sources do not make it clear why tribalism is not visible in the early Seljuqid period. The history of Chinggis Khan and Tamerlane is better documented. Both rose to power in tribally organized societies and later deliberately suppressed tribal organization in their armies. All these armies also included numerous settled soldiers. Thus, all three conquering powers created mixed armies with a chain of command largely independent of tribes and, in the Mongol and Timurid cases, famous for their discipline.

The three steppe dynasties of the Middle Period laid claim to broad territory and adopted the bureaucratic culture created by the 'Abbasids, administered largely by Persian bureaucrats. While adopting much of Islamic tradition they also brought in new ideas, each creating a new charismatic lineage which survived well beyond the dynasty itself. The Mongols in particular introduced traditions and structures developed in the steppe which were added to the institutions developed by the caliphate. Just as military activity was not limited to steppe nomads, administration was not entirely in the hands of Persian bureaucrats. In the Mongol and the Timurid realm, Turco-Mongolian emirs were active in the *dīwān*, presumably not in the more technical posts, but nonetheless involved in running the state.

Legitimation and State Ideology

Both the Bedouin and the steppe nomads made important contributions to state ideology. Though the Bedouin had little tradition of state building, they did provide a useful image for the nascent Muslim ruling class. While encouraging their followers to settle in garrison cities and give up the life of the desert, the Muslim ruling class also sought to differentiate itself from its more sophisticated subjects. The Bedouin image, already well developed in Arabic poetry and lore, proved popular and useful, better suited to an emerging aristocracy than the more modest ethos of town and merchant that became enshrined in the *ḥadīth*. Thus the image of the Arab as a martial nomad, simple in habits but brave and generous, became part of court culture in the Umayyad period and retained its charm long thereafter. At the same time, the tribal tradition proved useful first as an organizational convenience in the new cities, and then more broadly as a way to distinguish the Muslims from the subjects of the Roman and Persian empires. The requirement that converts become clients (*mawālī*) of tribes both helped to discourage conversion and retained a formal superiority for the new conquerors, while the development of tribal genealogies gave the Arabs pedigrees to match those of the established elites of their new territories.

The arrival of the steppe nomads brought in a new imperial tradition which first rivalled and then combined with the Islamic one. This ideology also enshrined the idea of nomad military prowess, with an origin and lifestyle distant from and superior to that of the settled and urban populations. Though the Seljuqs did not claim imperial status and legitimated their rule primarily through Islamic institutions, they did introduce a new dynastic legitimation, and the lineage of their rulers achieved a stature that lasted for centuries, particularly in Anatolia where the memory of the Rum Seljuqs continued to be invoked well into the Ottoman period.

The Mongols of course came in as a fully imperial power with their own tradition, and for a while reduced much of the Middle East to provincial status, introducing new offices and institutions which were frankly foreign to the region. Most importantly perhaps they created a uniquely charismatic dynasty which first rivalled and then overthrew the caliphate. For almost a century the descendants of Chinggis Khan were the only people who could claim legitimate sovereign power within the Mongol lands, which included much of the central Islamic territory, and the Mongol *yasa* was held up beside the shari'a. With the end of the unified Mongol Empire and the gradual conversion of the western Mongolian Empire to Islam, the two traditions became closely intertwined despite their apparent contradictions, and Mongol heritage became part of dynastic legitimation. The synthesis was completed by the rise of the Timurid dynasty which produced a dynastic founder claiming both Muslim identity and Chinggisid connections, and also a brilliant court culture in which innovations brought by the Mongols combined with the rise of a sophisticated literature in the Turkic language and a continued flowering of Persianate art and culture. The Turks and Turco-Mongolians were now fully part of the Islamic world and its political culture. The figure of Tamerlane remained useful as a source of dynastic legitimation through the eighteenth century.

Successor States and Conquest from Inside

The period of steppe dominance was followed by a new set of nomad conquests and the creation of the great regional empires – the Ottoman, Safavid, Uzbek and Mughal – made possible through the destruction of the caliphate. These states were based on Turkic power, the Uzbek and Timurid from the Turco-Mongolian tradition and the Ottoman and Safavid from Turkmen – Turks who shared the steppe tradition but did not belong to the Chinggisid enterprise. We see two major differences from the earlier period. First, the conquest came from within, now from the largely Turkic and nomadic population of Anatolia, which was energized by the rivalry of the states on its borders. The other difference was that tribalism became a significant element in state development. The Aqqoyunlu and Qaraqoyunlu were tribally organized and the Safavids followed them in using tribal structure as an organizing principle, in stark contrast to the earlier Seljuqs, Mongols and Timurids. It is unlikely that tribes had ceased to exist in the middle periods. Although tribal powers did not play a part in the early campaigns of the Seljuqs, they do appear later, perhaps through the continued influx of Oghuz nomads from the steppes. Under the Mongols and Timurids, tribes ceased to be an active organizing principle in the army or regional politics and for that reason they are largely absent from contemporary histories. It is probable nonetheless that they continued to play a role in social and economic life and in local politics, just as regional settled elites did. We know that some tribes, like the Oyirad, remained intact in the Mongol period, and in the later period a number developed out of Mongol contingents, particularly in the regions less fully under central control – Anatolia in the west, and to the east, in Khorasan and Transoxiana. In the Timurid histories we find a few continuing mentions of the tribes that had been active before and during Temür's rise, and in the struggles of the later Timurid period tribalism became a more important factor.

With the conquest of Iran first by the Turkmen confederations and then by the Safavids, the nomad population again increased, particularly in southern Iran, and tribalism became a major force in both provincial and military organization. Although the Ottomans pursued a very different strategy in their central regions, in Anatolia and the Arab provinces, Turkmen, Kurdish and Arab nomadic tribes remained prominent. Thus, the Middle East entered the modern period with a large population of tribally organized nomads.

Nomad Military Prowess

Nomads are seen as exceptionally good soldiers and as such were both useful and threatening to the settled powers they interacted with. The steppe nomads were excellent mounted archers; the Bedouin were likewise hardy and mobile, often better fighters than their settled neighbors. However, we should recognize that nomad military superiority was far from absolute; when tribal nomad armies met the army of a strong settled state, they generally lost. One problem was that of discipline and control. Soldiers who were paid in booty might simply cease fighting and start plundering; likewise if they encountered a setback, they could not necessarily be counted on to remain loyal. Tribal troops could succeed very well in local campaigns and could likewise be effective in raids either for booty or to extract concessions, but the most powerful armies were those not tribally organized and not exclusively nomadic. This was true of those serving settled states, which often included nomads, and equally of the armies of nomadic powers. As we have seen, the three conquests from the steppe – Seljuq, Mongol and Timurid – were all accomplished with armies in which tribes did not fight as units under their own leaders.

All of the major armies of conquest likewise included a large number of soldiers of settled origins. The Seljuq Toghril soon acquired local allies who fought for him, and added mamluk cavalry to his army; mamluks became an important and central part of the Seljuq army, particularly during the reign of Malik Shah. Chinggis Khan began to use soldiers from settled regions in his army early on. The troops he brought with him on his initial conquest included contingents from Eastern Turkestan, as well as Chinese siege engineers. To these he added levies of soldiers from the cities he conquered, which began as cannon fodder but soon fought alongside the Mongols. A significant number of local soldiers also joined the Mongol army, taking part in most of their campaigns in the central Islamic lands. Tamerlane appears to have started with a primarily nomad army, but he quickly added settled contingents as allies or as vassals. Both the Mongols and the Timurids likewise introduced systematic conscription from the settled population, and regional armies became a significant part of their military manpower.

It makes sense that a mixed army would be an advantage. In some cases, it may have been a matter of discipline and an attempt to limit the power of nomads or tribes; this has been adduced (but also questioned) in the case of the Seljuqs, and it is clear that the Safavids added both artillery and *ghulāms* in order to curtail the power of the tribally organized Qizilbash. In the case of the Mongols and Timurids, discipline was not a significant problem, and settled soldiers were brought in for different reasons. Soldiers of different background could bring complementary skills and could cope with a variety of terrain. Furthermore, while a purely nomad army enjoyed greater mobility and could survive without the amount of grain required for a settled army of infantry or heavy cavalry, it did require extensive pasture, something that was not always available.

Nomad societies have sometimes been described as nations at arms, in which all adult males could act as soldiers. Certainly, both the Bedouin and the steppe nomads were trained from early on in skills useful for war. However, not all men were equally trained or equally active. It appears that in most nomadic societies, chiefs have had small standing armies of trained soldiers separate from the tribe as a whole. For individual campaigns a much larger body of troops could be assembled but might not always be retained for a long period. One should keep in mind also that there were central nomad occupations which competed with sustained military activity: pastoralism, the guidance of caravans, the guarding of routes and collection of taxes, for instance. Military service was one source of income and of prestige, but not the only one, and war could be destructive to the nomadic economy as well as the settled one.

In some ways nomads were less vulnerable than settled agriculturalists because they could retreat before an army, and pasture suffers less from the passage of troops than do the crops of the farmer. However, they also had vulnerabilities. For the Bedouin the more vulnerable period was the summer when they required significant sources of water, often in or near settled districts. If water was denied them, if their wells were poisoned – a common practice in war – or if they were pushed out into the desert, then they and their animals would die of thirst. For the nomads raising sheep, goats, and horses the vulnerable season was the winter, and particularly the lambing season in early spring. At this time of the year, they were more closely gathered, often in an area around a river offering winter grass and water, and were vulnerable to attack. Another weakness of nomads was their need to migrate. This appears particularly clear in the modern period. From the seventeenth century on the Ottomans often used the limitation of migration to control and weaken nomad groups, and in the twentieth century this became an important tool in combatting nomad power both in Iran and in the former Ottoman territories.

Social and Economic Life

Medieval and early modern sources elucidate only a small percentage of nomad activities, placing strong emphasis on the military actions which are the central interest of most early historical works. The everyday economic and political relationships among the population receive very little attention. We should recognize nonetheless that the economic relationship between settled populations and pastoral nomads went well beyond the exchange of livestock products. Nomads also gained money from the services they provided: the guidance of caravans; the transport of goods, including taxes in kind; and the protection of trade and pilgrimage routes. In regions controlled by nomads, tribes were often able to collect taxes from villages in return for protection. It is likely that in premodern as well as modern times, nomads also provided day labor for farming and even state projects. Another important source of income for nomads was military service, whether in the core army or as auxiliaries. Thus, the production and sale of livestock products was only one of many sources of income and influence for the premodern pastoral nomad.[1]

While we can learn much about nomad society and economy from the excellent ethnographic studies of twentieth-century nomads, we must be careful about projecting all aspects of the current lifestyle onto the past. It is

---

[1] See, for instance, Kurt Franz, "The Bedouin in History or Bedouin History?" *Nomadic Peoples* 15, no. 1 (2011): pp. 27, 31–32, 35–36.

important to remember that by the mid-twentieth century, when most ethnographic studies were carried out, pastoral nomads had ceased to be a military force and had lost several other sources of income. With the decline of the caravan trade, they no longer guided caravans, collected regional dues or held responsibility for the safety of trade and pilgrimage routes. For this reason, I have, for instance, not attempted to estimate the flock sizes of earlier times on the basis of modern calculations of the number of animals needed per family. Although in the twentieth century the income from the sale of livestock products would probably have constituted the main household income – sometimes with the addition of wage labor – in the premodern period other sources of income were more important and may have affected both the kind and the number of animals raised.

In the early nineteenth century, the economy of pastoral nomadism probably resembled the premodern system more closely. We have few ethnographic studies from the period, but archives and travelers' accounts do provide some information. This period therefore is probably a better one from which to reconstruct earlier habits and structures. Although the nineteenth century was a period of rapid change, and scholarship often emphasizes the impact of new market forces and growing government interference, there are some indications that many of the structures and institutions seen in that period may also have existed earlier. The possession of tribal territories or *dīras* and the collection of tax or protection money (*khuwwa*) mentioned for this time are certainly well attested for the early modern period, and allusions in the sources suggest strongly that the same system existed in the medieval period, if not earlier.

It is clear for the nineteenth and early twentieth centuries that the tribal aristocracy did not live exclusively within tribal territories but formed part of the wider elite, holding agricultural land and properties in cities or their suburbs. There are references in the Mongol and Timurid period to nomad elites building garden palaces and contributing to city edifices, and also to their involvement in the life of the court. Thus, we should not see the distance between the ordinary nomad and the tribal elite as a new phenomenon created by modern market conditions. The striking disparity between the wealthy nomad elite and the sometimes impoverished nomad subjects, noted in some places in the nineteenth century, echoes Rashid al-Din's and al-'Umari's descriptions of impoverished Mongol nomads at a time when Mongol *noyans* collected taxes at will.

The Decline of Nomad Power

There are many reasons for the decline of nomad power in the late nineteenth and the twentieth centuries, most of them connected with modernization, the growth of state power, and changing concepts of the relationship between the state and its subjects. In the nineteenth century, although nomads still played a part in Ottoman armies and dominated those of the Qajars, we see less feeling of connection. The nomads are no longer seen as part of the ruling group, except for a small elite. Legitimation was now based more on ideas of nation and citizenship and less on military prowess and dynastic origin, in both of which nomads had played a part. As modernization became an increasingly important goal, nomads were seen as holdovers from a past that was being discarded. Earlier they had maintained independence from the center and thus hindered the direct imposition of state control but in return had kept some sort of order in remote and inaccessible areas.

The goal of direct rule over the population and the move to register land made communal pasture rights obsolete, helping to concentrate land in the hand of tribal shaykhs and city merchants who found more profit in agriculture than in pastoralism. Inclusion in the world market likewise encouraged large-scale agriculture. With the development of modern weapons and military organization, the role of nomads in warfare declined, while the state armies gained powerful weapons against them. From the middle of the nineteenth century guns, which could now be reloaded on horseback, were clearly superior to the bow and arrow. This development did not destroy nomad independence in itself, since the tribes soon gained access to firearms and had new possibilities for outside alliances with the British presence in the Gulf. However, with World War I ushering in the development of the machine gun and the airplane, cavalry lost its role in war after nearly three millennia of dominance. The machine gun could destroy a mounted charge in a matter of minutes and the airplane could pursue nomads into otherwise inaccessible regions.

Above all, it was the development of motorized transport which constricted the sphere of nomad activity, severely reducing traditional sources of income and influence. The introduction of steamships in the 1830s marked the beginning of this shift but still left many trade routes dependent on the camel, and river routes could still be protected and taxed by local nomads. The railroad was a greater threat and was recognized as such by many nomads. The most important change, however, was the discovery of oil and the development of motorized wheeled transport. The jeep and truck opened new terrain to the settled powers, who no longer had to depend on the horse and camel for transport and the nomad powers for guidance and protection. The market for both camels and horses collapsed, while additional income from guidance and local taxes dried up. What was left were the livestock products – meat, milk, leather and wool – which have continued to support a smaller and weaker nomad population.

The nomads not only lost income, they also lost their usefulness to the states of the Middle East. Previously both nomad manpower and the animals they raised had been indispensable for the practice of trade and war, central to all states. The steppes, mountains and deserts so common in the central Islamic lands could not be fully controlled or safely traversed without them. Despite frequent conflicts with nomad tribes, states could not do without them, and had to come to an accommodation allowing them a separate sphere of power. In the contemporary Middle East nomads occupy only a small niche, but the history of the region cannot be well understood without including them. We should recognize that their role was not peripheral but central, and that it was not only a negative but also a positive one.

Bibliography

Abrahamian, Ervand. *Iran between Two Revolutions*. Princeton, NJ: Princeton University Press, 1982.

Aigle, Denise. *Le Fārs sous la domination mongole: politique et fiscalité, XIIIe–XIVe s.* Studia Iranica, Cahier 31. Paris: Association pour l'avancement des études iraniennes, 2005.

"Mongol Law *versus* Islamic Law. Myth and Reality." In *The Mongol Empire between Myth and Reality: Studies in Anthropological History*, edited by Denise Aigle, 134–156. Leiden: Brill, 2015.

Al-e Ahmad, Jalal. *Plagued by the West (Gharbzadegi)*. Translated by Paul Sprachman. Delmar, New York: Caravan Books, 1982.

Alexandrescu-Dersca, Marie-Mathilde. *La campagne de Timur en Anatolie (1402)*. Bucharest: Imprimeria Nationala, 1942.

Allawi, Ali A. *Faisal I of Iraq*. New Haven, CT: Yale University Press, 2014.

Allouche, Adel. *The Origins and Development of the Ottoman-Ṣafavid Conflict (906–962/1500–1555)*. Berlin: K. Schwarz Verlag, 1983.

Allsen, Thomas T. "Biography of a Cultural Broker, Bolad Ch'eng-Hsiang in China and Iran." In *The Court of the Il-khans 1290–1340*, edited by Julian Raby and Teresa Fitzherbert, 7–22. Oxford: Oxford University Press, 1996.

"Changing Forms of Legitimation in Mongol Iran." In *Rulers from the Steppe: State Formation and the Eurasian Periphery*, edited by Gary Seaman and Daniel Marks, 223–241. Los Angeles: Ethnographics Press, 1991.

Commodity and Exchange in the Mongol Empire: A Cultural History of Islamic Textiles. Cambridge: Cambridge University Press, 1997.

Culture and Conquest in Mongol Eurasia. Cambridge: Cambridge University Press, 2001.

"Maḥmūd Yalavač (?–1254); Masʿūd Beg (?–1289); ʿAlī Beg (?–1280); Buir (fl. 1206–1260)." In *In the Service of the Khan*, edited by Igor de Rachewiltz. Wiesbaden: Harrassowitz, 1993.

Mongol Imperialism: The Policies of the Grand Qan Möngke in China, Russia, and the Islamic Lands, 1251–1259. Berkeley: University of California Press, 1987.

"Notes on Chinese Titles in Mongol Iran." *Mongolian Studies* 14 (1991): 27–39.

"The Rise of the Mongolian Empire and Mongolian Rule in North China." In *Cambridge History of China*, vol. 6, edited by Herbert Franke and Denis Twitchett, 321–413. Cambridge: Cambridge University Press, 1994.

"Spiritual Geography and Political Legitimacy in the Eastern Steppe." In *Ideology and the Formation of Early States*, edited by Henri J. M. Claessen and Jarich G. Oosten, 116–135. Leiden: Brill, 1996.

"The Yüan Dynasty and the Uighurs of Turfan in the 13th century." In *China among Equals*, edited by Morris Rossabi. Berkeley: University of California Press, 1983.

Amanat, Abbas. *Pivot of the Universe: Nasir al-Din Shah Qajar and the Iranian Monarchy, 1831–1896*. Berkeley: University of California Press, 1997.

Amitai-Preiss, Reuven. *Mongols and Mamluks: The Mamluk-Īlkhānid War, 1260–1281*. Cambridge: Cambridge University Press, 1995.

Amitai, Reuven. "Continuity and Change in the Mongol Army of the Ilkhanate." In *The Mongols' Middle East*, edited by C. P. Melville and Bruno De Nicola, 38–52. Leiden: Brill, 2016.

"Did the Mongols in the Middle East Remain Pastoral Nomads?" In *Seminar at Max Planck Institute, Halle, Germany*. Internet: Academia.edu.

Anooshahr, Ali. *Turkestan and the Rise of Eurasian Empires: A Study of Politics and Invented Traditions*. Oxford: Oxford University Press, 2018.

Anscombe, Frederick F. *The Ottoman Gulf: The Creation of Kuwait, Saudi Arabia and Qatar*. New York: Columbia University Press, 1997.

Arberry, A. J. *The Seven Odes: The First Chapter in Arabic Literature*. London; New York: G. Allen & Unwin; Macmillan, 1957.

Aubin, Jean. "Comment Tamerlan prenait les villes." *Studia Islamica* 19 (1963): 83–122.

Émirs mongols et vizirs persans dans les remous de l'acculturation. Studia Iranica. Cahier 15. Paris; Leuven, Belgique: Association pour l'avancement des études iraniennes; Diffusion Peeters Press, 1995.

"L'avènement des Safavides reconsidéré." *Moyen Orient et Océan Indien. Middle East and Indian Ocean XVIe–XIXe siècles* 5 (1988): 1–130.

"La propriété foncière en Azerbaydjan sous les Mongols." *Le monde iranien et l'Islam* 4 (1976–1977): 79–132.

"Le qurlitai de Sultân-Maydân (1336)." *Journal Asiatique* CCLXXIX (1991): 175–197.

"Les princes d'Ormuz du XIIIe au Xve siècle." *Journal Asiatique* 24 (1953): 77–137.

"Réseau pastoral et réseau caravanier. Les grand' routes du Khurassan à l'époque mongole." *Le Monde iranien et l'Islam* 1 (1971): 105–130.

"Révolution chiite et conservatisme. Les soufis de Lâhejân, 1500–1514 (Études Safavides II)." *Moyen Orient et Océan Indien. Middle East and Indian Ocean XVIe–XIXe siècles* 1 (1984): 1–40.

Avery, Peter. "Nādir Shāh and the Afsharid Legacy." In *Cambridge History of Iran*, vol. 7. *From Nadir Shah to the Islamic Republic*, edited by Gavin Hambly, Peter Avery, Charles Melville, 3–62. Cambridge: Cambridge University Press, 1991.

Avni, Gideon. *Nomads, Farmers, and Town-Dwellers: Pastoralist-Sedentist Interaction in the Negev Highlands, Sixth-Eighth Centuries C.E.* Jerusalem: Israel Antiquities Authority, 1996.

Axworthy, Michael. "The Army of Nader Shah." *Iranian Studies* 40, no. 5 (2007): 635–646.

———. *The Sword of Persia: Nader Shah, from Tribal Warrior to Conquering Tyrant.* London; New York: I. B. Tauris 2006.

Ayalon, David. "The Auxiliary Forces of the Mamluk Sultanate." *Der Islam* 65 (1988): 13–37.

———. *Eunuchs, Caliphs and Sultans: A Study in Power Relationships.* Jerusalem: Magnes Press, The Hebrew University, 1999.

Babayan, Kathryn. *Mystics, Monarchs, and Messiahs: Cultural Landscapes of Early Modern Iran.* Cambridge, MA: Distributed for the Center for Middle Eastern Studies of Harvard University by Harvard University Press, 2002.

Babur, Ẓahīr al-Dīn Muḥammad. *Baburnama: Chaghatay Turkish Text with Abdul-Rahim Khankhanan's Persian Translation.* Translated by W. M. Thackston. Sources of Oriental Languages and Literatures. Cambridge, MA: Harvard University, Department of Near Eastern Languages and Civilizations, 1993.

Bar Hebraeus, Gregory. *The Chronography of Gregory Abû'l Faraj, the Son of Aaron, the Hebrew Physician, Commonly Known as Bar Hebraeus: Being the First Part of His Political History of the World.* Translated by E. A. Wallis Budge. 2 vols. London: Oxford University Press, 1932.

Barfield, Thomas J. *The Nomadic Alternative.* Englewood Cliffs, NJ: Prentice Hall, 1993.

Barkan, Ömer Lûtfi. "Research on the Ottoman Fiscal Surveys." In *Studies in the Economic History of the Middle East from the Rise of Islam to the Present Day*, edited by Michael A. Cook, 162–171. London: Oxford University Press, 1970.

Bartol'd, V. V. *Turkestan down to the Mongol Invasion.* Translated by Mrs. T. Minorsky. London: Luzac, 1968.

Bashir, Shahzad. "The Origins and Rhetorical Evolution of the Term Qizilbāsh in Persianate Literature." *Journal of the Economic and Social History of the Orient* 57, no. 3 (2014): 364–391.

Bashīr, Sulaymān. *Arabs and Others in Early Islam.* Princeton, NJ: Darwin Press, 1997.

Bayhaqī, Abū'l Faḍl Muḥammad. *The History of Beyhaqi (The History of Sultan Mas'ud of Ghazna, 1030–1041).* Translated by C. Edmund Bosworth. 3 vols. Cambridge, MA; Washington, DC: Ilex Foundation and Center for Hellenic Studies, 2011.

———. *Tārīkh-i Bayhaqī.* Edited by Manūchihr Dānishpazhūh. Tehran: Intishārāt-i Hīrmand, 1997–1998.

Baykara, Tuncer. "Society and Economy among the Anatolian Seljuks and Beyliks." In *The Turks*, edited by Hasan Celâl Güzel, C. Cem Oguz, Osman Karatay, 610–629. Ankara: Yeni Türkiye Publications, 2002.

Baypakov, Karl M. "La culture urbaine du Kazakhstan du sud et du Semiretchie à l'époque des Karakhanides." *Cahiers d'Asie Centrale* 9 (2001): 141–175.

Bazin, Louis. "Que était Alp Er Tonga, identifié à Afrâsyâb." In *Pand-o Sokhan. Mélanges offerts à Charles-Henri de Fouchécour*, edited by Claire Kappler, Christophe Balaÿ, Ziva Vesel, 37–42. Tehran: Institut français de recherche en Iran, 1995.

Beck, Lois. "Economic Transformations among Qashqa'i Nomads, 1962–1978." In *Continuity and Change in Modern Iran*, edited by Michael E. Bonine and Nikki R. Keddie, 85–107. Albany: State University of New York Press, 1981.

The Qashqa'i of Iran. New Haven, CT: Yale University Press, 1986.

Bernardini, Michele. *Mémoire et propagande à l'époque timouride*. Studia Iranica. Cahier 37. Paris: Association pour l'avancement des études iraniennes, 2008.

Bianquis, Th., S. Shamma. "Mirdās,– Mirdās b. Udayya." In *Encyclopaedia of Islam, Second Edition*. Edited by P. Bearman et al. Leiden: Brill, 1960–2005.

Bikhazi, Ramzi Jibran. "The Ḥamdānid Dynasty of Mesopotamia and North Syria 254–404/868–1014." Unpublished PhD dissertation, University of Michigan, 1981.

Binay, Sara. *Die Figur des Beduinen in der arabischen Literatur 9.-12. Jahrhundert*. Wiesbaden: Reichert, 2006.

Biran, Michal. *Chinggis Khan*. Oxford: Oneworld, 2007.

"The Mongols in Central Asia from Chinggis Khan's Invasion to the Rise of Temür: The Ögödeid and Chaghadaid Realms." In *The Cambridge History of Inner Asia: the Chinggisid Age*, edited by Allen J. Frank, Nicola Di Cosmo, Peter B. Golden, 46–66. Cambridge: Cambridge University Press, 2009.

"Qarakhanid Studies: A View from the Qara Khitai Edge." *Cahiers d'Asie Centrale* 9 (2001): 77–89.

Black, J. A., G. Cunningham, G. Fluckiger-Hawker, E. Robson, G. Zólyoni. *The Electronic Text Corpus of Sumerian Literature*. Oxford 1998–. https://etcsl .orinst.ox.ac.uk/

Blaum, Paul A. "Children of the Arrow: The Strange Saga of the Iraqi Turkmens." *The International Journal of Kurdish Studies* 15, no. 1–2 (2001): 137–163.

"A History of the Kurdish Marwanid Dynasty A.D. 983–1085, Part I." *International Journal of Kurdish Studies* 5, no. 1–2 (1992): 54–68.

"A History of the Kurdish Marwanid Dynasty, A.D. 983–1085, Part II." *International Journal of Kurdish Studies* 6, no. 1–2 (1993): 40–65.

Bombaci, Alessio. *Histoire de la litérature turque*. Paris: C. Klincksieck, 1968.

Bonner, Michael. "The Waning of Empire, 861–945." In *New Cambridge History of Islam*, vol. 1, *The Formation of the Islamic World, Sixth to Eleventh Centuries*, edited by Chase Robinson, 305–359. Cambridge: Cambridge University Press, 2010.

Bosworth, C. E. "Azerbaijan IV: Islamic History to 1941." In *Encyclopædia Iranica*. Vol. I–. London, 1982–.

The Ghaznavids: Their Empire in Afghanistan and Eastern Iran 994:1040. 2nd ed. Beirut: Librairie du Liban, 1973.

"Iran and the Arabs before Islam." In *Cambridge History of Iran*, vol. 3 pt. 1. *The Seleucid, Parthian and Sasanian Periods*, edited by Ehsan Yarshater, 593–612. Cambridge: Cambridge University Press, 1983.

"Malik-Shāh." In *Encyclopaedia of Islam, Second Edition*. Edited by P. Bearman et al. Leiden: Brill, 1960–2005.

"Mazyad, Banū, or Mazyadids." In *Encyclopaedia of Islam, Second Edition*. Edited by P. Bearman et al. Leiden: Brill, 1960–2005.

"The Persian Impact on Arabic Literature." In *Arabic Literature to the End of the Umayyad Period*, edited by T. M. Johnstone, A. F. L. Beeston, R. B. Sergeant, G. R. Smith, 483–496. Cambridge: Cambridge University Press, 1983.

"The Political and Dynastic History of the Iranian world (A.D. 1000–1217)." In *Cambridge History of Iran*, vol. 5. *The Saljuq and Mongol Periods*, edited by J. A. Boyle, 1–202. Cambridge: Cambridge University Press, 1968.

"Sādjids." In *Encyclopaedia of Islam, Second Edition*. Edited by P. Bearman et al. Leiden: Brill, 1960–2005.

"Sandjar." In *Encyclopaedia of Islam, Second Edition*. Edited by P. Bearman et al. Leiden: Brill, 1960–2005.

"'Uḳaylids." In *Encyclopaedia of Islam, Second Edition*. Edited by P. Bearman et al. Leiden: Brill, 1960–2005.

Bowersock, G. W. *Roman Arabia*. Cambridge, MA: Harvard University Press, 1983.

Boyle, John A. "Dynastic and Political History of the Īl-Khāns." In *Cambridge History of Iran*, vol. 5. *The Saljuq and Mongol Periods*, edited by J. A. Boyle, 303–421. Cambridge: Cambridge University Press, 1968.

Briant, Pierre. *État et pasteurs au Moyen-Orient ancien*. Cambridge; Paris: Cambridge University Press; Maison des sciences de l'homme, 1982.

Broadbridge, Anne F. *Kingship and Ideology in the Islamic and Mongol Worlds*. Cambridge: Cambridge University Press, 2008.

"Marriage, Family and Politics: The Ilkhanid-Oirat Connection." *Journal of the Royal Asiatic Society* 26, no. 1–2 (2016): 121–135.

Bruinessen, Martin van. *Agha, Shaikh, and State: The Social and Political Structures of Kurdistan*. London: Zed Books, 1992.

Buell, Paul D. "Early Mongol Expansion in Western Siberia and Turkestan (1207–1219): A Reconstruction." *Central Asiatic Journal* 36, no. 1–2 (1992): 1–32.

"Sino-Khitan Administration in Mongol Bukhara." *Journal of Asian History* 13, no. 2 (1979): 121–147.

"Tribe, 'Qan' and 'ulus' in Early Mongol China: Some Prolegomena to Yüan History." Unpublished PhD dissertation, University of Washington, 1977.

"Yeh-lü A-hai (ca. 1151-ca.1223), Yeh-lü T'u-hua (d. 1231)." In *In the Service of the Khan*, edited by Igor de Rachewiltz. Wiesbaden: Harrassowitz, 1993.

Bulliet, Richard W. *The Camel and the Wheel*. New York: Columbia University Press, 1990.

Bürgel Ch. and R. Mottahedeh. "'Ażod al-Dawla." In *Encyclopædia Iranica*. Vol. I–. London, 1982–.

Cahen, Claude. "Atabak." In *Encyclopaedia of Islam, Second Edition*. Edited by P. Bearman et al. Leiden: Brill, 1960–2005.

"Eretna." In *Encyclopaedia of Islam, Second Edition*. Edited by P. Bearman et al. Leiden: Brill, 1960–2005.

The Formation of Turkey. The Seljukid Sultanate of Rūm: Eleventh to Fourteenth Century. Translated by P. M. Holt. Harlow: Longman, 2001.

"History and Historians." In *Religion, Learning and Science in the 'Abbasid Period*, edited by J. D. Latham, R. B. Sergeant, M. J. L Young. *Cambridge*

History of Arabic Literature, 188–233. Cambridge: Cambridge University Press, 1990.

"Le Malik-nameh et l'histoire des origines seljukides." *Oriens* 2 (1949): 31–65.

"Les tribus turques d'Asie Occidentale pendant la période seljukide." *Wiener Zeitschrift für die Kunde des Morgenlandes* 51, no. 1–2 (1948): 178–187.

"The Turkish Invasion: The Selchükids." In *A History of the Crusades*, edited by Kenneth Setton, 135–176. Philadelphia: University of Pennsylvania Press, 1955.

Canard, Marius. "al-Basāsīrī." In *Encyclopaedia of Islam, Second Edition*. Edited by P. Bearman et al. Leiden: Brill, 1960–2005.

Histoire de la dynastie des H'amdanides de Jazîra et de Syrie. Paris: Presses universitaires de France, 1953.

Ceylan, Ebubekir *The Ottoman Origins of Modern Iraq: Political Reform, Modernization and Development in the Nineteenth-Century Middle East*. London: I. B. Tauris, 2011.

Charpin, Dominique. "The History of Ancient Mesopotamia: An Overview." In *Civilizations of the Ancient Near East*, edited by Jack M. Sasson, 807–829. New York: Simon Schuster McMillan, 1995.

Chase, Kenneth Warren. *Firearms: A Global History to 1700*. Cambridge: Cambridge University Press, 2003.

Chatty, Dawn. *From Camel to Truck: the Bedouin in the Modern World*. New York: Vantage Press, 1986.

Christian, David. *A History of Russia, Central Asia, and Mongolia*. Blackwell History of the World. Malden, MA: Blackwell Publishers, 1998.

Cole, Donald P. "Where Have the Bedouin Gone?" *Anthropological Quarterly* 76, no. 2 (2003): 235–267.

Commins, David. *The Mission and the Kingdom: Wahhabi Power behind the Saudi Throne*. London: I. B. Tauris, 2016.

Connermann, Stephan. "Volk, Ethnie oder Stamm? Die Kurden aus mamlükischer Sicht." *Asien und Afrika. Beiträge des Zentrums für asiatische und afrikanische Studien der Christian-Albrechts-Universität zu Kiel* 8 (2004): 27–68.

Conrad, Jo-Ann. "Dede Korkut: Reintegrating the Historic, the Heroic, and the Marvelous." *Turcica* 33 (2001): 243–275.

Crone, Patricia. "The Early Islamic World." In *War and Society in the Ancient and Medieval Worlds. Asia, the Mediterranean, Europe and Mesoamerica*, edited by Kurt Raaflaub and Nathan Rosenstein, 309–332. Washington, DC: Center for Hellenic Studies, Harvard University, 1999.

"The First-century Concept of Hiǧra." *Arabica* 41 (1994): 352–387.

Meccan Trade and the Rise of Islam. Princeton, NJ: Princeton University Press, 1987.

"Quraysh and the Roman Army: Making Sense of the Meccan Leather Trade." *Bulletin of the School of Oriental and African Studies* 70, no. 1 (2007): 63–88.

Slaves on Horses. Cambridge: Cambridge University Press, 1980.

"Were the Qays and Yemen of the Umayyad Period Political Parties?" *Der Islam* 71 (1994): 1–57.

Cronin, Stephanie. *Armies and State-Building in the Modern Middle East: Politics, Nationalism and Military Reform*. London: I. B. Tauris, 2014.

Tribal Politics in Iran: Rural Conflict and the New State, 1921–1941. London: Routledge, 2007.

Dalley, Stephanie. "Ancient Mesopotamian Military Organization." In *Civilizations of the Ancient Near East*, edited by Jack M. Sasson, 413–422. New York: Simon and Schuster McMillan, 1995.

Davidovich, E. A. "The Karakhanids." In *History of Civilizations of Central Asia*, edited by M. S. Asimov and C. E. Bosworth, 119–143. Paris: UNESCO Publishing, 1998.

Davis, Dick. "Iran and *Aniran*: The Shaping of a Legend." In *Iran Facing Others: Identity Boundaries in a Historical Perspective*, edited by Abbas Amanat and Farzin Vejdani, 37–48. New York: Palgrave Macmillan, 2012.

De Nicola, Bruno. *Women in Mongol Iran: The Khātūns, 1206–1335*. Edinburgh: Edinburgh University Press, 2017.

Dehqan, Mustafa and Genç, Vural. "Kurds as Spies: Information-Gathering on the 16th-Century Ottoman-Safavid Frontier." *Acta Orientalia Academiae Scientiarum Hungaricae* 71, no. 2 (2018): 197–230.

Deringil, Selim. "'They Live in a State of Nomadism and Savagery': The Late Ottoman Empire and the Post-Colonial Debate." *Comparative Studies in Society and History* 45, no. 2 (2003): 311–342.

The Well-Protected Domains: Ideology and the Legitimation of Power in the Ottoman Empire 1876–1909. London: I. B. Tauris, 1998.

DeWeese, Devin A. *Islamization and Native Religion in the Golden Horde: Baba Tükles and Conversion to Islam in Historical and Epic Tradition*. Hermeneutics, studies in the history of religions. University Park: Pennsylvania State University Press, 1994.

Di Cosmo, Nicola. *Ancient China and Its Enemies: The Rise of Nomadic Power in East Asian History*. Cambridge: Cambridge University Press, 2002.

"Ancient Inner Asian Nomads: Their Economic Basis and Its Significance in Chinese History." *The Journal of Asian Studies* 53, no. 4 (1994): 1092–1126.

Diakonoff, I. M. "Media." In *Cambridge History of Iran*, vol. 2. *The Median and Achaemenid periods*, edited by Ilya Gerschevitch, 36–148. Cambridge: Cambridge University Press, 1985.

Dickson, Martin. "Sháh Ṭahmásb and the Úzbeks (The Duel for Khurásán with 'Ubayd Khán: 930–46/1524–1540)." Unpublished PhD Dissertation, Princeton University, 1958.

Digard, Jean-Pierre. "À propos des aspects économiques de la symbiose nomades-sedentaires dans la Mésopotamie ancienne." In *Nomads and Sedentary Peoples. XXX International Congress of Human Sciences in Asia and North Africa*, edited by Jorge Silva Castillo. Mexico City: Colegio de México, 1981.

Dixon, Abd al-Ameer Abd. T*he Umayyad Caliphate, 65–86/684–705: (A Political Study)*. London: Luzac, 1971.

Donner, Fred M. "The Bakr b. Wa'il Tribes and Politics in Northeastern Arabia on the Eve of Islam." *Studia Islamica* 51 (1980): 5–38.

"Dolafids." In *Encyclopædia Iranica*. Vol. I–. London, 1982–.

The Early Islamic Conquests. Princeton, NJ: Princeton University Press, 1981.

"Muḥammad's Political Consolidation in Arabia up to the Conquest of Mecca: a Reassessment." *The Muslim World* 69, no. 3 (1979): 229–247.

Muhammad and the Believers at the Origins of Islam. Cambridge, MA: Belknap Press, Harvard University Press, 2010.

Narratives of Islamic Origins: The Beginnings of Islamic Historical Writing. Princeton, NJ: Darwin Press, 1998.

"Umayyad Efforts at Legitimation: The Umayyads' Silent Heritage." In *Umayyad Legacies: Medieval Memories from Syria to Spain*, edited by Antoine Burrut and Paul M. Cobb, 187–211. Leiden: Brill, 2010.

Donohue, John J. *The Buwayhid Dynasty in Iraq 334 H./945 to 403 H./1012: Shaping Institutions for the Future.* Leiden: Brill, 2003.

Durand-Guédy, David. "Goodbye to the Türkmens? The Military Role of Nomads in Iran after the Saljūq Conquest." In *Nomad Military Power in Iran and Adjacent Areas in the Islamic Period*, edited by Kurt Franz and Wolfgang Holzwarth, 107–136. Wiesbaden: Reichert, 2015.

Iranian Elites and Turkish Rulers: A History of Iṣfahān in the Saljūq Period. London: Routledge, 2010.

"Ruling from the Outside: A New Perspective on Early Turkish Kingship in Iran." In *Every Inch a King: Comparative Studies on Kings and Kingship in the Ancient and Medieval Worlds*, edited by Lynette Mitchell and Charles Melville, 325–342. Leiden: Brill, 2013.

"The Türkmen-Saljūq Relationship in Twelfth-Century Iran: New Elements Based on a Contrastive Analysis of Three inšā'documents." *Eurasian Studies* IX, no. 1–2 (2011): 11–66.

Eckmann, János. "Die kiptschakische Literatur." In *Philologiae Turcicae Fundamenta, vol. II*, edited by Louis Bazin, Alessio Bombaci, Jean Deny, Tayyib Gökbilgin, Fahir Iz, Helmuth Scheel. Aquis Mattiacis: Steiner, 1964.

Edward McEwen, Robert L. Miller, Christopher A. Bergman. "Early Bow Design and Construction." *Scientific American*, June (1991): 76–82.

el-Tayib, Abdulla. "Pre-Islamic Poetry." In *Arabic Literature to the End of the Umayyad Period*, edited by A. F. L. Beeston, 27–109. Cambridge: Cambridge University Press, 1983.

el-Tayib, Abdullah. "Abū Firās al-Ḥamdānī." In *'Abbasid Belles-lettres*, edited by Julia Ashtiany, T. M. Johnstone, J. D. Latham, R. B. Sergent, C. Rex Smith. *Cambridge History of Arabic Literature*. Cambridge: Cambridge University Press, 1990.

Enderwitz, Susanne. *Gesellschaftlicher Rang und ethnische Legitimation: der arabische Schriftsteller Abū 'Uṯmān al-Ǧāḥiz (gest. 868) über die Afrikaner, Perser und Araber in der islamischen Gesellschaft.* Freiburg im Breisgau: Schwarz, 1979.

Ercilasun, Ahmet B. "Language and Literature in the Early Muslim Turkish States." In *The Turks*, edited by C. Cem Oğuz Hasan Celâl Güzel and Osman Karatay, 347–372. Ankara: Yeni Türkiye Publications, 2002.

Erdem, Ilham. "Eastern Anatolian Turkish States." In *The Turks*, edited by C. Cem Oğuz, Hasan Celâl Güzel and Osman Karatay, 477–506. Ankara: Yeni Türkiye Publications, 2002.

Fabietti, Ugo, "State Policies and Bedouin Adaptation in Saudi Arabia, 1900–1980." In *The Transformation of Nomadic Society in the Arab East*, edited by

Martha Mundy and Basim Musallam, 82–9. Cambridge: Cambridge University Press, 2000.

al-Fahad, Abdulaziz H. "The *'Imama vs.* the *'Iqal:* Hadari-Bedouin Conflict and the Formation of the Saudi State." In *Counter-Narratives: History, Contemporary Society, and Politics in Saudi Arabia and Yemen,* edited by Madawi al-Rasheed and Robert Vitalis, 35–75. New York: Palgrave Macmillan, 2004.

Faroqhi, Suraiya. *Pilgrims and Sultans: The Hajj under the Ottomans, 1517–1683.* London; New York: I. B. Tauris 1996.

Faṣīḥ Khwāfī, Aḥmad b. Jalāl al-Dīn. *Mujmal-i Faṣīḥī,* edited by Muḥammad Farrukh. Mashhad: Bāstān, 1960–61.

Fattah, Hala Mundhir. *The Politics of Regional Trade in Iraq, Arabia, and the Gulf, 1745–1900.* Albany: State University of New York Press, 1997.

Finkelstein, J. J. "The Genealogy of the Hammurapi Dynasty." *Journal of Cuneiform Studies* 20 (1966): 95–118.

Fleischer, Cornell H. *Bureaucrat and Intellectual in the Ottoman Empire: The Historian Mustafa Âli (1541–1600).* Princeton studies on the Near East. Princeton, NJ: Princeton University Press, 1986.

Flemming, Barbara. "Old Anatolian Turkish Poetry and Its Relationship to the Persian Tradition." In *Turkic-Iranian Contact Areas: Historical and Linguistic Aspects,* edited by Lars Johanson and Christine Bulut, 49–68. Wiesbaden: Harrassowitz, 2006.

Floor, Willem. "The *Khalifeh al-Kholafa* of the Safavid Sufi Order." *Zeitschrift der deutchen morgenländischen Gesellschaft* 153, no. 1 (2003): 51–86.

"The Rise and Fall of the Banū Kaʻb. A Borderer State in Southern Khuzestan." *Iran* 44 (2006): 277–315.

The Economy of Safavid Persia. Iran-Turan Bd. 1. Wiesbaden: Reichert, 2000.

Foran, John. "The Long Fall of the Safavid Dynasty: Moving beyond the Standard View." *International Journal of Middle East Studies* 24 (1992): 281–304.

Fragner, Bert. "Social and Internal Economic Affairs." In *Cambridge History of Iran,* vol. 6. *The Timurid and Safavid Periods,* edited by Peter Jackson and Laurence Lockhart, 491–565. Cambridge: Cambridge University Press, 1986.

Franz, Kurt. "The Bedouin in History or Bedouin History?" *Nomadic Peoples* 15, no. 1 (2011): 11–53.

Vom Beutezug zur Territorialherrschaft. Beduinische Gruppen in mittelislamischer Zeit. Wiesbaden: Reichert, 2007.

Frye, Richard N. "The Sāmānids." In *Cambridge History of Iran,* vol. 4, edited by Richard N. Frye, 136–161. Cambridge: Cambridge University Press, 1975.

Gandjeï, Tourkhan. "Turkish in Pre-Mongol Persian Poetry." *Bulletin of the School of Oriental and African Studies* 49, no. 1 (1986): 67–75.

Gardet, L. and J.-C. Vadet. "Kalb." In *Encyclopaedia of Islam, Second Edition.* Edited by P. Bearman et al. Leiden: Brill, 1960–2005.

Garthwaite, Gene R. *Khans and Shahs: A Documentary Analysis of the Bakhtiyari in Iran.* Cambridge: Cambridge University Press, 1983.

Gaube, Heinz, and Thomas Leisten. *Die Kernländer des 'Abbāsidenreichs im 10./11. Jh.: Materialien zur TAVO-Karte B VII 6.* Beihefte zum Tübinger Atlas des

Vorderen Orients. Reihe B, Geisteswissenschaften; Nr. 75. Wiesbaden: L. Reichert, 1994.

Gibb, H. A. R. *The Arab Conquests in Central Asia.* New York: AMS Press, 1970.

"An Interpretation of Islamic History." In *Studies on the Civilization of Islam,* edited by Stanford Shaw and William R. Polk, 3–33. Boston: Beacon Press, 1962.

"The Social Significance of the Shuubiya." In *Studies on the Civilization of Islam,* edited by Stanford J. Shaw and William R. Polk, 62–73. Boston: Beacon Press, 1962.

Golden, Peter B. "The Peoples of the South Russian Steppe." In *The Cambridge History of Early Inner Asia,* edited by Denis Sinor, 256–284. Cambridge: Cambridge University Press, 1990.

An Introduction to the History of the Turkic Peoples: Ethnogenesis and State-Formation in Medieval and Early Modern Eurasia and the Middle East. Turcologica, Bd. 9. Wiesbaden: Harrassowitz, 1992.

Nomads and Sedentary Societies in Medieval Eurasia. Essays on global and comparative history. Washington, DC: American Historical Association, 1998.

Goldziher, Ignaz. *Muslim Studies.* Translated by C. R. Barber and S. M. Stern. 2 vols. London: Allen and Unwin, 1967–1971.

Gordon, Matthew. *The Breaking of a Thousand Swords: A History of the Turkish Military of Samarra, A.H. 200–275/815–889 C.E.* Albany: State University of New York Press, 2001.

Goriacheva, Valentina D. "À propos des deux capitales du khaghanat karakhanide." *Cahiers d'Asie Centrale* 9 (2001): 91–114.

Graf, David Frank. "Rome and the Saracens: Reassessing the Nomadic Menace." In *Rome and the Arabian Frontier: From the Nabataeans to the Saracens,* edited by David Frank Graf. Aldershot: Variorum, 1997.

Haarmann, Ulrich W. "Ideology and History, Identity and Alterity: the Arab Image of the Turk from the 'Abbasids to Modern Egypt." *International Journal of Middle East Studies* 20, no. 2 (1988): 175–96.

Haase, Claus-Peter. "Untersuchungen zur Landschaftsgeschichte Nordsyriens in der Umayyadenzeit." Unpublished PhD dissertation, Universität Hamburg, 1975.

Habib, John S. *Ibn Sa'ud's Warriors of Islam: The Ikhwan of Najd and Their Role in the Creation of the Sa'udi Kingdom, 1910–1930.* Leiden: Brill, 1978.

Hamori, A. "al-Mutanabbī." In *'Abbasid belles-lettres,* edited by Julia Ashtiany, T. M. Johnstone, J. D. Latham, R. B. Sergent, C. Rex Smith. Cambridge History of Arabic Literature, 300–314. Cambridge; New York: Cambridge University Press, 1990.

Haneda, Masashi. *Le châh et les Qizilbāš: le système militaire safavide.* Islamkundliche Untersuchungen Bd. 119. Berlin: K. Schwarz, 1987.

Hanioğlu, M. Şükrü. *Atatürk: An Intellectual Biography.* Princeton, NJ: Princeton University Press, 2011.

Hartog, François. *Le miroir d'Hérodote: essai sur la représentation de l'autre.* Bibliothèque des histoires. Paris: Gallimard, 1980.

Hawting, Gerald. *The First Dynasty of Islam: The Umayyad Caliphate AD 661–750.* Carbondale; Edwardsville: Southern Illinois University Press, 1987.

Haykel, Bernard. "Western Arabia and Yemen during the Ottoman Period." In *New Cambridge History of Islam*, vol. 2. *The Western Islamic World Eleventh to Eighteenth Centuries*, edited by Maribel Fierro, 436–449. Cambridge: Cambridge University Press, 2010.

Heidemann, Stefan. *Die Renaissance der Städte in Nordsyrien und Nordmesopotamien: städtische Entwicklung und wirtschaftliche Bedingungen in ar-Raqqa und Ḥarrān von der Zeit der beduinischen Vorherrschaft bis zu den Seldschuken.* Islamic history and civilization. Studies and texts, v. 40. Leiden; Boston: Brill, 2002.

"Numayrid ar-Raqqa: Archaeological and Historical Evidence for a 'Dimorphic State' in the Bedouin Dominated Fringes of the Fāṭimid Empire." In *Egypt and Syria in the Fatimid, Ayyubid and Mamluk Eras. The 9th and 10th International Colloquium at the Katholieke Universiteit Leuven in May 2000 and May 2001*, edited by U. Vermeulen and J. van Steenbergen. Orientalia Lovaniensia Analecta, 85–105. Leuven, Belgium: Peeters, 2005.

Heinkele, Barbara Kellner. "The Turcomans and Bilād aš-Šām in the Mamluk Period." In *Land Tenure and Social Transformation in the Middle East*, edited by Tarif Khalidi, 169–80. Beirut: American University of Beirut, 1984.

Hillenbrand, Carole. "Islamic Orthodoxy or Realpolitik? Al-Ghazālī's Views on Government." *Iran* 26 (1988): 81–94.

"Women in the Seljuq Period." In *Women in Iran from the Rise of Islam to 1800*, edited by Guity Nashat and Lois Beck, 103–120. Urbana and Chicago: University of Illinois Press, 2003.

Hinds, Martin. "Kûfan Political Alignments and Their Background in the Mid-Seventh Century A.D." *International Journal of Middle East Studies* 2 (1971): 346–367.

Hoffmann, Birgitt. *Waqf im mongolischen Iran: Rašīduddīns Sorge um Nachruhm und Seelenheil.* Stuttgart: F. Steiner, 2000.

Hope, Michael. *Power, Politics, and Tradition in the Mongol Empire and the Īlkhānate of Iran.* Oxford: Oxford University Press, 2016.

Hoyland, Robert G. *Arabia and the Arabs. From the Bronze Age to the Coming of Islam.* London; New York: Routledge, 2001.

Hsiao, Ch'i-ch'ing. *The Military Establishment of the Yuan Dynasty.* Cambridge, MA: Council on East Asian Studies, Harvard University: distributed by Harvard University Press, 1978.

Humphreys, R. Stephen. *From Saladin to the Mongols: The Ayyubids of Damascus, 1193–1260.* Albany: State University of New York Press, 1977.

Hütteroth, Wolf D. "Ottoman Administration of the Desert Frontier in the Sixteenth Century." *Asian and African Studies* 19 (1985): 145–155.

Ibn al-Athīr, 'Izz al-Dīn. *The Annals of the Saljuq Turks: Selections from al-Kāmil fī'l-Ta'rīkh of 'Izz al-Dīn Ibn al-Athīr.* Translated by D. S. Richards. London: RoutledgeCurzon, 2002.

Ibn al-Nadīm, Muḥammad ibn Isḥāq. *The Fihrist of al-Nadīm: A Tenth-Century Survey of Muslim Culture.* Translated by Bayard Dodge. New York: Columbia University Press, 1970.

Ibn Ḥawqal, Muḥammad ibn ʿAlī. *Configuration de la terre (Kitab surat al-ard)*. Translated by Johannes Hendrik Kramer and Gaston Wiet. Beirut: Commission internationale pour la traduction des chefs d'oeuvre, 1965.

al-Kāshgharī, Maḥmūd. *Compendium of the Turkic Dialects*. Translated by Robert Dankoff. Sources of Oriental Languages and Literatures, vol. 7. Cambridge, MA: Harvard University Press, 1982.

Ibn Khaldūn, ʿAbd al-Raḥmān. *The Muqaddimah: An Introduction to History*. Translated by Franz Rosenthal. Abridged ed. Princeton, NJ: Princeton University Press, 1967.

Imber, Colin. *The Ottoman Empire, 1300–1650: The Structure of Power*. 2nd ed. Houndmills, Basingstoke, Hampshire; New York: Palgrave Macmillan, 2009.

Inalcik, Halil. "Meḥemmed I." In *Encyclopaedia of Islam, Second Edition*. Edited by P. Bearman et al. Leiden: Brill, 1960–2005.

"Meḥemmed II." In *Encyclopaedia of Islam, Second Edition*. Edited by P. Bearman et al. Leiden: Brill, 1960–2005.

"Tīmār." In *Encyclopaedia of Islam, Second Edition*. Edited by P. Bearman et al. Leiden: Brill, 1960–2005.

"The Yürüks, Their Origins, Expansion and Economic Role." In *Oriental Carpet and Textile Studies*, edited by R. Pinner and H. Inalcik, 39–65. London: HALI, 1986.

Inalcik, Halil, and Donald Quataert. *An Economic and Social History of the Ottoman Empire, 1300–1914*. Cambridge: Cambridge University Press, 1994.

Irwin, Robert. *The Middle East in the Middle Ages: The Early Mamluk Sultanate, 1250–1382*. London: Croom Helm, 1986.

Jabbur, Jibrail Sulayman, Suhayl Jibrail Jabbur, and Lawrence I. Conrad. *The Bedouins and the Desert: Aspects of Nomadic Life in the Arab East*. Albany: State University of New York Press, 1995.

Jackson, Peter. *The Mongols and the Islamic World from Conquest to Conversion*. New Haven, CT: Yale University Press, 2017.

Jacobsen, Thorkild. *The Treasures of Darkness: A History of Mesopotamian Religion*. New Haven, CT: Yale University Press, 1976.

Jāḥiẓ, al -. *Nine essays of al-Jahiz*. Translated by William M. Hutchins. New York: P. Lang, 1989.

al-Juhany, Uwaidah M. *Najd before the Salafi Reform Movement*. Reading, UK: Ithaca, 2002.

Juwaynī, ʿAlāʾ al- Dīn ʿAṭā-Malik. *The History of the World-Conqueror*. Translated by John Andrew Boyle. Manchester: Manchester University Press, 1958.

Jūzjānī, Minhāj Sirāj. *Ṭabaḳāt al-Nāṣirī: A General History of the Muhammadan Dynasties of Asia, including Hindustan; from A. H. 194 (810 A.D.) to A.H. 658 (1260 A.D.) and the Irruption of the Infidel Mughals into Islam*. Translated by H. G. Raverty. New Delhi: Oriental Books Reprint Corp.; exclusively distributed by Munshiram Manoharlal, 1970.

Kaegi, Walter Emil. *Byzantium and the Early Islamic Conquests*. Cambridge: Cambridge University Press, 1991.

Kafadar, Cemal. *Between Two Worlds: The Construction of the Ottoman State*. Berkeley: University of California Press, 1995.

Kafesoğlu, Ibrahim. *A History of the Seljuks: Ibrahim Kafesoğlu's Interpretation and the Resulting Controversy*. Translated by Gary Leiser. Carbondale: Southern Illinois University Press, 1988.

Kamola, Stefan. "History and Legend in the Jāmiʿ al-tawārīkh: Abraham, Alexander and Oghuz Khan." *Journal of the Royal Asiatic Society* 25, no. 4 (2015): 555–577.

Karev, Yuri. "From Tents to City. The Royal Court of the Western Qarakhanids between Bukhara and Samarqand." In *Turko-Mongol Rulers, Cities and City Life*, edited by David Durand-Guédy, 99–148. Leiden: Brill, 2013.

Kasaba, Reşat. *A Moveable Empire: Ottoman Nomads, Migrants, and Refugees*. Seattle: University of Washington Press, 2009.

al-Kāshgharī, Maḥmūd. *Compendium of the Turkic Dialects*. translated by Robert Dankoff and James Kelly, vol. 1, Sources of Oriental Languages and Literatures Cambridge, MA: Harvard University, 1982.

Kastritsis, Dimitris J. "The Ottoman Interregnum (1402–1413): Politics and Narratives of Dynastic Succession." Unpublished PhD dissertation, Harvard University, 2005.

Kennedy, Hugh. *The Armies of the Caliphs: Military and Society in the Early Islamic State*. London: Routledge, 2001.

The Early Abbasid Caliphate: A Political History. London; Totowa, NJ: Croom Helm; Barnes & Noble, 1981.

The Prophet and the Age of the Caliphates: The Islamic Near East from the Sixth to the Eleventh Century. London; New York: Longman, 1986.

"The Uqaylids of Mosul: The Origins and Structure of a Nomad Dynasty." In *Actas del XII congreso de la Union européenne d'arabisants et d'islamisants (Málaga, 1984)*, 391–402. Madrid: Union Européenne d'Arabisants et d'Islamisants, 1986.

Khalik, Nancy A. "From Byzantium to Early Islam: Studies on Damascus in the Umayyad Era." Unpublished PhD dissertation, Princeton University, 2006.

Khazanov, A. M. *Nomads and the Outside World*. 2nd ed. Madison: University of Wisconsin Press, 1994.

Khazeni, Arash. *Tribes & Empire on the Margins of Nineteenth-Century Iran*. Seattle: University of Washington Press, 2009.

Khoury, Dina Rizk. *State and Provincial Society in the Ottoman Empire: Mosul, 1540–1834*. Cambridge: Cambridge University Press, 1997.

Khoury, Philip S. *Syria and the French Mandate: The Politics of Arab Nationalism 1920–1945*. Princeton: Princeton University Press, 1987.

"The Tribal Shaykh, French Tribal Policy, and the Nationalist Movement in Syria between Two World Wars." *Middle Eastern Studies* 18, no. 2 (1982): 180–193.

King, G. R. D. "The Distribution of Sites and Routes in the Jordanian and Syrian Deserts in the Early Islamic Period." In *Proceedings of the Twentieth Seminar for Arabian Studies held at London on 1st-4th July 1986*, 91–105. London: Seminar for Arabian Studies, Institute of Archaeology, 1987.

"The Umayyad Qusur and Related Settlements in Jordan." In *The IVth International Congress of the History of Bilad al-Sham*, edited by Muhammad 'Adnan al-Bakhit and Ihsan 'Abbas. Amman: al-Jami'a al-Urduniya, 1987.

Kister, M. J. "Al-Ḥīra: Some Notes on Its Relations with Arabia." *Arabica* 15 (1968): 143–169.

"Mecca and the Tribes of Arabia." In *Studies in Islamic History and Civilization in Honour of David Ayalon*, edited by M. Sharon, 33–57. Leiden: E.J. Brill, 1986.

Klausner, Carla L. *The Seljuk Vezirate: A Study of Civil Administration, 1055–1194*. Harvard Middle Eastern monographs, 22. Cambridge, MA: Distributed for the Center for Middle Eastern Studies of Harvard University by Harvard University Press, 1973.

Kliashtorny, S. G. "Les Samanides et les Karakhanides: une étape initiale de la géopolitique impériale." *Cahiers d'Asie Centrale* 9, Études Karakhanides (2001): 35–40.

Koca, Salim. "Anatolian Turkish Beyliks." In *The Turks*, edited by C. Cem Oguz, Hasan Celâl Güzel, Osman Karatay, 507–553. Ankara: Yeni Türkiye Publications, 2002.

Kochnev, Boris D. "Les frontières du royaume des Karakhanides." *Cahiers d'Asie Centrale* 9 (2001): 41–48.

Komaroff, Linda, and Stefano Carboni. *The Legacy of Genghis Khan: Courtly Art and Culture in Western Asia, 1256–1353*. New York; New Haven, CT; London: Metropolitan Museum of Art; Yale University Press, 2002.

Kostiner, Joseph. "The Hashimite Tribal Confederacy of the Arab Revolt, 1916–1917." In *National and International Politics in the Middle East: Essays in Honour of Elie Kedourie*, edited by Edward Ingram, 126–143. London: F. Cass, 1986.

"On Instruments and Their Designers: the Ikhwan of Najd and the Emergence of the Saudi State." *Middle Eastern Studies* 21, no. 3 (1985): 298–323.

Kraemer, Joel L. *Humanism in the Renaissance of Islam: The Cultural Revival during the Buyid Age*. Leiden: Brill, 1986.

Kuhrt, Amélie. *The Ancient Near East: c. 3000–330 B.C.* London: Routledge, 1995.

Kunke, Marina. *Nomadenstämme in Persien im 18. und 19. Jahrhundert*. Islamkundliche Untersuchungen Bd. 151. Berlin: K. Schwarz, 1991.

Lamberg-Karlovsky, C. C. *Archaeological Thought in America*. Cambridge; New York: Cambridge University Press, 1989.

Lambton, Ann K. S. "Aspects of Saljūq-Ghuzz Settlement in Persia." In *Islamic Civilization, 950–1150*, edited by D. S. Richards, 105–125. Oxford: Cassirer, 1973.

Continuity and Change in Medieval Persia: Aspects of Administrative, Economic, and Social History, 11th–14th century. Columbia lectures on Iranian studies; no. 2. Albany, NY: Bibliotheca Persica, 1988.

"The Internal Structure of the Saljuq Empire." In *The Cambridge History of Iran*, vol. 5. *The Saljuq and Mongol Periods*, edited by J. A. Boyle, 203–282. Cambridge: Cambridge University Press, 1968.

"Mongol Fiscal Administration in Persia, pt. II." *Studia Islamica* 65 (1987): 97–123.

Landau-Tesseron, Ella. "Review of F. McGraw Donner, *The Early Islamic Conquests*, Princeton 1981." *Jerusalem Studies in Arabic and Islam* 6 (1985): 493–512.

Lane, George. *Early Mongol Rule in Thirteenth-Century Iran: A Persian Renaissance*. Studies in the history of Iran and Turkey. London: RoutledgeCurzon, 2003.

Larsson, Göran. "Ignaz Goldziher on the Shu'ūbiyya." *Zeitschrift der deutche morgenländische Gesellschaft* 155, no. 2 (2005): 365–372.

Lassner, J. "Hilla." In *Encyclopaedia of Islam, Second Edition*. Edited by P. Bearman et al. Leiden: Brill, 1960–2005.

Lecker, Michael. *The Banū Sulaym: A Contribution to the Study of Early Islam*. Jerusalem: Hebrew University of Jerusalem, 1989.

Lecomte, Gérard. *Ibn Qutayba (mort en 276/889). L'homme, son oeuvre, ses idées*. Damascus: Institut français de Damas, 1965.

Leder, Stefan. "Towards a Historical Semantic of the Bedouin, Seventh to Fifteenth Centuries: a Survey." *Der Islam* 92, no. 1 (2015): 85–123.

Leick, Gwendolyn. *A Dictionary of Ancient Near Eastern Mythology*. London: Routledge, 1991.

Lemche, Niels Peter. "The History of Ancient Syria and Palestine: an Overview." In *The Civilizations of the Ancient Near East*, edited by J. M. Sasson, 1195–1218. New York: Simon & Schuster Macmillan, 1995.

Lewis, Norman N. *Nomads and Settlers in Syria and Jordan, 1800–1980*. Cambridge: Cambridge University Press, 1987.

Lindner, Rudi. "Anatolia, 1300–1451." In *Cambridge History of Turkey*, vol. 1. *Byzantium to Turkey, 1071–1453*, edited by Kate Fleet, 102–137. Cambridge: Cambridge University Press, 2009.

Lindner, Rudi Paul. *Explorations in Ottoman Prehistory*. Ann Arbor: University of Michigan Press, 2007.

Nomads and Ottomans in Medieval Anatolia. Bloomington: Research Institute for Inner Asian Studies, Indiana University, Bloomington, 1983.

Littauer, M. A., and J. H. Crouwel. *Wheeled Vehicles and Ridden Animals in the Ancient Near East*. Leiden: Brill, 1979.

Løkkegaard, F. "Fay." In *Encyclopaedia of Islam, Second Edition*. Edited by P. Bearman et al. Leiden: Brill, 1960–2005.

Luther, Kenneth A. "Alp Arslān." In *Encyclopædia Iranica*. Vol. I–. London, 1982–.

MacDonald, M. C. A. "North Arabia in the First Millennium BCE." In *Civilizations of the Ancient Near East*, edited by Jack M. Sasson, 1355–1369. New York: Simon & Schuster Macmillan, 1995.

Madelung, Wilferd. "Has the *Hijra* Come to an End?" In *Mélanges offerts au professeur Dominique Sourdel. Revue des Études Islamiques*, vol. LIV, 226–237. Paris: Paul Geunther, 1986.

"Deylamites, ii, In the Islamic Period." In *Encyclopædia Iranica*. Vol. I–. London, 1982–.

Maeda, Hirotake. "The Forced Migrations and Reorganization of the Regional Order in the Caucasus by Safavid Iran: Preconditions and Developments Described by Fazli Khuzani." In *Reconstruction and Interaction of Slavic Eurasia and Its Neighboring Worlds, in Slavic Eurasian Studies*, edited by Ieda Osamu and Uyama Tomohiko, 237–271. Hokkaido: Research Center, Hokkaido University, 2006.

Malbran-Labat, Florence. "Le nomadisme à l'époque néoassyrienne." In *Nomads and Sedentary Peoples. XXX International Congress of Human Sciences in Asia and North Africa*, edited by Jorge Silva Castillo, 57–76. Mexico City: El Colegio de México, 1981.

Manz, Beatrice F. "The Development and Meaning of Čagatay Identity." In *Muslims in Central Asia: Expressions of Identity and Change*, edited by Jo-Ann Gross. Durham: Duke University Press, 1992.

"Mongol History Rewritten and Relived." In *Figures Mythiques des mondes musulmans, special issue of Revue des mondes musulmans et de la Méditerranée*, edited by Denise Aigle, 129–150. Aix en Provence: Édisud, 2001.

"Multi-ethnic Empires and the Formulation of Identity." *Ethnic and Racial Studies* 26, no. 1 (2003): 70–101.

"Nomads and Regional Armies in the Middle East." In *Nomad Military Power in Iran and Adjacent Areas in the Islamic Period*, edited by Kurt Franz and Wolfgang Holzwarth, 1–28. Wiesbaden: Reichert, 2015.

Power, Politics and Religion in Timurid Iran. Cambridge: Cambridge University Press, 2007.

The Rise and Rule of Tamerlane. Cambridge: Cambridge University Press, 1989.

"Tamerlane and the Symbolism of Sovereignty." *Iranian Studies* 21, no. 1–2 (1988): 105–122.

"Temür and the Problem of a Conqueror's Legacy." *Journal of the Royal Asiatic Society* series 3 vol. 8, no. 1 (1998): 21–41.

Martin, Vanessa. *The Qajar Pact: Bargaining, Protest and the State in Nineteenth-Century Persia*. London: I. B. Tauris, 2005.

Martinez, A. P. "Some Notes on the Īl-Xānid Army." *Archivum Eurasiae Medii Aevii* VI (1986): 129–242.

Masters, Bruce. "Egypt and Syria under the Ottomans." In *The New Cambridge History of Islam, vol. 2. The Western Islamic World Eleventh to Eighteenth Centuries*, edited by Maribel Fierro, 411–435. Cambridge: Cambridge University Press, 2010.

"Semi-autonomous Forces in the Arab Provinces." In *The Cambridge History of Turkey, vol. 3. The Later Ottoman Empire, 1603–1839*, edited by Suraiya N. Faroqhi, 186–206. Cambridge: Cambridge University Press, 2006.

Masuya, Tomoko. "Ilkhanid Courtly Life." In *The Legacy of Genghis Khan: Courtly Art and Culture in Western Asia, 1256–1353*, edited by Stefano Carboni and Linda Komaroff, 74–104. New York; New Haven, CT: Metropolitan Museum of Art and Yale University Press, 2002.

Matthee, Rudi. "Between Arabs, Turks and Iranians: The Town of Basra, 1600–1700." *Bulletin of the School of Oriental and African Studies* 69, no. 1 (2006): 53–78.

Persia in Crisis: Safavid Decline and the Fall of Isfahan. London: I. B. Tauris, 2012.

"Relations between the Center and the Periphery in Safavid Iran: The Western Borderlands v. the Eastern Frontier Zone." *The Historian* (2015): 431–463.

"The Safavid-Ottoman Frontier: Iraq-i Arab as Seen by the Safavids." In *Ottoman Borderlands: Issues, Personalities and Political Changes*, edited by

Kemal Karpat and Robert W. Zens, 157–173. Madison: University of Wisconsin Press, 2003.

"Unwalled Cities and Restless Nomads: Firearms and Artillery in Safavid Iran." In *Safavid Persia*, edited by Charles Melville, 389–416. London: I. B. Tauris, 1996.

May, Timothy. *The Mongol Art of War: Chinggis Khan and the Mongol Military System*. Barnsley, England: Pen & Sword Military, 2007.

"The Mongol Conquest Strategy in the Middle East." In *The Mongols' Middle East*, edited by C. P. Melville and Bruno De Nicola, 13–37. Leiden: Brill, 2016.

Mazzaoui, Michel M. *The Origins of the Ṣafawids: Šīʿism, Ṣūfism and the Ġulāt*. Wiesbaden: F. Steiner, 1972.

Meadow, Richard H. "Inconclusive Remarks on Pastoralism, Nomadism, and Other Animal-Related Matters." In *Pastoralism in the Levant*, edited by Ofer Bar-Yosef and A. M. Khazanov, 261–69. Madison, WI: Prehistory Press, 1992.

Meisami, Julie Scott. *Persian Historiography to the end of the Twelfth Century*. Edinburgh: Edinburgh University Press, 1999.

Melikian-Chirvani, A. S. "Conscience du passé et résistance culturelle dans l' Iran mongol." In *L'Iran face à la domination mongole*, edited by Denise Aigle. *Bibliotèque iranienne*, 135–177. Tehran: Institut français de recherche en Iran, 1997.

Melville, C. P. "Between Tabriz and Herat: Persian Historical Writing in the 15th Century." In *Iran und iranisch geprägte Kulturen*, edited by Raliph Kauz, Birgitt Hoffmann, Markus Ritter, 28–39. Wiesbaden: Reichert, 2008.

Melville, Charles. "Anatolia under the Mongols." In *Cambridge History of Turkey*, vol. 1. *Byzantium to Turkey, 1071–1453*, edited by Kate Fleet, 51–101. Cambridge: Cambridge University Press, 2009.

"From Adam to Abaqa: Qāḍī Baiḍāwī's Rearrangement of History." *Studia Iranica* 30, no. 1 (2001): 67–86.

"Čobān." In *Encyclopædia Iranica*. Vol. I–. London, 1982–.

"The Itineraries of Sultan Öljeitü." *Iran* 28 (1990): 55–70.

"The *Keshig* in Iran: The Survival of the Royal Mongol Household." In *Beyond the Legacy of Genghis Khan*, edited by Linda Komaroff, 135–164. Leiden: Brill, 2006.

"Pādshāh-i Islām: the conversion of Sultan Maḥmūd Ghāzān Khān." *Pembroke Papers* 1 (1990): 159–177.

Melyukova, A. I. "The Scythians and Sarmatians." In *The Cambridge History of Early Inner Asia*, edited by Denis Sinor, 97–117. Cambridge: Cambridge University Press, 1990.

Merçil, Erdoğan. "History of the Great Seljuk Empire." In *The Turks*, edited by C. Cem Oguz, Hasan Celâl Güzel, Osman Karatay, 147–170. Ankara: Yeni Türkiye Publications, 2002.

Michalowski, Piotr. "History as Charter: Some Observations on the Sumerian King List." *Journal of the American Oriental Society* 103 (1983): 237–248.

Mieroop, Marc Van De. *A History of the Ancient Near East*. Oxford: Blackwell, 2003.

Minorsky, Vladimir. "The Aq-Qoyunlu and Land Reforms." *Bulletin of the School of Oriental and African Studies* XVII (1955): 449–462.

"A Civil and Military Review in Fārs in 881/1476." *Bulletin of the School of Oriental and African Studies* X (1940–1942): 141–178.

"Kurd, Kurdistan, iii. B History: The Islamic period up to 1920." In *Encyclopaedia of Islam, Second Edition.* Edited by P. Bearman et al. Leiden: Brill, 1960–2005.

Tadhkirat al-mulūk: A Manual of Ṣafavid Administration (circa 1137/1725), Persian text in facsimile (B.M. Or. 9496). E. J. W. Gibb memorial series. London: Luzac, 1980.

Minorsky, Vladimir, V. V. Bartol'd and Clifford Edmund Bosworth. *Ḥudūd al-'Ālam: "The regions of the world": A Persian Geography, 372 A.H.-982 A.D.* 2nd ed. London: Luzac, 1970.

Mitchell, Colin P. *The Practice of Politics in Safavid Iran: Power, Religion and Rhetoric.* London: I. B. Tauris, 2009.

Montgomery, James E. *The Vagaries of the Qaṣīdah: The Tradition and Practice of Early Arabic Poetry.* Cambridge: E. J. W. Gibb Memorial Trust, 1997.

Morgan, David O. "The 'Great yasa of Chinggis Khan' revisited." In *Mongols, Turks, and Others*, edited by Reuven Amitai and Michal Biran, 291–308. Leiden: Brill, 2005.

"Mongol or Persian: The Government of Īlkhānid Iran." *Harvard Middle Eastern and Islamic Review* 3, no. 1–2 (1996).

"Rašīd al-Dīn and Ġazan Khan." In *L'Iran face à la domination mongole*, edited by Denise Aigle. *Bibliotèque Iranienne*, 179–188. Tehran: Institut Français de Recherche en Iran, 1997.

Morimoto, Kazuo. "An Enigmatic Genealogical Chart of the Timurids: A Testimony to the Dynasty's Claim to Yasavi-'Alid Legitimacy?" *Oriens* 44 (2016): 145–178.

Morony, Michael G. *Iraq after the Muslim Conquest.* Princeton, NJ: Princeton University Press, 1984.

Mottahedeh, Roy P. "The Shu'ûbîyah Controversy and the Social History of Early Islamic Iran." *International Journal of Middle East Studies* 6 (1976): 161–182.

Loyalty and Leadership in an Early Islamic Society. Princeton, NJ: Princeton University Press, 1980.

Murphy, Rhoads. *Ottoman Warfare, 1500–1700.* New Brunswick, NJ: Rutgers University Press, 1999.

"The Resumption of Ottoman-Safavid Border Conflict, 1603–1638: Effects of Border Destabilizaton on the Evolution of Tribe-State Relations." In *Shifts and Drifts in Nomad-Sedentary Relations*, edited by Stefan Leder and Bernard Streck, 307–323. Wiesbaden: Reichert, 2005.

"Some Features of Nomadism in the Ottoman Empire: A Survey Based on Tribal Census and Judicial Appeal Documentation from Archives in Istanbul and Damascus." *Journal of Turkish Studies* 8 (1984): 189–197.

Mustawfī, Qazwīnī, Ḥamd Allāh. *The Geographical Part of the Nuzhat-al-qulub.* Leiden; London: E.J. Brill; Luzac, 1919.

Nagel, Tilman. "Buyids." In *Encyclopædia Iranica.* Vol. I–. London, 1982–.

Najmabadi, Afsaneh. *The Story of the Daughters of Quchan: Gender and National Memory in Iranian History*. Syracuse, NY: Syracuse University Press, 1998.

Nasawī, Muḥammad ibn Aḥmad. *Histoire du sultan Djelal ed-Din Mankobirti, prince du Kharezm, par Mohammed en-Nesawi: texte Arabe publié d'apres le manuscrit de la Bibliotèque Nationale*. Translated by O. Houdas. 2 vols. Vol. 2. Paris: E. Leroux, 1891–95.

Nawā'ī. 'Abd al-Ḥusayn, ed. *Asnād wa makātibāt-i tārīkhī-i Īrān*. Tehran, 2536/1977.

Nawā'ī, Mīr 'Alī Shīr. *Muḥākamāt al-lughatayn*. Translated by Robert Devereux. Leiden: Brill, 1966.

Newman, Andrew J. *Safavid Iran: Rebirth of a Persian Empire*. London: I. B. Tauris: Distributed in the U.S.A. by Palgrave Macmillan, 2006.

Nieuwenhuis, Tom. *Politics and Society in Early Modern Iraq: Mamlūk Pashas, Tribal Shaykhs and Local Rule between 1802 and 1831*. The Hague: Martinus Nijhoff, 1982.

Niẓām al-Mulk. *The book of Government or Rules for Kings: The Siyar al-muluk or Siyasat-nama of Nizam al-Mulk*. Translated by Hubert Darke. 2nd ed. London: Routledge & K. Paul, 1978.

Oberling, Pierre. *The Qashqāī Nomads of Fārs*. The Hague: Mouton, 1974.

Ochsenwald, William. *Religion, Society and the State in Arabia: The Hijaz under Ottoman Control, 1840–1908*. Columbus: Ohio State University Press, 1984.

O'Kane, Bernard. "Persian Poetry on Ilkhanid Art and Architecture." In *Beyond the Legacy of Genghis Khan*, edited by Linda Komaroff, 346–354. Leiden: Brill, 2006.

Ölçer, Nazan. "The Anatolian Seljuks." In *Turks: A Journey of a Thousand Years*, edited by David Roxburgh, 102–145. London: Royal Academy of Arts, 2005.

Oppenheim, Max, Freiherr von. *Die Beduinen*, vol. 2, 3. Leipzig: Harrassowitz, 1939–1952.

Orthmann, Eva. *Stamm und Macht: die arabischen Stämme im 2. und 3. Jahrhundert der Hiǧra*. Wiesbaden: Reichert, 2002.

Parker, Geoffrey. *The Military Revolution: Military Innovation and the Rise of the West, 1500–1800*. Cambridge: Cambridge University Press, 1988.

Paul, Jürgen. "Karakhanids." In *The Turks*, edited by C. Cem Oguz, Hasan Celâl Güzel, Osman Karatay, 71–78. Ankara: Yeni Türkiye Publications, 2002.

"Mongol Aristocrats and Beyliks in Anatolia. A Study of Astarabādi's *Bazm va Razm*." *Eurasian Studies* IX, no. 1–2 (2011): 105–158.

"Nouvelles pistes pour la recherche sur l'histoire de l'Asie centrale à l'époque karakhanide (Xe-début XIIIe siècle)." *Cahiers d'Asie Centrale* 9 (2001): 13–34.

"The Role of Ḥwārazm in Seluq Central Asian Politics, Victories and Defeats: Two Case Studies." *Eurasian Studies* VII (2007–8): 1–17.

The State and the Military: The Samanid Case. Bloomington: Indiana University Research Institute for Inner Asian Studies, 1994.

Paviot, Jacques. "Les marchands italiens dan l'Iran mongol." In *L'Iran face à la domination mongole*, edited by Denise Aigle. *Bibliotèque iranienne*, 71–86. Tehran: Institut français de recherche in Iran, 1997.

Peacock, A. C. S. "Court and Nomadic Life in Saljuq Anatolia." In *Turko-Mongol Rulers, Cities and City Life*, edited by David Durand-Guédy, 191–222. Leiden: Brill, 2013.

Early Seljūq History: A New Interpretation. London: Routledge, 2010.

The Great Seljuk Empire. Edinburgh: Edinburgh University Press, 2015.

Pellat, Charles. *Le milieu baṣrien et la formation de Ǧāḥiẓ*. Paris: Librairie d'Amérique et d'Orient Adrien-Maisonneuve, 1953.

The Life and Works of Jāḥiẓ. Berkeley: University of California Press, 1969.

Perry, John R. "The Zand Dynasty." In *The Cambridge History of Iran*, vol. 7. *From Nadir Shah to the Islamic Republic*, edited by Gavin Hambly, Peter Avery, Charles Melville, 63–103. Cambridge: Cambridge University Press, 1991.

"Forced Migration in Iran during the Seventeenth and Eighteenth Centuries." *Iranian Studies* 8 (1975): 199–215.

Karīm Khān Zand: A History of Iran, 1747–1779. Chicago: University of Chicago Press, 1979.

Peters, F. E. *The Arabs and Arabia on the Eve of Islam*. Brookfield, VT: Ashgate, 1998.

Petrushevskiĭ, I. P. "The Socio-Economic Condition of Iran under the Īl-Khāns." In *The Cambridge History of Iran*, vol. 5. *The Saljuq and Mongol Periods*, edited by J. A. Boyle, 483–537. Cambridge: Cambridge University Press, 1968.

Zemledelie i agrarnye otnosheniia v Irane XIII–XIV vekov. Leningrad: Izd-vo Akademii nauk SSSR, Leningradskoe otd., 1960.

Pfeiffer, Judith. "Conversion to Islam among the Ilkhans in Muslim Narrative Traditions: The Case of Ahmad Tegüder." Unpublished PhD dissertation, University of Chicago, 2003.

Potts, Daniel T. *Nomadism in Iran, From Antiquity to the Modern Era*. Oxford: Oxford University Press, 2014.

Quinn, Sholeh Alysia. *Historical Writing during the Reign of Shah 'Abbas: Ideology, Imitation, and Legitimacy in Safavid Chronicles*. Salt Lake City: University of Utah Press, 2000.

Rachewiltz, Igor de. *The Secret History of the Mongols: A Mongolian Epic Chronicle of the Thirteenth Century*. Leiden: Brill, 2006.

"Yeh-lü Ch'u Ts'ai (1189–1243); Yeh-lü Chu? (1221–1285)." In *In the Service of the Khan: Eminent Personalities of the Early Mongol-Yüan Period*, edited by Igor de Rachewiltz, Hok-lam Chan, Hsiao Ch'i-ch'ing, Peter W. Geier. Wiesbaden: Harrassowitz, 1993.

al-Rasheed, Madawi. *A History of Saudi Arabia*. Cambridge: Cambridge University Press, 2010.

Politics in an Arabian Oasis: The Rashidi Tribal Dynasty. London: I. B. Tauris, 1991.

"Shammar." In *Encyclopaedia of Islam, Second Edition*. Edited by P. Bearman et al. Leiden: Brill, 1960–2005.

Rashīd-al-Dīn. *Rashiduddin Fazlullah's Jami'u't-tawarikh: Compendium of Chronicles*. Translated by W. M. Thackston. Cambridge, MA: Harvard University, Dept. of Near Eastern Languages and Civilizations, 1998.

Rashīd al-Dīn Ṭabīb. *The History of the Seljuq Turks from the Jāmi' al-tawārīkh: an Ilkhanid adaptation of the Saljūq-nāma of Ẓahīr al-Dīn Nīshāpūrī*. Translated by Kenneth A. Luther. Richmond, Surrey: Curzon, 2001.

Ratchnevsky, Paul. *Genghis Khan, His Life and Legacy*. Translated by Thomas Nivison Haining. Oxford: Blackwell, 1992.

Retsö, Jan. *The Arabs in Antiquity: Their History from the Assyrians to the Umayyads*. London: RoutledgeCurzon, 2003.

"The Domestication of the Camel and the Establishment of the Frankincense Road from South Arabia." *Orientalia Suecana* 40 (1991): 187–219.

Richard, Jean. "D'Älğigidäi à Ġazan: la continuité d'une politique franque chez les Mongols d'Iran." In *L'Iran face à la domination mongole*, edited by Denise Aigle, 57–69. Louvain: Peeters, 1997.

Ripper, Thomas. *Die Marwāniden von Diyār Bakr: eine kurdische Dynastie im islamischen Mittelalter*. Würzburg: Ergon, 2000.

Robinson, B. W. *Fifteenth-Century Persian Painting: Problems and Issues*. New York: New York University Press, 1991.

Robinson, Chase F. "Tribes and Nomads in Early Islamic Northern Mesopotamia." In *Continuity and Change in Northern Mesopotamia from the Hellenistic to the Early Islamic Period*, edited by Karin Bartl and Stefan R. Hauser, 429–452. Berlin: Dietrich Reimer, 1996.

Roemer, Hans Robert. *Persien auf dem Weg in die Neuzeit: iranische Geschichte von 1350–1750*. Beirut: Orient-Institut der deutschen morgenländischen Gesellschaft, 1989.

"The Safavid Period." In *The Cambridge History of Iran*, vol. 6. *The Timurid and Safavid Periods*, edited by Laurence Lockhart and Peter Jackson, 189–350. Cambridge: Cambridge University Press, 1986.

Rogan, Eugene. *The Arabs: A History*. New York: Basic Books, 2009.

The Fall of the Ottomans: The Great War in the Middle East. New York: Basic Books, 2015.

Frontiers of the State in the Late Ottoman Empire: Transjordan, 1850–1921. Cambridge: Cambridge University Press, 1999.

Röhrborn, Klaus. *Provinzen und Zentralgewalt Persiens im 16. und 17. Jahrhundert*. Berlin: de Gruyter, 1966.

Rothstein, Gustav. *Die Dynastie der Laḥmiden in al-Ḥīra: ein Versuch zur arabisch-persischen Geschichte zur Zeit der Sasaniden*. Hildesheim: G. Olms, 1968.

Rotter, Gernot. *Die Umayyaden und der zweite Bürgerkrieg (680–692)*. Wiesbaden: Steiner, 1982.

Rowton, Michael B. "Economic and Political Factors in Ancient Nomadism." In *Nomads and Sedentary Peoples, XXX International Congress of Human Sciences in Asia and North Africa*, edited by Jorge Silva Castillo, 25–36. Mexico City: Colegio de México, 1981.

Sadr, Karim. *The Development of Nomadism in Ancient Northeast Africa*. Philadelphia: University of Pennsylvania Press, 1991.

Safargaliev, M. G. *Raspad Zolotoĭ Ordy*. Saransk: Mordovskoe knizhoe izd-vo, 1960.

Şahin, Ilhan. "The Oguz Turks in Anatolia." In *The Turks*, edited by Hasan Celâl Güzel, C. Cem Oguz, Osman Karatay, 418–429. Ankara: Yeni Türkiye Publications, 2002.

Saʿīdī Sīrjānī, ʿA. A. "Baḵtīārī; Ḥājī ʿAlīqolī Khan Sardār Asʿad." In *Encyclopædia Iranica*. Vol. I–. London, 1982–.

Savory, Roger. *Iran under the Safavids*. Cambridge: Cambridge University Press, 1980.

Schwarz, Glenn M. "Pastoral Nomadism in Ancient Western Asia." In *Civilizations of the Ancient Near East*, edited by Jack M. Sasson. New York: Simon Schuster Macmillan, 1995, pp. 249–58.

Shahid, Irfan. "Ghassān." In *Encyclopaedia of Islam, Second Edition*. Edited by P. Bearman et al. Leiden: Brill, 1960–2005.

"Lakhmids." In *Encyclopaedia of Islam, Second Edition*. Edited by P. Bearman et al. Leiden: Brill, 1960–2005.

"Tanūkh." In *Encyclopaedia of Islam, Second Edition*. Edited by P. Bearman et al. Leiden: Brill, 1960–2005.

Shamma, Samir. "Mirdās." In *Encyclopaedia of Islam, Second Edition*. Edited by P. Bearman et al. Leiden: Brill, 1960–2005.

Sharon, Moshe. "The Political Role of the Bedouins in Palestine in the Sixteenth and Seventeenth Centuries." In *Studies on Palestine during the Ottoman Period*, edited by Moshe Ma'oz, 5–31. Jerusalem: Magnes Press, 1975.

Shaw, Brent D. "'Eaters of Flesh, Drinkers of Milk': The Ancient Mediterranean Ideology of the Pastoral Nomad." In *Rulers, Nomads and Christians in Roman North Africa*, edited by Brent D. Shaw, 5–31. Aldershot: Variorum, 1995.

Shaw, Stanford J. and Ezel Kural Shaw. *History of the Ottoman Empire and Modern Turkey*. Cambridge: Cambridge University Press, 1977.

Shoufani, Elias. *Al-Riddah and the Muslim Conquest of Arabia*. Toronto: University of Toronto Press, 1973.

Shryock, Andrew. *Nationalism and the Genealogical Imagination*. Berkeley: University of California Press, 1997.

Simon, Róbert. *Meccan Trade and Islam: Problems of Origin and Structure*. Budapest: Akadémiai Kiadó, 1989.

Sinclair, Tom. "The Ottoman Arrangements for the Tribal Principalities of the Lake Van Region of the Sixteenth Century." *International Journal of Turkish Studies* 9, no. 1–2 (2003): 119–143.

Sinor, Denis. *The Cambridge History of Early Inner Asia*. Cambridge: Cambridge University Press, 1990.

"The Establishment and Dissolution of the Türk Empire." In *Cambridge History of Early Inner Asia*, edited by Denis Sinor, 285–316. Cambridge: Cambridge University Press, 1990.

Smith, John Masson. "Mongol Nomadism and Middle Eastern Geography: Qīshlāqs and Tümens." In *The Mongol Empire and Its Legacy*, edited by Reuven Amitai-Preiss and David O. Morgan, 39–56. Leiden: Brill, 2000.

Smoor, P. "al-Ma'arrī." In *Encyclopaedia of Islam, Second Edition*. Edited by P. Bearman et al. Leiden: Brill, 1960–2005.

Sneath, David. *The Headless State: Aristocratic Orders, Kinship Society, and Misrepresentations of Nomadic Inner Asia*. New York: Columbia University Press, 2007.

Sommerfeld, Walter. "The Kassites of Ancient Mesopotamia: Origins, Politics and Culture." In *Civilizations of the Ancient Near East*, edited by Jack M. Sasson, 917–930. New York: Simon Schuster Macmillan, 1995.

Tübinger Atlas des Vorderen Orients. Wiesbaden: Reichert, 1977, maps AX1 and AX11.

Stark, Sören. *Die Alttürkenzeit in Mittel- und Zentralasien: archäologische und historische Studien*. Wiesbaden: Reichert, 2008.

Stetkevych, Jaroslav. *The Zephyrs of Najd: The Poetics of Nostalgia in the Classical Arabic Nasīb*. Chicago, IL: University of Chicago Press, 1993.

Stetkevych, Suzanne Pinckney. *The Poetics of Islamic Legitimacy: Myth, Gender, and Ceremony in the Classical Arabic Ode*. Bloomington: Indiana University Press, 2002.

Storey, C. A. and Yuri Bregel. *Persidskaia literatura, bio-bibliograficheskiĭ obzor*. 3 vols. Moscow: "Nauka," 1972.

Stewart, F. H. "Khuwwa." In *Encyclopaedia of Islam, Second Edition*. Edited by P. Bearman et al. Leiden: Brill, 1960–2005.

Stump, Ayfer Karakaya. "Subjects of the Sultan, Disciples of the Shah: Formation and Transformation of the Kiszilbash/Alevi Communities in Ottoman Anatolia." Unpublished PhD dissertation, Harvard University, 2008.

Subtelny, Maria. *Timurids in Transition: Turko-Persian Politics and Acculturation in Medieval Iran*. Leiden: Brill, 2007.

"Bābur's Rival Relations: A Story of Kinship and Conflict in 15th–16th Century Central Asia." *Der Islam* 66, no. 1 (1989): 102–118.

Sulimirsky, T. "The Scyths." In *Cambridge History of Iran*, vol. 2, *The Median and Achaemenid Periods*, edited by Ilya Gershevitch, 149–199. Cambridge: Cambridge University Press, 1985.

Sümer, Faruk. "Döger." In *Encyclopaedia of Islam, Second Edition*. Edited by P. Bearman et al. Leiden: Brill, 1960–2005.

"Karā-Koyunlu." In *Encyclopaedia of Islam, Second Edition*. Edited by P. Bearman et al. Leiden: Brill, 1960–2005.

"Karamān-oghullarï." In *Encyclopaedia of Islam, Second Edition*. Edited by P. Bearman et al. Leiden: Brill, 1960–2005.

Oğuzlar (Türkmenler): tarihleri, boy teşkilatı, destanları. 4. baskı. ed. Istanbul: Türk Dünyası Araştırmaları Vakfı, 1999.

Szombathy, Zoltan. "Fieldwork and Preconceptions: The Role of the Bedouin as Informants in Mediaeval Muslim Scholarly Culture (second-Third/Eighth-Ninth Centuries)." *Der Islam* 92, no. 1 (2015): 124–147.

Szuchman, Jeffrey, "Integrating Approaches to Nomads, Tribes, and the State in the Ancient Near East," in *Nomads, Tribes, and the State in the Ancient Near East: Cross-Disciplinary Perspectives*, edited by Jeffrey Szuchman, 1–14. Oriental Institute Seminars # 5, Oriental Institute of Chicago, IL, 2009.

Szuppe, Maria. *Entre Timourides, Uzbeks et Safavides: questions d'histoire politique et sociale de Hérat dans la première moitié du XVIe siècle*. Studia Iranica. Cahier 2. Paris: Association pour l'avancement des études iraniennes, 1992.

"Kinship Ties between the Safavids and the Qizilbash Amirs in Late Sixteenth-Century Iran: A Case Study of the Political Career of Members of the Sharaf al-Din Oghli Tekelu Family." In *Safavid Persia: The History and Politics of an Islamic Society*, edited by Charles Melville, 79–104. London: I. B. Tauris, 1996.

"L'évolution de l'image de Timour et des Timourides dans l'historiographie safavide, XVIe–XVIIIe siècles." In *L'Héritage timouride Iran – Asie centrale – Inde XVe–XVIIIe siècles*, edited by Maria Szuppe. *Cahiers D'Asie centrale*, 313–331. Tashkent, Aix-en-Provence, 1997.

Tall, Tariq. "The Politics of Rural Policy in East Jordan, 1920–1989." In *The Transformation of Nomadic Society in the Middle East*, edited by Martha Mundi and Basim Musallam, 90–98. Cambridge: Cambridge University Press, 2000.

Tapper, Richard. *Frontier Nomads of Iran: A Political and Social History of the Shahsevan.* Cambridge: Cambridge University Press, 1997.

Tatiana Zerjal, Yali Xue, et. al. "The Genetic Legacy of the Mongols." *American Journal of Human Genetics* 72 (2003): 717–721.

Tekin, Talât. *A Grammar of Orkhon Turkic.* Bloomington: Indiana University Uralic and Altaic Series, 5,1968.

Thackston, W. M. *Album Prefaces and Other Documents on the History of Calligraphers and Painters* [in Original Persian texts and parallel English translations]. Leiden: Brill, 2001.

Thesiger, Wilfred. *Arabian Sands.* New York: Dutton, 1959.

Ṭihrānī Iṣfahānī, Abū Bakr, *Kitāb-i Diyārbakriyya*, edited by N. Lugal and F. Sümer. Ankara: Türk tarih Kurumu Basımevi, 1962–1964.

Togan, Isenbike. *Flexibility and Limitation in Steppe Formations: The Kerait Khanate and Chinggis Khan.* Leiden: Brill, 1998.

Togan, Zeki Velidi. "Timurs Osteuropapolitik." *Zeitschrift der deutschen morgenländischen Gesellschaft* 108 (1958): 279–298.

Tor, Deborah G. *Violent Order: Religious Warfare, Chivalry, and the 'Ayyār Phenomenon in the Medieval Islamic World.* Würzburg: Ergon, 2007.

"The Mamluks in the Military of the Pre-Seljuq Persianate Dynasties." *Iran* 46 (2008): 213–225.

Tousi, Reza Ra'iss. "The Persian Army, 1880–1907." *Middle Eastern Studies* 24, no. 2 (1988): 206–229.

Tripp, Charles. *A History of Iraq.* Cambridge: Cambridge University Press, 2007.

Tucker, Ernest. *Nadir Shah's Quest for Legitimacy in Post-Safavid Iran.* Gainesville: University of Florida Press, 2006.

Turan, Fikret. "The Mamluks and Their Acceptance of Oghuz Turkic as a Literary Language: Political Maneuver or Cultural Aspiration?" In *Einheit und Vielfalt in der türkischen Welt: Materialien der 5. Deutschen Turkologenkonferenz Universität Mainz, 4.–7. Oktober 2002*, edited by Hendrik Boeschoten and Heidi Stein. Wiesbaden: Harrassowitz, 2007.

al-'Umarī, Aḥmad ibn Yaḥyā ibn Faḍl Allāh. *Das mongolische Weltreich. Al-'Umarī's Darstellung der mongolischen Reiche in seinem Werk Masālik al-abṣār fī mamālik al-amṣār.* Translated by Klaus Lech. Wiesbaden: Harrassowitz, 1968.

Vassiliev, Alexei. *The History of Saudi Arabia.* London: Saqi Books, 1998.

Väth, Gerhard. *Die Geschichte der artuqidischen Fürstentümer in Syrien und der Ǧazīra'l Furātīya (496–812/1002–1409).* Berlin: K. Schwarz, 1987.

Velud, Christian. "French Mandate Policy in the Syrian Steppe." In *The Transformation of Nomadic Society in the Arab East*, edited by Martha Mundi and Basim Musallam, 63–81. Cambridge: Cambridge University Press, 2000.

Venzke, Margaret L. "The Case of a Dulgadir-Mamluk Iqṭā': A Re-assessment of the Dulgadir Principality and Its Position within the Ottoman-mamluk Rivalry." *Journal of the Economic and Social History of the Orient* 43, no. 3 (2000): 399–474.

Vinogradov, Amal. "The 1920 Revolt in Iraq Reconsidered: The Role of Tribes in National Politics." *International Journal of Middle East Studies* 3, no. 2 (1972): 123–139.

Vogelsang, Willem. "Medes, Scythians and Persians: The Rise of Darius in a North-South Perspective." *Iranica Antiqua* 33 (1998): 195–224.

Vryonis, Speros. *The Decline of Medieval Hellenism in Asia Minor and the Process of Islamization from the Eleventh through the Fifteenth Century.* Berkeley: University of California Press, 1971.

Waines, David. "The Third Century Internal Crisis of the Abbasids." *Journal of the Economic and Social History of the Orient* 20, no. 3 (1977): 282–306.

Watson, Oliver. "Pottery under the Mongols." In *Beyond the Legacy of Genghis Khan*, edited by Linda Komaroff, 325–345. Leiden: Brill, 2006.

Watt, W. Montgomery. *Muhammad at Mecca.* Oxford: Clarendon Press, 1953.
Muhammad at Medina. Oxford: Clarendon Press, 1956.

Wellhausen, Julius. *The Arab Kingdom and Its Fall.* Translated by Margaret Graham Weir. Calcutta: University of Calcutta, 1927.

Wensinck, A. J. and Patricia Crone. "Mawla." In *Encyclopaedia of Islam, Second Edition.* Edited by P. Bearman et al. Leiden: Brill, 1960–2005.

White, Sam. *The Climate of Rebellion in the Early Modern Ottoman Empire.* Cambridge: Cambridge University Press, 2011.

Williamson, John Frederick. "A Political History of the Shammar Jarba Tribe of al-Jazirah: 1800–1958." Unpublished PhD dissertation, Indiana University, 1974.

Wing, Patrick. "Between Iraq and a Hard Place: Sulṭān Aḥmad Jalāyir's Time as a Refugee in the Mamluk Sultanate." In *Mamluk Cairo, A Crossroads for Embassies: Studies on Diplomacy and Diplomatics*, edited by Frédéric Bauden and Malika Dekkiche, 163–175. Leiden: Brill, 2019.
The Jalayirids: Dynastic State Formation in the Mongol Middle East. Edinburgh: Edinburgh University Press, 2016.

Wood, Michael. "A History of the Balqā' Region of Central Transjordan during the Umayyad Period." Unpublished PhD dissertation, McGill University, 1995.

Woods, John E. *The Aqquyunlu: Clan, Confederation, Empire.* Rev. and expanded ed. Salt Lake City: University of Utah Press, 1999.
"The Rise of Tīmūrīd Historiography." *Journal of Near Eastern Studies* 46, no. 2 (1987): 81–108.
"Timur's Genealogy." In *Intellectual Studies on Islam: Essays written in Honor of Martin B. Dickson*, edited by Michael Mazzaoui and Vera B. Moreen, 85–126. Salt Lake City: University of Utah Press, 1990.

Yarshater, E. "Afrāsīāb." In *Encyclopædia Iranica.* Vol. I–. London, 1982–.

Yazdī, Sharaf al-Dīn 'Alī, *Ẓafarnāma*, ed. Muḥammad 'Abbāsī. Tehran: Amīr Kabīr, 1957.

Yıldız, Sara Nur. "Aydınid Court Literature in the Formation of an Islamic Identity in Fourteenth-Century Western Anatolia." In *Islamic Literature and Intellectual*

Life in Fourteenth- and Fifteenth-Century Anatolia, edited by A. C. S. Peacock and Sara Nur Yıldız, 197–242. Würzburg: Ergon Verlag, 2016.

"Mongol Rule in Thirteenth-century Seljuk Anatolia: The Politics of Conquest and History Writing, 1243–1282." Unpublished PhD dissertation, University of Chicago, 2006.

"Post-Mongol Pastoral Polities in Eastern Anatolia during the Late Middle Ages." In *At the Crossroads of Empires: 14th–15th Century Eastern Anatolia. Proceedings of the International Symposium Held in Istanbul, 4th-6th May 2007*, edited by Deniz Beyazit. *Varia Anatolica* 27–48. Paris: De Boccard, 2012.

Yūsuf Khāss Ḥājib. *Wisdom of Royal Glory: A Turko-Islamic Mirror for Princes*. Translated by Robert Dankoff. Chicago, IL: University of Chicago Press, 1983.

Zakkār, Suhayl. *The Emirate of Aleppo, 1004–1094*. Beirut: Dar al-Amanah, 1971.

Zimansky, Paul E. "The Kingdom of Urartu in Eastern Anatolia." In *Civilizations of the Ancient Near East*, edited by Jack M. Sasson, 1135–1146. New York: Simon and Schuster McMillan, 1995.

Index

Note: Page numbers with the suffix n indicate a footnote and those in italic denote illustrations.